Are the origins of the synagogue to be sought in a reaction to the centralisation of worship in Judaism, or in a wider context? When did prayer become central to Jews and how are the conflicts and tensions of the talmudic period reflected in the history of its liturgy? Did Christianity and Islam have something to do with the emergence of the first Jewish prayer codices? Can one identify in today's Hebrew prayers the influences of the massive demographical changes in the distribution of the Jewish people and of the establishment of the State of Israel? In this first attempt for almost three quarters of a century to provide a scientific overview of Jewish liturgical history, the latest scholarship and the most original sources are carefully identified and exploited. The result is a book that will prove attractive to both scholarly and lay opinion, and which makes liturgical research accessible to modern readers.

JUDAISM AND HEBREW PRAYER

JUDAISM AND HEBREW PRAYER

New perspectives on Jewish liturgical history

STEFAN C. REIF

Director of Genizah Research and Head of the Oriental Division of the University Library, University of Cambridge

Published by the Press Syndicate of the University of Cambridge
The Pitt Building, Trumpington Street, Cambridge CB2 1RP
40 West 20th Street, New York, NY 10011–4211, USA
10 Stamford Road, Oakleigh, Melbourne 3166, Australia

First published 1993
First paperback edition 1995
Transferred to digital printing 1998

Printed in the United Kingdom by
Antony Rowe Ltd, Chippenham, Wiltshire

A catalogue record for this book is available from the British Library

Library of Congress cataloguing in publication data

Reif, Stefan C., 1944–
Judaism and Hebrew prayer: new perspectives on Jewish liturgical history / Stefan C. Reif.
p. cm.
Includes bibliographical references and index.
ISBN 0 521 44087 4 (hardback)
ISBN 0 521 48341 7 (paperback)
1. Judaism – Liturgy – History. 2. Prayer – Judaism. I. Title
BM660.R45 1993
296.4 – dc20 92–1709 CIP

ISBN 0 521 48341 7 paperback

לזכר נשמת אבי מורי

ר׳ פינחס ב״ר צבי אריה הכהן

נולד בקאלוש גליציא תרע״א

נלב״ע בטורונטו קנדה תשמ״ט

ת. נ. צ. ב. ה.

Contents

Preface

Of the various books and numerous articles that have appeared over my name in the course of twenty-three years of scholarly publication, none has given me so much satisfaction in its completion as the volume here being prefaced. It has been my ambition for a number of years to offer such an overview of Jewish liturgical history and, given my many other commitments, it has been no easy task to find the time and energy to effect its realisation. Now that the final touches have been put to the text submitted to Cambridge University Press a few months ago, I can only express the hope that the study proves as useful and acceptable to the student, non-specialist and scholar in its reading as it has proved absorbing and challenging to me in its composition.

Some earlier versions of sections of the book have appeared in a number of publications and I welcome the opportunity of thanking the editors and publishers for kindly granting their permission to incorporate that material here. The first half of chapter 1 appeared as 'Jewish Liturgical Research: Past, Present and Future' in the *Journal of Jewish Studies* 34 (1983), pp. 161–70, edited by Geza Vermes and published by the Oxford Centre for Postgraduate Hebrew Studies; an earlier draft of chapter 3 was submitted to Cambridge University Press in December 1986 and will appear in the third volume of the *Cambridge History of Judaism* edited by Louis Finkelstein and W. D. Davies; a substantial proportion of chapter 4 was published in *Studia Liturgica* 15 (1982–3), pp. 188–206, now edited by Paul Bradshaw for Societas Liturgica. Paul also included an earlier version of chapter 5 as 'The Early History of Jewish Worship' in *The Making of Jewish and Christian Worship* edited by him and Larry Hoffman for the University of Notre Dame Press (Notre Dame and London, 1991), pp. 109–36; and a small part of chapter 6 was delivered as a lecture at a congress of the European Association for Jewish Studies held in Troyes in 1990 and is scheduled to appear in its proceedings being edited by Gabrielle Sed-Rajna of the Centre National de la Recherche Scientifique in Paris.

I am also indebted to a number of institutions and scholars whose assistance has been invaluable but who are of course in no way responsible for the manner in which I have made use of it. The Lady Davis Fellowship Trust in Jerusalem generously made it possible for me to spend a semester as a visiting professor at the Hebrew University in 1989, where I taught an MA course in Jewish liturgy and benefited from the Jewish National and University Library, from the responses of my students, and from discussions with my friends Ezra Fleischer, Menahem Ben-Sasson, Robert Brody and Tsvi Groner. I lectured to the evening MA class at Jews' College in London for three terms in 1990–1 and gained important insights during these sessions; I was also assisted by academic and library staff there and in Leo Baeck College, the British Library, the Brotherton Library at the University of Leeds, and the John Rylands Research Institute at the University of Manchester. My colleagues here in Cambridge, in the University Library (particularly in the Genizah Research Unit) and in the Faculties of Oriental Studies and Divinity (especially the Old Testament Seminar), have generously provided comments and information, and specific enquiries have met with the kind responses of Robert Attal of the Ben-Zvi Institute in Jerusalem, Eleazar Gutwirth of Tel Aviv University, Chaim Milikowsky of Bar-Ilan University, Philip Scheim of Toronto, and Louis Jacobs, Abraham Levy, Raphael Loewe, Naftali Loewenthal and Michael Weitzman in London. Warm thanks are also due to my secretary, Sandra McGivern, for typing daunting scripts, and to the staff at Cambridge University Press, especially the religious studies editor, Alex Wright, and my copy-editor,

Glennis Foote, for applying their various skills to the production of the volume.

The original inspiration for my interest in the subject of Jewish liturgy came from an outstanding scholar and teacher, Naphtali Wieder, while the everyday inspiration for all my efforts comes from my closest colleague, collaborator and friend, my wife Shulie. My late father would have taken great pleasure in handling this volume and it is fitting that it should be dedicated to his memory and, through him, to the memory of the Eastern European world in which our forbears were raised. I sign this preface on a date which serves as the *yahrzeit* for a number of them.

14 Menaḥem Av 5752 = 13 August 1992 S.C.R.

CHAPTER I

On Jewish liturgical research

Research into the history of daily Hebrew prayers may justifiably be said to warrant total scholarly attention or none at all. With a presence in each period of Jewish history, a relationship with almost every area of scientific as well as traditional Hebrew and Jewish studies, and a relevance to the wider analysis of religion and religions, it may be argued that the liturgy of the Jews, in its various forms, deserves the closest scrutiny on the part of students of all these disciplines. On the other hand, it is easily understood why the very comprehensive nature of the subject might lead to its neglect as an independent topic. Given that it occurs within so many areas of research, it is a simple matter to restrict it to such contexts and deny it any specific, critical treatment. This latter policy is clearly not one that commends itself to the author of this book but it may not be obvious how a need for the present study has emerged in recent years, in which ways it relates to other overall examinations of the subject, and what ground it expects to cover. It is to be hoped that as the reader becomes acquainted with the volume such matters will become clear. In the mean time the purpose of this introductory chapter is to set the tone for the remainder of the book by referring briefly to major developments in the Jewish liturgical research of the modern and contemporary periods and by offering a summary of the methodology and theory that underlie the eight chapters that follow it. It is divided into five parts: (i) Zunz and Elbogen; (ii) Later work; (iii) Some problems; (iv) The way forward; (v) Methodology and theory.

ZUNZ AND ELBOGEN

Although there are some respects in which Leopold Zunz (1794–1886) benefited from earlier efforts at arriving at a systematic, if not critical study of Jewish liturgy, he may still justifiably be described as the father of all modern research in this field. He bequeathed to his scholarly heirs a wealth of material and a scientific method that continue to influence contemporary work and his bibliographical study of the prayer-book remains seminal. As well as tracing the central role played by Torah-study in the history of Jewish worship, he analysed the historical development of specific prayers and of the rites in which they occurred. His work also covered the adjustments made in liturgical language, form and content, and in synagogal customs, as a result of internal and external factors.

Yet there was undoubtedly a *tendenz* in that work. Behind his early studies lay the desire for liturgical reform in the Germany of his day and the interest in presenting Judaism to liberal Europeans as a respectable culture. He consequently contrasted the lateness of *piyyuṭ* (liturgical poetry) with the antiquity of the fixed daily prayers and stressed the centrality of the homily. At a later stage of his work, however, he acknowledged the cultural value of these poems and viewed them as a mutation of the original homily form. He saw the differences in rites in terms of poetic additions and paid a growing degree of attention to the personalities of the poets and their influence on the literary genre. What he never did was to develop his basic idea about the regular prayers into either a history of the prayer-book or an analysis of its concepts, or to distinguish between the citation of a prayer and its exact wording. The study of poetry thus became an independent and fruitful subject of research while the history of the major prayers was relatively neglected.[1]

Ismar Elbogen (1874–1943) redressed the balance between prayer and poetry in the comprehensive German work, published in its final form in 1931, which built on the theories of his teacher, Israel Lewy, as well as expanding and refining

Zunz's basic treatment of Torah, *tefillah* and synagogue, but was stylistically accessible to both layman and scholar.[2] Starting out from linguistic definitions of liturgical terms, he detailed the major debts owed by Jewish liturgy to biblical precedent, Temple practice and sectarian tendencies, and acknowledged that it was only slowly that a fixed liturgy developed in the talmudic and post-talmudic periods. He pointed to divergencies between Babylonian and Palestinian practice and followed Solomon Schechter in making significant use of Genizah material for the history of rites and texts. Forty years after its appearance, the work was still important enough (or progress in the wider field unimpressive enough) to warrant a Hebrew translation of the German, albeit with corrections and updated annotations.[3]

On the less creditable side, Elbogen was still biased towards liturgical reform, negative about mysticism and tending towards the devotional. The Ashkenazi rite is too central for historical comfort and little treatment is offered of theology, *halakhah* and vestigial cultic elements. Principal aspects of the major prayers are historically analysed but little attention is paid to the textual, linguistic and literary development of the remainder of such prayers and to more minor compositions. Elbogen acknowledges the existence of more than one 'Ur-type' but nevertheless oversimplifies and exaggerates the talmudic trend towards a fixed formal liturgy. What particularly attracts contemporary criticism are his claims that Jewish prayer was innovative only in the first and third periods of its existence, namely before 600 and after 1800 CE, and that in the intermediate period that innovative ability moved from prayer to *piyyuṭ*.[4]

LATER WORK

In spite of Elbogen's provision of a more comprehensive treatment of Jewish liturgy, or perhaps because of the way in which his treatment was widely regarded as definitive, further research over the next forty years was predominantly of the highly specialised and individual variety.

Jacob Mann and, to a lesser extent, Simḥa Assaf illuminated the Jewish liturgical developments of the geonic and post-geonic periods in Palestine and Babylon by their discovery and publication of numerous Genizah texts.[5] Daniel Goldschmidt described little-known manuscripts, editions, rites and personalities and produced critical editions of major works.[6] Naphtali Wieder, to whom the writer owes his training in liturgical research, devoted his earliest work to Islamic influences on Jewish worship and to the reconstruction of Saadya's prayer-book and has more recently traced the detailed textual history of expressions and formulations, the basic sense and origin of which have long been forgotten.[7]

Much as these excellent researches were appreciated by the few experts in the field they did little to advance the general history of Jewish liturgy beyond the stage reached by Elbogen or to force the subject back into the centre of the Jewish academic scene. Educational and devotional literature gradually came to an awareness of Elbogen's findings but there was little additional work of the comprehensive type to offer further guidance for those in search of the historical prayer-book.[8]

The pendulum began to swing in the opposite direction about a quarter of a century ago and there have been signs since then of an interest in intensively analysing the subject in whole or in part, establishing how it is to be studied and following Elbogen's lead in widening its scope. At that time Goldschmidt and Joseph Heinemann began a lively exchange of views about the nature of liturgical research the significance of which remains major in spite of the deaths of both scholars. Goldschmidt continued to stress the need for thorough manuscript research, the importance of sound philological method and the close study of the various rites. Heinemann followed Arthur Spanier and argued that the philological approach was out of date and should be replaced by the form-critical method which had been so useful to biblical research and was now being applied to rabbinic texts. For him the only remaining function of the philological approach was in the completion of some outstanding points of detail. His own form-critical studies led him to the conclusion that there were equally valid variations, rather than a correct 'Ur-text', from the very beginning of rabbinic prayer, and he devoted his efforts to identifying the *Gattungen* (types) of prayer and their *Sitz im Leben* (original context).[9]

Heinemann's views gradually came to dominate in Israel and no major challenge to their whole essence was issued until the recent Hebrew article by Ezra Fleischer 'On the Beginnings of Obligatory Jewish Prayer'.[10] Fleischer, whose major work had been primarily in the field of mediaeval Hebrew poetry, increased his research interest in the history of the prayer-book itself in the 1980s and published an excellent description of the Palestinian rite as discovered in the Genizah manuscripts.[11] Now arguing that obligatory worship was a Temple activity and that there was no communal prayer in the synagogue before the destruction of the Jerusalem shrine, he placed the whole responsibility for the change on Rabban Gamliel as the innovator and fashioner of statutory rabbinic prayer. Taking issue with Heinemann's view that alternative texts, as found in the Genizah, reflected equally valid versions that had been orally transmitted, he argued for an early commitment to writing and fixed form and explained the alternatives as the result of cantorial and poetic expansions in the post-talmudic period. Fleischer's forceful expression of opinion reopened the debate about the general origin and history of rabbinic prayers and amounted to a rejection of the many moves around the world to build on Heinemann's theories.[12]

In the USA, Jakob Petuchowski took a similar position to that of Heinemann and co-operated with him in a number of projects. He did much to encourage the study of liturgy, at both the scholarly and popular levels, by his publications[13] and the postgraduate researches of his students. One of these students, Richard Sarason, in a most useful summary of the history of Jewish liturgical scholarship published fourteen years ago,[14] made a clear-cut distinction between traditional philologists and form-critics, and seemed to favour the view that the latter held the key to future developments. Indeed, the fact that his article made no mention of Wieder in seventy-six pages of printed text and had only two references to Mann and one for

Assaf in 370 footnotes, could in itself have been seen as an indication of such a preference on the part of the author. In two later articles, however,[15] he moved away from such a polarised presentation of future developments and argued for a more comprehensive approach to the study of the subject. In addition, he demonstrated convincingly the complex and multifarious nature of Jewish worship by pointing to the liturgical aspects of traditional Jewish study, practice and mystical pietism. Interestingly, the writer's own thoughts on the future of Jewish liturgical research, as expressed in a Hebrew lecture given at the Eighth World Congress of Jewish Studies held in Jerusalem in 1981, also tallied with the promotion of the comprehensive approach, and a paper first delivered to the Cambridge Theological Society in 1977, and later published in *Studia Liturgica*, independently paralleled Sarason's definitions of Jewish worship.[16]

Another student of Petuchowski, Lawrence Hoffman, analysed fifty-nine liturgical controversies among the geonim in order to reconstruct the history of the move towards standardisation of the prayers.[17] He rightly pointed to the differences between Eretz Yisrael and Babylon at that time, and to the tensions and disagreements within Babylon itself, but his neat packaging of the liturgical history of geonic Babylon into three distinct periods was perhaps a trifle too simple a solution. Whatever his attitude to the traditional, philological approach, and *pace* the view of Sarason about the 'freshness' of his thesis,[18] Hoffman was substantially indebted to scholars such as Mann and Wieder for the basic research on which he built his theories. Five years ago Hoffman produced a more general study of Jewish liturgy, more indebted to social studies and religious phenomenology, and identifying the 'sacred myths' to be traced through its history. Among the prayers and patterns analysed were *havdalah*, *'avodah*, mysticism, American Reform liturgy and the 'chavurot' (prayer groups) phenomenon, and the theories, though intriguing, were by definition somewhat speculative.[19]

One has come to expect the encouragement and promotion of novel approaches to various aspects of Jewish studies from

Jacob Neusner and his school, and in the liturgical field too a thought-provoking piece was produced by Tzvee Zahavy in 1980.[20] Zahavy's article sets out clearly the new directions in which he believes the study of early Jewish prayer should proceed and, interestingly enough, no mention is made of form-criticism, but a wide, interdisciplinary approach to the problem is proposed. The prayer-texts themselves should be studied without preconceived notions about their accurate transmission, early standardisation and historical background. The evidence from material remains is to be given a central place in reconstructing the nature of rabbinic acts of prayer and must be cautiously correlated with the evolution of literary traditions dealing with liturgical subjects. A clear distinction requires to be made between the religious theory and legal philosophy underlying rabbinic prayer on the one hand, and the rites and practices recorded in the talmudic–midrashic literature on the other. Once again there are interesting parallels with the writer's own notions.[21] In connection with such matters as the early intent of the *shema'*, the structure of some synagogues in Roman Palestine and the search for original prayers, Zahavy seems to err on the side of iconoclasm rather than caution. Similarly, there is no doubt that forms of Jewish law other than the rabbinic existed in Roman Palestine, but his implication that no overriding importance may be attached to talmudic traditions in the analysis of rabbinic prayer must be open to question. It should also be noted that he has restricted his remarks to early Jewish prayer and offered no comment on the remaining fifteen centuries of development. Nevertheless, Zahavy's emphasis on the 'interdisciplinary nature of this problem' and his call for the integrated use of 'philological study, literary criticism, archaeology, art history, history of religions, and the history of law' represented a sensible and welcome development in the field. Since penning that general article he has produced a study of the mishnaic tractate *Berakhoth* and some thought-provoking (though not necessarily convincing) theories of the original provenances of the *shema'* and the *'amidah*.[22] There is also cause for satisfaction in the fact that the subject of 'prayers and blessings' in the

Encyclopedia Hebraica was treated in a similarly variegated fashion rather than in the narrow way characteristic of many earlier Jewish encyclopaedias.[23]

SOME PROBLEMS

A researcher into the origins of the Christian daily office made the following comment some ten years ago:

> Such work as has been done has on the whole been pursued in separate, seemingly watertight, compartments: Jewish scholars have worked largely in isolation from New Testament scholars, New Testament scholars largely in isolation from liturgical scholars, and so on, with the result that hardly at all have the findings in one area been related to those in another. Even among liturgical scholars study has tended to be restricted to small areas of the subject, and the effects of new perspectives and discoveries in one historical period or geographical area upon the understanding of the office at other times and in other places have rarely been considered or worked out in full.[24]

The criticism was as applicable to the study of Jewish prayer as it was to researches in Christian liturgy. The high degree of specialisation in certain areas, the failure to approach the subject as a whole or in all its aspects, and the tendency to follow one fashionable approach and to regard others as outdated, have all led to an unacceptable degree of fragmentation. Perhaps the potential student is discouraged by the fact that Jewish liturgical scholarship touches on so many aspects of Jewish and related studies that it demands, for coping with it, an education that is at once both intense and broad. The answer to the problem is not to treat the subject in a piecemeal fashion but either to train specifically for it or to conduct the research by way of teams and projects. At least there have been some hopeful developments during the last decade in the matter of the cross-fertilisation of ideas. Jewish and Christian scholars have begun to make greater use of each other's research and to benefit from scholarly dialogue and liturgists have been looking wider than the texts of the prayers for explanations. Paul Bradshaw, who made the remark, arranged a highly successful conference on Jewish and Christian worship at Notre Dame in 1988 and two volumes of essays have been published as a result.[25]

As far as the intensive study of Jewish liturgy is concerned, it is still not taken sufficiently seriously in the wider academic community. In Israeli universities there appears to be some doubt whether the subject is entitled to an independent existence and scholarly respectability and, if so, where it truly belongs. To the extent that it receives attention, this is provided in the context of related disciplines and not as an independent academic entity, or with distinctly traditional overtones and intentions. In the many university departments teaching Hebrew and Jewish studies outside Israel, little or no time or effort is devoted to the subject. The rabbinical seminaries have a practical interest in providing an adequate training in the field, and yet there are at the moment perhaps only two or three of those institutions that could justifiably claim to be providing satisfactory encouragement for the serious and advanced study of Jewish prayer. It is not therefore surprising that in comparison with similar areas of study, the number of articles and books on the subject as a whole is few, courses are rare, progress in research is slow and spasmodic, and the interest of learned societies and academic conferences is distinctly limited.[26] Given, in addition, the current financial crisis in which all these centres of learning find themselves, the prospect of a significant expansion of this branch of scholarship in the near future does not appear likely.

The close association of study and practice has also proved a stumbling-block to the acceptance of the subject as a serious academic discipline. It has been too closely connected with traditional observance of Jewish religious customs for it to be above suspicion among academics who take a pride in their espousal of freedom of enquiry and their advocacy of objective judgement. The problem is not unique to Judaism. It has been written of the North American Academy of Liturgy that it 'represents a tension between the two end-points of the spectrum, for according to its constitution, while it hopes its work redounds to the good of the churches, the NAAL is an independent scholarly and professional organization and it does not take on its research for the sake of the churches'.[27] Even those interested in praying, and in providing spiritual guidance for those who would make most of their prayers, have not necessarily been interested in the serious study of prayer. A Dean of St Paul's Cathedral was once asked if he studied liturgiology: 'No, he did not, nor did he collect postage stamps.'[28] But then it should be said, however flippant it sounds, that the critical study of Jewish liturgy is in any case too important to be left exclusively to the 'daveners'!

Researchers must always face the problem of the assumption that has become almost axiomatic, and the long history of Jewish prayer has attracted more than its fair share of unjustified generalisations. When one such cherished supposition concerns the origins of a major world faith and the significant development of its mother religion, it is not so easily refuted. It is often claimed that the earliest Christian liturgy was based on Jewish forms of prayer as preserved in the rabbinic tradition; and yet serious questions are now being raised about the basic and relative natures of Jewish and Christian worship that may ultimately lead to a complete reappraisal of this particular sacred cow, and a consequent revision of an important aspect of Jewish and Christian religious history.[29] A good example is Arnold Goldberg's brief but important article in which he argues that rabbinic and synagogal worship is not liturgy in the Christian sense. It is a substitute for the suspended Temple liturgy which 'shows liturgical aspects, but it is . . . not a liturgy but rather a worship of the heart'.[30] Goldberg is not justified in regarding this view as characteristic of the rabbis in general, but there is no doubt that it was of major significance in the evolution of the standard rabbinic theology about prayer. Suddenly it becomes clear that the basic work in Jewish liturgy has, after all, not been definitively completed. *Au contraire*, even the most basic facts about the early liturgical relationship between Jews and Christians must be rethought.

THE WAY FORWARD

The search for the solution to the subject's problems must surely be by way of the comprehensive approach. All the scholarly means at our disposal should be used to expand our basic knowledge, to sharpen our understanding of the different elements, and to trace historical developments induced by both internal and external factors. At the same time, the concrete and factual must be made to serve the needs of the historian of ideas and sight should never be lost of the subject's larger and wider context. Co-operative courses and projects should be initiated between faculties, institutions and, indeed, religious groups, so that advantages can accrue to both the study of the subject itself and to all the aspects of learning on which it touches. In which particular department Jewish liturgy operates will depend on the nature of the institution teaching it, but it surely warrants more than a mention in the passing in such subjects as Hebrew language and literature, Jewish history, *halakhah*, kabbalah, archaeology and art, musicology, Jewish religious thoughts and phenomenology and social anthropology.

There have indeed been some interesting developments in the last few years that point the way forward in at least some restricted areas. M. Greenberg has attempted a new definition of biblical prose prayer, which stresses its democratic nature, and M. Haran has offered a comprehensive study of the more elitist Temple, priesthood and formal worship in ancient Israel.[31] The structure, purpose and evolution of the synagogue in the homeland and the diaspora has received close attention from L. I. Levine and a number of collaborators as well as from J. G. Griffiths and L. L. Grabbe,[32] while the sources in the Apocrypha, Pseudepigrapha and Qumran scrolls have been combed for their liturgical content by J. Charlesworth, D. Flusser and M. Weinfeld.[33] Students of Jewish mysticism have begun to sketch in more detail the background to its impact on the statutory prayers and in this connection the work of J. Dan, M. Bar-Ilan, P. Alexander, R. Goetschel and P. B. Fenton have indicated the future direction of research.[34] Much of I. Ta-Shema's recent research has concentrated on explaining the origins and development of mediaeval Ashkenazi customs such as, to cite only one example, the recitation of the orphan's *qaddish*.[35] The role of women in the history of Jewish worship has finally been examined, in the way that Schechter said it should about a century ago, and interesting surveys have been produced by B. Brooten, A. Weiss and J. Baskin.[36] On the sociological front, S. C. Heilman's close studies of synagogue activity and study groups have been fascinating as well as scholarly,[37] while the writer himself has tried to assess the degree to which linguistic and grammatical considerations lie behind controversy about liturgical formulation.[38]

Where then do we go from here? Elbogen's division of Jewish liturgical development into three periods may profitably be increased in number, and important work remains to be done in each. The biblical period certainly contains important evidence in Israel and outside it about the original forms of Jewish worship and how they relate to the earliest rabbinic traditions. Are the origins of the synagogue to be sought in a reaction to the centralisation of worship in Judaism, or in a wider context? The theological conflicts and tensions of the talmudic period should be clearly identified and defined, and the place of prayer, as well as the whole concept of worship, in rabbinic and non-rabbinic groups, carefully compared. Was Kohler perhaps right in looking to Christianity and Essenism for some degree of impetus, and when did prayer become a central obligation for Jews? Is it now possible to look at liturgical developments in the geonic period and to characterise them more accurately? Did Christianity again have something to do with the emergence of the first Jewish liturgical codices? Did Islamic practices influence their later contents? In the mediaeval period we have yet properly to trace the origins of the Old French and Ashkenazi rites and their relationship with the Italian and Palestinian and to distinguish clearly the old North African rite from the Sefardi version which ousted it. How much cross-fertilisation was there, linguistically and otherwise, between statutory prayer, mysticism and poetry? And what of the modern influences on the prayer-book of the massive demographical changes in the distribution of the Jewish people and the establishment of the State of Israel?

If that is the programme, it is a very full and demanding one and the current book can make only a limited contribution to implementing it. It is, however, important that a beginning be made in the construction of a new Jewish liturgical history that takes into account all these and other innovations and developments and offers guidance and encouragement to future students of the subject. Before the task here in hand is undertaken it will be useful to indicate at least briefly what will and will not be attempted and by which means.

METHODOLOGY AND THEORY

Given that the present volume is the first attempt at providing an overall scientific treatment of Jewish liturgical history for almost three-quarters of a century, it is self-evident that the aim will be to start out at the period of the Hebrew Bible, even if it predates the existence of a Hebrew prayer-book, and to trace developments up to and including the last few decades, even if many are as much a matter of speculative assessment as they are of solid analysis. Dealing with literary, linguistic and cultural problems over such a wide period is a challenging exercise and the writer is conscious not only that there are few scholars rash enough to undertake it but that anyone who does so is open to criticism from those who occupy themselves with the highly specialised exposition of a single aspect of development at a particular point in history. If, however, the results of the latest scholarship of such a specialised variety are incorporated into the overall treatment, there is the prospect of presenting an up-to-date picture throughout and of meeting thereby a need that is being widely felt by scholars and lay people. This is not to say that the same approach is consistently being used for each topic or period. There is here a conviction of the existence in Jewish religious and cultural history of more than an element of continuity and an awareness of the artificial nature of many of the strict divisions commonly made between times, places, groups and ideas. Nevertheless, no historian worthy of the title would for a moment deny that each historical entity, in whatever way it is linked to its fellows, is deserving of an individual type of treatment and an invitation to it to speak for itself. Common themes will always emerge but, as different questions are posed, so individual answers will be forthcoming and the characteristics of each age will be identified. The cost of excessive compartmentalisation is a failure to trace the inevitable red threads that permeate the patchwork quilt of history. At the same time, it requires constant scholarly caution if one is to avoid the pitfalls of making assumptions about one element in history on the basis of one's knowledge of another. Whether in the matter of terminology, or custom, or formal practice, it is altogether too simple a matter to presuppose that what was standard in one period must have enjoyed the same status in earlier or later generations. To make such a presupposition is to deny many individuals and communities their contribution to the long process of religious and cultural development. Religions often engage in imposing current ideas and fashions on their pasts, thereby winning for them an increased respectability and this is part of an inner dynamic rather than any conscious effort to deceive. It is, however, the historian's duty to separate the continuous theme from the innovative development as far as scholarly ability permits and to appreciate the fact that the biblical, rabbinic, geonic, mediaeval and modern periods may have to be examined in different ways and that such examination may yield unexpected results. Later concepts may turn out to be based on earlier precedents and may have to be redated but, in the absence of proof, no unsupported assumptions may be made of this nature.

It is of course now freely admitted that no researcher can ever be totally dispassionate and that scholarship does not exist in a human vacuum. Jewish or Christian, modernist or post-modernist, Orthodox or Reform – whatever one's convictions, they may well underlie one's interpretation of the evidence, but every effort should still be made for scientific detachment. Whether or not the findings of the historian are relevant to current approaches to the theory and practice of Judaism and to plans for their future is a matter for rabbis, theologians, and communal leaders to determine and not for academics on which to pontificate. For all that historians know, the lessons of yesterday may be precisely the wrong guidance for tomorrow but the reconstruction of all our yesterdays remains an imperative, for its own sake if for no other, and each chapter in this volume should ideally be able to function as a self-contained treatment of a particular part of Jewish liturgical history, with an inevitable degree of overlap between aspects of them all.

An overall approach such as the present one will inevitably exploit the classical sources of Jewish theological and halakhic expression as source material as well as dealing with such disparate matters as general history, mysticism, codicology and social studies. Such a wide understanding of cultural history is an important factor in exchanging nineteenth-century interpretations for their equivalents as we approach the twenty-first century. Much of the historical work of the scholars of the *Wissenschaft des Judentums* of the last century was based on their fresh examination of old rabbinic sources and their extrapolation from these of the building bricks for reconstructing the events of the past. Although great credit belongs to them for transforming traditional texts into scientific accounts, their methods now appear somewhat parochial. In more recent times students of Jewish history have sought to acquaint themselves not only with Jewish sources but also with non-Jewish materials and have ranged much more widely than rabbinic literature in their search for documentation. The liturgist too must now follow this lead and bring a broad spectrum of scholarship to bear on his presentation of the prayers and their development so that instead of a one-way traffic from primary Jewish sources to general history there is also a movement in the opposite direction.

However wide and comprehensive the analysis, or perhaps because of its extensive nature, it will be necessary to be eclectic about what receives attention. Clearly, although the majority of the relevant prayers, authors and works will be touched upon, only a volume twice or three times the size could provide guidance about everything relevant. While major developments of the past are here being treated, it is also the intention to set an agenda for future liturgical study and to leave detailed analysis for other contexts. Many questions will be asked and some will be answered; others will remain to be posed and to attract the required responses at a later date. Liturgical poetry will hardly feature at all for the simple reason that it has had more than its fair share of scholarly attention for a century and a half. For an age that was most anxious to stress its commitment to cultural phenomena that would attract the admiration of the dominant environment, the discovery, decipherment and attractive publication of the products of the Hebrew lyrical genius were a matter of national pride. Statutory prayers, particularly when influenced by mystical trends, could be embarrassing and were more a matter for internal contemplation. Strangely, this scholarly tendency has remained a feature of Jewish liturgical study throughout the twentieth century. It is true that Jewish mysticism has been rehabilitated but for the dominant Scholem school the religiosity of that phenomenon has been presented almost as independent of standard rabbinic ideology and practice, even in contrast to them. The mystical tail has therefore been made to wag the liturgical dog, much as liturgical poetry was given an unbalanced degree of importance by the Maskilim. The object here is to take account of mysticism but to try to place it in its rabbinic context on the assumption that in those instances when it truly became independent it virtually ceased to affect the daily religious activities of the ordinary Jewish community.

By the same token, it is the *siddur* (daily prayer-book) of traditional rabbinism that is the primary concern here and the whole presentation will very much be taken up with descriptions of the contexts in which it was used, altered and retained. Since biblical and Qumranic evidence is very relevant to the emergence of the earliest rabbinic prayers, due attention is given to these sources but since the liturgies of the Samaritans and the Ethiopian Jews are of quite a different order and do not to any significant degree make an impact on the *siddur*, they are not included in the discussion. Karaism, too, represents a rejection of the rabbinic tradition in favour of what is seen as the biblical one and reference is made to that interpretation of Judaism only briefly in the passing. As far as modern, non-Orthodox versions of Judaism are concerned, the liturgical preferences of the major movements are discussed in some detail in the final two chapters because they took the traditional *siddur* as their starting-point and, even when proposing radical adjustments, still constructed their alternative versions with close reference to the original. In any event, those pressures for change also made a powerful impact on the form and content of the *siddur* in Orthodox circles, whether at one extreme, where mild reforms were sanctioned or smuggled in, or at the other, where only the physical presentation of the traditional text was modernised.

While manuscripts were available to the researchers of the nineteenth and early twentieth centuries, the situation today is an even happier one with additional collections now available for the first time, others becoming progressively more accessible, and Genizah fragments no longer lying crated, neglected and unconserved in forgotten corners of libraries, much as they had once lain dormant in Cairo. There is therefore the opportunity of making use of primary material and its novel exploitation, and of stressing the view adopted here that the Genizah material is a reflection of normative reality, and not of fringe interests, part of a continuous historical development rather than indicative of revolutionary propensities. While there are innovative interpretations, some of which will undoubtedly be regarded by some as controversial, the object has not been to succumb to the temptation of allowing the footnotes to force the text into a subordinate role in the manner that is sometimes encountered in certain kinds of scholarship. The preferred alternative has been to use a judicious blend of the primary and the secondary, of the narrative text and the documentation, and of the Hebrew and the European sources in order to achieve an overview that will, without ever being dogmatic, offer the reader a soundly based consensus, the opportunity of independently pursuing some topics, and some fresh insights into the whole subject. The hope is that this volume will enthuse some to search and others to research, the intention being not only to cater for specialists seeking helpful summaries for themselves and their students but also to update scholars in other fields who wish to keep abreast of developments, and to inform the intelligent lay person with an interest in unravelling the *siddur*'s various layers of history.

In the course of the preparation of this work, a number of

recurrent themes have been identified that in a sense represent the theory that underlies the explanations here being offered of the process of liturgical history. A brief allusion to them will alert readers to what may be expected of the remaining chapters and invite them to apply their own minds to the problems, either to support or to challenge the interpretations here being offered. It should not of course be thought that these themes are here being identified for the first time; far from it. Many will be familiar to students of Jewish liturgy, but their rehearsal here and the inclusion of other, perhaps more novel ideas, will assist with the creation of the *überblick* that is the declared aim.

Perhaps the currently best recognised theme of Jewish liturgical history is that of tensions between opposing principles. Is participation in worship ideally to be formal, communal and dominated by males, or is it at its best when it constitutes the spontaneous act of an individual, regardless of sex? Do the *Tanakh*, the Hebrew language and the land of Israel stand at the heart of Jewish prayer, or are the Talmud, vernacular and the current domicile the factors that control its essence? Should one strive for a mystical and esoteric communion with the divine through intensive expressions of praise, in emulation of the celestial world, and risk the prospect that success will be granted only to an elite? Is it preferable to lay down rational legislation that caters for simple human requests and thanksgiving as well as praise and is capable of being more popularly followed? It need hardly be emphasised that the possible equations are innumerable and that, whatever their constituent parts, there is an inbuilt balance of forces that maintains the tension.

There are also various contexts that compete for dominance in liturgical matters. The home as the centre of ordinary activity and the observances that go with it makes its bid for central recognition, offering the table as the altar and the family members as the priests. The house of study argues for the teaching and learning of Torah as the most important forms of worship, suggesting that the studied text is the liturgy and the scholar the worshipper. The synagogue presses its claim as the purpose-built location for an exclusive concern for praising, thanking and importuning God and develops a set of functionaries who are devoted to ensuring the religious efficiency of the exercise. Not only do each of the central elements of Judaism and many of their minor details all present themselves as service of God but the texts that are composed reflect a variety of Jewish religious and cultural endeavour and the cycle of the Jewish calendar provides opportunities for the indulgence of each different aspect of liturgical need. Perhaps most significant of all, the Jewish encounter with God may at one extreme consist of a total negation of the self but at the other extreme it may challenge him in litigious fashion, daring to see the struggle as one of equals.

Today's greatest expert in the detailed textual study of mediaeval Hebrew liturgy, Naphtali Wieder, used to refer in his Jews' College lectures of thirty years ago to the importance of understanding that Judaism always had an excellent digestive system, and that its liturgy was capable of absorbing all manner of content at different periods. What emerges from an overall analysis of historical developments is the extent to which the Christian and Islamic worlds not only borrowed from Jewish liturgy but also had both positive and negative effects on the mother religion's own prayers. This is just as true in the modern world as it was in the mediaeval, even when the dominant influence is more often a secular than a religious one. What is remarkable is that no matter how fierce the battle over the acceptance of a new text or custom, a final victory for the argument in favour of absorption ultimately brings with it a canonicity for the novelty which alters it from yesterday's threatening heresy to today's established tradition. New convincing reasons for its importance will appear and may also be bolstered by an attribution to a major figure of Jewish liturgical or, indeed, general history.

The fate of proposed alternatives also depends on the particular historical circumstance and atmosphere in which they come to the fore. There are crests and troughs in matters of authority, centralisation and unification. In one generation the move may be in the direction of such principles; in others the preference may be for variation and more individual communal expression. Similarly, the tendency of one centre or generation to ritualise prayers, ceremonies, functionaries, artefacts and buildings may be matched by the rebellion of another against what they might regard as an artificially imposed discipline. A group that is regarded or regards itself as dominant in one sense or another may succeed in imposing the acceptance of its rites and customs on another group even if the former is a newcomer and in a minority.

The problem for the researcher is that such developments are not of course seen as such, or not at least described as such, in the relevant or in subsequent generations. Once new customs or rites are legitimately established, they are redefined in the light of their new status and acquire an authority and history that cover the original evidence with layers of later deposits. The historian is therefore obliged to be sceptical about the arguments and comments made by later authorities in favour of a development and about the degree to which it may be assumed that what is regarded by them as a well-established principle or policy was always the reality in earlier situations. This is by no means an attempt to mislead or to suppress evidence on the part of those in positions of religious authority at any particular time. They too have simply been deceived by the manner in which an inner dynamic has led to adjustments that can no longer be easily explained in the light of the dominant attitudes. Novel suggestions are therefore put forward, generally in innocence and with conviction, to provide the explanation required, and the most commonly proposed reasons for change relate to tragedy, insecurity and persecution. Just as researchers must be wary of simplistic categorisations of the different rites and historical periods that forget or blur the differences that once existed, so must they learn to question any prima-facie case for attributing liturgical change to the 'lachrymose element' in Jewish history. It is just as common for Judaism to devise its own means of making progress as it is for it to have its future path charted for it by its enemies' activities. This is not to say that death, suffering and martyrdom do not have a major impact on Jewish liturgical development in each age. The centrality of such human problems forced a significant degree of attention to them in the *siddur* and thereby found their expression in liturgical terms, as did popular folklore even when opposed by rabbinic sentiment. This is, however, quite a different matter from explaining the origin in times of persecution of customs that have in themselves nothing to do with such suffering and are in no way a direct reflection of it. There are clues scattered about Jewish liturgical history that can assist the historian in locating the real reasons for developments but they are not always adequate for a full reconstruction. Until they are, one must simply remain suspicious and sceptical when dealing with explanations of a *post-eventum* nature.

It should also be noted in conclusion that the method of transmission has had a considerable influence on the history of the Hebrew prayers. Silver, papyrus, leather and paper have been among the materials used for recording texts and stone and wood may also have played a part. Textuality, in the sense of a fixed and formal composition, may also have been orally communicated and this fact must also be taken into account when tracing the history of prayers. The physical structure has at various times been the amulet, the scroll, the codex and the printed volume, and the changes from one medium to another have inevitably left their mark on the literary form. The ability to add halakhic guidance, glosses and commentaries in the Middle Ages and the availability of quick copying and transmission of one sort or another in the contemporary world are clearly significant features that deserve closer attention than has been possible in the current volume.[39] Now that these introductory remarks have been made on methodology and theory, the way is open for an examination in eight chapters of what it has been possible to include in the present context.

CHAPTER 2

The biblical inspiration

The purposes of this chapter are to describe briefly the wider historical and cultural setting in which the earliest manifestations of liturgical activity among the Hebrews and Jews are to be placed and to summarise the nature of that activity as it is recorded in both the pre-exilic and post-exilic books of the Hebrew Bible on the one hand and in the wider literature of the Second Temple period on the other. Establishing precisely the *terminus a quo* for Jewish worship is a matter that must remain controversial since it is bound up with the problem of identifying the relationship between Hebrews, Israelites and Jews and offering a judgement on the degree of religious continuity that one may genuinely trace from the biblical into the rabbinic period. It is the view of the writer that in the area of worship there is sufficient evidence of some degree of continuity to justify commencing this treatment from at least the period of the Hebrew monarchy. Aspects of the terminology, vocabulary, ritual, and the organisation of personnel and formulae which have their origins in the older, if not oldest, parts of the Hebrew Bible may still be traced, even if sometimes in mutated form, in the prayer-books that were written almost two thousand years later. Furthermore, attempts by the ancestors of the Jews to find the most efficacious way of communicating with God and to challenge the equitable basis of their relationship with him may justifiably be said to lie behind a number of the tensions that characterise the development of Jewish liturgy through the many centuries from the Hebrew Bible until modern times.

There is, of course, always the danger of reading backwards

instead of forwards in the historical analysis of religious trends and care must be taken to avoid the trap of assuming that what a later form of religious practice claims as its earliest precedent is accurately to be identified as such. It is indeed part of the stock-in-trade of the major faiths through the centuries that they rarely claim to be innovating but almost always to be returning to their roots and their authentic origins. The paradox with worship, perhaps more than with any other element of religious expression, is that until the modern period it could only ever be revolutionary by presenting itself as intensely conservative. While exercising caution, then, one must nevertheless be conscious of the fact that the Hebrew Bible always constituted a major source of Jewish liturgical theory and practice in their generality, however much the details of their application might vary from generation to generation and between one centre and another. Consequently, this treatment considers early biblical Hebrew texts before it moves on to that Second Temple period in which some scholars of the last century preferred to seek the origins of Judaism, while they appropriated for the histories of their own faiths what they regarded as the finest ideals of pre-exilic times.

Having offered some justification for setting the chronological parameters of this study the way that one has done, one may be forgiven for regarding it as self-evident that some reference, however brief, should be made to the liturgical activities of the surrounding peoples. This, after all, is the starting-point for so much scientific study of the institutions and culture of ancient Israel that it would seem strange to rule it out of order in the present context. Nevertheless, a number of challenges to this approach may be anticipated, not only from the circles of those who are generally loath to see the Hebrew Bible as anything but the directly mediated message of God, but also from others who are either wary of the dangers of 'parallelomania' or would argue that the customs of other Near Eastern peoples in such a religiously sensitive issue as prayer are no more or less relevant than those of African pygmies or Oceanian headhunters.[1]

It may be argued that a response validating a critical

approach to religious texts is unnecessary for those who accept the need for scientific methodology in the historical analysis of all cultural traditions and pointless for those who reject it. But this is to take too pessimistic a view. The matter of liturgical origins in any event touches upon no dogmas of traditional Judaism, the talmudic rabbis themselves, as will become apparent in a later chapter, having expressed themselves in a variety of contradictory ways on the subject, and their mediaeval successors having acknowledged the influences, for one reason or another, of the surrounding environment upon the emergence and development of what they nevertheless regarded as Torah concepts.[2] As far as Christian religious history and dogma is concerned, not only do the liturgical practices of the ancient Near Eastern peoples so antedate these as to be less relevant than the mystery religions and the pagan practices of the classical world but there is even little firm knowledge about Christian liturgy and its required form in the early centuries of its existence.[3] There will always be Jews and Christians of fundamentalist leanings who will remain unconvinced by these disclaimers but they are in any case unlikely to be exclusively swayed by rational and historical arguments alone in matters of religious history.

More to the point in the current context is the fear of drawing parallels almost for parallels' sake, an exercise that has drawn justified criticism within academic circles in recent years. Here it should be pointed out that the object is not to trace the direct source of one people's rituals and customs in those of another, nor of making judgements about their relative value, religiously or otherwise. A study such as this simply proceeds on the assumption that ancient peoples who lived in close proximity to each other, sometimes occupied each other's territory, and/or spoke languages that belonged to the same general group are likely to have exercised influence on each other's ways of life, either positively leading to emulation or negatively resulting in polemical disassociation. It is only by establishing the wider context that one can arrive at such conclusions about the significance of particular developments within sections of that context.

If the phenomenology of religious rites were here the major concern, one might follow James Frazer's example and seek parallels through world culture, but the methodology in this case is rather an historical one, with due attention to phenomenological, form-critical and other scientific factors, and the overall intention of producing a more comprehensive overview than has hitherto been attempted.[4] Consequently, it is essential to place geographical, chronological and cultural limits on the areas to be regarded as relevant in arriving at an understanding of the background against which the earliest aspects of documented liturgy among the Hebrews made their appearance. Before attempting such an understanding it is perhaps necessary to stress that what is being viewed here is not only the individual elements of prayer or ritual or liturgical ideology but a combination of them all. Although the ultimate aim is to understand the synagogue and the *siddur*, it is central to the thesis of this book that this cannot be successfully undertaken without previously making reference to a wide variety of practices within the overall sphere of Hebrew, Israelite and Jewish worship.

What then are the overall impressions to be gained from an examination of sample texts and scientific summaries relating to the liturgical activities of the major civilisations of the Egyptians, Hittites, Mesopotamians and Canaanites?[5]

The rich variety of extensive material available to the researcher is immediately apparent. As far as cultic activities are concerned, sacrifices of animals and the varied disposal of their sundry parts are virtually ubiquitous, while it is no less common to encounter offerings of incense as well as of staple food and drink to ensure a happy frame of mind on the part of the divine recipient. Ritual acts are often linked with a calendrical cycle, be it daily, monthly, seasonal or annual, and the rites are performed or supervised by a royal, priestly or senior figure. Ministering vestments are recorded, as are images, precious stones and special vessels used for cultic purposes. Prescriptions for theurgical activities and instructions for ritual ablution are laid out and there are details of numerous ceremonials, some of them acted out in the manner of passion plays, others involving the use of everyday items, usually of mineral or vegetable origin, for the purposes of achieving aims through sympathetic magic. Singing, dancing and the composition of poetry are features of some acts of worship and there are often texts, at times of a formulaic nature, that are recited as an integral part of the cultic activity. Such texts may take the form of blessings or curses, invocations, praises, lamentations and entreaties but they are generally related to the formalities of communal liturgy.[6]

What then of hymns and prayers of the more personal kind, recited by the individual or group of 'lay' individuals, and so familiar to the adherents of the world's major, monotheistic religions in later times? The reader of inscriptions from the world of the ancient Near East does encounter forms that may, at first sight, be seen as the antecedents of personal prayer. In some compositions, gods and goddesses, both senior and junior, either singly or jointly, are extravagantly praised for their operation of the natural world, while in others, somewhat rarer, they are extolled for their defence of justice and protection of the underprivileged. Before making his or her request, the suppliant may adopt a particularly humble pose, begging forgiveness and expressing repentance, or confident claims may be made that, to the best of the petitioner's knowledge, all religious requirements have been fully and correctly carried out in the past, no wrongdoing perpetrated and, consequently, there is no justification for divine disfavour. The god's mercy is invoked and entreaty made for an end to ill health or unhappiness, the reputation of the deity and the supplicant's continued loyalty to him are predicated upon the successful outcome of these prayers, and blessing and prosperity are solicited for oneself and the opposite for one's enemies. It is in this area of blessings and curses that it becomes apparent that, even in those more 'personal' prayers, the homeland, the people, the capital city and the shrine often play a major part. The enemy is commonly the military adversary of the nation, the god or goddess may be the nation's own special deity, and the composition and recitation of the hymn is the prerogative of a priest, priestess or other temple or palace official.[7]

Such hymns and prayers are so similar to what is found in the formal, institutional cult and so bound up with it in many ways that it is difficult to make any meaningful distinction between the texts used in the two contexts. Perhaps this is what Lichtheim has in mind when she offers the following characterisation of Egyptian liturgical texts: 'the elaborate hymns that came from the cultic context stand side by side with the short hymns and prayers of humble individuals.'[8] Certainly as far as the Sumerian, Assyrian and Babylonian liturgies are concerned, it is clear that Schmökel's judgement is of major importance in essaying a comparison with the equivalent sections of the Hebrew Bible: 'in contrast to the OT, the religious literature of ancient Mesopotamia rarely presents free, personal prayer – this is most likely to be found, if at all, on the lips of rulers and kings, and particularly in their votive inscriptions and those on new buildings; in that case the prayer is addressed to the deity to whom a gift is offered or for whom the particular building has been erected or restored.'[9] One should certainly not lose sight of the possibility that the documents preserved for later generations are, by definition, those emanating from the royal court and the national shrine and that there is no obvious context in which the more individual prayers of the masses, assuming that they did exist, might have been perpetuated. The fact is, however, that by choosing to preserve the forms of expression that they did, rather than any other, the dominant transmitters of Mesopotamian culture were betraying their views on the superior merit of those forms for their religious values, much as the editors of the biblical books may be said to have done in their choice of Hebrew and Israelite traditions.

Attention may now be focussed on these traditions and an attempt made to delineate the general liturgical situation as it obtained from, say, the middle of the monarchial period. It is notoriously difficult to fix the precise dates of biblical material but if a policy is pursued of limiting both general statements and particular examples to what, in their essence, may be regarded as fairly uncontroversial from the chronological point of view, the most obvious pitfalls will probably be avoided.

There did once exist a chronologically helpful tendency to see a progressive development in liturgical, as well as all other aspects of ancient religious behaviour, from the natural, through the historical, to the formal, and the evolution of theory and practice was traced accordingly. Current scholarship is justifiably more wary of such a Hegelian philosophy and is consequently more inclined to see a combination of such elements from the earliest period, with crests and troughs occurring in connection with the predominance of each of these and in accordance with the changing circumstances of the passing generations. In that case, the dating of material has to be based on the literary, linguistic and historical clues that it offers rather than on its degree of systematic theology. Given that in some cases early narrative traditions are said to have undergone later editorial and redactional treatment, one must be cautious about relying too much on their exact formulation. Nevertheless, where the basic structure, vocabulary and message betray little evidence of such treatment and still presuppose an environment compatible with the period of the monarchy, one is perhaps entitled to regard the evidence of such texts as valid for building a picture of much of the documented pre-exilic period.[10] What must first be addressed, then, are the various forms of liturgical expression that are recorded in the earliest parts of the Hebrew Bible.

There can be no doubt that the sacrifice of animals and the offering of gifts, with the associated use of specially designed and designated implements, constituted an important means of promoting the relationship with God by way of appeasement, apology or gratitude; that women had at least a limited role in such activities; and that the communal or family meals attendant on such rituals strengthened the ties of those who shared a belief in him. It is clear from the later, prophetic struggles to restrict the Canaanite influences on Israelite worship that the Hebrews had borrowed much from their pagan neighbours in this as well as in other areas of religious practice. Be that as it may, the monotheistic theory served to adjust the nature of such practice and to temper its excesses from whenever it may be stated to have taken hold. The narratives relating to such places as Shechem, Bethel, Gilgal, Tabor, Beersheba, Mizpah, Shiloh and Carmel provide ample evidence of the multiplicity of cultic centres in ancient Israel, even after Jerusalem acquired a special, central role. Older traditions relating to the tent of meeting appear to indicate the existence of an even less permanent shrine, perhaps once a moveable structure for a nomadic family or tribe. Prophets, priests and levites, as well as the heads of households are seen to be active in the performance of sacrificial rites, which are regarded as the best means of inducing mystical piety and a feeling of proximity to the divine. There is royal involvement, particularly in the case of David, but this appears to have been considerably less central among the Israelites than it was among some of their neighbours.[11]

Whether or not it has to do with the consistency of the climate, the natural calendar and its seasons stood at the centre of much of the ritual of the ancient Near East. The Hebrews, too, had their special festivities to mark spring, autumn, the new moon and the various harvests, and historical and theological elements combined with agricultural ones to lend multifarious significance to their observance. The feast of the Passover is perhaps the best example of such a complex, liturgical phenomenon, combining as it did ceremonies relating to the barley harvest, the sacrifice of a lamb, the inauguration of a new season and the people's memory of a major religio-historical event that came to be identified as the exodus from Egyptian slavery. In connection with the liturgical function of the calendar, it should be noted that the sun itself, as distinct from its effect on the seasons, is given little attention in the Hebrew Bible, perhaps because of the centrality of the sun-god in so many Semitic pantheons, and solar language for God is fairly limited. Furthermore, the sabbath has no true parallel among any neighbouring peoples and introduces a new element, unrelated to the natural calendar, into Israelite practice and, ultimately, worthy of special liturgical attention.[12]

The use of musical instruments, as well as of singing and dancing, to induce a mood of rejoicing and even of ecstacy is also documented. There were, no doubt, both spontaneous and formal manifestations of this kind of sprituality.[13] The declamation of formulae, the recitation of poetry, and the reading/chanting of prayers would also be rhythmic activities that one would naturally look for in the communal liturgical contexts legally and specifically prescribed in the Pentateuch, particularly since they occur in geographically proximate cultures. The remarkable fact is that on a strict reading of the relevant texts there appears to be few or none of such activities directly associated with formal Temple practices, a circumstance that requires closer investigation and explanation. In order to meet this requirement it will be necessary to examine what there is of these types within the cult and outside it.

Two formulae connected with the Temple are to be found in Numbers 6:22–7 and Deuteronomy 26:1–12. The former constitutes the famous priestly benediction, clear-cut support for the existence of which in the pre-exilic period has recently come from the discovery in Jerusalem excavations of a silver amulet containing a version of its text and dated to the seventh century BCE.[14] The liturgical use of this same benediction in the Second Temple period, as documented in both internal and external sources, will later be noted.[15] The latter formula is that to be recited by the farmer on bringing his first ripe fruits to the Temple. It bears all the literary and linguistic hallmarks of a ritual declaration originating in Israel's earliest history and containing significant historical, agricultural and theological references.[16] Other recitations that may be regarded as having become ritualised are the historical explanation that the father must give to his son for the paschal sacrifice, recorded in both Exodus and Deuteronomy, and the reading of 'this Torah' to the assembled people – men, women and children – on the Festival of Tabernacles at the end of each sabbatical year and during the pilgrimage to the Temple.[17] But whatever their connections with the Temple, whether through the first fruits, the priests, the paschal offering or the pilgrimage, none of these formulae are actually a part of the sacrificial cult, or a necessary ingredient of its internal ceremonial. In fact, both these ceremonial recitations may be understood more as educational exercises within a liturgical framework than as liturgies with historical content. The explanation of the Passover is pedagogical and domestically based while the Torah reading is specifically aimed at the wider public temporarily present for the festival. This didactic element in early Israelite liturgical ceremonial is not an insignificant one in view of subsequent developments. As will become clearer in later chapters, Torah not only had a part to play in worship but was at times so central to the faith that it threatened the development of formulated prayer or at least attempted to occupy a more exalted theological position. The only direct reference to some statement being made during the worship by the priest or the layman initiating the offering is to be found in the requirement that he 'confesses' or 'acknowledges' his sin, or that of those he is representing, before completing the ritual.[18] It is a moot point whether the texts are described as early by a large enough consensus of modern scholars to allow them to be universally regarded as significant but, whatever their date, they make no reference to any actual words of a prayer and may imply no more than a formula of two or three words at most or, possibly, an acceptance of the *need* for atonement before the arrangement for its availability is undertaken. The theophany described in Isaiah's famous vision in the sixth chapter of the book includes references to what later became the famous trisagion ('holy, holy, holy') and to burning coals on an altar and it could be argued that the prophet's image is borrowed from Israelite Temple practice. Ranged against such an argument, however, are the facts that such prophetic visions rarely reflect reality, that the image of God is that of a king being praised in his palace, and that the altar is mentioned in a separate sequence of the narrative. Indeed, according to V. Hurowitz, the whole passage is a distortion of a legal-cultic situation similar to those acted out in many Mesopotamian rituals, rather than a reflection of any standard Israelite practice.[19]

What then of verbal expressions of what may be called the liturgical communion between man and God outside the central sacrificial cult, in so far as they are preserved in the Hebrew Bible? Clearly, the book of Psalms merits some close attention but before this is undertaken other texts which are early and are not to be found in contexts that are by definition hymns, praises and the like, should be analysed for their prayer content. The Hebrew root *pll* in the *hithpa'el* conjugation and its equivalent substantival form, translated 'pray' and 'prayer', are used to describe appeals to humans, idols and God. The appeal, which may be on behalf of oneself or someone else, is usually for the removal of physical problems or the granting of favours and the format sometimes resembles a kind of negotiation rather than a direct request. There are also instances in which miraculous vision, forgiveness and the punishment of an adversary are sought and in which the petitioner asks for consideration of his previous, good behaviour. The setting is not usually a temple or a holy place, with the interesting exception of Isaiah 16:12 which describes Moab's unsuccessful prayers as taking place at his sanctuary after a similar failure at a high place.[20]

There are certainly many cases in which a similar form of appeal is made to God, with a record of the alleged wording, but without the actual use of the technical term *hithpallel*, and it will be instructive to analyse in brief a few samples of these. Abraham's statements before God in Genesis 18:22–33 smack of theological challenge and judicial debate although they are made on behalf of the wicked of Sodom and include some technically humble terminology. The dedication of Bethel by Jacob in Genesis 28:16–22 is fairly straightforward but is followed by an oath according to the literal sense of which he proposes to strike a bargain with God that in return for a protected journey, sustenance and a safe homecoming, he will acknowledge the Lord as his God and offer him tithes. The same patriarch is credited with a simpler request for protection from his brother Esau in Genesis 32:12 but, if the surrounding verses (10–13) are not to be taken as literary expansions, both ancestral merit and previous, divine promises are cited, however delicately, as pressing reasons for a favourable response. Similar considerations apply in the cases of Moses' entreaty on behalf of Israel in Exodus 32:11–14 where God's right to be angry is starkly challenged and successfully refuted.

His request for the healing of Miriam is altogether more simple, a polite but direct cry to the Lord to cure her (Numbers 12:13). While the supplication of Joshua in Joshua 7:6–9 and its physical manifestations seem real enough, the apparent inconsistency of God's policy towards Israel is once again brought into question and the possibility raised of damage to his reputation if the people he has brought over the Jordan meet with ignominious defeat.

Such inconsistency also troubles Samson when, having achieved a splendid military victory over the Philistines, he seems about to perish of thirst (Judges 15:18), although his final prayer is a simple appeal for the power to avenge the gouging out of his eyes by his Philistine captors (Judges 16:30). The teachers of the Babylonian Talmud already recognised in Hannah's prayers referred to in 1 Samuel 1:10–16 the *locus classicus* for the correct behaviour in undertaking such a religious exercise.[21] Anguish, desperation and distraught tears accompany her entreaty for a son of her own but, even in such circumstances, she is cool enough to offer God a bargain that he will find it difficult to refuse, namely, a child devoted to his service. Her exultant psalm has, of course, to be considered with all other forms of the genre in a later paragraph.[22] The formal, literary structure of the prayers of David (2 Samuel 7:18–29) for the survival of his dynasty, and of Solomon (1 Kings 3:5–15), raise at least some doubts about provenance and date but what is clear from these, as well as from the simple form of Hezekiah's appeal for recovery (2 Kings 20:1–3), and other similar texts, is that prayer is direct and personal, totally outside the realm of the institutional cult, and often dialectical enough to be characterised almost as an exchange between equals.[23] Rather than taking its place among priestly rituals, such a form of communication with God seems more closely related to the personal invocation of blessings and curses or the individual's imposition on himself of oaths and vows. It is indeed difficult in some of the older poetic texts such as the blessings of Jacob (Genesis 49) and Moses (Deuteronomy 33) to distinguish between prophesy, blessing, prayer and admonition. What certainly cannot be identified in such passages, however, is an obvious involvement of the text in the formal cult or vice versa, and there is no indication of a stereotypical, linguistic or literary pattern. Be that as it may, there are theories about the function of such poetry and of the psalm form in the communal, liturgical context which necessitates some consideration of these types of biblical literature within the present discussion.

It would be difficult to argue with the claim that many of the biblical psalms are related to the Temple. Some of them make direct reference to the psalmist's desire to undertake the pilgrimage to the sanctuary (42, 84 and 122) while others stress the centrality, beauty and spirituality of Mount Zion and the city of Jerusalem (20, 48 and 87). There are chapters in the book of Psalms such as 24, 99 and 150 that would have read well as accompaniments to a triumphal and/or ceremonial entry on to the Temple Mount and a batch of psalms prefaced with the word *ma'aloth* (120–34) that have been explained as the songs that were chanted by those ascending the steps (regarded as the translation of *ma'aloth*) that led up to the Temple itself. Some scholars have gone further and, seeing in the Psalms the Israelite version of ancient Semitic myths that accompanied annual rituals, have characterised the whole book as a kind of hymn-book attached to formal worship from the Israelite conquest of Canaan until Second Temple times, and have seen in these compositions an exalted and delicately constructed literary form that served as a paradigm on which were based the more vulgar and simple efforts of the ordinary people to pray when they had no access to the Temple.[24] Alternatively, such primitive prayers were taken by the Temple composers and recast into the beautiful poetry that they now constitute so that they would be suitable for the more elevated style required by communal worship at the national shrine. There are indeed some psalms such as 5, 27, 54 and 56 in which the psalmist makes references to both prayer and sacrifice. He looks forward greatly to a regular appearance in the Temple and undertakes to fulfil the vows he has made and to bring the offerings he has promised. At the same time, he mentions the spoken or chanted word as well as physical obeisance as acts of worship. All such evidence might be said to identify the formal, sacrificial cult conducted by the priests as a centre of personal prayer.

Such a conclusion goes beyond the evidence of the psalm texts cited and is of a considerably speculative nature. What is clearly demonstrated by the sources is that some Israelites were enthusiastic participants in the cult, as well as keen reciters of prayers, and that, on their way to indulge that former interest, they might well have given expression to their fondness for the latter. Such texts as 1 Samuel 15:22 and Isaiah 1:11–15 demonstrate an anxiety on the part of at least some to ensure that the sincerity and spontaneity associated with personal prayer be present in equal measure in the functioning of the sacrificial rituals. There were Israelites who associated the holy places with a nearness to God and found the environs of a temple conducive to what one may go so far as to designate a communal version of personal worship. Zion and Jerusalem were consequently of special significance to their religious lives and attracted special praise in this connection. The vast majority of psalms, however, relate to matters that can be exclusively linked with a formal cult, particularly in its sacrificial aspect, only by the stretch of a vivid imagination, since it is just as likely that such types of composition as praises and laments, expressions of gratitude or celebrations of happy events were recited away from the Temple Mount as on it. Precisely when and how to date the psalms, what possible *Sitz im Leben* they originally had among the Israelites and/or their close neighbours, and whether 'cultic' psalms inspired personal prayer or vice versa, are, in any case, all questions to which only the most theoretical and hypothetical answers have been given.[25] Such answers may or may not be correct in stressing a link between oral expressions of the relationship with God on the one hand and their cultic equivalents on the other. One may certainly define the psalm as a liturgical genre with formal and structural elements that was in existence over much of the biblical period, but that does not necessarily mean that it was closely attached to the Jerusalem cult. It may even be possible that the psalm form was widely used as a eulogy at alternative acts of worship, perhaps of a syncretistic kind, in ancient Israel and that it was only in the post-exilic period that it became associated with the central Temple and appeared in greater number. What remains clear, even unequivocal, is that no text in the Hebrew Bible reports the recitation of a personal prayer or psalm as an integral part of the internal operation of prescribed Temple rituals.

Although this is a perfectly valid reading of the evidence, the idea that major ceremonials in an impressive place of worship could have been conducted in virtual silence is one that obviously troubles scholars more familiar with the chants, responses, choral performances and lectionaries of the grand centres of communal prayer that later became a feature of the major monotheistic religions. H.-J. Kraus somewhat cavalierly transports the statements of various emotions made in some of the psalms into the sacrificial system itself and, following von Rad but with no more warrant than his predecessor, defines sections of verses describing elements of the cultic rites as the spoken part of the Temple liturgy:

> The sacrificial system in the Old Testament, however, is . . . not merely a sphere of silence. It shows us the praying and worshipping community, from the expressions of joy at the *zbḥ* to the expressions of homage, thanksgiving and petition at the *mnḥh* and the *ʿwlh* . . . and the prayers do not remain unanswered. The studies in form criticism of recent decades have shown more and more clearly that there are formulae and expressions in the cultic traditions of the Old Testament in which the priest declares God's pleasure at the offerings . . . There was a whole series of 'declaratory formulae' by means of which the priest pronounced an authoritative judgement on the sacrificial animal and the sacrificial action.[26]

H. H. Rowley, too, in this connection, indulges in what can, in all honesty, be no more than a fanciful conjecture necessitated by an inability to see an essential distinction between liturgy as sacrificial cult on behalf of the community and liturgy as the personal prayer of the individual: 'Here I would observe that there is every reason to believe that the ritual acts were accompanied by the recital of liturgical texts, which were designed to make the ritual acts the vehicle of the spiritual worship of the people . . . and when men came to worship, it was not just to watch a sacrificial act but to participate in an approach to God.' Unfortunately, the phrase 'every reason to believe' appears to substitute in that statement for hard facts and textual support. Nor is such a desire to find the formulation of spoken prayer in the context of the Temple ritual confined to Christian scholars. The nineteenth-century German rabbi who inspired much of modern Orthodoxy, S. R. Hirsch, shares such a view. When discussing worship in his overall presentation of Jewish religious practice, he also argues that 'the word was not missing in the act of sacrifice', pointing to the confession, thanksgiving and levitical singing as evidence of such verbalisation.[27]

From what has just been argued, it follows that there is no valid reason for denying the more independent and personal nature of the prayers earlier recorded in the name of various biblical personalities. However edited and redacted, they constitute a particular form of Israelite spirituality that is essentially different from that achieved by the formal, sacrificial cult and do not therefore have to be identified as the forerunner or the successor of that type of worship. Moshe Greenberg has recently expressed this definition in a way that is both convincing in itself and of singular importance for the later history of Jewish liturgy. He points to the uniqueness of *improvised* prose prayer in the Hebrew Bible, indicates parallels in the patterns of commonly used speech forms, and argues the democratic and egalitarian nature of such a method of approaching God. The distinction between the personal and the cultic in this respect is clearly summarised by him:

> The formulated prayers follow a simple pattern, consisting basically of address, petition, and motivating sentence, with freedom to add and subtract elements. The content of the prayers is tailored to the circumstances in which it arises; hence the prayers cannot be reused. These features distinguish the embedded petitionary prayers from institutionalized forms of worship – sacrifice and other temple rituals and psalms. These are the properties of experts; their details are fixed and prescribed. A unit of them – a given sacrifice, a given psalm – is infinitely reusable or repeatable, since it is not determined by specific circumstances.[28]

While this summary of the situation fits well the prayer texts earlier cited and, whatever the interesting and extensive parallels, permits a meaningful differentiation to be made between the liturgical customs of Israel and her neighbours, it makes no mention of any historical developments within the larger biblical period or the possibility of analysing what are obviously the latest liturgical texts in the Hebrew Bible in order to identify and characterise adjustments and modifications of the Israelite approach. An attempt will now be made to fill this gap.

A good starting-point are the books of Ezra, Nehemiah, Chronicles and Daniel since there is no controversy about dating them well after the exile.[29] A prayer text such as that recorded in Ezra 9:5–15 presents a distinctly different picture from those considered above. The lengthy nature of the entreaty is itself a factor and it is noteworthy that the prayer is formally begun at the onset of evening, after fasting and the rending of garments, and is accompanied by such physical acts as genuflection, prostration, weeping and the spreading out of the palms. In the course of an introductory confession, the suppliant makes use of a fairly varied vocabulary to describe the guilt and shame felt by him and his people and the punishments meted out because of their misbehaviour. In spite of God's kindness in returning them from exile and restoring them to their land, they have again abandoned his precepts and intermarried with the local pagans. The prayer ends with an admission of guilt, a firm commitment to do better and an acknowledgement of God's justice. Mournful weeping over a lengthy period and a fast also precede Nehemiah's prayer in 1:4–11. In addition to the admission of guilt, there is on this occasion a somewhat formulaic recital of God's attributes, an intricate request for a response and a reminder of God's promise that repentance would bring restoration to the homeland, just as rebellion had invited dispersal among the nations. In the well-known passage in Daniel 6:11, Daniel continues to pray in his usual way in spite of the decree requiring exclusive worship of King Darius. Three times a day he still gets down on his knees in front of open windows facing

Jerusalem and contritely offers prayer to God. The lengthy prayer of Daniel in 9:3–19 is highly reminiscent of the Ezra passage cited above. Here too, supplicatory prayer is preceded by fasting but on this occasion sackcloth and ashes are also mentioned. An introductory confession, equally rich in suitable terminology, is made on behalf of Jews in both the homeland and the diaspora and the warnings of the Pentateuch are cited as the justification for Israel's historical punishments. In a variety of expressions, God's forgiveness is sought, not because it is deserved, but for the sake of God's reputation. The passage then moves from the liturgical into the apocalyptic, with the appearance of the angel Gabriel, again at the onset of evening, with prophesy and instructions. What should perhaps be stressed about all these post-exilic prayers is that while certain individual aspects of the worship described may be found earlier it is only these late sources that contain lengthy and complex amalgams of so many such elements.

Other texts of interest for Jewish liturgical history concentrate on different aspects of worship. The earliest unequivocal reference to a formal and public reading of the Pentateuch occurs in Nehemiah 8:1–8.[30] From a special platform, Ezra, with a retinue of dignitaries, blesses God, and the assembled men and women raise their hands, prostrate themselves and exclaim *'amen*. He reads to them from the Pentateuch and explanations are then apparently offered by the levites. An invitation to bless God marks the beginning of a long declamation by the levites in Nehemiah 9:5–37, the first section of which reports God's favours to Israel from Abraham until the Sinaitic revelation and the remainder of which, in stark and vivid language, acknowledges Israelite recalcitrance in the wilderness and after the conquest of Canaan. By contrast, God's patience, righteousness and mercy are applauded and Israel's present, miserable state is bewailed. In the report offered in 1 Chronicles 29:10–22 of David's designation of his son Solomon as his successor, the king's prayer is opened with a formal benediction reminiscent of later formulae, namely, 'You are blessed, God of Israel, our Father, from everlasting until everlasting.'[31] God's manifold attributes are contrasted with the people's lowliness, and, as the God of Abraham, Isaac and Israel, he is entreated to guide Solomon in the right ways and inspire him to complete the building of the new Jerusalem capital. The people bless God when formally invited to do so by David and prostrate themselves to him and before the king. Here, interestingly enough, sacrifice follows prayer the next day and a joyous feast is held to celebrate the proposed accession and Solomon's anointment. Also put into the mouth of David, in 1 Chronicles 15 and 25 is an instruction to appoint men and women of levite families as singers and players to make joyous music in the sanctuary.

It will now be instructive to examine some earlier sources in the light of the later passages just cited. It is clear, for instance, that Solomon's prayer at the dedication of the Temple in 1 Kings 8:22–53 has more in common with such passages than it does with the simpler personal prayers reported in the names of earlier personalities. The technical vocabulary used for various aspects of prayer, the length, the reference to non-Israelites and the punishment of exile, the formulaic repetition of various kinds of request and the author's views on theodicy clearly indicate that scholars are justified in seeing here a mixture of late pre-exilic and early post-exilic elements.[32] The constant references to the centrality of 'this house' may conceivably be early and deuteronomic but they are at least placed in contexts that contain many later characteristics. The role of non-Jews in Israelite worship of the future is also a theme touched upon in Isaiah 56:7 where it is claimed that their offerings are destined for approval when they come to the Temple Mount and, in a happy frame of mind, make use of that shrine as a universal place of prayer. Here there clearly occurs the fusion of the cult and the personal worship which was manifestly missing in earlier sources and which supports, as so much else in 'Trito-Isaiah', a post-exilic date for much of the content.[33] Jeremiah's prayer (32:16–35) in response to God's invitation to purchase property in the Holy Land, in spite of the Babylonian occupation, also raises problems of dating. Here are all the combined elements of the later passages of Ezra, Nehemiah and Chronicles, namely, technical terminology, a theology of reward and punishment, potted history, and a justification for Israel's punishment by conquest and yet there is also a prophetic style about parts of the text. Are we then dealing with an early manifestation from prophetic circles of what later became more widespread? The fact that this passage appears to have Jeremiah ask the question about the need for the purchase that has already been assumed by God in the previous passage, and rehearse an event that has already taken place, has led scholars to characterise the prayer as a later interpolation. If this is correct, much of the text of the prayer fits well with what has above been cited from books that are clearly much later.[34] As far as Ezekiel is concerned, even the temple of the future will still be exclusively for cultic purposes. In 44:15–31 he offers a detailed description of the future sanctuary, replete with technical details, and guidance for the priests as teachers and judges, but there is no mention of any prayer-texts to be recited by them. For him apparently this is still a matter for the individual. Finally, brief note should be taken of Job's concluding prayer in 42:1–6. A simple theology of reward and punishment is rejected in favour of a view of God and his activities as beyond human ken. There is nothing for the suppliant but to pursue humility and obedience.[35]

It will now perhaps be useful to summarise the overall developments that took place with regard to Jewish liturgy from the time of the exile into the first half of the Second Temple period. The cult was restored and again played a dominant role while the priests operated politically, nationally and educationally, as well as in the Temple. At the same time, the personal prayer of earlier centuries expanded in content, form and function and began to take on some of the characteristics of what may be called the psalm genre. It attracted to itself various ceremonials and tended to make use of more formulaic language and vocabulary. Elements of the phraseology that later became part of rabbinic prayers made their first appearance and such themes as confession, the lessons of Israelite history and the need for forgiveness and improvement tended to occur and recur. Theological content increased and contrasted God's numerous attributes with humanity's failings and a simple view of reward and punishment gave way to an acceptance of the inscrutability of God's actions. It will not have gone unnoticed by the observant reader that a number of these developments are reminiscent of the liturgical trends that were earlier identified in the wider Near Eastern context and they may consequently owe their inspiration to the exposure of the Israelite community to wider religious ideas and practice during their exile.[36] The small, tightly knit group that organised the return and ran the affairs of the numerically and politically insignificant country of Judah was apparently able to make some moves towards merging the ideas and practice relating to individual prayer and institutionalised communal worship that had existed more separately in earlier times and to add to these concepts developed in the wider context of the diaspora. As a result, formal, communal, elements were incorporated into personal prayers and the Temple Mount gradually became the centre for more than the sacrificial cult, but these prayers bear the hallmark of literary productions or adaptations and there is no reason to presuppose, as will shortly become apparent, that improvised, personal entreaties had become any less popular than they had earlier been. Of any form of fixed liturgy outside the Temple on the part of the Judahite community there is simply no evidence at this stage.

It should not, however, be forgotten that there still existed Jewish communities outside Judah and seemingly beyond the influence of this gradual move in the direction of a more united and uniform tradition. In the fifth century BCE, for example, a community of Jewish mercenaries in Elephantine, on the east bank of the Nile opposite Syene (the modern Aswan), built their own temple to its own specifications, with its own priests and worship of Yahu as well as some other deities, prayed for the government, observed the sabbath and celebrated the Passover by eating unleavened bread and abstaining from all leaven. Although it is not known whether the Elephantine Jews had collections of psalms, there is a report of at least one formal gathering for mourning, fasting and praying but no indication of anything more structured in the way of formulae.[37] The Aramaic documents that testify to the whole phenomenon also indicate tensions with the 'establishment' in Judah but the real challenge to the comfortable situation in the homeland and its capital was yet to come. When it did, it represented a Greek rather than an Egyptian cultural onslaught and was destined to influence Jewish religious ideas and practice for many centuries. In order to assess its significance in terms of Jewish liturgical developments in the middle of the Second Temple period, when the last books of the Hebrew Bible were being written or had made their appearance, the literature written in and around that time, in Hebrew, Aramaic and Greek, will have to be examined. The main question to be addressed will be whether there was any fixed liturgy inside or outside the cult and, if so, among which of the numerous Jewish groups that came to flourish in the Hellenistic and Roman periods.

Since the late biblical books mentioned above are in any case at least contemporaneous with the earliest works cited in the Apocrypha and Pseudepigrapha, it is hardly surprising to find that much of the content and style in passages of relevance to liturgical history is common to them both. The literary or possibly liturgical use of certain technical phrases, some of which later occur in rabbinic literature; the more sophisticated theodicy and theology; the centrality of the supplicatory element and the special significance of prayer closely linked with the Temple Mount – all these factors continue to be found throughout the apocryphal and pseudepigraphical works, to a greater or lesser extent, depending, presumably, on how closely related the author was to the circles that produced the books that were then, or later, accepted as canonical. But the most exciting aspect of these works is that as they move more into the period of Hellenistic and, later, Roman dominance, when what was tantamount to the dominant world culture touched and even seriously affected the lives of the Jews on a daily basis, so do they come to represent a much wider and more varied body of religious opinion and expression in the Jewish communities of Palestine and the diaspora. It should not indeed be forgotten that some of the books date from the first centuries of the Christian era and may even reflect a Hellenistic Jewish syncretism of the diaspora that was less pronounced in the Holy

Land. This is not to say that all or any modifications in Jewish liturgical practice were directly inspired, either through emulation or rejection, by the Greek example. Such a judgement may ultimately be seen to have a basis but the required research has not yet been undertaken. Until then all that may safely be done is to point out those areas in which some developments took place, what general form they took and where some examples may be found.[38]

Simple entreaties to God for such major gifts as rescue in war (1 Maccabees 4:30–3), deliverance from an oppressor (Judith 13:4–7), the end of a drought through the prayer of a righteous person (Judith 8:31), the restoration of health or fertility (Testament of Simeon 2:13 and Testament of Judah 19:2) and the welfare of the gentile authorities (1 Baruch 1:11) are fairly common and they continue to be personally expressed and circumstantially inspired. There are, however, also some texts that seek God's blessing in more ordinary and everyday situations such as a journey (Tobit 4:19, if this is to be understood literally) or a meal time (Aristeas, 183–5) and others that presuppose a somewhat different cosmology by requesting an end to the power of evil spirits over mankind (Jubilees 10:5–6). The structure of many of these requests is as much the benediction as it is the prayer and there is little to indicate a formal and communal liturgical context outside the Temple. When one reads the Psalms of Solomon, however, one is again faced with the question of the context of such poetic compositions and at least parts of the texts, such as 17:23–4, which are beginning to resemble common motifs in the earliest rabbinic liturgies and probably date from the first century BCE, could conceivably have been recited formally and communally. Certainly when one encounters the formal praises of such later literature as 2 Enoch, 2 Baruch and 4 Ezra, which take us comfortably into the Christian era, the whole atmosphere is different and the worshipping group, emulating the presupposed activities of its heavenly counterpart, is the most conceivable context.[39]

Indeed, angelological, eschatological and mystical themes appear in far greater number in the books of the Apocrypha and Pseudepigrapha than perhaps in any other period of Jewish history and seem to have flourished in an ever-increasing degree as political and social conditions deteriorated. While the later books mentioned in the previous paragraph are particularly rich in references to angels, they are not an uncommon phenomenon in earlier texts, in which they respond favourably to the requests of such righteous individuals as Tobit and Sarah (Tobit 3:16, 17), Abram (Jubilees 12:22–4) and Judah the Maccabee (2 Maccabees 10:25–30). The eschatological is well represented in Ben Sira 36:1–17, a passage that makes use of a number of phrases that became part of the standard rabbinic prayers and seems more nationally and publicly orientated than many of the other prayers. The mystical trend is continued in later books such as the Testament of Job, Joseph and Asenath and the Apocalypse of Abraham, where music and poetry are also strongly represented, and David Flusser has suggested that these literary compositions may reflect the liturgy of a Jewish Hellenistic group living in Egypt in about the second century CE.[40]

As far as more general liturgical topics are concerned, those familiar from earlier periods recur throughout. Confession, God's attributes (especially his justice), the history of Israel's recalcitrance, and the people's ultimate pardon and rescue by God stand at the centre of Baruch's prayer (1:13–3:8), much as they did in the prayers earlier cited from Ezra, Nehemiah and Daniel. But the didactic element is also not neglected, with prayers for wisdom, understanding and Torah (Aristeas 256, Wisdom 9:1–18 and 15:3, and Ben Sira 51 and 24:23–7). Whatever the developments in the form and content of Jewish prayer in general, the cultic centre in Jerusalem remained of major significance for the total liturgical picture throughout the Second Temple period. The temporary loss of the Temple during the occupation by Antiochus Epiphanes was the subject of formal acts of mourning and prayer by the supporters of the Maccabees, both male and female (1 Maccabees 4:38–40 and 2 Maccabees 3:19–20), and when it was restored there was music, worship and praise by all the people (1 Maccabees 4:54–5) and a special hymn was composed known as the Song of the

Children. Ben Sira devotes a long passage to the glories of the high priest, Simeon ben Yoḥanan, and his cultic activities (50:5–21). There are also associations made between the cult and other aspects of religious expression. Sincerity and honesty are a *sine qua non* for acceptable sacrifice (Ben Sira 34:20–6); sacrifices are accompanied by rejoicing, feasting and praising God (2 Enoch 68:5–7); music and hymns are part of the Temple ritual (Ben Sira 47:8–10); the restoration and rededication of the Temple are followed by processions of celebrants carrying *lulavim* (2 Maccabees 10:7); and Aaron relieves the situation after the episode of the golden calf by offering prayer and incense (Wisdom 18:21). The location of prayers wherever they are needed, in, for instance, Hebron (2 Baruch 47:1–2), Ptolemais in Egypt (3 Maccabees 7:20) and Babylon (1 Esdras 4:58–63), is not surprising, whether it is a continuation of the earlier concept of personal prayer or some kind of anti- or post-Temple reaction.[41] What is highly significant is the assumption in some of the texts that prayer took place in or around the Temple. Judith 4:9–15 describes how all the population of Jerusalem, including women and children, fasted, supplicated and prayed before the Temple and put sackcloth on the altar. According to 2 Maccabees 1:21–30, the restoration of the sacred fire for the sacrifices achieved by Nehemiah was accompanied by a prayer recited by the priests during the sacrifices and reported in the text, and was followed by their singing of hymns. Even more striking is the claim made in 2 Maccabees 3:15 that during Heliodorus' attack on Jerusalem the priests, in their ceremonial robes, flung themselves in front of the altar, entreating God to save the holy Temple treasure from the invader.

It turns out, then, that in the circles represented by the books of the Apocrypha and Pseudepigrapha one may detect a more extensive, even everyday use of the personal prayer, hymn-psalm and benediction. There are technical aspects to both the content, themes and vocabulary that have roots in the later biblical books as well as adumbrating some of the earliest rabbinic liturgy. If any compositions are to be regarded as having been employed in a formal liturgical setting, these are most likely to be the hymnic, psalmic or poetic praises and the mystical formulations that appear to be thrusting themselves on to the scene during this period. Prayers continued to be recited wherever there were Jews but there is not yet any concrete evidence of a fixed communal liturgy, particularly not of a proto-rabbinic variety.[42] Especially significant are the reports that there were times when elements of personal prayer were imported into the Temple precincts by both priests and laymen and even made their way into the inner sanctum of the altar area. It is not clear whether this is a reflection of a new liturgical reality or of a few special circumstances, nor whether it testifies to practice or to the views of the authors. Whatever its origin, it seems to be a departure from earlier biblical custom that could conceivably owe its origin to influences that began to bear upon the Jewish community with the arrival of Hellenistic and related culture.

Although the evidence from Philo and Josephus will be incorporated into the overall presentation offered in the next chapter, when the history of *synagogal* worship receives attention, it will perhaps be useful in the present context to complete the picture by taking note of what they have to say about Jewish prayer in their day. Both writers make frequent references to individual prayers, even of a regular nature, to the special role of the High Priest, and to assemblies at which prayers were recited, Torah was studied and thanksgiving was offered. The synagogue (or equivalent institution) is not, however, presented as the exclusive location or exclusively used for this and although the *shema*ʿ could well have been what they sometimes had in mind, that is of course a collection of pentateuchal readings and not a fixed prayer-text as such. The apparently long-standing tradition of assembly on the sabbath was also related as much, if not more, to study than to prayer and priests still played a role in such assemblies even if the latter were unconnected with the Temple ritual. Particularly worthy of note is the interest taken by Philo and Josephus in the traditional prayers communally recited by the Essenes and the Therapeutae, as if they had some special significance for being different from other religious practices.[43]

Some comparison should now be made between the findings reported above and the evidence available about Jewish prayer from the Qumran scrolls. It should first be acknowledged that there are clear similarities between the contents of the scrolls and the texts to be found in late biblical, apocryphal and pseudepigraphical and early rabbinic literature. The *Hodayoth* are psalms or hymns of thanksgiving and praise often introduced by the Hebrew *'wdk*. There are *Benedictions*, using the Hebrew term *brwk*, to be recited by the Instructor (*Maskil*) and addressed to the community, the priests and the 'Prince' (*Nasi'*), probably the future Davidic Messiah. Similarly, there are prayers said in times of distress that refer to rescues in the past and promise repentance that will, it is hoped, lead to forgiveness; and Psalms scrolls of unusual order and content, possibly of liturgical significance. Eschatological themes, cosmological speculation and angelology are also present, as in earlier apocalyptic and later *merkavah* materials.[44]

The presence of such and similar liturgical types and texts in the Qumran corpus indicates a close concern on the part of the sect with this form of religious expression. It is not easy to establish, on the basis of such evidence alone, in which context such compositions were utilised and precisely for what purpose. They may have been private devotions or public recitations and the intention may have been didactic or liturgical. The distance, both geographical and theological, that the members of the sect had put between themselves and the Jerusalem cult, may have inspired a greater concern with the creation of their own formal system of worship that put angelic praise, rather than Temple ritual, at its centre. A number of other Qumran texts, that go beyond those summarised above, and, consequently, beyond the other canonical and 'deutero-canonical' literature earlier cited, appear to indicate that this was the case.

Perhaps the most interesting formulations in this respect are those that are related to a specific occasion in the calendar. The 'Angelic Liturgy', for instance, contains songs for recitation with every sabbath offering of the Essene calendrical year. As is clear from later rabbinic texts, these need not have had any other than a sentimental connection with the actual Jerusalem

Temple. Various angels in a number of heavens are involved in the liturgy and the impression given is, as it is in later mystical liturgies of the *merkavah* type including the *qedushah* (trisagion), that humans are following the angelic example. The composition of such texts in fact constitutes evidence that angels are being credited with the kind of ideal liturgical behaviour that would presuppose their original recitation of such formulae. There are also manuscripts found in Cave Four that explicitly associate the recorded prayers with *Yom Kippur* and *Yom Ha-Bikkurim*, others that list evening and morning benedictions for each day of the month, and some, in a work entitled by the scribe *Divrey Ha-Me'oroth* ('The Words of the Luminaries'), that contain texts for communal worship on such specific days as Wednesday and the sabbath. References to rituals of purification and of marriage have also been identified by some scholars.[45]

As far as content is concerned, here too close examination of the texts by Qumran scholars has produced considerable discussion about possible parallels with parts of the later rabbinic *'amidah*, *taḥanun* and *widduy*. Such subjects as the choice of Israel and its special role, the centrality of the Zion theme in hymns, the obliteration of evil from the world, and the survival of the saints, certainly all figure prominently in the earliest synagogal liturgy for the festivals. The masterful music of David in praise of God has even been identified as the inspiration for one of the psalms in the *Psalms Scroll* and described by Flusser as a counterpart to the talent of the Greek musician Orpheus as known in Jewish and early Christian art.[46]

It is no new theory to associate advances in Jewish attitudes to prayer and later rabbinic developments with such sects. Kaufmann Kohler already made the connection with the Essenes almost a century ago.[47] Certainly the Qumran scrolls provide the earliest testimony to liturgical formulations of a communal nature designated for particular occasions and conducted in a centre totally independent of Jerusalem and the Temple, making use of terminology and theological concepts that were later to become dominant in Jewish and, in some cases, Christian prayer. Such prayer texts as those recorded in Luke 1:68–79 and 2:25 and the 'Lord's Prayer' (Matthew 6:14–15) are continuations of the expression of personal prayer found in earlier generations and may also owe some of their apparent centrality to attitudes cultivated by such groups as the Qumran sect. But sufficient evidence has already been cited from other sources to make it clear that such influences, while clearly significant, were by no means the only ones, and that the background for later developments has to be sought in a much wider context.

It remains only to summarise the findings of this chapter before proceeding to the topic of the synagogue liturgy itself. The need for a comparative approach that took the early period of the Hebrew Bible as its starting point was first argued. It was then clearly seen that parallels for much of Israel's centralised cultic activity exist among the preserved records of its major neighbours, expecially with regard to the sanctuary; the sacrifice of animals; the implements, utensils and vessels; and the calendar. On the other hand, not only is the theology regarding the nature of the deity being worshipped considerably different, but there also appears to have been a less central role for both magic and the king among the Israelites. Even more significantly, singing, dancing and the recitation of formulae do not appear to have accompanied most of the rituals enacted in the Jerusalem Temple, as prescribed in the pentateuchal legislation. What formulae there were may be characterised as benedictory, didactic or historical rather than institutionally cultic. While prayers were part of formal, communal worship among various cultures of the ancient Near East, they would seem to have been quite separate from such an institution in Israel's central shrine, constituting a freer and more personal expression of religiosity. Closely associated with oaths, curses, blessings and prophesy, such prayers in the early parts of the Hebrew Bible followed common speech patterns rather than formulaic structures and often amounted to spirited challenges or exchanges rather than formal obeisance. The relationship between prayer and worship may therefore have been one of tension rather than of integration.

By the time that they had returned from exile the Jews had clearly made adjustments in their liturgical arrangements, whether or not as a result of their more international contacts is difficult to state definitively. Certainly a move towards the greater integration known in other cultures can be detected in the early Second Temple period. Formal techniques were introduced into the preparation for and the recitation of personal prayer and more rigid patterns of vocabulary and specific themes began to emerge. The vast theological gap between man and God was acknowledged and the lessons of history were regularly rehearsed. The cultic centre was used more widely for communal activity, apparently by men and women, and the priests operated politically and educationally as well as ritually but, unless some credence is given to speculative theories about the use of the psalms in that period, the sacrificial cult itself remained an area of virtual silence and there was no fixed and standard form of communal liturgy outside the Temple.

The wider circles represented by the books of the Apocrypha and Pseudepigrapha both continued the biblical practices and adumbrated some elements of the later rabbinic traditions. There was still no fixed liturgy among most groups but there were more benedictions, hymns and praises, mystical formulations of considerable variety, a concern for the absorption of Torah knowledge and a growing use of the Temple precincts on special liturgical occasions. According to Philo and Josephus, individual and assembled Jews prayed and studied in various contexts, at times with priestly guidance or involvement, especially on the sabbath, and there were particular groups for whom the formal, communal aspects of such activities took on a central significance. The *shema'* was also in individual use, as will be noted in the next chapter.

The evidence from Qumran is even more interesting. The members of that sect looked upon their liturgies as reflections of the angelological variety and designated particular prayers for specific sabbaths and festivals. They used concepts and formulations that do occur in later rabbinic liturgy but it has not yet been convincingly demonstrated that the link was a direct one.

What is fairly clear is that the sect had its own formal worship outside the Temple and used ritual ablutions as an integral part of its ceremonials. Within the Judaean establishment and outside it there were obviously differences of opinion and tensions about what constituted the most efficacious form of Jewish worship. With communities inside and outside Jerusalem following their own liturgical practices, and the expansion and development of the communal aspects of education and personal prayer, it now seems reasonable to enquire about the nature of the synagogue and its function in the period before the destruction of the Temple.

CHAPTER 3

The early liturgy of the synagogue

INTRODUCTION

The precise nature of Jewish liturgical expression in the period immediately preceding the destruction of the Second Temple and the loss of any semblance of Jewish political independence in 70 CE is clearly of interest to a wide body of scholarship. Historians of Jewish religious practice, analysts of Christian origins, and students of the cultic forms in existence in the Hellenistic and Roman worlds all have sound reasons for seeking to reconstruct for themselves what may for the moment, pending the more accurate assessment and definition that will shortly be offered, be referred to as 'the early liturgy of the synagogue'.

In pursuit of this reconstruction, liturgists have sometimes turned for guidance to the authoritative Jewish prayer-books of almost a thousand years later, or even of the more modern period, and sought to extrapolate backwards, making assumptions that defy the vast chasms of history, geography and ideology that separate one millennium from another. Those who have adopted such a position have transplanted some or all of the rabbinic rites and customs of tenth-century Babylon or early mediaeval Europe to first-century Judaea and the surrounding Jewish diaspora and have declined to distinguish the continuity of some liturgical traditions from the patent novelty of others. While this kind of analysis is particularly misguided in connection with the text of the liturgy, it also has its dangers in the scholarly search for the central theological concepts of Jewish liturgy, tending, as it does, to presuppose that ideas and terminology that are similar may be defined as conveying the identical religious message. However methodologically untenable the theory underlying such an approach, the picture painted by its proponents of proto-rabbinism and its liturgical practice was generally a clear one, unobfuscated by doubts and complications.[1]

Recent, more reliable research in the field tends, on the other hand, to stress the lack of concrete evidence, the inadmissibility of sources dating from even one or two centuries after the destruction of the Temple, and the complex nature of Judaism in the time of Jesus and Hillel, thus shying away from a commitment to simple description and taking refuge in a welter of doubt and hesitancy. For his part, Ezra Fleischer, in an important article published after much of this chapter had been the subject of public lectures and most of this book was already in typed draft, has gone even further and argued for a totally new version of Jewish prayer after the destruction of the Temple. Such a view seems unnecessarily iconoclastic and attempts will later be made to refute aspects of its more extreme elements. At the same time it should be stressed that much of what Fleischer has to say about the Second Temple period is not at all at odds with what is here being suggested. As a consequence of such variety and complexity of opinion, the less specialised scholar is left unenlightened about the general situation that obtained with regard to Jewish liturgy in the first century, and with many unanswered questions about its particular aspects.[2]

The object of the present chapter is to complement recent scholarly studies in the areas of Temple, synagogue, theology and piety. A number of well-documented contributions to the subject have touched upon the theme of liturgy in diverse ways but, with the possible exception of the article by Fleischer just cited, it has not been their task to stand back and survey the whole scene or to identify all the various trends and tensions.[3] The intention here is to build on such detailed research and bibliography and, by offering some further comments of a methodological, historical, ideological and linguistic kind, to clarify for the reader the topic that stands at the head of this chapter.

METHODOLOGY

The scholar in search of first-century Jewish ideology and practice in the field of liturgy faces the same problems as his colleagues concentrating on the alternative areas of law, biblical interpretation, or the history of personalities and events. The major difficulty is constituted by the absence of any primary sources that may categorically be classified as contemporary. The origins of the whole vast network of talmudic–midrashic literature remain shrouded in mystery and there is no scholarly consensus about the method of dating traditions, particularly not their earliest pre-literary forms, or the way of testing the reliability of ascriptions. Although most (but not all) specialists would today eschew the talmudic tradition's own version of its early history, they would, at the same time, remain reluctant to declare the whole of that tradition an invalid witness to earlier customs and ideas, recognising that traditions in Jewish religious law, for instance, may well be much older and of wider historical relevance than the tannaitic formulations in which they ultimately survived. The preliminary observations of Yaakov Sussmann on 4QMMT have recently demonstrated with clarity the central role of a strict and harsh form of *halakhah*, possibly of Sadducean origin, in the life of the Qumran sect.[4] However much it complicates the task of the researcher, today's scholarly preference must surely be for the *ad hoc* analysis of each tradition, or at least each group of traditions, particularly by way of the historical study of the manuscripts that have transmitted them.[5]

This complication is further compounded for the student of Jewish liturgy by the existence of a number of other factors that have special application to that area of study and generally concern the matter of definition. Certain attitudes to prayer, its form and its centrality, became almost axiomatic in the talmudic–midrashic literature and indeed, to a certain extent, in the wider Judaeo-Christian system of religious values. By the same token, the rabbinic Hebrew terminology for such concepts as synagogue, prayer, benediction and scriptural reading that became such a familiar part of daily Jewish life was assumed to convey that particular meaning and those special characteristics that they appear to have acquired during the talmudic era. A further assumption, unwarranted from a purely scientific viewpoint, was and is that, when a named prayer is cited in an early rabbinic source, its overall content and detailed text are identical with what they came to be in one or other of the rites known to us from the mediaeval period. The fact is that only rarely is any more than the introductory and concluding phraseology recorded in the tannaitic and amoraic literature.

Wary as he must be of reading later talmudic meanings back into earlier rabbinic texts, the scholar must be equally cautious about taking for granted that those alternative Jewish sources that predate the talmudic–midrashic literature necessarily guide him in his search for the liturgical practice of first-century Judaism.[6] Earlier as much of their literary form may be, the Dead Sea Scrolls, the Apocrypha and Pseudepigrapha, the Jewish–Hellenistic corpus (particularly represented by Philo and Josephus) and the New Testament, while of major importance for the general history of Jewish liturgy, as previously demonstrated, give no guarantee that any or all of the attitudes that underlie their approaches to worship in its widest sense provide us with the missing link between the late Old Testament books and tannaitic traditions. It must constantly be borne in mind that at least some rabbinic ideas and traditions may well have their origins in some form of oral transmission or, indeed, a lost textual form and that no one alternative Jewish ideology is necessarily to be defined as having once been the dominant or central one that influenced all the others. Consequently, the interpretation of the various sources for a better understanding of Jewish liturgical history, while following basic principles of historical research and avoiding the unjustified presuppositions already mentioned, cannot be done on a blanket basis but must be, to a certain extent, *ad hoc* in nature.

This accounts for the variety of approaches adopted in scholarly books and articles on the subject and explains why no definitive analysis has yet proved possible.

HISTORICAL CONTEXTS

It is of primary importance to recall that there was no one exclusive medium for the expression of the Jewish need to communicate with God in the period under discussion. A dispassionate survey of all the available sources that may be regarded as relevant reveals a remarkably variegated set of contexts in which some form of liturgy was conducted. The Second Temple certainly seems to have stood at the centre of such contexts, in a daily and pervasive manner as far as Jerusalem and the immediate environs were concerned, and on special occasions for Jews living at less commutable distances. Sacrifices were offered and rituals enacted with the use of sacred implements on behalf of the people of Israel as a whole in order to demonstrate its allegiance to the requirements of pentateuchal legislation and to cement its relationship with God. Individuals could play a role in these formal acts by donating sacrifices and defraying Temple costs but it was only the hereditary priesthood, at its various levels, that was responsible for what might be termed the actual acts of worship. Only a small minority of the rituals included the recitation, at some stage and in some part of the Temple precincts, of certain formulae but on special occasions the milling crowds declaimed responses to an act of worship and there were times when spontaneous, penitential or laudatory prayers were offered there.[7] Tannaitic sources (e.g. Mishnah, *Tamid* 5.1) speak of the daily recitation of an introductory benediction, the Ten Commandments, the *shema'*, the priestly blessing, and, if any of the later rabbinic liturgy had already entered part of the Temple service by this period, these elements, as well as sections of the Psalms, by virtue of their incontrovertible antiquity and immediate relevance, seem the most likely candidates for inclusion, as will later be argued. R. Hammer has made a good case for regarding the *Tamid* passage as evidence of the kernel of later synagogal liturgy, constituting a call to bless God, blessings of the people, and Torah readings. Though speculative in his reconstruction of the nature of these blessings of the people, he is right to point to the ambiguity of the evidence and to the danger of accepting talmudic definitions of each part of the ceremony described. The historical authenticity of other talmudic claims about the content of the Temple liturgy (perhaps with the exception of some references to festival prayers) also remains a moot point because of the remark earlier made about the uncritical projection of later customs on to earlier generations and institutions.[8] By the same token, the talmudic reference to the existence of a synagogue as part of the Temple complex has long been the subject of scholarly scepticism but, in view of what was earlier noted about the gradual encroachment of personal prayer customs on to the territory of public worship, the earliest form of such an institution could conceivably have existed by the first Christian century. If it did, it represents another example of the phenomenon whereby popular custom gradually encroached upon the more elitist rituals of the Temple Mount. There are certainly tannaitic sources that testify to tensions between Pharisees on the one hand and Sadducees/Essenes on the other about the permissibility of bringing Israelites further into the Temple precincts and removing Temple utensils outside of them during the pilgrim festivals.[9]

A further link was forged between the Temple and the common people by the existence of an institution known as the *ma'amad* according to which those who did not make the journey to Jerusalem when a particular group of priests and levites (*mishmar*) took its turn at officiating in the Temple would gather in their home towns to fast, to recite scriptural passages and, apparently, to pray, albeit not in the formal fashion of later times.[10] The remnants of information available to us in the talmudic sources about such an institution are not paralleled in other literature but smack of the authentic, particularly since there was no reason to wish such an arrangement into retrospective existence after the Temple had been destroyed. Perhaps, indeed, it continued to exist even after that catastrophic event. Equally authentic and also demonstrating a practical interaction between the cultic centre and the wider populace are the descriptions of the involvement of the people in the Passover ceremony in which the statutory lamb is offered at the Temple to the accompaniment of a *hallel* recited by the levites and is then consumed at home in an atmosphere of feasting and thanksgiving and with references to the relevant biblical texts.[11]

It has already been noted that the association of fasting with the recitation of special prayers was an established practice from at least as early as the immediate post-exilic period[12] and this clearly provides us with another liturgical context in the late Second Temple period. On such distressing occasions as droughts, the people would congregate to perform acts normally associated with mourning, and to make special appeal through supplicatory prayers, readings and fasting, for relief from their adversity.[13] These acts of popular piety, which presumably had their equivalents on joyful occasions, were played out in public places, but not necessarily in a synagogue or similar institution, a fact to which further reference will be made later in this chapter. Where there were leaders of the group's devotions, they were either communal dignitaries or men of special piety whose reputation encouraged the public to believe that their appeals to God would be more likely to succeed and about whose miraculous powers in matters of supplicatory prayer many old folk-tales came to be recorded.[14] Just as some of the prophets of old appear to have alternated spells of communal activity with periods of intense asceticism experienced within a group of peers or even in isolation,[15] so these men of devotion (*ḥasidim*) appear to have had both a public and a private side to their religious endeavours. Perhaps it is not unfair to say too that the common people saw the special value of such pietists in terms of magic, with the stress on wonders and miracles, while they themselves were attempting to give expression to that strong element of 'mysticism' that scholarship has recently traced through the whole history of Jewish religious ideology. It is to that element that Judaism ultimately owes the composition of those liturgical formulae that stress apocalyptic, angelological and cosmological themes and that are already recorded in some of the apocryphal and pseudepigraphical books. Although the rabbinic versions of these incorporated into the standard prayer-book are of later vintage and should only with great caution be used for the earlier history of Jewish mystical liturgy, they would appear to have their generic origins in the Second Temple period.[16]

The praising or blessing of God, either for his powers in general or for their particular manifestation, counts as another form of Jewish worship that continued from earlier times into the axial age. Before the tannaitic teachers of the late first and early second centuries began the process of legislation and standardisation that was eventually to lead to their 'authorised' form, these benedictions were a popular form of religious expression, possibly with more than a tinge of superstition attached to them. They were employed as a means of thanking God for his bounty by those who felt that it was an act of ingratitude, or possibly a dangerous provocation, to enjoy the benefits of the creation without acknowledging the role of its creator.[17] It was particularly apt to introduce them at communal meals, where the gratitude could be publicly acknowledged, or at noteworthy events of an especially happy or social kind, and the basic format was no more than a praise of the Supreme Being followed by a brief reference to the attribute for which praise was deserving.[18] No doubt, individuals or groups expressed preference for their own formulation and the context in which the whole custom operated was a wide and popular one. It is from this context that the nineteen benedictions of the *'amidah* subsequently emerged and there are interesting parallels in apocryphal and Qumranic sources to the concepts expressed in that central prayer of tannaitic and later Judaism.[19] There is, however, no convincing evidence that even the earliest known text of the *'amidah* itself predates the destruction of the Temple and only on the basis of intelligent and informed speculation can it be argued that some of the introductory and concluding benedictions were in existence as such at that time.

Even if blessings of the type just discussed were at times pronounced in a public or communal setting, they surely belong in essence and in origin to the area of private rather than public prayer. As pointed out in the previous chapter, ample evidence attests to an extensive practice of private prayer from the time of the earliest books of the Hebrew Bible and to a complicated interplay between the spontaneous devotions of the individual, on a regular basis or on occasions of special need, and the formal liturgy of the cult throughout the early history of Judaism.[20] It may well be that, as will shortly be noted, the resultant compromises reached in the homeland were not those that appealed to the communities of the diaspora. In this context, as in all the other contexts mentioned above, one should not think (as so many scholars seem mistakenly to do) of watertight, discrete groups occupying separate contexts. One should rather presuppose the existence of dominant religious trends that might express themselves internally in different ways and even at times coalesce with each other, and of a variety of forms that commended themselves to particular people at specific times but that were never mutually exclusive or beyond reciprocal influence.[21] The exclusive identification of recognisable sets of people with particular characteristics is often the predeliction of later historians rather than the tendency of contemporary witnesses to events. In order better to understand the place that these forms of expression occupied in the Jewish life of the period under discussion it will be necessary to comment on some of the theological concepts that lay behind the liturgical practices at that time. Before this is undertaken, however, some attention will have to be given to a topic that has been mentioned a number of times in passing, namely, biblical readings and interpretations.

HEBREW BIBLE

It is not surprising that the Jews, who saw history as God's plan for his people and particular events as his response to the degree of loyalty currently being displayed by them to him, should lay emphasis on the acquisition of a sound knowledge of the texts that described that history. The Hebrew Bible itself constantly makes reference to the transmission of its message from father to son and the need for it to be understood and conscientiously absorbed, and to the importance of learning theological lessons from what were seen as the sacred records of a special relationship. Only a limited number of texts make reference to the public reading of scrolls or of specific sections of the written tradition but, taken together with the enthusiasm for religious education already noted and the evidence that some later biblical traditions reveal a reworking of their earlier counterparts, they provide a fairly clear picture of the general situation, if not its detailed constituents, in the period of the Second Temple.[22]

The transmission of the Jewish people's authoritative sources was accomplished by the copying of scrolls, the recitation of their contents in family and larger social groups, and the exegesis of the tradition in a language that would be understood by the public rather than exclusively by an elite and in a manner that would make their message relevant to the spiritual dilemmas of the day. The *ḥakham* and *sofer*, perhaps predominantly in circles that later became closely identified with pharisaic groups, will surely have made a significant contribution to this process, the ideas common to the 'wisdom movement' of the ancient Near East and the scribal customs leaving their mark on its development.[23] For various groups of Jews the concept of wisdom was not one that was expressed merely in intellectual stimulation or exercise. It was religious knowledge *in toto*, in other words, the Torah, and Israel's preoccupation with it was an act of piety as well as a reflection of the people's love of the word. The study of the biblical traditions was, as the work of Michael Fishbane has convincingly demonstrated, more than an act of education or a commitment to historical continuity; it was the reflection of a dynamic religious philosophy.[24]

The clash between the Jewish way of life and the Hellenistic civilisation must also have prodded the traditionalists into strengthening the preservation of their inherited texts and traditions by seeking opportunities to recite and interpret them, as it inspired their more symbiotically inclined co-religionists to clothe their religious inheritance in the garb of Greek language and philosophy.[25] The evidence of this blossoming of biblical recitation, interpretation and adaptation is all-pervasive, occurring as it does in almost all the literature emanating from Jewish circles in the later pre-Christian and early Christian eras. The Greek and Aramaic translations of the Hebrew Bible that were the basis of what later became the familiar *targumim* and the Septuagint; the *pesher* system of exegesis that the Qumran sect used for underpinning their philosophy of life and their prognostications; the allegories that the Jewish scholars of Alexandria employed to lend a new relevance to an old message; the use made of scripture by Jesus and his followers to expound and justify their religious claims; and the earliest *midrashim* of the rabbis – all point to a preoccupation with sacred writ. In addition, there is ample testimony to the use of scriptural verses in such religious accoutrements as *tefillin* and *mezuzoth*, whether (if the distinction is meaningful) of a prophylactic or of a devotional nature, and whichever collections of passages they actually contained.[26]

It hardly seems possible to imagine a situation in which such significant and extended use was made of scriptural texts without seeing a concomitant recitation of these as a regular feature of Jewish communal activity. Whether such regularity can be traced back as far as Ezra, as the talmudic tradition would have it, is a matter of some doubt; what seems indubitable is that scriptural readings were familiar to many Jews of the Greek and Roman periods. Various minor contexts in which such readings were undertaken have already been noted and have included the *ma'amad*, Passover *Haggadah*, and occasions of special liturgical import. To these should also be added the sabbath which appears to be the most likely occasion on which Jews first gathered to read the Hebrew Bible.[27]

If the exegesis of scripture was as popular as has just been argued, and there were occasions when readings were part of a ceremony, it seems reasonable to assume that, on the one hand, a regular lectionary would evolve and that, on the other, the expounding of the biblical text would attach itself to such liturgical expressions. Attempts at locating the most original form of such a lectionary and identifying its primary characteristics have been made for almost a century and received a particular boost from the discovery of a number of unknown systems in the manuscripts and fragments located in the Cairo Genizah.[28] Such systems, though recorded no earlier than the early mediaeval period, were quickly seen by many scholars as the remnants of reading cycles that had been in existence in tannaitic times.

The fact is, however, that none of the suggested reconstructions is convincing and that these texts are now seen to bear witness to the existence of a variety of systems for pentateuchal and prophetic readings, some very short, others much longer, that existed, side by side, in Palestine and Babylon until a century or two after the end of the geonic period and that failed to agree even on the time to be taken to complete a cycle, let alone what precisely to include in it. The question about which there remain diametrically opposed views is whether the annual and triennial cycles have an equally hoary talmudic pedigree or whether one of them represents the authentic original, subsequently challenged by the other.[29]

What may be identified at the end of the Second Temple period, then, is the gradual incorporation into various liturgical contexts of a preoccupation with scriptural reading and study that may originally have belonged elsewhere. If there ever was an original, independent and major context from which such borrowing could have been made, it must surely have been the religio-educational one to which reference has already been made.

It will now be necessary for us to make further reference to those wider liturgical traditions already shown to have been in existence in the century before the destruction of the Temple. Such a reference will, in general terms, shed light on the context in which it was possible for new and different liturgical priorities to emerge and develop and, more particularly, will clarify why a merger between the liturgical and the scriptural came to be effected.

LITURGY AND THEOLOGICAL PRIORITIES

Our way of establishing the place occupied by liturgy in the theological hierarchy of first-century Judaism will be to remind ourselves of the situations presupposed in the Hebrew Bible, in the numerous Jewish works of the 'inter-testamental period', at Qumran, and in the talmudic–midrashic literature and, by combining these findings with what has already been said about the intervening period, to reconstruct the ideological developments that appear to have taken place in the period being discussed.

With regard to biblical prayer, it will be recalled that Moshe Greenberg has argued convincingly against two opposing views: one that sees the spontaneous, personal prayer as the impetus for the development of communal worship and the other that takes the formal liturgy of the community as the paradigm on which the individual based his own devotions. He prefers to postulate the contemporaneity of private prayer and communal worship and assumes their parallel existence throughout biblical history. That parallel existence was not, however, without its tensions. Popular religion always preferred the direct and simple method of individual communication and was uneasy with a form of worship that had to be mediated by a priesthood on behalf of a whole community and that savoured of the magical. This preference laid the foundations of a democratisation of worship that came to fruition in post-biblical Judaism.[30]

While this assessment is important and helpful it should not be assumed that personal prayer and communal worship failed to exercise influences on each other, especially in the post-exilic period. The restoration of the Second Temple not only provided the tiny country and small population of Judah with a focal point for their religious identity but also permitted the extension of sacerdotal authority into the political sphere and, paradoxically, encouraged parallel cultic developments elsewhere. Personal prayer attracted to itself the more formal elements of technical content, characteristic terminology and sophisticated theology while at the same time looking ever more strongly towards the Temple precincts as a specially favoured area for communication between man and God. As is the way with such tensions, there were as many positions of compromise as there were trends towards further polarisation.

Such a state of affairs became even more complicated and variegated towards the end of the pre-Christian period when additional interchanges took place between the two areas and new trends also made their appearance. The sincerity and religiosity of the cultic ceremonies became a greater issue and spontaneous acts of prayer and intercession came to be performed on the Temple Mount. Perhaps the recitation of formulae and praises began to play a greater part in Temple ceremonials; certainly their wider use is clearly attested. Although the structure of many prayers resembled the benediction and the request rather than a formulaic liturgy, elements of fixed form were creeping in, albeit without yet becoming dominant. Liturgy, whether in the form of biblical readings or of individual prayer, was becoming a feature of communal ritual, although it is clear that neither the location, the recitation nor the timing were yet restricted by the expression of a standard authoritative opinion. The situation at Qumran, at least physically separated from the wider community, was different and there formal worship, prayer, praise and benediction were in the process of merging.[31] The question that has yet to be asked, let alone answered, is whether that process is to be understood as a unique feature of the way of life represented at Qumran, which was later adopted and adapted by the rabbinic inheritors of Jewish religious practice, or as an example of popular liturgical piety that was common to various Pharisaic and Essenic groups and subsequently survived in the tannaitic traditions. It should not be forgotten that other groups also came to prefer what might be called a form of religious escapism or otherworldliness, giving a central function to mystical themes in their prayers, placing the stress on man's total unworthiness or looking to Torah and the intellectual dimension as the means of reaching out heavenwards.

In the next chapter it will be pointed out that the rabbis of the post-destruction era were also forced to reach some urgent conclusions about the religious way forward. There was considerable controversy among them about the relative merits of Torah-study, worship and good deeds, and arguments were put forward in favour of each of these as the essential element of Judaism. This is not to say that there was any serious attempt to abandon one or other of these forms of religious expression; rather that they felt the need to establish their order of theological priority. Ultimately, Torah-study appears to have been the victor and this had an effect on all subsequent interpretation, particularly since the reason for its pre-eminence was given as its ability to win people over to practice. What is more important for our present purpose is that it emerges from that analysis that there were considerable doubts among the rabbis about the nature of Jewish liturgy. For some it was identified as rabbinically formulated prayer and to be seen as the natural successor to the Temple cult in as many respects as possible, while for others it was to be sought in Torah-study. Just as the sacrificial system had once cemented the special relationship between God and Israel in a manner that bore an element of the mysterious, so would the study of the Torah or, for others, the practice of good deeds now fulfil the same function. In that case, the true liturgy, or service of God, was no longer to be found in formal, public worship. This latter exercise was, in the absence of the Temple, now limited to prayer, which was simply one of a number of precepts, possibly but not necessarily one of those central requirements later defined as Torah-based rather than rabbinically ordained, enjoined upon the observant Jew. As such, it had to be performed in a prescribed manner, but there was no unanimity about the precise injunctions to be followed. Public or private, synagogal or domestic, towards Jerusalem or heavenwards, lengthy or brief, daily or occasional – it took a number of centuries for these issues to be finally settled. Even Fleischer, who argues strongly that Rabban Gamliel fixed the standard text of the *'amidah* after the destruction of the Temple, is forced to admit that there were those who chose to maintain or develop some variations from it. Similarly, the nature of prayer was the subject of controversy, some arguing for its magical effect and therefore its transmission to God by a man of special piety, while others settled for a daily recitation by ordinary individuals as a requirement of the faith.[32] It should, of course, be stressed that as liturgy developed into the geonic and later periods these controversies remained part of the argument about prayer, but often had to give way to a tendency towards formalisation, authorisation and prescription, but this is a subject for later treatment.[33]

Indeed, it is clear from what have already been listed as the liturgical contexts relevant to that age, that the dissatisfaction felt by those who were geographically distant from Jerusalem which led them to express themselves in less centralised ways was a sentiment shared by their later counterparts. There were certainly those who bitterly criticised the Second Temple and its priesthood as corrupt and evil and would have nothing to do with it and others who perhaps looked to men of special piety and mystical flair as an alternative medium of contact with heaven. There even appears to be some evidence of attempts to retain or reactivate elements of religious status in a number of the older cultic centres.[34] But even among those larger numbers who might still send their annual half-shekel for Temple maintenance or manage to undertake a journey to Jerusalem on one of the three annual pilgrimage festivals, there was enough interest in some form of independent expression to encourage, as has already been pointed out, the development of the *maʿamad*, the prayer gathering, the individual devotion, and what we might call the Bible reading group. While for some, then, the Temple cult, even if modified, remained central during the Second Temple period, and for others there was at least an ambivalence about its position among Israel's theological priorities, there were groups who sought their major liturgical expression in a different context.

It does not require a very thorough reading of the contemporary Jewish literature in order to encounter some of the reasons for the disenchantment with the Temple. The divide between the aristocracy and the common people that often seemed to be perpetuated there; the political machinations of the Hasmoneans and their successors that were bound up with the abuse of the high priesthood; and the growing distances between Jerusalem and the diaspora, in more senses that the geographical – all contributed to the drift towards alternative liturgical centres. It should be stressed that certain pentateuchal obligations could be met only by making use of the Temple's facilities and that there was consequently an enforced attachment between the established cult and the majority of the populace who, it would seem, would not go to the length of such groups as the Dead Sea sect in denying the validity of the service as then carried out on Mount Zion. Nevertheless, the doubts that had existed from biblical times grew and the more that certain priestly factions assimilated to Hellenistic ways, the more would the worship conducted by them be open to suspicion. With the introduction of Greek and Roman elements into the architecture of an expanding building there were surely those who feared the growing similarity with at least the outward appearance of pagan cults and, possibly, some who were growing progressively more impatient with rituals that were not without their mystery and magic.[35] The characteristic features of individual devotion that had sometimes been relegated to a secondary role were bidding once again to become dominant among the various reactions to the Temple's assumed centrality in the liturgical *status quo*.

That it was a multifarious rather than a single response that was made in the wake of such gnawing doubts is clear from the contemporary sources that have already been listed. One obvious solution was to stress the role of the family and the home in offering a simpler and more direct means of communication with one's creator. If the theory recently championed by Baruch Bokser is correct, and the origins of the *Seder* service and Passover *Haggadah* are to be sought in the transformance of a biblical ritual tied to the Temple sacrifice into a domestic celebration with liturgical and pedagogic elements, there is no reason to assume that this transformation commenced only after the destruction of the Temple. Indeed, in the earliest textual witnesses to a ritual being conducted at home the existence of that institution is certainly presupposed.[36]

Whether such a domestic liturgy was being conducted in scribal circles, pietistic groups, or among a more proletarian or rustic segment of the population, is difficult to judge and any conclusion would inevitably be dependent on the degree to which credence is lent to the simple division of the Jews of the period into Pharisees, Sadducees and Essenes, or into Hellenists and nationalists, or into plebeians and patricians – the list of possible divisions has grown as historians of the period have multiplied and new historical theories have been propounded. Perhaps the suggestion made earlier to speak of composite trends rather than clearly definable groups will allow the discussion to proceed without committing itself to a definitive assessment. It will also once again point out the danger of presupposing the existence of a systematic, religious philosophy on the part of any section of society in a period of social, political and spiritual flux. Wherever it originated, the development of a domestic alternative to the Temple is paralleled by other such tendencies. The emphasis laid by Jesus and/or his followers on good deeds rather than assisting the operation of the cult by providing a system of money-changing may be defined as a pietistic or proletarian response[37] while the swift substitution of intellectual discussions for sacrificial rituals made by the generation of the early tannaim may betoken an earlier and fundamental preoccupation with Torah-study that welcomed the revolution as an evolution.[38] The events of the Jewish Revolt and the later defeat by the Romans also lent support to those patterns of thought that had already questioned the simplistic systems of theodicy that associated physical comfort with devoutness and suffering with evil and had thereby driven a philosophical wedge between appeals to God and actual human experience, between petitions and the response to them. Perhaps scholastic circles were in this way opting for a novel view of man's communication with the Divine. Expressed in different terms, what is here being suggested is a religious ferment among the majority of the people which provided the opportunity for liturgical innovation that took diverse forms in a variety of contexts. However motivated, all these developments give testimony to a changing system of priorities and the reconsideration of the nature of liturgy, worship and prayer.

DEFINITION OF LITURGY

The quest for the origins of Jewish rabbinic, Christian and Muslim prayer customs in the immediate pre-Christian period has, paradoxically, been blighted by scholarly acquaintance with such customs and the presuppositions that underlie them. For the scholar in Christianity, liturgy calls to mind the eucharist, or its equivalent, an act that confirms the believer's status as an adherent of the faith in good standing and, through a mysterious process, unites him with its founder. A colleague concentrating on Jewish liturgy will think of a prescribed number of recitations of the *shema'* and the *'amidah* each day with accompanying lectionaries on many occasions, while a student of Islam will be reminded of the central requirement to acknowledge the unity of God and the uniqueness of Muḥammad's prophecy five times daily. It will be supposed that synagogues, churches and mosques are the ideal centres for such liturgy; that the act of worship is best performed communally; that there are officials to act as mediators or leaders; and that authoritative formulations are a *sine qua non* of the ceremonial. The very use of the Greek term that refers to the performance of the public service of the gods by the priests (*leitourgia*) is in itself an indication of a somewhat preconceived notion. It takes for granted that the Hebrew word employed by the tannaim, and presumably their predecessors, to describe the Temple service, namely *'avodah*, which is the equivalent of the Greek *leitourgia*, adequately describes Jewish worship in its totality during the Second Temple period.

As has been pointed out, there was no unanimity during that period about what constituted the most effective and essential means of performing a public service of God, this being determined by the theological propensities of a particular gathering, group or occasion, whether spontaneous or prearranged. Acts of mystical piety, Temple offering, study, benediction or praise might each lay claims to such a distinction and could equally be referred to as a liturgy of Second Temple Judaism. The term 'liturgy' must therefore either be abandoned in the present context as a deceptive misnomer or given a much wider definition that avoids anticipating the existence of what later became the standard, authoritative theory and practice and rather refers to all aspects of Jewish worship and prayer, whatever their origin, milieu and ideological basis.

Since the term is widely used in connection with the history of pre-rabbinic Judaism, it has been retained in the title of this chapter on the understanding that it soon becomes apparent to readers that only the latter of the two senses just offered tallies with the views here being expressed. What must now be tackled is the definition of the word 'synagogue' and whether its use too has tended to mislead students of its early history.

DEFINITION OF SYNAGOGUE

It is widely recognised that the origins of the synagogue are shrouded in mystery and that there is little concrete evidence available to enable scholars to plot its history with any great confidence before the beginning of the Christian era. This shortcoming has not, however, prevented historians of the institution from commonly making a number of questionable assumptions about the impetus for its creation and about its physical state, its functions and its relationship with the Temple.

Its earliest form is traced to pre-exilic Israel as a means of providing a place of worship for those who were deprived of their cultic shrines after the centralisation of the liturgy in the Jerusalem Temple,[39] or had become disenchanted with that centre, or to the Babylon Jewish communities established after the destruction of the first Temple which had no prospect of making the pilgrimage to Jerusalem.[40] It is seen as a smaller copy of the Temple (*miqdash me'aṭ*), incorporating various elements of the original institution and providing a centre for regular communal worship.[41] The Greek terms *sunagoge* and *proseuche* are identified as the equivalents of the Hebrew *beth tefillah* or *beth ha-keneseth*, often without reference to any geographical, historical or functional distinction. Where public prayers by Jews are recorded, it is sometimes taken for granted that these are being conducted in at least an earlier equivalent of the synagogue. The architectural designs that are known from archaeological discoveries to have existed in the early centuries of the Christian era are cited in the presentation of the synagogue's pre-Christian history and encourage the view that it is a specific type of building that should be imagined when consideration is given to its earliest form. The truth is, however, that before the late first century BCE there is no definitive source that indicates the existence of such a specific building in the Holy Land or in Babylon, no archaeological site in those countries that can be identified as a synagogue, and no evidence of a centre for public service in Hellenistic Judah that somehow matched that of the Temple. What historians can refer to are Greek inscriptions from third-century BCE Egyptian sites that make mention of *proseuchai*, or prayer-places, during the reign of Ptolemy III.[42]

It may well then be the case that the earliest precursor of the synagogue was the creation of the Hellenistic diaspora, not exclusively as a place of public worship (the Jews actually had temples at Araq el-Amir, Elephantine and Leontopolis) but as an assembly point for the local community where they could express themselves as Jews in a variety of social and religious ways, including scriptural readings, study, prayer and the performance of other traditional Jewish customs. Interestingly enough, the earliest Palestinian inscription to refer to such an institution, recording the construction of a synagogue by Theodotos, mentions reading of the Torah, observance of the religious precepts and hospitality for visitors but says nothing of communal prayer.[43] While such an institution in the diaspora might wish to imitate the Temple practices of Jerusalem and would *faute de mieux* be applauded for doing so, its equivalent in the homeland would be less likely to do so. For those for whom the Jerusalem Temple alone stood paramount this would be offensive and those with doubts about aspects of the sacrificial cult would no doubt prefer to develop institutions and practices that provided more distinctly alternative means of expression. The reason why no synagogue has been found that may even tentatively be dated earlier than the late first pre-Christian century in Palestine is that there was no such specific building. Jews came together for benedictions, prayers, Bible reading and interpretation, or for the *ma'amad*, if the mishnaic account is historically accurate, and what they thereby constituted might well be referred to in Greek as a synagogue, but, just as the context differed, depending on the group and the situation, so the site was not necessarily a fixed one nor subject to the same physical requirements on each occasion. If the word *keneseth* that occurs in the Mishnah in the context of Temple liturgy (*Yoma* 7.1 and *Soṭah* 7.7–8) has to be seen as the equivalent of *bet ha-keneseth* and therefore a reference to a synagogue, it may well be an anachronistic gloss. More likely, both historically and linguistically, is that the sense borne by this use of the noun amounts to no more than a description of a formal assembly or congregation of Israelites and conveys precisely the same as its Greek equivalent.

In the first century CE, possibly as more external influences on the whole of Judaean society made themseves felt, and when, as we have seen, a variety of forms of Jewish liturgical expression flourished side by side in the homeland, the diaspora synagogue also took root in that milieu and actual buildings gave form to the previously less tangible concept. This understanding of the situation would explain why there are so many varieties of physical structure used for synagogues in the early Christian centuries and why it took so long for a standard format to emerge.[44] It was only when the tensions between the Temple and the various alternative expressions of Jewish worship disappeared after the destruction of the former that the synagogue in Palestine was able to consider absorbing within its own infrastructure not only all these various expressions but also major elements of Temple ritual. That this was not done without objection and controversy is a matter for discussion when the later history of Jewish worship is considered. In the present context it need only be stressed that while for the Jews of the Hellenistic diaspora the synagogue may well have constituted a characteristic building, the equivalent concept for their brethren in the Judaean homeland probably conveyed no more than the sense of a gathering. If that is indeed the case then the 'early liturgy of the synagogue' must be redefined to refer to the various means used by the Jews during the Second Temple period for expressing the closeness that they felt to God and his revealed word.

OPPOSING TRENDS

So much has been said about the unacceptability of uncritically assuming the existence of second-century CE tannaitic prayers and prayer customs in the latter part of the Second Temple period that a few remarks should also be made about those elements of controversy that characterise the tannaitic and, indeed, to a large extent, the amoraic attitudes to liturgy in its widest sense and owe their origin to dissenting opinions and varying priorities that already existed before the Jewish Revolt. These will serve as a corrective to any impression that might have been given of an overall lack of continuity and will demonstrate that there was a long process of liturgical development during the whole of which variety and uniformity were vying with each other and exercising a mutual influence. However revolutionary a particular adjustment to an aspect of Jewish liturgy, it is rare indeed to find no precedent at all for it in at least the ideology, if not in the practical arrangements of the past. Indeed, it could strongly be argued that the essence of Jewish liturgy is that it carries within it all these competing tendencies and successfully absorbs them all.[45]

Clearly, the relative roles of the individual and the community, and of spontaneity and formality, stand at the centre of such controversies. While the Temple service, with all its cultic paraphernalia, was performed on behalf of the entire community, present and absent, it was conducted by a relatively small number of priests of the required heredity and needed to find the popular dimension through such contrastingly simple and unadorned devices as the *ma'amad*. On the other hand, petitions, supplications and benedictions that were originally expressed by individuals ultimately served as the foundation of a system of prayers that became progressively more formal and ceremonial. As was pointed out in the previous chapter, such a system began in the latter part of the Second Temple period, to include specific days and times and to develop a complete liturgical calendar, a move that was bound to disturb those concerned with the importance of the spontaneous element. As far as poetic praises and psalms are concerned, it is not definitively established that they are consistently to be related to formal Temple services but it is clear that they represent one end of the linguistic and literary spectrum at the other end of which stand prosaic prayers and entreaties of a less structured kind. In spite of the existence of both Temple and synagogue in the first century CE, important liturgical activity took place, as has been noted, among individuals, in public places, at home, or in centres deliberately chosen for their inaccessibility. Remnants of alternative *loci* are still to be found long after rabbinic Judaism has established the synagogue as the major centre of worship.[46] The fact that the Temple was virtually in permanent action must have made the occasional prayer, or even regular benediction, appear, especially to pietists, a somewhat parsimonious act of religiosity and was no doubt one of the factors that led to the growth of three daily sessions of communal worship and the argument between its expansion and abbreviation.

It was inevitable that the diaspora synagogue would have a large number of members that preferred Greek to Hebrew and that, even in Judaea, Aramaic would be regarded as the more popular tongue in certain areas. The status of the language of the Hebrew Bible as against the practical advantage of a widely understood vernacular was destined to become a recurrent theme in the halakhic discussions of the rabbis concerning the precise form in which various prayers were to be recited. Distinctions between the homeland and the diaspora extended from language to ritual. It only becomes clear from sources dating from the talmudic period that such variations exist but it is not unreasonable, in view of what has been suggested above about the synagogue and the Greek language, to assume that at least some of these distinctions had their origins in late Temple times.[47] It should be noted that these distinctions between the Holy Land and the diaspora ranged well beyond the matter of language and ultimately extended into matters of synagogal architecture, decoration and administration.[48]

In his various publications J. Heinemann seriously questioned the notion that research in Jewish liturgy must be devoted to the discovery of *the* original text of each of the prayers and convincingly demonstrated that in many cases it is a number of original texts that are to be sought. Such reasoning would support the assumption that as soon as there were communal prayers in more than one centre there had to be a variety of oral versions. However widespread a religious idea in that period of religious ferment before the rise of tannaitic Judaism, conditions were such that it would be unlikely to find identical expression among different groups of Jews. One is therefore tempted with regard to that stage of pre-rabbinic history to refer to oral versions rather than written ones. Indeed, as far as the attitude that continued into the early rabbinic tradition is concerned, there could be no Jewish prayer *texts* that were not directly borrowed from the Hebrew Bible. For the rabbis they had to be either biblical and written or rabbinic and oral and Fleischer's recent attempt to play down the significance of orality in the development of early rabbinic liturgy is unconvincing. This is not to say that there was no structure to Jewish prayer as far as the talmudic rabbis were concerned and that expression was totally free. The sources indicate at least a basic, and even hardy framework, and differences of opinion about precisely how to complete the picture. Those who argued for a fixed format attempted to lay down the details; those who preferred spontaneity argued the need for the constant introduction of novel elements.[49] But, given the efficiency of the oral transmission of the time, such a framework by no means required to be committed to writing to ensure its adoption and survival. The sect from the Dead Sea thought differently and preserved written versions of their prayers that imitated the biblical style and idiom but clearly adopted their own linguistic characteristics, so that here too there is controversy.[50] Presumably, the oral transmitters' basic objection lay in giving a written form and authority to something other than the Hebrew Bible, and only after the consigning of the talmudic traditions to writing did it become inevitable that the *siddur* would follow suit.[51] But it was almost a thousand years before the first rabbinic prayer-books made their appearance and during that time the successors of the Dead Sea sect, the Karaites, and, presumably, any sects that existed in the generations between them but have yet to be discovered and identified, staunchly maintained what was apparently a minority view.[52] Here too, then, there is a millennium of divergent predisposition in a major matter of liturgical policy.

The controversy about ritual ablutions before prayer may be described in similar terms. One trend was towards the maintenance of such a symbol of purification long after the loss of the Temple, to which it was originally most relevant, and the other gradually restricted its use to a few specific areas. Here, rabbinic Judaism through the centuries remained ambivalent and there appear from time to time major revivals of such stringencies in line with the Qumran community and the Islamic tradition, while for the most part the ritual ablution is left to the devotees of the mystical element in Judaism, which in itself has from earliest times made various forays into Jewish liturgy, with no small degree of success in its effects on the formulation of the prayers and the practice of various rituals.[53] A preoccupation with cosmology, angels and the *eschaton* can be identified in some texts from as early as the late Hebrew Bible period, at about the same time as there appeared the powerful intellectual and didactic trend that scholars have so often identified, but not necessarily with complete justification, as its antithesis.

Even the current debate about the role of women in acts of worship has a precedent in the varying Jewish responses to this question in the late Second Temple period. While there were Essenes who are reported to have admitted no women to their company and while the Qumran sect are seen to have accorded them no status in 'the purity of the many', there was a women's court in the Jerusalem Temple and there were occasions when men and women participated there in the same ceremony, albeit in segregated arrangement.[54] Again, the diaspora synagogues appear to take what today might be called a more egalitarian line in connection with the involvement of women, not necessarily segregated, in synagogue attendance and in the bestowal of honorific synagogal titles. If, as has been suggested by Bernadette Brooten, these titles betray a functional as well as an honorific role, and if the relevant inscriptions from the first few Christian centuries also reflect an earlier situation, this would necessitate a reconsideration of the place of women in the early synagogue.[55] Similarly, later rabbinic views about the possibility of women playing a part in Torah reading and study and in their own communal grace but not in leading the prayers for men might be a continuation of the different attitudes originally taken in the educational and devotional contexts, but the evidence is lacking and any conclusion must remain in the realm of speculation.[56] At any rate, enough is known to indicate that there was no uniform stance about the degree of female participation in liturgical acts, and that when new circumstances led different varieties of the Jewish religious experience to take up contrasting positions on the subject, they were each able to claim some support from historical precedent.

LITURGICAL LANGUAGE

Since the language of the Hebrew prayer-book is sometimes cited as an important link between the earlier classical and the later rabbinic form of the language, a brief treatment of that subject will not be out of place here. It will also enable us to see how each of the particular liturgical contexts that have been touched upon makes use of its own type of language and how elements of these were eventually absorbed into what became the basic structure of the rabbinic prayer-book. There is of course the danger of circular argument. One cannot at the same time declare a form to be early because of its language and a language to be early because of its form. What will rather be done here is to make some general points about liturgical language in the latter part of the Second Temple period, following the assumptions already made and documented about the larger historical situation, without using the conclusions reached as a foundation on which to build such assumptions.

It needs to be stated at the outset that any theory that postulates a line of direct development from biblical Hebrew through liturgical Hebrew to mishnaic Hebrew is based on a misunderstanding of the history of language in general and of the Hebrew language in particular. All manner of environmental factors affect language in diverse ways at different times and written sources that have come down to us do not tell the whole story. It is now well recognised that the language of the Hebrew Bible can represent no more than a 'frozen section' of a dialect or a dialectical tendency in the period of classical Hebrew and that mishnaic Hebrew may have originated in a different linguistic context and preserved all manner of characteristics that had once existed side-by-side with that form that subsequently became associated specifically with the Hebrew Bible. One is therefore obliged to view the differences between the two forms of the language in a synchronic as well as a diachronic fashion and to be wary of plotting a graph with a single line of development. In that case, liturgical Hebrew too, in its widest definition, must be seen to contain a variety of linguistic elements originating in the period under discussion, each of them representative of the context in which it was being used.[57]

Before turning to Hebrew one should immediately acknowledge that it was not the only liturgical language being employed. Ubiquitous as it is in one form or another in the contemporary literature, and predominant as it was becoming among the Jewish communities of the diaspora, Greek inevitably found its way into the synagogues of Jews for whom Hebrew was a foreign language, as would appear to be demonstrated by Jewish Hellenistic literature, the evidence of the early tannaitic sources about its liturgical use, and the ultimate preferences of the early Christian Church.[58] Aramaic, too, was employed in similar contexts. The private prayers of common people, particularly those living in Galilee or other less central areas, were couched in Aramaic, not only because it was the vernacular and more widely understood but also because there may have been among them a feeling that it was in the reading and transmission of sacred scripture that the 'holy tongue' was most suitably employed. The same logic, drawing as it did a distinction between scripture and the vernacular, was used by those who instituted, for recitation in the study centre or *beth ha-midrash*, special prayers that still carry the mark of this original, educational context.[59]

It was not entirely or universally clear, however, that the language that we now refer to as mishnaic Hebrew was to be regarded as identical with the medium used for scripture and therefore capable of being confused with it and the later rabbis certainly made a distinction between the two.[60] In that case, any objection to the wider use of the language of scripture did not necessarily apply to mishnaic Hebrew. What is more, the use of Aramaic may essentially have been geographical rather than ideological, so that only in the north would it have been the norm for popular liturgical expression. It is therefore not surprising to find that some of the earliest prayers were recited in the mishnaic dialect. Certain Temple responses, where they were not actually catenae of biblical Hebrew passages and verses, appear to have been recited in mishnaic Hebrew and this precedent seems to have been followed in such public contexts as the *maʿamad*, *Haggadah*, fast-day and grace after meals, if the earliest versions available to us of what they contained are to be trusted.[61] It is of course possible that there was an exchange of secondary Aramaic for original Hebrew in certain areas but since Aramaic passages were later incorporated into the liturgy without obvious embarrassment one would have to wonder why the change was made in some cases and not in others. Perhaps the process of standardisation towards mishnaic Hebrew, just as the later tendency to 'correct' that language to what had come to be regarded as more accurate biblical Hebrew,[62] (both of which trends were inspired by a desire to establish an independent religious identity) was never comprehensively achieved.

Some of the oldest Temple prayers have indeed been classified as *piyyuṭim*, that is, liturgical Hebrew poetry, a view that would make that genre of Jewish liturgical expression as old, if not older, than the more prosaic Hebrew texts that are characteristic of the rabbinic prayer-book. Heinemann details the simple and repetitive *hoshaʿanoth* and the *seliḥoth* among such prayers and argues that their form and content retain some of the earliest patterns of Jewish liturgical expression used in the Temple. It should, however, be noted that such a definition could be regarded as anachronistic and that a more cautious view would prefer to classify these forms as the predecessors of *piyyuṭ* rather than their earliest example.[63]

The simple benediction directly addressed to God and describing him as blessed was based on biblical Hebrew precedent, particularly the language of the later books of the Hebrew Bible, and, therefore, in its earliest form did not deviate from its original pattern, although it may originally have had an Aramaic equivalent in certain circles. The more complicated it became, and the more innovative its style and content, the more it veered towards mishnaic Hebrew.[64] Perhaps it is here that we can detect the growing schism between such groups as that of Qumran and the forerunners of the tannaitic rabbis. The former also based their original prayers on the precedent of biblical Hebrew, especially that of the Psalms, deliberately eschewing what they recognised as the more vernacular form of the language and adjusting the content rather than the linguistic style, while the latter made a more radical alteration, choosing to couch their prayers, even when they became more formal and communal, in terms that were more familiar to the common people and more closely identified with them as a discrete religious group.[65]

CONCLUSIONS

In spite of the complex and indefinite nature of the situation just described, it would be churlish to conclude this chapter without attempting, by way of summary of the arguments and evidence presented above, to catalogue those elements of the later synagogal liturgy that are to be found in the period before the destruction of the Temple and to suggest the form that they took at that stage. Since it has already been explained that there was no one context in which they all coexisted and that there was an interplay between the various ideas and practices, and since identification has been made of the original setting of each of the tendencies as far as the evidence permits, no further definition of who contributed what is necessary and these remarks may justifiably be limited to a brief description of the prototypes for what became standard elements in the rabbinic prayers. It should not be forgotten that there was no unanimous conviction that public prayer, other than that which might have existed in the Temple, deserved a central place in the religious commitments of the ordinary Jew and that it was probably only in the diaspora that an actual synagogue building provided a central setting for such and related activities. This lack of formal structure applied to the frequency, order and composition of Jewish devotions as much as to their location.

The substantial archaeological and literary evidence for the use of the *shema*ʿ, together with the equally theologically significant Ten Commandments, as a form of amulet, and as a daily prayer in the Temple and outside it, clearly establishes Deuteronomy 6:4 as one of the earliest forerunners of synagogal liturgy.[66] Indeed, the traditional recitation of the sentence 'blessed be the name of his glorious kingdom for ever and ever', which is a Temple response in origin, immediately after that verse, may be seen as confirming the authenticity of the claim about the *shema*ʿ's use in the Temple.[67] Whether the whole passage (6:4–9) and the second paragraph (Deuteronomy 11:13–21) were also recited is a more controversial point. The earliest tannaitic discussions support the contention that the first paragraph was an early adoption and that the third paragraph (Numbers 15:37–41) had not yet achieved an equal status in the second century CE.[68] It has been suggested that benedictions preceding and following the *shema*ʿ may have predated the destruction[69] but the lack of conclusive evidence about the content of the *shema*ʿ itself makes it unlikely that its liturgical setting had been so far defined, and, even when benedictions did begin to attach themselves to its recitation in, say, the latter part of the first Christian century, their oral nature and lack of standardisation meant that they could be no more than brief and simple.

For all the approximate parallels that have been suggested for the contents of the daily *ʿamidah*, there was still controversy about the precise number and contents of the benedictions in the early tannaitic period and if a skeletal form did exist at an earlier period it probably constituted no more than prototypes of some or all of the first three and last three benedictions that later became integral to all forms of the *ʿamidah*. Covering as they do the importance of the ancestral traditions, the after-life, divine holiness, worship, thanksgiving and peace, these benedictions are sufficiently 'neutral' in content to reflect a pre-rabbinic stage but there is no doubt that they were later modified to meet standard criteria laid down by the tannaim.[70] Since daily public prayers appear to be later than those attached to special occasions of sadness and joy, it is not surprising to find what appear to be early prayers attached to fast-days, sabbaths and festivals in the earliest rabbinic literature.[71] Another factor militating against any tendency to see the joint daily recitation of the *shemaʿ* and the *ʿamidah* as predating the tannaim is to be identified in the strenuous efforts made by the latter scholars to insist on their linkage by stressing the supreme importance of joining the latter benedictions to the paragraphs of the *shemaʿ* and their doxological conclusion to the beginning of the *ʿamidah*, efforts that would otherwise have been unnecessary.[72] Furthermore, the tannaitic requirements in the case of the *shemaʿ* are not identical with those of the *ʿamidah* and demonstrate that the former was a common custom attached to the beginning and end of the day while the latter was a more concentrated act of pious devotion.[73] It is of course possible that these two central pillars of the later rabbinic liturgy originated in different contexts. There are certainly enough of these, be they cultic, devotional, ascetic, intellectual, mystical or personal, to provide the relevant sources but, as yet, insufficient information to permit any more than undocumented speculation. Zahavy's linkage of the *shemaʿ* to scribal circles and the *ʿamidah* to the priesthood is certainly forced and strong arguments could be raised for precisely the opposite attribution.[74]

Another common custom was the recitation of benedictions in the context of daily life and these were simply constituted as praises directed to God. Only in the tannaitic period did they begin to acquire a more lengthy and complicated structure, as the essence of the form moved from a personal act of thanksgiving or blessing to a structured prayer. It is possible that the invitation to the community to praise God (*barekhu*), used to introduce prayer sessions, was an important stage in that development. The earliest benediction with formal overtones is the grace after meals, as is clear from the difficulties later encountered by the rabbis in accommodating it to the pattern that they were constructing for less established doxologies.[75] The priestly blessing is of course of a different order altogether and it would make sense to assume that it entered the proto-rabbinic liturgy from Temple use where it must surely have had a very respectable pedigree.[76] The recent discovery of a seventh-century BCE silver amulet with a form of the benediction, however, indicates an even wider use from an early date.[77]

Among other elements of the liturgy that appear to have moved from Second Temple to synagogue were certain biblical Psalms and those selections of them known as *hallel* (Psalms 113–18), the Ten Commandments (about the inclusion of which there continued to be controversy for many centuries),[78] perhaps versions of the poetic *seliḥoth* and *hoshaʿnoth* and certain rituals of the High Priest on the Day of Atonement.[79] It is not unlikely that they and their like were introduced into the Temple in the first place under the pressure of the populace for recitations to be attached to the cultic service. Be that as it may, they may be counted among those items that may justifiably be regarded as part of the Second Temple's institutions in the latter part of its existence. In view of their obvious suitability to the synagogal context, there was no matter of principle involved in their transfer, the issue of the Ten Commandments being related to polemics against heretics rather than matters of liturgical principle, but the same cannot be said for other Temple institutions. It is reasonable to suggest that such ceremonies as the blowing of the *shofar* and the waving of the *lulav* were not incorporated into the synagogal liturgy without considerable controversy, some believing that they could only ever be part of an authentic Temple service and others preferring to preserve their practice in the only context available after 70 CE.[80] These suggestions will have to be pursued elsewhere at greater length but they are relevant here to the extent that they may provide further evidence that the early synagogue was as much the Temple's contender as its imitator. Ultimately, and paradoxically, the less realistic and desirable the restoration of such a Temple service became, the more successful were the efforts to emulate its example in the synagogue.

Although Jews certainly came together for the reading and study of scripture in the early first century CE, there is no possibility, on the basis of the evidence currently available to us, of establishing precisely which passages were read on which occasions. One may only speculate that the readings were linked with the manner of the occasion being marked, so that festivals and fasts must early have attracted their own readings, both on the dates themselves and on sabbaths preceding them. There is clear evidence in the tannaitic sources, for instance, that the four readings on sabbaths around the time of *Purim* and Passover were early versions of a cycle of readings and not additions to one. The more formal the synagogal liturgy became, the more control was exercised over what was read and how it was translated and interpreted, but remnants always persisted of earlier attempts to match the biblical readings with the events of the Jewish calendar.[81]

While the mystical element in the rabbinic liturgy was once thought to be among its later accretions, the current tendency to trace that element through the whole of Jewish religious history encourages the view that there were among those who pressed for the development of Jewish public prayer pietists who had felt their spiritual sensitivity heightened by mystical experiences. They not only adopted aspects of emerging talmudic prayer in their own devotions but also saw a place for the introduction of mystical formulations into the rabbinic liturgy.

Such pietists will have included those who composed the earliest forerunners of the later *hekhaloth* hymns.[82] The rabbis remained ambivalent on the subject for many generations, ultimately absorbing elements of such hymnology into the standard prayers, but there is no reason to assume that the controversy about the place of mysticism in public Jewish prayer was not already present when its nature was first being debated.

Whatever the attractions of the developing synagogue, the home always remained an important centre of Jewish ritual and liturgy, the dietary laws, sabbath and festival customs such as the *qiddush* and *havdalah* in their earliest forms,[83] and the traditional education of children necessitating the performance of various precepts in the domestic context. The best example is of course the *Seder* service on the first evening of Passover and the development of the Passover *Haggadah*, the earliest aspects of which certainly belong to the century before the destruction of the Temple. And no matter what transpired in the realm of public worship, and regardless of the pressure on the Jew to transfer the private to the communal, individual prayers and supplications were always an ingredient of Jewish religious practice. Daniel's example of fervently praying three times a day (Daniel 6:11), as many other such individual acts of piety, ultimately became archetypal for public worship in Judaism, but its motivation was a personal need for support and inspiration that would never be displaced by the formalised service, whatever its degree of expansion and acceptance. The tension between personal prayer and public worship is one of a number of such competing trends in Jewish liturgical history, some of which will receive attention in the next chapter.

CHAPTER 4

Some liturgical issues in the talmudic sources

INTRODUCTION

The situation with regard to Jewish liturgical history after the destruction of the Temple is in some respects in stark contrast to that which obtained in the periods of the Hebrew Bible and the Second Temple. In these earlier periods the researcher has to utilise a variety of sources that clearly emanate from different contexts and that have been brought together in the literature not because of their original significance and function but because of the way in which later generations chose to interpret and employ them. It is difficult, indeed unwise, to try to present the relevant texts as reflections of one systematic and consistent approach to matters of religion since their origin, history and provenance are very much open to debate. All that can be done (and it is hoped that this has been achieved in earlier chapters) is to identify certain characteristics, relate them speculatively to particular circles, and offer a broad description of the various types of liturgical expression that existed before rabbinic Judaism and Christianity carried the tradition forward in their separate ways. As with theology, so with liturgy, today's scholar prefers plurals to singulars in the description of past religious phenomena. It is safer to speak of biblical liturgies than of Jewish liturgy in the biblical period; similarly with regard to the era of the Second Temple.

When we pursue the history of Jewish liturgy into and through the tannaitic and amoraic periods, the image presented to us in the talmudic–midrashic literature is of quite a different order. Although the basic content of such central items as the *shema'* recitation and the *'amidah* is becoming established, there is decidedly no fixed prayer-book for the rabbinic community at large and no uniform approach to matters of detail among its various groupings. Nevertheless, one can be confident that one is dealing with a specific form of Judaism with variant tendencies within it, rather than a variety of interconnected Judaisms with insufficient evidence to draw clear-cut lines of demarcation between them. Rabbinic Judaism's identity at that time was still in the early stages of its development and was by no means monolithic but the richness of the literary heritage that it bequeathed from as early as the second and as late as the sixth century permits much more precise conclusions about the nature of much of its *Weltanschauung*. All the evidence to date points to the fact that the talmudic interpretation of the meaning of Jewish religious existence was on its way to becoming the dominant one and the familiarity of its ideology and practice makes it a simple matter, perhaps sometimes too simple and consequently a little misleading a matter, to trace a direct line of continuity into the geonic and mediaeval eras.[1]

What is to be attempted in this chapter, then, is an overview of the attitudes to prayer revealed by the talmudic–midrashic sources, which will provide insights into how the early rabbis dealt with the subject in the formation of their overall theology and help to explain what tended to be taken as axiomatic by scholars in post-talmudic generations. One must, of course, bear in mind that, given the nature of Judaism, the accurate treatment of any topic in the realm of Jewish studies is unlikely to smack of the theologically systematic. Israel Abrahams put it most succinctly when declaring that 'Rabbinic theology is a syncretism, not a system'[2] and thereby raising the question whether such religious ideas, failing as they do to constitute a system, may in the strictest sense be defined as theology. Whatever one's view of what is or is not theology, there can be little doubt that an examination of the attitudes to liturgical issues in a particular religious tradition provides an important key to the understanding of that tradition and will, in this specific case, help us to establish the precise contribution made by the tannaim and amoraim to the general development of Jewish liturgy.

Fortunately, much of the basic analysis of Jewish prayer in the talmudic period, at least as a whole, if not in the layers of its history, has already been completed. As well as dealing with the wider history of individual services, prayers, poems and customs within the various post-talmudic rites, and the communal and synagogal contexts in which they developed, Ismar Elbogen also gave some attention to the characteristic elements of the tannaitic and amoraic periods. He sketched the historical background to the adjustments then made and identified which parts of the prayer-book might be dated from these early centuries of rabbinic Judaism.[3] The more recent work of Joseph Heinemann complemented Elbogen's historical survey with a form-critical treatment of the sources.[4] He characterised the different genres of prayer and located their origins in Temple, synagogue, academy, law court and personal life, while at the same time offering important guidance on matters of linguistic style and literary pattern. Elbogen's original German and Heinemann's original Hebrew have been translated into Hebrew and English respectively[5] and have influenced the popular books on the subject that have recently appeared, although Heinemann's clear caution that one should think of an elastic and pliable form rather than of a more solid structure has sometimes been ignored and has recently been subjected to considerable criticism by Fleischer.[6] There is still work to be done on the linguistic, literary and historical background to liturgical developments in the period but the contribution to be made here will be more on the ideological side. It seems to the writer that, even after Heinemann, insufficient attention has been paid, either by negligence or by design, to the lack of theological or ideological consistency in the talmudic sources' discussions of liturgical issues, with the attendant danger that much of the organisation and centralisation that are the product of a later age may be wrongly attributed to this earlier period. If a detailed, diachronic treatment of the whole period and an attendant dating of the numerous layers of its tradition history are left for later scholarship, one may in the mean time concentrate on pointing out the intensive dialectic that engaged the early rabbis on matters of liturgical principle. The hope is that such a treatment, briefly commenced in this chapter, will complement earlier scholarship and exercise some influence on future directions in the field.

METHOD

It should be stated at the outset that consistency and completeness demand that this chapter will at times cover what may be regarded by some specialists as well-trodden ground. By way of compensation, the presentation may induce even such specialists to look afresh at certain problems and thus contribute to their general understanding of what is a vast subject.

After some brief remarks about the general background to rabbinic prayer, the central part of this chapter will be devoted to an examination of almost a hundred selected sources, nearly all of them talmudic, dealing with the complicated spiritual phenomenon of prayer. The use of such talmudic sources always requires caution. In the words of a doyen of rabbinic studies in an earlier generation, the late Louis Ginzberg, 'the devil, according to Shakespeare, quotes Scripture. But if he is really as clever as he is reputed to be, he ought to quote the Talmud, as there is hardly any view of life, for and against which one could not quote the Talmud.'[7] Such a situation has elicited various kinds of response through the ages. Mediaeval Jewish scholars devised ingenious means of harmonising different views and bringing them into line with the codified *halakhah*, while their Christian antagonists demonstrated a penchant for the most bizarre ideas they could find and utilised them to discredit Judaism. Although such standpoints have not entirely disappeared in our own times, modern scholarly opinion seems to range from a position which postulates the existence of a normative rabbinism from which certain groups and individuals deviated from the late Second Temple period to the post-talmudic era, through a gamut of more moderate opinion to the other extreme, which prefers to post-date the emergence of any authoritative interpretation as much as possible and to upgrade any recorded view at variance with this interpretation. Clearly, to arrive at an accurate assessment of the views of the tannaim and amoraim and of their development during the talmudic period, generalisations, religious preconceptions and what have been called 'fanciful conjectures and unfounded explanations'[8] must be abandoned in favour of a comprehensive survey of the sources which combines the best of traditional interpretation, form- and text-criticism, and historical analysis. To accept uncritically the historicity of all talmudic reports, particularly as they relate to events in the pre-Christian period, and the attribution of all statements and policy changes to particular personalities[9] is as misguided as the approach that claims that all previous studies are antiquated and distinguished talmudists now obsolete and refuses to credit the rabbis with any reliable information about the origin of their own religious traditions.[10]

Ultimately, then, no historically sound study of rabbinic attitudes to prayer will be possible until the talmudic literature has been critically and comprehensively studied with all available research tools. This does not, however, mean that the kind of overview being attempted in this book is beyond the researcher's scope as far as the talmudic period is concerned. On the contrary, the identification of the basic themes of each major period of Jewish liturgical history is precisely the aim here. Indeed, the more general treatment of a sufficiently broad sample of talmudic sources is, in its totality, as likely to serve that aim as the detailed textual, historical and linguistic analysis of each of its constituents. Without doubt, such an intensive examination is a desideratum and one that is not ruled out as a later supplement to the present study. If properly undertaken, however, it would take us well beyond the range of this volume and surely requires a complete monograph in its own right. In a brief article Tzvee Zahavy has recently attempted to begin such a process of analysis by relating liturgical issues to Jewish political, economic and social history in the first two centuries and has identified three periods of development. Until the literary and linguistic study of the relevant texts is further advanced and/or more external evidence becomes available, such an exercise must remain a speculative one but, meanwhile, some of the points he makes are important and others will encourage debate.[11] With regard to the general historical and methodological problems of studying Jewish liturgical history in the talmudic period, the necessary discussions are included in the chapters that precede and follow this one, thus permitting a concentration here on the overall impression conveyed by the sources themselves. In the mean time, therefore, and for the purposes of this modest chapter, it is possible to make initial progress by identifying various themes that occur throughout the talmudic literature, while leaving their precise, historical development within the period of that literature and the uncovering of the literary layers in which they are preserved for later analysis. Where dates and personalities are cited they will be those that are presupposed in the talmudic text and not necessarily those that will ultimately be accepted as scientifically authenticated, but it should be remembered that even a view that argues for a later formulation of all such texts would be hard-pressed to prove that the nuclei of traditions did not originate in earlier centuries. By a temporarily synchronic explanation of a selection of talmudic sources, then, an impression will be conveyed of some of the tensions, controversies, stresses and strains that accompanied early rabbinic Judaism's attempt to define the place of prayer in the framework of its religious ideology, to reveal that the matter is not as uncomplicated as it is sometimes portrayed, and to provide some guidelines for future work.

BACKGROUND

It appears that in liturgy, no less than in other fields, the talmudic rabbis inherited a welter of concepts and forms that they attempted to remould in accordance with their own emergent ideology. It will be recalled that from at least as early as the time of Jesus, and probably earlier, there existed numerous prayer contexts already overlapping to a considerable degree and exerting a strong influence on the contemporary Jew. The Temple rituals in their wider ramifications had attracted to themselves some formulaic recitations (e.g. Ten Commandments and priestly benediction) while the people had learned to express themselves liturgically outside the Temple (as in the case of the *ma'amad*) while the offerings were made in it; a formal liturgy for special festive and solemn occasions, quite independent of the sacrificial cult, had developed in certain circles; a liturgical dimension was being added to the social and pedagogical aspects of the synagogue, and the first attempts were being made to regulate this spontaneous expression of popular religiosity; the individual devotions of pious folk-heroes were held in high esteem, and they were credited with the ability to intercede with God and bring about miracles; and special groups, coming together for Torah-study and communal meals, were evolving sets of formulae suitable for introducing and concluding such sessions and for expressing their gratitude to God for his bounty. All these were of course in addition to the outpourings of the individual at times of intense emotion such as are recorded in the Bible.[12] A statement by R. Joshua ben Ḥananiah may be interpreted either in a literal fashion as an eye-witness report of this pluralistic state of affairs obtaining during the first Christian century or, more minimally, as evidence of an awareness of its existence on the part of later transmitters of such a tradition. Either way, and with due account being taken of the textual variants, the statement notes the parallel existence of what may loosely be described as festival rituals in Temple, synagogue, academy and home so that there was barely any respite from religious activity on the part of those participating in the water-drawing ceremony on the festival of *Sukkoth*.[13] In the reassessment of their spiritual values and commitments that was forced on the tannaim by the destruction of the Temple and the almost equally catastrophic Bar Kokhba revolt, they were called upon to pronounce on which elements among the inherited traditions were likely to contribute most to Jewish spiritual survival and how best to preserve them. The central position accorded by them to a system of *halakhah* is well known. In order to give prayer a place in the system, its general importance had to be evaluated and its function defined, decisions had to be made on such matters as the relative merits of public and private, as well as spontaneous and fixed prayer, and opinions had to be offered on such practical aspects as the best time and place for one's devotions. The lively response elicited by this challenge should become apparent from the sources about to be examined. These are treated here under three main headings: The theological status of prayer, The essential nature of prayer, and The mechanics of prayer.

THE THEOLOGICAL STATUS OF PRAYER

Whether or not its attribution to Simeon the Just is authentic, the statement at the beginning of the first chapter of *'Avoth* that the existence of the world is dependent on a continuous Jewish commitment to the triad of Torah, *'Avodah* (Temple-service) and Good Deeds, is a clear testimony to the theological priorities of the early tannaim. With the destruction of the Temple, one third of this spiritual structure lay in ruins and the search for an alternative got underway. One obvious solution was to claim that the loss could be made good by a corresponding elevation of one or other of the two remaining elements. Evidence of such a claim is available to us in an interesting commentary on Simeon's statement that records, on the one hand, an anonymous view that God is more enamoured of Torah-study than of burnt-offerings and, on the other, an alleged assurance given by Rabban Yoḥanan ben Zakkai to R. Joshua that the means of atonement for sins had not, as the latter imagined, disappeared with the destruction of the Temple, but had been transferred to the practice of Good Deeds.[14] Although the expression of such views may partly reflect what Julius Guttmann described as 'the growth of theoretical reflection on the contents of religion',[15] as well as a homiletical tendency to stress aspects of the faith that required bolstering in difficult situations, the establishment of religious priorities had an important practical application in times of persecution. The *locus classicus* for the age-old rabbinic discussion on whether, in the final analysis, Torah-study or Good Deeds takes precedence, describes the deliberations of a high-level conference possibly summoned during the Hadrianic persecutions to offer guidance at a time of national emergency.[16] The same location, in the Nitza home in Lod, is given elsewhere for an equally fraught discussion about the Jewish religious principles for which one is obliged to suffer martyrdom.[17] In the instance here being cited, the view of R. Akiva in favour of Torah-study over Good Deeds won the day because, in his words, 'study leads to deeds' and not vice versa, but no final settlement was reached. E. E. Urbach's summary of the situation deserves to be quoted: 'Just as the problem of the livelihood of the Sages in the framework of the question of studying Torah and practising a craft did not cease troubling, complicating and confusing the circles of the Sages, so, too, no unambiguous solution was found to the question of the relationship between learning Torah, on the one hand, and performing good works and occupying oneself with communal needs, "both religious and mundane", on the other.'[18] Even the recitation of the *shema'* was pressed into the service of those anxious to miss no opportunity of listing the major principles of Judaism. For the second- to third-century Palestinian teacher, R. Levi, the first two paragraphs were recited each morning and evening not so much to mark the beginning and end of the day as to remind the Jew of each of the Ten Commandments, to which he found allusions in the *shema'*'s various phrases.[19]

Those scholars of subsequent generations who did follow the view of R. Akiva felt no compunction about stressing the superiority of Torah-study over prayer. In their case, of course, they were able, and indeed anxious, to fulfil their obligations in both respects, but by their statements and actions they left their co-religionists in no doubt about which preoccupation was to take precedence. Although his own private prayers are reputed to have brought rain when it was needed, the early third-century amora from Lydda, R. Joshua ben Levi ruled that a synagogue could be converted into a *beth ha-midrash* (loosely rendered 'academy'), apparently because the latter possessed a higher degree of sanctity, thereby implying that a conversion in the opposite direction was not permissible.[20] More specifically, the same teacher has God interpreting the verse in Psalms 84:11 to mean that one day of David's Torah-studies pleases him more than a thousand burnt-offerings to be made by Solomon, his son. A contemporary, R. Eleazar ben Pedat, went so far as to claim that the attainment of education was tantamount to the rebuilding of the Temple.[21] One particular folio, 8a, of the tractate *Berakhoth* in the Babylonian Talmud is a rich source of similar attitudes. It records that although there were thirteen synagogues in Tiberias, the leading scholars of the town, R. Ammi and R. Assi, would recite their prayers only on the premises where they did their studying. Another report there reveals that such tendencies were not restricted to the rabbis of the Holy Land. The fourth-century Babylonian amora, R. Shesheth, who was blind, grew so impatient with the public Torah reading that he literally turned away, and proceeded with his studies. In a third passage a delightful remark is attributed to Rafram ben Papa, whose teacher, R. Ḥisda, was a contemporary of the R. Shesheth already mentioned. On being requested to repeat some of the fine things that his teacher had said on synagogal matters, he cited a view of his that interpreted a Psalm verse to mean that God prefers centres of *halakhah*-study to synagogues. Rava, to whose views and those of his colleague Abbaye, so much of the Babylonian Talmud is devoted, was so powerful an advocate of the supremacy of Torah-study that the prolonged prayers of R. Hamnuna inspired him to declare: 'Such people are abandoning eternal life in order to engage in mundane matters!' A comment immediately following Rava's declaration in this talmudic text and probably made by the redactor of the passage, demonstrates an awareness of the opposing viewpoint. It explains that R. Hamnuna was of the opinion that Torah and Prayer each had its separate time. Similarly, an aggadic interpretation of Isaiah 55:6 recorded in the name of the third generation amora R. Abbahu has it that God is particularly to be found in the houses of both prayer and study. That even sabbath prayers were conducted on an *ad hoc* basis among scholars rather than in a formally designated synagogue is obvious from the report of R. Dimi about the Palestinian group, probably in the third century, that forgot to arrange the removal of a Torah scroll on a Friday in preparation for the statutory reading the next day.[22] As a final example of the view that gave Torah-study precedence over Prayer, it will be helpful to cite from the same source the riposte of R. Zera, a Babylonian rabbi who had emigrated to the land of Israel, to the action of his pupil, R. Jeremiah, who was anxious to adjourn his lesson for prayer. He applied to him the verse in Proverbs 28:9: 'He that turneth his ear away from learning Torah, even his prayer shall be an abomination.' The authentic successor to the Temple liturgy and, thus, the ideal form of worship is being portrayed as Torah-study, and Prayer is accorded no more than a junior place in comparison.

If, as has been indicated, the intensified acclamation of Torah-study and Good Deeds represented one response to the disappearance of the *'Avodah* or Temple-service, it was accompanied from the outset by what must surely have seemed a more revolutionary assertion, namely that the distinguished place of *'Avodah* was now to be taken by *Tefillah*, Prayer. A tannaitic interpretation of the injunction in Deuteronomy 11:13 'to serve' God clearly sets forth the two alternatives of how this *'Avodah* or service is now to be understood. The passage characteristically challenges its own opening statement that *'Avodah* means Torah-study by arguing for a literal meaning of *'Avodah*, i.e. 'work', on the basis of the verse in Genesis 2:16 which describes how God placed Adam in the Garden of Eden *le'ovdah uleshomrah* 'to work it and look after it'. The literal interpretation is rejected on the grounds that Adam was required to undertake such labour only later as a punishment for his disobedience, and *'Avodah* is therefore explained as Torah-study and *shemirah* ('looking after') as observance of the precepts. The alternative is then offered that *'Avodah* refers to Prayer, and the literal interpretation is here rejected on the grounds that the service of God demanded by the verse is to be with all one's heart and soul and that such service can only be Prayer, a view later repeated in the Babylonian Talmud in *Ta'anith* f. 2a. The argument concludes with the unequivocal statement that as the altar-service was called *'Avodah* so Prayer is called *'Avodah*. It is not without significance that the passage then includes a statement by R. Eliezer ben Jacob which presupposes that *'Avodah* still refers to the Temple-service. With his close association and acquaintance with the Temple, this tanna was perhaps unwilling to cede the distinction of being designated as *'Avodah katexochen* to any usurper.[23] Of similar interest is the statement by the tanna R. Judah ben Batyra that the festive joy once represented by the eating of the sacrificial meat is now, after the destruction of the Temple, achieved by the drinking of wine and not, apparently, by the eating of non-sacrificial meat.[24]

It was the view that *Tefillah* was the natural successor of the Temple *'Avodah* that made it possible for so many of the latter's rituals to be given a new attachment to Prayer and incorporated into the synagogue service. It is at the same time clear from the talmudic sources that the process was not altogether a smooth one, and that attempts were made to limit the new roles of the rituals so that they could not quite match their former cultic splendour. With regard to the priestly benediction, for instance, its incorporation into the synagogal liturgy brought with it changes in the form of the ritual. For the tanna R. Simeon (of whatever patronym) it was not priesthood but a good reputation that had maintained an attractive religious function and the *mishnah* in *Berakhoth* 5.4 seems to regard the priestly benediction as separate from the standard prayer context but others preferred a compromise to such a categorical differentiation. The discussion concerning the details of the benediction recorded in BT, *Soṭah* ff. 37b–39b provides clear evidence of changes in the use of the Divine Name, the ritual of raising the hands in blessing, the nature of the accompanying rituals and the Israelite constituency to whom the formula is addressed. It may here be added that the role of the priest himself, once so central to the liturgy, always had to struggle to maintain a significant place in the worship of rabbinic Judaism in the face of the growing participation of the learned or the ordinary Jew.[25] Similar adjustments in the form or use of Temple formulae may be detected in connection with the history of the expressions *min ha-ʿolam weʿad ha-ʿolam* and *barukh shem kevod malekhuthow leʿolam waʿed* whether or not the talmudic explanations themselves are scientifically convincing.[26] It is in the light of such gradual adjustments that the halakhic history of such customs as sounding the *shofar*, waving the *lulav* and reciting the *hallel* should be examined, as is clear from the fourth chapter of the tractate *Rosh Ha-Shanah* and has been suggested in an earlier chapter. It is clear from the evidence carefully supplied by S. Safrai that the absorption of Temple customs into the growing ritual of the synagogue was a lengthy and controversial process.[27] R. Abbahu cites the view of R. Eleazar that the correct fulfilment of the precept to wave the *lulav* is the equivalent of building an altar and offering a sacrifice on it but he omits to mention that the ideas about such a fulfilment current in his own day had come a long way from their original and narrow altar context. There is indeed some evidence of an opinion that sacrifices too had not totally disappeared among Jews with the destruction of the Temple but had simply been limited to other locations.[28]

The conviction that Prayer had inherited the prominent position in the theological triarchy hitherto occupied by the Temple-service was never without strong support. Indeed, the third-century amora, R. Eleazar ben Pedat, was not content with such a status for Prayer but went further, declaring it to be superior to offerings, as he proves on the basis of the first chapter of Isaiah, and greater than Good Deeds, as demonstrable from the fact that only Moses' Prayer and not his good deeds obtained for him God's answer (Deuteronomy 3:26–7). It is clear from a number of passages that R. Yoḥanan was a keen supporter of such views. In his interpretation of 56:7 in Isaiah, he makes the daring claim that God himself prays, apparently for his mercy to overcome his anger.[29] Removed as they were from their originally lofty status, details of the Temple-service found a way to return to the centre of attention by obtaining an important place in the very form of worship that had replaced them. The idea that God would credit the Jews with offering the sacrifices if they recited their specifications ensured the inclusion of such passages among the prayer forms that would ultimately constitute the written prayer-book.[30] For some there is even the hint not only that prayer is superior to offerings but that a prayer context other than the Temple may have advantages over that august institution. This would appear to be the message behind the daring homily of the Babylonian amora R. Ḥinena ben Papa based on the verse in Psalms 33:1. Understanding the last two words of the verse as meaning 'a place of praise', he uses a biblical text and a rabbinic tradition to imply that the places of worship of neither Moses nor David met the same terrible fate that befell the Temple. Is it too far-fetched to identify here a discreet evaluation of the synagogue that gives it a superior status to the Temple?[31]

The divergent views of the rabbis of Eretz Yisrael themselves on the origins of the statutory *'amidoth*, or standing prayers, to be recited every morning, afternoon and evening, are also of relevance to our discussion of the theological status of prayer. It seems that they reflect not only an awareness of the different prayer-contexts which had existed from Temple times, and to which reference has already been made, but also the desire to establish a relationship between what had become the central element in the talmudic liturgy and those earlier contexts. In this way the rabbis may have been pronouncing on the position of Prayer in their own religious ideology although, in the absence of more than the occasional statement, and with the difficulties involved in verifying each attribution, caution must be exercised in attempting a precise definition of that position for any one rabbi. When, for instance, R. Joshua ben Levi, who has been mentioned as one of those acknowledging the precedence of the academy over the synagogue, and who elsewhere reports that Jerusalem's centrality in the cult has been replaced by its common occurrence in the prayers, notes that the three statutory prayers correspond to the daily Temple-offerings, he is certainly admitting the debt owed by formal prayer to the cult. He may even be expressing agreement with those who describe prayer as the *'Avodah* of their own day, although he would not quite put it on a par with Torah-study.[32] The same passage that records his view also provides the alternative opinion of a younger contemporary, R. Yose ben Ḥanina, to the effect that the Patriarchs instituted these prayers and provides fuller explanations and supporting evidence for each view that need not here concern us. R. Yose's rejection of the link with the Temple in favour of a link with those whom he regarded as the founding fathers of Judaism is, however, important. It takes its place among those talmudic statements that enhance the standing of rabbinic traditions by claiming that the Patriarchs fulfilled the precepts of the Oral Torah in their entirety. For R. Yose, therefore, the matrix of rabbinic prayer was presumably to be sought in the institution that best preserved these traditions, i.e. the synagogue. It seems a likely corollary of this view, though not a necessary one, that formal prayer is to be counted not with Torah and Good Deeds as a principle of rabbinic Judaism but among the 613 Torah precepts or, indeed, the remaining rabbinic laws that traditionally comprise its practical observance.[33] A third alternative is reported in the Yerushalmi in the name of a student of R. Joshua ben Levi, R. Samuel ben Naḥman. For him the three prayers give expression to the individual's need to affirm his gratitude to the Almighty for having vouchsafed to him his continued existence through each of the natural divisions of the day. R. Samuel's reputation as a poet is confirmed by the manner in which he expresses his view: 'In the morning a man should declare, "I give thanks to thee, O Lord my God, and the God of my fathers, for having brought me out of darkness into light"; in the afternoon, "I give thanks to thee O Lord my God, and the God of my fathers, for now having found me worthy of beholding the sun in the west as I earlier beheld it in the east"; in the evening, "May it be thy will, O Lord my God, and the God of my fathers, that you bring me once more out of darkness into light".'[34] According to such a view, even formal prayer arose out of the individual and not the institutional context, and is therefore neither a matter of theological principle nor ritual requirement but of personal devotion. This leads us neatly into our second major theme.

THE ESSENTIAL NATURE OF PRAYER

Whatever its enemies may say about the 'dry legalism' of talmudic Judaism, efforts to legislate and standardise were always complemented by more emotional and esoteric tendencies, and this is nowhere truer than in the sphere of prayer. In order to deal with the present theme, the first task will be to trace such tendencies and the place accorded to them in the sources and in the evolution of talmudic *halakhah*. Since they are most characteristically and unambiguously represented by the successful entreaties and miraculous achievements of particularly pious individuals, it will be instructive to note the activities of these mystics and what have been called their 'law-court prayers' as reported in one of the richest sources of such material, the third chapter of tractate *Ta'anith* in the Babylonian Talmud. The best known tale is of course that of Ḥoni who, when asked to pray for rain during a particularly severe drought, drew a circle and swore to God that he would not leave it until Divine mercy had been shown to his people. Not only were his endeavours blessed with success but he was even able to achieve a reduction in the force of the rain when it arrived. No less admirable were the feats of Naqdimon ben Gurion who borrowed water from the local Roman general to provide water for a Temple ceremony on the Festival of Tabernacles and was able to repay it by the stipulated time only by imploring God to send rain and to delay the sunset. Similarly miraculous manipulations of weather conditions are reported in the name of R. Ḥanina ben Dosa and various members of Ḥoni's family.[35] What is important for our purpose is not the achievements that are claimed for these personalities, since every people has its folk-heroes for whom it makes such claims, but the manner in which they are reported in the Talmud. The wonder-working is not attributed to the hero but to God and the means is not magic but the sincere prayer of a saintly scholar.[36] In this form the mystical element in prayer is carried forward into the talmudic sources, and some of the tannaim and amoraim are credited with the ability to create such a close personal relationship with God through their spontaneous prayers that their requests to Him meet with a positive response.

While the prayers of his colleague, R. Eliezer ben Hyrcanus, had failed to have the required effect, R. Akiva had no sooner commenced his supplications on behalf of the community than the rain descended. The same passage which reports this event hastens to add that a Heavenly Voice allayed any possible suspicion against R. Eliezer by declaring that the reason for R. Akiva's success lay in his forbearing disposition. This gloss, at whatever stage it was made, seems to presuppose a view that efficacious prayer is the prerogative of the privileged few and not something to be achieved through formal liturgical means. Similarly, Rava who, it will be recalled, criticised R. Hamnuna for prolonging his prayers, was forced to admit that although R. Judah ben Ezekiel's scholarly competence did not match his own, he needed only to take off his shoe in preparation for the special penitential prayers in times of drought for the rain to arrive.[37] Indeed, this might suggest that his criticism of R. Hamnuna was less motivated by a low estimate of prayer as such than by a conviction that for most supplicants the exercise would be fruitless and the time therefore better spent in study. This idea is adumbrated in a number of rulings which, while taking for granted the obligation of formal prayer, follow the principle established in the Mishnah that solemnity is a prerequisite for undertaking it. Rav's interpretation of this principle is not a mystical one and he declares simply that such prayer should not be undertaken in the absence of a suitably composed state of mind. The most extreme position appears to be that adopted by R. Eliezer and the father of Samuel who, perhaps because of their high opinion of prayer, believed that on one's return from a journey one should refrain from prayer for three days. An anonymous tannaitic teaching concerning the frame of mind required for the recitation of the *'amidah* is, however, hardly less demanding. The disqualifying moods, in at least the textual form found in the Babylonian Talmud, are listed as sorrow, lethargy, levity, loquaciousness, frivolity and shallowness, and the desirable emotion as the joy of performing a religious precept.[38]

Whether this joy is best achieved by occupying oneself with another religious precept before proceeding to prayer, as the commentators suggest, or is expected to arise out of a determined will, is not stated. That the ideal for those making such strict requirements was represented by the custom of the *ḥasidim rishonim*, the 'early pious men', is made clear by the *mishnah* in *Berakhoth* 5.1. Demanding a serious frame of mind, it refers approvingly to their habit of spending a whole hour before prayer in directing their minds towards their Father in heaven. R. Simeon the Pious (*ḥasida*) demanded that one engaged in prayer should conduct himself as if the Divine Presence (*shekhinah*) was before him. Ritual ablution would also have been a prerequisite of prayer for such pietists and there are still remnants of such attitudes in the Mishnah as, for instance, when it limits the prayers that may be recited by one who has discharged semen.[39] Whatever identification scholars may today suggest for these *ḥasidim*, those rabbis anxious to stress the mystical element in prayer seem to have put them in a category similar to that of such saintly individuals as Ḥoni and Ḥanina ben Dosa, discussed earlier. According to a recent analysis by M. D. Swartz, mystics and non-mystics in the talmudic period had their own forms of prayer but did not shrink from borrowing elements of content and structure from each other. Whether or not it was among the pietistic circles that prayers and benedictions were committed to writing is a moot point. It may be argued that they saw prayer as an act of spontaneous piety arising out of deep concentration and that texts were unlikely to encourage this. On the other hand, it is possible that a belief in the mystical and magical powers associated with the names of God and with scriptural verses was the impetus for the earliest transcription of liturgical texts among some groups. Either way, there were those among the rabbis who held that such texts need not be rescued from a fire on the sabbath and that those who wrote them down were in effect consigning them to flames. The argument here is that the rabbinic objection to such a commitment to liturgical textuality was not exclusively aimed at sectarian groups in the manner argued by Fleischer. To take such a position is to beg the very question of the degree of uniformity of Judaism in the talmudic period. To argue, as Fleischer does, that the context of such condemned texts may be presupposed to be sectarian by a definition of their elements in terms of authoritative rabbinic *halakhah* is to prejudge the constitution of Jewish prayer at that period. What seems more historically convincing is that rabbinic objections to textuality were as much an internal as an external defence mechanism and succeeded in delaying its adoption for a number of centuries.[40]

Those who are over-generous with their praise for the spiritual levels attained by their predecessors are sometimes at a loss to understand why their own efforts are not blessed with similar success. Some statements in the Talmud demonstrate that there were amoraim whose positive view about what could be achieved by sincere prayer forced them to explain why devotions could so often be ineffective. R. Eleazar who, it will be remembered, declared Prayer greater than offerings and Good Deeds, postulated a revolutionary change in the nature of prayer after the destruction of the Temple. As soon as this event occurred, he stated, the gates of prayer were closed, but not the gates of tears. One means of access to God had been removed and prayer thus made more difficult, but a channel of communication was still available for those sufficiently moved to weep. R. Ḥama ben Ḥanina advised those whose prayers had not been answered to repeat the process, presumably until they achieved success, while Rava stated categorically that only when God listens to Israel's prayers is he demonstrating his love for that people.[41] The poetic R. Samuel ben Naḥman, by explaining that the gates of prayer were only sometimes open while those of repentance never closed, was presumably suggesting to his enquiring student that lesser mortals were better advised to rely on a contrite spirit than to speculate with such a mysterious phenomenon as prayer. Needless to say, the opposing view is also to be found. R. Anan ben Yose refused to accept that the gates of prayer were ever closed.[42] Perhaps his view was a more pragmatic one, and he believed that, whatever its form, prayer would serve a useful religious function. Be that as it may, the tendency to question what might be called the pietistic, or even ascetic, approach and to offer something more within the reach of the ordinary adherent to the faith is found in the earliest sources and will now receive further attention.

The unease that some rabbis felt at setting up the activities of Ḥoni and his like as models for their own liturgical endeavours may be detected in the concluding section of the Ḥoni story that contains some serious criticism of his spiritual excesses. The words are put into the mouth of Simeon ben Shetaḥ who is reputed by the talmudic rabbis to have been among the precursors of the tannaim in the second century BCE, but this attribution is of no particular significance in this context. What is significant is that Ḥoni is said to deserve excommunication for interfering with God's arrangements and his behaviour described as that of a petulant child before his father, insisting on having his way. A preference for a more practical system also lies behind the puzzlement expressed at the prayer-customs of the early *ḥasidim*, of whom note has already been taken. When a report is made that these saintly men used to spend an hour in meditation after each of the three daily prayers as well as before them, the question is asked, almost tongue-in-cheek one feels, how, if they spent nine hours a day in this way, did they find time for their studies and their occupations. The answer is revealing and its implication obvious. Since *they* were *ḥasidim*, it was possible for *them*.[43] From the more average Jew the tannaim expected less, but efforts were made to ensure that however little it might be, it would be regular, consistent and religiously meaningful. It might be true that the ministering angels' praises of God on high are activated by those of Israel below but for the practical purposes of prayer the Jewish worshipper should presuppose that the influence is in the opposite direction and regulate his praises accordingly. When R. Shesheth declares it an act of hubris on the part of anyone who enumerates his sins, is he perhaps directing his criticism at those pietists in his day whose prayers were prefaced or accompanied by self-humiliating lists of their religious misdemeanours and by a consequent assumption of unworthiness?[44]

It was not only the matter of the place of pietism that occupied the rabbis in their deliberations about the nature of liturgy and consequently exercised an influence on the ultimate formulation of prayers. Other expressions of Jewish religiosity played a part in laying the foundations of what was ultimately to become the fixed liturgy. The controversy cited in the names of the academies of Shammai and Hillel on whether one should literally stand up or lie down to recite the morning and evening *shema'* respectively was a disagreement about whether the recitation of such a passage was essentially symbolic and mainly intended to constitute a general act of prayer or to be taken literally and left in a state of close association with the acts of rising and retiring. Perhaps this dilemma was only ultimately resolved by the adoption of a *shema'* attached to the morning benedictions and another reserved for recitation at the bedside, both of them in addition to the formal, liturgical benedictions.[45] The talmudic arguments about the degree to which doxologies should be recited over the study of Torah passages and rabbinic teachings; the attempt to find a biblical authority for such blessings as the grace after meals; and the suggestion that a benediction sometimes requires a rabbinic presence – all these reveal a move towards the fusion of the intellectual or didactic element into the essential composition of the liturgical structure.[46] Even when parts of such a structure are devoted to the grave matter of appealing to God on New Year for a favourable judgement, the Jews are reminded by R. Hamnuna and R. 'Oshaya that joy, confidence and a festive spirit are the order of the day rather than the more morbid approach apparently dictated by some groups of pietists.[47] However universal sounding some of the tannaitic prayers, there is at the same time a desire on the part of some to protect Israel's spiritual relationship with God from encroachment by other elements claiming the right to an equal share. The *Mekhilta* commentary on Song of Songs 5:10 records the view that Israel has the exclusive right to its special praises of God, thus revealing an apparent need to withstand contradictory philosophies on the part of competitive communities such as, perhaps, that of the early Christians.[48]

The formulation of benedictions to be recited on enjoying different aspects of God's bounty and, indeed, on tasting his displeasure, the evolution of special Beth Ha-Midrash prayers, the organisation of the daily liturgy and its contents, and rulings on what constituted the basic halakhic requirement, were among the matters that received the attention of those second-century leaders anxious to provide a definitive framework for future development. The regular recitation of the *shema'* and *'amidah* was part of this framework. To the one who omitted prayer either in the morning or in the evening, the formalists applied the verse in Ecclesiastes 1:15: 'That which is crooked cannot be made straight, and that which is wanting cannot be numbered.'[49] Not that any more than the basic guidelines were drawn. The written prayer-book was still many centuries away, and precise formulation, even if there were those who pressed hard for it, was still a matter of no little controversy. The process towards a fixed liturgy was, however, under way and brought with it a considerable divergence of opinion among the rabbis as to the relative merits of spontaneous and fixed prayer. This controversy is exemplified by numerous sources of which only a very few need be cited in the present context. The four opinions expressed in the fourth chapter of Mishnah *Berakhoth*, for instance, represent an interesting range of views among the tannaim of the early second century CE on the form to be taken by the daily *'amidah*. Rabban Gamliel, the president of the Sanhedrin and something of a champion of organised liturgy, favoured eighteen complete benedictions, while his colleague, R. Joshua, was less stringent, content with an abstract which briefly alluded to the contents of each of the benedictions. R. Akiva offered a compromise by restricting Rabban Gamliel's requirement to those who were fluent enough to recite all eighteen benedictions satisfactorily, while R. Eliezer ben Hyrcanus, in somewhat characteristic fashion, went his own way by stating categorically that fixed prayer was bound to lose the supplicatory quality.[50] The clashes between Rabban Gamliel, the aristocratic and rather authoritarian leader, and R. Joshua, the impoverished and rather tolerant scholar, seem calculated to capture the imagination of academics of all generations, and the most famous of them led to the deposition, at least temporarily, of R. Gamliel, and a permanent diminution of his power. It again concerned a liturgical matter, the nature of the evening prayer. R. Gamliel wished to establish it as obligatory, while R. Joshua regarded it as voluntary.[51] The determination of many of the tannaim and amoraim to follow R. Gamliel and build a formal structure of Jewish prayer may be detected in their strenuous efforts to bring together its originally disparate elements. It was clearly not enough for them that the biblical *shema'* was recited twice a day; the rabbinic *'amidah* three times; benedictions formulated about the natural day and about Israel's redemption from Egypt; the *tefillin* donned; and one's working day preceded by attention to practical and spiritual aspects of one's toilet – true, comprehensive worship required a combination of all of these.[52] Nevertheless, however formal the recitation of the *shema'* had become, there was still scope in fifth-century Babylon for its more mystical or magic employment. A tradition recorded in the name of Ravina advises the recitation of the *shema'* as a prophylactic for someone suddenly stricken with fear. What appears to have happened by this time is that there had been a move towards the incorporation of elements of the mystical into the general body of the more authoritative.[53]

An interesting discussion in BT, *Rosh Ha-Shanah* f. 35a revolves around the question of prior preparation of one's prayers. One view suggests the general application of such a procedure while another restricts preparation to special occasions when the prayers are less familiar to the individual. One typically daring piece of aggadic exegisis of Exodus 34:6, in the name of R. Yoḥanan, leaves no room for doubt about the ideal quality of fixed prayer. God is said to have wrapped himself in a *ṭallith* and to have indicated to Moses the precise order of the *Tefillah* to be followed by the Jews in order to obtain forgiveness for their sins.[54] The Palestinian Talmud in *Berakhoth* (4.3, f. 8a) in apparent reaction to the growing tendency to recite fixed formulae, records views stressing the importance of including some innovative element in the daily prayers and the example set by certain rabbis in this respect. King David's trusted counsellor, Aḥitophel, seen as he is as a rabbinic prototype, is even made to recite three new prayers each day.[55] As the official nature of Jewish prayer became less spontaneous, so the efficacy of prayer was made less dependent on the level of meditation by the individual at the time of prayer and more on his general standards of religious behaviour, of which regular prayer was seen as an integral part. This seems to be the philosophy underlying the statement cited in *Devarim Rabbah* 7.3 to the effect that God's arrangement with Israel is that if they hearken to his precepts He will hearken to their prayer.

Whatever advances were made towards the formalisation of prayer in the talmudic period, and whatever was laid down about the overall nature of each benediction, the one leading the congregation in prayer was often left to his own devices with regard to the precise, internal wording used for the praise of God. The opportunity for public self-expression consequently existed for both those who wished to adhere to the more normative formulations as well as for the mystic circles that came to be closely associated with the *hekhaloth* literature. The latter, in Urbach's words, 'created hymns and prayers, basically composed of praise and glorification of God, by repeating and duplicating the honorific epithets, and the monotony of their rhythm was intended to induce in the worshipper a state of enthusiasm and ecstasy, and to arouse in him the *mysterium tremendum* towards the Holy King'.[56] Such prayer is recorded without objection in the name of the third-century Meturgeman, R. Judah ben Naḥman, and was recited at the invitation of no less a personage than R. Simeon ben Laqish, better known as Resh Laqish. It ran: 'God, who is great in the abundance of his greatness, mighty and strong in the multitude of his awe-inspiring deeds, who revives the dead with his word, does great things that are inscrutable and wondrous works without number.'[57] On the other hand, a similar attempt to apply a long list of epithets to God met with the disapproval of R. Ḥanina who permitted the three regular epithets only because they were sanctioned by their biblical use and their introduction into the liturgy by earlier authorities. He derided the inadequacy of all human eulogy of God and compared it to praising a king who possessed millions of gold coins by referring to his silver cash. Similar sentiments are recorded in the names of three other amoraim, each of them clearly anxious to limit the praise of God to statutory proportions. For R. Eleazar, adequate praise is in any case impossible; R. Yoḥanan threatens severe punishment for over-indulgence; and in the view of R. Dimi, brevity is the soul of devotion.[58]

The second section of this survey will now be concluded with a brief reference to some sources which, though admittedly difficult to interpret, may reflect tannaitic controversy about another aspect of the nature of prayer. The operative expression is *ʿIyyun Tefillah*, literally 'looking closely into prayer'. Such a preoccupation meets with the enthusiastic approval of R. Yoḥanan who is reported as having included it among those meritorious acts for which a man receives reward both in this world and the next. From this source it even seems to have found its way into some texts of the Mishnah itself, no mean attestation to the importance with which it was regarded. Furthermore, R. Judah is reported to have expressed the hope that he would be rewarded for having engaged in this exercise.[59] Conversely, *ʿIyyun Tefillah* is included by Rav among the three transgressions from which no man escapes even for a single day, and by R. Isaac among the three things that draw attention to a man's iniquities, and the same R. Yoḥanan who praised it is reputed to have said that one who prolongs his prayer and subjects it to *ʿIyyun* will ultimately suffer pain.[60] The traditional commentaries attempt to harmonise these conflicting sources by arguing that the rabbis are advocating concentration in prayer but criticising concentration on a particular aspect of the prayers in the hope of an immediate and beneficial response.[61] An alternative explanation sees *ʿIyyun Tefillah* in some of its occurrences as bearing precisely the opposite meaning to the usual, i.e. absence of concentration, an explanation that might conceivably be grammatically justified by reference to similar noun-forms constructed from the *piʿel* conjugation and bearing a privative sense.[62] Neither of these explanations is satisfactory and it may therefore be worthwhile to make the tentative suggestion that the negative view of *'Iyyun Tefillah* is but a remnant, no longer clearly recognisable, of an earlier tannaitic suspicion, and even rejection, of the role of meditation in prayer, perhaps because it was closely associated with other sects, perhaps for more internal reasons. If such meditation had indeed originated in groups outside tannaitic circles, one would be justified in enquiring to what degree the growing respect for communal prayer resulted from the spiritual influences of such groups; this too is certainly a line of enquiry to which one will be obliged to return in future studies. Be that as it may, in a chronologically or geographically different milieu the term *'Iyyun Tefillah* came to be used for the more ordinary 'concentration in prayer' i.e. *kawwanah* demanded by the rabbis, and this received a more positive evaluation. A recent article by Israel Ta-Shema has suggested that the term means the composition of liturgical poetry, or was at least understood as such in geonic times.[63] Whether the term refers to poetic expansion or mystical meditation (and both suggestions have merit without appearing conclusive), the evidence points to a talmudic ambivalence about an aspect of liturgical expression.

THE MECHANICS OF PRAYER

The purpose of this final section is to complete the picture which, if this chapter has not entirely failed in its task, should by now be emerging. To do this, it will be necessary to refer briefly to the views expressed in the sources on such practical aspects of talmudic prayer as its ideal recitation, duration and location. It has been pointed out in an earlier chapter that in the late Second Temple period Jewish prayer was being recited in a number of languages, not the least of them Greek. Anyone familiar with the work of the late Saul Lieberman will know how far that language entered into the soul of rabbinic as well as Hellenistic Judaism. In the time of R. Judah, the editor of the Mishnah, there appears to have been a lively discussion as to whether such a central declaration as the *shema'* could be recited in any tongue, he himself arguing for the original language of the text while his colleagues permitted translation into any form understood by the worshipper.[64]

Little is known about the precise way in which the leaders of the communal prayers over the whole talmudic period interacted with the congregation of participants but there are early traditions relating to the *shema'* and the *hallel*. In the case of the former some division into units is presupposed because of the use of a technical term *prs* but there is no clear indication of what precisely this entailed, antiphonal arrangements and simpler responses having been among the suggestions. As far as the *hallel* is concerned, R. Akiva, R. Eliezer ben Yose and R. Nehemiah all accept an interpretation of Exodus 15:1 that compares its declamation with that of the Song at the Red Sea, namely, antiphonally by leader and community, but each has a different concept of the precise form that such an exchange takes. The very fact that there was soon no clear idea of what either of these traditions precisely meant indicates either that there were various customs or that the original custom was soon abandoned or modified. It certainly calls into question any claim that liturgical custom had already been formally and authoritatively structured in wide circles.[65]

With regard to the amount of time spent in prayer there are two remarkable statements that deserve to be cited. The former is the express wish of R. Yoḥanan that man would spend the whole day in prayer, the latter the report that R. Judah ben Ezekiel, whose prayers were so effective, prayed only once in thirty days.[66] That efforts were made to introduce more regular devotions than this among the people at large is clear from the sources already cited, but a passage included in the *Tanḥuma* also demonstrates opposition to the pietistic notion about continuous prayer given expression by R. Yoḥanan. Having enquired of R. Judah the Patriarch why prayers should not be recited every hour, the Emperor Antoninus was unimpressed with the reply that such a procedure would amount to a frivolous treatment of God. In order to prove the validity of his reply, R. Judah greeted him as Emperor regularly every hour, first in Greek, then in Latin, finally in

Hebrew, until he was told that such behaviour was a mockery of his Imperial Highness. He was then able to point out to the Emperor that he himself had validated R. Judah's original reply.[67]

The tanna, R. Eliezer ben Hyrcanus, is said to have taken up a rather tolerant position on this issue. When his students complained to him that one of their colleagues was prolonging the service more than he might, he pointed, in mitigation, to the example of Moses who had spent forty days and nights in prayer on Sinai, no doubt inviting some relief that their own plight would not be of that duration. On another occasion, when a colleague's brevity had distressed them, he again found a biblical precedent, this time in the simple plea of Moses for Miriam's restoration to health: 'Please God, heal her now' (Numbers 12:13).[68] Examples of R. Akiva's tendency to find compromise positions in controversial matters have already been encountered with regard to the superiority of Torah-study and the *'amidah* benedictions. Here too he found a personal compromise between lengthy and brief prayer. When he prayed alone he allowed himself to be carried away with all manner of genuflections and prostrations, but when with the community he abbreviated his devotions to avoid imposing lengthy proceedings on the congregation.[69] The transference of such physical accompaniments of one's devotions from the spontaneous to the formal is reflected in the various talmudic views about the required degree and manner of the worshipper's genuflections, reverential bowings and foot movements.[70]

It is clear from what has just been said that there were occasions on which the statutory prayers were recited by the individual in private. The Talmud also records the numerous personal prayers composed in the first person by famous scholars and inserted into the formal liturgy, the most familiar being the one that was destined to be appended to the *'amidah*, that is, *'elohay neṣor*. A number of them are conveniently available in English in the most useful compilation of C. G. Montefiore and Herbert Loewe, and it should also be noted that specific acts of prayer are recorded on the part of women.[71] There was, however, a strong desire during the talmudic period to centralise all statutory worship in the synagogue and to stress the 'we' rather than the 'I' of prayer. The general principle was well expressed by Abbaye, the fourth-century Babylonian teacher: 'A man should always associate himself with the congregation.'[72] Those in support of such a philosophy expressed themselves in very strong terms and a set of comments records a number of what may be described as rather extravagant claims made on behalf of communal prayer. One view is that a man's prayer will never be answered unless it is recited in the synagogue and/or during communal prayer and another describes God's pleasure when Jews enter the synagogue or the academy and recite 'May God's great name be blessed'. Other statements, in somewhat daring fashion, describe God's anger when he enters a synagogue and fails to find the statutory ten men required for the public recitation of certain elements of the liturgy and his interest in establishing the reason for the absence from the quorum of a regular attender. God's presence is, however, assured when ten Jews come together to pray, three to judge Jewish law and two to study Torah. The familiar theological triangle of Torah, charitable acts and communal prayer is again cited in a claim that a preoccupation with these activities is equivalent to the rescue of God and his children from the power of the gentile nations. The Babylonian amora, R. Huna, obviously played on the passionate desire of some men for impressive obituaries. He promised him who regularly worshipped in the same place that when he died it would be said of him: 'Such a humble man! So pious! A disciple of our father Abraham!'[73] As early as the Mishnah a ruling is recorded that *musaf* may be recited only in some form of communal context (the meaning is unclear) rather than, presumably, by the individual.[74]

Communal worship did not, however, always bring with it the assurance of total uniformity since there might be among the worshippers those with different ideas or customs about what to recite. This was particularly true, and is widely reflected in the talmudic sources, with regard to the differences between Eretz Yisrael and Babylon. One case will serve to exemplify a situation that must have been multiplied when rabbis from one centre visited their colleagues in the other. During a stay in Babylon (probably the city), Rav attended synagogue on a communal fast. Favouring his own rather than the local custom, he prefaced but did not conclude his reading of the Torah with a blessing and he did not join the community when they prostrated themselves in supplication.[75]

But there are always those who refuse to be browbeaten into theological conformity. It is known from a number of sources that the early-fourth-century Babylonian amora, Naḥman ben Jacob, was no slouch when it came to asserting his independence, and the general impression is strengthened by a report of a discussion he had with his friend R. Isaac possibly when he was residing with him while on a visit from the Holy Land. On being asked why he failed to attend synagogue, he answered simply, 'I cannot'. On being further challenged with the suggestion that he arrange for communal prayer to be held in his home, he replied bluntly: 'That would be too much trouble'![76] Although communal services gradually became the dominant context for Jewish liturgical expression, the alternative was sufficiently well established to avoid suppression. A charming *midrash*, reflective of halakhic compromise rather than confrontation, records that the Holy One Blessed be He declared to Israel: 'I say to you, when you would pray, attend the synagogue in your city; if you are unable to pray there, pray in your field; if that is not possible, pray at home; if you cannot do this, then pray on your bed; if even this is impossible, then devote your thoughts to prayer.'[77]

An illustration of the timelessness of certain theological controversies may be offered by way of conclusion. When, in the work already cited, C. G. Montefiore discusses the rabbinic rules for the direction in which one should face when praying, he comments, with what may surely be characterised as a nineteenth- rather than a twentieth-century self-assurance: 'To us moderns, all this seems very needless, as if it mattered a pin whether our bodies face one way or another.' Herbert Loewe was no fundamentalist, but this produced the following sharp rebuke: 'Mr Montefiore's "pin" sticks in my gizzard! In one sense, it certainly does not matter which way we face, when we pray, so long as our hearts are set towards our Father in Heaven. Still worse, if such a detail as direction is given undue importance! And yet the Christian has his "Eastward Position" and the Muslim his *Ḳiblah*. Turning to a given place is an old and natural idea.'[78] This controversy about the suitable direction in which to pray and how it compares with alternative practices, and whether the whole idea is invalidated by a recognition of God's omnipresence, already occupied the talmudic rabbis. According to the Mishnah the priests participating in the joyous water-drawing ceremony would, when they reached the east-facing gate, turn around to face the Temple and, having referred to the opposite custom of their ancestors recorded in Ezekiel 8:16 to turn their backs on the Temple and face eastwards towards the sun, declare that *their* eyes were turned to God. There is here a clear rejection of the eastern direction which is regarded as pagan, although one might argue whether the west was chosen simply to stress God's omnipresence or as a preference for worship towards the Temple. The discussion is continued in the Babylonian Talmud where arguments in favour of both the east and west are proposed and followed by a declaration that God's presence is to be found everywhere. The blind R. Shesheth shared this view and had no objection to the direction in which his servant stood him for prayer except that he did prefer not to be facing eastwards because this was the custom of the *minim*, the heretics, possibly meaning the Christians. The issue is given a further airing in another passage where scriptural support is offered for the directing of both one's physical and mental faculties towards Jerusalem from 1 Kings 9:3 ('My eyes and heart shall always be there') and towards heaven from Lamentations 3:41 ('Let us lift up our heart with our hand'). The compromise view with which we are left is that which attempts to comply with both verses by ruling that one should look towards Jerusalem but concentrate on heaven. And one's physical position on earth while reciting the *'amidah* should literally be a lowly one. Tannaitic traditions object to prayer being offered from some artificially raised position and Psalms 102:1 is cited in favour of a humble posture.[79]

The sources cited above clearly reveal lively differences of opinion about the status, nature and mechanics of prayer and provide some of the raw material necessary for the kind of comprehensive treatment of the subject that will produce a historically accurate account of early rabbinic attitudes to the whole topic. In the mean time it may confidently be asserted that the dominant message of these sources is that there was no monolithic approach to prayer in talmudic times and that attempts to generalise on the basis of the views of this tanna or that amora are doomed to failure.

The idea and practice of communal worship were certainly widespread and the basic forms of the central prayers were already established but it is here being argued, along with Heinemann, that varieties of formulation still existed side by side and, in spite of the efforts of some major personalities, various attitudes had not yet given way to one central, dominant approach. It must be admitted that there have always been scholars, and among them to be counted today is the distinguished historian of liturgical poetry, Ezra Fleischer, who prefer to argue that the Jewish liturgy was fixed, in all but minor details and later additions, in the talmudic period, that the arguments in the talmudic sources are theoretical rather than reflections of reality, and that the divergent views of individuals are recorded not because they had an equal validity in the eyes of the codifiers but simply as part of an oral tradition that transmits less significant ephemera as well as central doctrine and practice. According to such a view, liturgy, as *halakhah* in general, was fixed in the talmudic period and references *en passant* to the standard prayers by the amoraim and their later use by the liturgical poets prove that their standard nature was already presupposed. Later changes to the public worship indicate a new iconoclasm that was not carried into the individual sphere, where standard texts remained. Sabbath texts were so well known that there was no danger of forgetting them; hence their public adjustment was not seen as threatening.[80]

In the view of the present writer such an interpretation of the evidence creates more problems than it solves. Had the rabbis felt confident that one fixed liturgy and one standard attitude to it, as indeed all aspects of more general *halakhah*, had been incontrovertibly established, they would surely have made less polemical statements about the need to do so and many of the alternative views would have quietly disappeared, certainly from the traditions as they were redacted in the post-talmudic period. Furthermore, it seems somewhat open to question whether the precise form and content of all the liturgical texts recorded in the Babylonian Talmud were the product of the talmudic rabbis rather than the contribution of their successors, and whether evidence of the promotion of *a* fixed text in the talmudic period may be employed to prove that such a text was the same as the one that became *the* fixed text in the geonic or a later period. Some comments in connection with the history of oral rabbinic traditions and its relevance to the standardisation of liturgy will be made in the next chapter. In addition, it should not be forgotten that at all other stages of the development of Jewish liturgical expression, whatever the dominant trend and the ultimate preference of the legislators, those arguing for a totally fixed and uniform structure were always being challenged by others at odds with such a view. The weak legal and historical basis of such a structure made it difficult to put it on a par with principles concerning the sabbath, festivals, dietary laws and the like and although attempts were made to do so, they never quite succeeded. Instead of presupposing that the liturgy of both individuals and the community was originally fixed by the talmudic rabbis and that later changes were made only to communal worship and only in those cases where the basic form was safely preserved, it seems less complicated to argue for an original elasticity in both spheres that came under greater control in Babylon than in Palestine. However strong that control, it was not successful in putting an end to the varieties and tensions that were so much a part of Jewish liturgy and the cantors and poets were sometimes able to base their compositions on forms that had been more generally accepted and at others to indulge an existing tendency towards diversity and even novelty. Above all, the presupposition of a fixed talmudic liturgy must carry with it the assumptions that in the geonic period there was a regression to pluralism, since there is often so much evidence of variation at that time, and that the geonim had to fight battles a second time that had earlier been won by their talmudic predecessors. A different outlook on the developments in the centuries that saw the rise of Islam will be presented in the next chapter.

CHAPTER 5

How the first Jewish prayer-book evolved

The function of this part of our discussion of the liturgical traditions of Judaism is to explain how a formal, authoritative liturgy committed to writing emerged in the history of rabbinic Judaism; when and where this process took place; and what the factors were that dictated the adoption of such an office among the religious commitments of the Jewish community at large. In order to achieve an adequate explanation of such developments it will obviously be necessary to take as our starting-point that period of Jewish religious history at which a recognisable form of rabbinic liturgy may be identified and up to which the story has already been told, and to describe in general terms the various characteristics of that form as contemporary research has identified them. A leap of some centuries will then be made to bring us to a situation when a Jewish liturgical codex was given a position of some respect among the literary sources of the religious tradition and therefore to a time at which it may no longer be doubted that there existed a written guide for regular communal worship sanctioned by a leading figure, or a number of such guides emanating from various such authorities.

A comparison, or rather a contrast, will then be drawn between the primitive form and the subtle shape that it later acquired and it will be possible to pinpoint the differences that had emerged in the intervening centuries. Reference will be made to the attempts of various generations of Jewish liturgical scholars to account for any differences that may be detected between the earlier and later sources and to their efforts to demonstrate, by and large, that these were of degree rather than of essence. By way of contrast, and as a result of recent research in the fragmentary manuscripts from the Cairo Genizah, it will be suggested that what may be traced here are pivotal developments in the history of Jewish liturgy that have only recently gained the attention of scholars and that indeed characterise a period of Jewish history that has yet to give up all its secrets to the researcher. It will then be possible to set such developments in a larger context and thereby to achieve the aims set for this chapter.

By the latter part of the fourth century of the Christian era it is fairly certain that there existed an authoritative body of tannaitic traditions relating to biblical interpretation and the application of Jewish law, and at least the early, dialectic responses, both supportive and disputatious, of the amoraim to these traditions. The process of developing these responses, or *talmud* as it came to be called, was under way in both Jewish Palestine and the major diaspora community of Babylon, and the Jewish religious reaction to the loss of its Temple, its holy city, its independent state and its Hebrew vernacular had had time to mature over a period of over three centuries.[1]

What is more, whatever the length of the period during which the Jews and the early Christians, or Jewish Christians, enjoyed close religious and social contact, they had by that time gone their separate ways. The situation, as has been shown in earlier chapters, had been much more fluid in the first Christian century than it is often presented. At that early stage, neither the founders of Christianity nor the precursors of the talmudic tradition had a definitive theory or practice with regard to worship outside the Jerusalem Temple and various competing forces had been seeking to dominate the liturgical scene. Whatever mutual influences were at work on the earliest recognisable forms of rabbinic and Christian liturgy, these are more likely to date from the second and third centuries, when the two communities were still operating in the same, or closely connected contexts. As far as the rabbinic practice during those centuries is concerned, its basic features and suggested degree of fluidity have been discussed in the previous chapter. Its Christian counterpart was already according a central role to baptism and the eucharist, as well as to sermons and biblical readings. Prayer for the followers of Jesus was, however, still more individual than communal and improvised rather than authoritatively structured, a state of affairs that in itself calls into question the views of those who would argue otherwise for the Judaism from which such followers derived so much. It was in the fourth century, with the imperial acceptance of Christianity, that profound changes were made in the form of Christian worship. By the end of that century, then, the schism was complete and later effects, positive and negative, whether the result of emulation or reaction, were those of one religion on another and not internal affairs. For all these reasons, it may be assumed that by the late fourth century the foundations had been laid of what ultimately became talmudic Judaism and that the liturgical customs in vogue by then may fairly be identified as the early form of what later evolved into the rabbinic prayer-book.[2]

It is the current scholarly consensus that the wide variety of prayers and blessings that are attested in the talmudic literature were normally recited from memory, and transmitted orally, and that there was a distinct preference not to commit them to an authoritative, written text. To argue that, in spite of the paucity of the references to any written form for the rabbinic traditions, there simply *must* have been a widespread practice of note-taking that supplemented and supported the oral record is to misunderstand the nature of both textuality and orality at that period, as will become apparent when these topics are discussed later in this chapter. While there is no doubt in the talmudic sources about the existence of specific items of liturgy, there are no unanimous views recorded there about its degree of importance in Jewish practice, its essential character and its detailed application. It was not without controversy that it was sometimes given a theological centrality equal to that accorded to Torah-study and charitable behaviour, and directly linked with the cultic obligations that had once been met in the Jerusalem Temple. Where, when, towards which site, how often, in which language, with whom and for how long the observant Jew (and possibly Jewess) should conduct his prayers, were questions that elicited a host of varied responses from the Babylonian and Palestinian rabbis. Even if specific rabbinic leaders had clear ideas of what constituted liturgy for them, no one such idea appears to have achieved a predominant status over all the existing alternatives. By the same token, the formalisation of the reading and interpretation of the Hebrew Bible was already a feature of synagogal activity but the precise content and structure of the lectionary was clearly open to debate and variant usage.[3]

As far as the synagogue itself was concerned, it was only gradually being transformed from a centre of social and intellectual activity, where Jewish religious identity could be asserted, to the successor of the Temple as *a* central but not *the* central focus of Jewish liturgical activity. It was attracting to itself more and more of the disparate elements of earlier Jewish expressions of worship and their symbols and growing in importance but it was still possible to argue for alternative sites, such as the home and the academy, perhaps even for alternative cultic sites in the form of Jewish temples, and to draw a distinction between prayer as the expression of individual piety and supplication and liturgy as the religious commitment of the community, whatever form that might have to take now that there was no Jerusalem Temple. The architecture and function of the synagogue was by no means standard and it is not even clear how women were accommodated and how much of a distinction existed between a 'house of prayer' and a 'house of study' but the trend was moving away from the simple towards the complex and from the functional to the symbolic. Although there were honorific titles and functions for leading members of the synagogue, the service could be led by any male congregant, no special mediator, professional or theological, being required.[4]

In the matter of prayer, as in so many other detailed elements of their daily religious activities, the rabbis of the Talmud, sometimes even more than those of the Mishnah, sometimes less, record views that are, if looked at in their entirety, reflective of a significantly pluralistic situation. This, of course, assumes that what each of them has to say is to be regarded as a reflection of what he viewed as important and worthy of widespread adoption in his day, rather than one of a collection of theoretical reflections of relevance only to an intellectual system of argumentation, and preserved only by the accident of literary transmission, long after the battle for implementation was lost and won. As has been argued at the end of the previous chapter, one should be wary of basing one's historical and theological theories on the authenticity of some talmudic statements while rejecting others, of an almost identical nature, as irrelevant to the reconstruction of the Jewish liturgical debate as it actually was. Among the individual talmudic rabbis, some stressed the mystical and the poetic while others opted for a more prosaic order and guidance, and it is highly dubious whether any one figure at a specific time succeeded in dictating to all his colleagues and successors the precise nature of all the major prayers. The student of liturgical issues in the oldest talmudic sources soon becomes aware of what were earlier described as 'the tensions, controversies, stresses and strains that accompanied early rabbinic Judaism's attempt to define the place of prayer in the framework of its religious ideology'. This is not to say that there were no halakhic requirements, no clear-cut views expressed, and that it was left entirely to the individual to treat prayer as he pleased. Some traditions had existed long enough among the ordinary folk to have acquired a popular status, others were clearly attached to special occasions of one sort or another, and there were certainly those that were treated as authoritative because of their origin in the Jerusalem Temple. No doubt groups of students also followed the practice of an esteemed master. In the detailed recitation, however, as well as in the degree of standardisation of all the customs and the theological assessment of their importance, there lay the substantial pluralism just noted. Although many specific items of prayer and prayer-custom are referred to, they often appear only as a title or as a few initial words, disembodied liturgy as it were, or they are offered in a variety of different forms. Types of prayer are mentioned and numbers of words are sometimes specified but, to the critical observer, it is not obvious where the individual rabbinic theory ends and the popular communal practice begins.[5] It should not be taken for granted at any stage of Jewish religious history that what a particular rabbi declared as the law was already the widespread, communal norm, even among his closest associates. There were certainly periods and areas in which centralised rabbinic authority was predominant but these were at least as often the exception as they were the rule. Talmudic statements may consequently reflect the struggle of particular individuals or groups of individuals to impose certain ideas and practices on the community and need not necessarily record a contemporary and unanimous communal reality that they were simply reporting. Conversely, it is possible that what some rabbis record as accepted custom may to an extensive degree include items that had their origin among the common folk rather than the intelligentsia. But until we have fuller liturgical texts, if we ever do, dating from that period, we can only speculate on the relative proportions of literary theory and practical application.[6]

Before an attempt is made to summarise what constituted the corpus of Jewish prayer in about the fourth century, one further point needs to be stressed. There were, of course, two major Jewish communities during the talmudic period, one in the Holy Land and the other in Babylon. There was considerable intercourse between the two and influence was exercised in both directions. It is possible that the Babylonians attached more importance to the synagogue than the Palestinians. There are also clues that in Eretz Yisrael, to put it in Heinemann's words, 'a certain amount of freedom and variety remained' and it may therefore be the case that the pluralism of the talmudic sources with regard to prayer will ultimately turn out to be a division between the popular, aesthetic and variegated traditions of one community against the elitist, standardised and authoritative preferences of the other.[7] In addition, however, there is the further complication of the existence of Jewish communities in the Greek-speaking diaspora which might have been more open to external influences than those in Babylon and Eretz Yisrael. Some inscriptions point in such a direction although it should not be forgotten that they do not represent a major source when compared to the Talmudim and *midrashim*. It would, for instance, be fascinating to know which Jewish groups in Syria influenced Greek Christian prayer in the third century and which historical institution in Jewish Alexandria inspired the report recorded in the Tosefta about the huge basilica with a double set of colonnades, with gold seats and a wooden platform, with space for thousands of worshippers, where a synagogue official had to wave a flag to indicate when the congregants should recite the *'amen*. Again, the necessary analysis remains to be undertaken and it is not certain that it can successfully be completed on the basis of the literary sources alone since these have obviously passed through the hands of various editors and redactors since they were first compiled. To take little account, however, of possible differences between the liturgical practices of Palestine, Egypt and Babylon, given their significantly variant backgrounds and influences, is to risk producing a naive interpretation of the history of Jewish prayer.[8]

Which Jewish prayers, then, were already in existence and use by the middle of the talmudic period? It seems clear that at least two paragraphs of the *shema'* were recited, morning and evening, and that a formal invitation to communal prayer, as well as benedictions concerning the natural order of the day and the unique role of Israel, preceded it. The *'amidah* was also to be recited in the morning and afternoon but there were still some doubts about its obligatory nature in the evening. Efforts were being made to ensure a continuity between the *shema'* and the *'amidah* by the adoption of passages, with suitable benedictions, expressing faith in God's special relationship with Israel, as demonstrated in the past, and confidence in his response to its more immediate needs. The daily *'amidah* recorded these needs but, in spite of the efforts of Fleischer to argue to the contrary, it is doubtful whether there was yet a definitive structure to each and every one of its eighteen (Palestinian) or nineteen (Babylonian) benedictions. No doubt the texts that later became standard had their origins at that time but together with numerous others that eventually disappeared. Perhaps the first three and last two or three were less fluid than the remainder. These were also recited on sabbaths, festivals and fasts together with one or more appropriate central benedictions relating in some way, also yet to be categorically defined, to the particular nature of the occasion.[9] In view of what we now know from manuscript sources to have been later developments, it is possible that the degree of elasticity with regard to these central benedictions was least pronounced in the case of New Year and the Day of Atonement and this perhaps indicates an early role for these festivals in the adoption of fixed liturgy. Certainly, the variety of central *'amidah* benedictions in use for the sabbath in late geonic times contrasts with the relatively standard overall appearance of the equivalent passages used on the High Holidays.[10] The matter depends on the interpretation of later sources, as well as earlier ones, and is consequently open to debate. Here, as elsewhere, are we dealing with a later, revolutionary tendency towards change and variety, or an earlier pluralism that is still reflected in Genizah manuscripts? Elements of what had originally been individual prayer and benediction were gradually becoming absorbed into communal or synagogal worship and remnants of the public ritual once carried out on Mount Zion were being adopted and adapted for more personal use. It was not, however, universally assumed that the formal patterns suitable for the liturgy of the community were necessarily applicable to private prayers. Much as some rabbis would have wished it so, any presupposition that what became fixed for the community was automatically adopted by the individual at his devotions must remain in the realm of the speculative. Some such devotions, generally of a pietistic or penitential nature, were associated with the names of individual rabbis and couched in the first person. Heinemann has also suggested that rabbinic liturgy retains in the *hosha'noth* and *seliḥoth* poetic supplications that may have originated in the Jerusalem Temple, but in this case van Bekkum may be right in questioning the force of his arguments.[11]

The other function of the synagogue – perhaps indeed its major and earlier function – was as a centre of Bible reading and instruction. Pentateuchal scrolls were publicly read and expounded on sabbaths, festivals, fasts and on the market days of Monday and Thursday and, while it was becoming customary to associate particular passages with related occasions, it is still anachronistic to refer to a fixed lectionary at this time. The existence is attested of both the annual and triennial cycles of pentateuchal readings, in Babylon and Eretz Yisrael respectively, but it is not clear at which stage these lectionaries emerged, whether each of these communities was exclusively committed to one cycle or, indeed, if the divisions of the cycles were quite as they later came to be. Although it is generally assumed that the Palestinian cycle was a triennial one, the possibility must also be considered that this was a later development and that the original format in that centre was the completion of the pentateuchal readings in one year. There was controversy about the place of the Ten Commandments and a tendency on the part of some communities to make a theological point against competing antinomian philosophies by abandoning its daily recitation in spite of its long and respectable pedigree. Translations from the Hebrew into Aramaic and interpretations of the text were a central part of what amounted to this system of regular religious education for the community. Parts of the prophetic and hagiographical books also played a part in such public readings but the process had yet to be liturgically formalised. The earliest manifestation of a custom to include a formal recitation of a set of psalms in the communal liturgy was the use of Psalms 113–18 as the *hallel* but the wider, indeed, extensive liturgical use in a communal context of what has often been viewed as the hymn-book of the second Jerusalem Temple was still a development of the future.[12]

As previously implied, liturgy for the talmudic Jew was not restricted to prayer but was expressed in the observance of *miṣwoth*, the study of Torah and in domestic customs. It therefore occasions no surprise to find the academy and the home as the normal settings for the remainder of talmudic prayer. Declarations of God's sanctity, with the use of the trisagion in the earliest forms of the *qedushah* and *qaddish*, and pious aspirations for the establishment of his kingdom, perhaps emanating from a variety of doxologies freely recited among groups of mystics who themselves used more standard rabbinic content and style for other devotions, were a feature of the praises that came to be associated with sessions of Torah-study. At home, the commencement and conclusion of sabbaths and festivals were marked by formulae that declared the sanctity of God, and of the special day, and distinguished between various examples of the holy and the profane. Some prayers were couched in Aramaic, others in Hebrew, and there was even no objection in principle to the use of Greek in certain contexts. Among the oldest Jewish liturgical forms are the Passover *Haggadah* and the grace after meals and it should not be forgotten that benedictions were used to acknowledge God's bounty in providing for human sustenance. Even the contract of marriage had, by talmudic times, developed its own set of benedictions on the themes of the creation of mankind, marital joy and the return to Zion, but the setting here was not the synagogue but the independent entity of wedding ceremony and feast. The benediction, like the oath and the vow, had evolved from its popular origins into a more formal structure and, as has been argued by Heinemann, was gradually being applied as such to various liturgical contexts.[13]

Since the earliest forerunners of what became the standard rabbinic prayer-book can be traced back to the period of the ninth to the twelfth centuries, it will now be necessary to move on to that era of Jewish history and describe how the emergence of a new liturgical situation was presided over by Jewry's outstanding religious leaders and how its characteristic features became predominant by the end of that period. It is a useful point of reference for other reasons too. It was during these years that the once dominant Jewish community of Babylon began to see its power drift away to new centres and that the Palestinian Jewish community which, for all its vicissitudes and crises, had always made its influence felt in the far-flung diaspora, and had even flourished again for a short time beforehand, was virtually destroyed by the Crusaders in many parts of the Holy Land and left only remnants of its customs among its liturgical heirs. Furthermore, the primary sources available to the researcher multiply significantly and the relative silence of a number of centuries is broken.[14]

It was in the context of that newly emerging liturgical situation that the Jewish prayer-book made its first appearance. Leading scholars, among them the later geonim, issued guidelines on what should constitute the regular blessings and prayers and answered questions about the validity of particular customs. They systematically applied the various principles that occur from time to time in the Talmud to numerous parts of the liturgy and offered definitions of what qualified to be included under the headings of each of the different, liturgical categories. They and their successors in a much wider geographical area, ultimately taking in countries as far apart as England in the west and Persia in the east, laid down detailed regulations for prayer and attempted to explain its theoretical basis and its historical evolution. Some types of accretion to the basic talmudic framework were firmly rejected while others were welcomed and sanctioned. Novelty was not always the critical issue; it might also be the matter of the thematic relevance of an interpretation to the basic content of the benediction. In those cases where what they regarded as an unsatisfactory custom had established itself too stubbornly to be dislodged, a new interpretation was given to it that could justify its retention even in the light of the strictest categorisations.[15]

Two new types of liturgical composition had made their way into the regular practice and were, during the centuries now under discussion, given specific places in the standard prayers. The *piyyuṭim* or liturgical poems, the earliest forms of which had first made their appearance in the Holy Land in the latter part of the talmudic age, having to a certain extent overcome much Babylonian animosity towards them, were incorporated into those sections of the liturgy with which they could incontrovertibly be linked. Their structure, content and language were, however, gradually brought under control in the process and their degree of creativity thereby reduced, with the result that their composers ultimately had to find other outlets for their originality and aesthetic expression. What started out as daring novelties sometimes ultimately ended their existence as irrelevant appendages to statutory prayer.[16] A similar limitation came to be imposed upon prayers of the more mystical bent. There was more than a little hesitation about the incorporation of such supernatural pieces as those to be found in the *hekhaloth* and *merkavah* literature. Certain compositions were allowed to enter, or remain, in such contexts as the recitation of the trisagion or *qedushah* (as standardised in the Babylonian rite in general) but there was a clear trend towards a policy of restricting any unfettered development and adoption in the synagogue. It is not yet established in which context mystical hymnology operated but there can be little doubt of its active relationship with more standard liturgy and of the fact that its originally Palestinian forms were adapted for wider use in Babylon. Systems of vocalisation and cantillation, albeit in more than one form, had been drawn up for the reading of the Hebrew Bible and the use of specific liturgical melodies was so well established by the twelfth century that the famous proselyte, Obadiah, known from various Genizah fragments, could record a number of these without the need for any explanation or introduction. There were even problems about the attempted importation of non-Jewish musical items.[17]

It was at this immediate post-geonic stage, too, that individual communities, or sets of communities, merged what they had inherited as their established liturgical custom with what they were told by their authorities was acceptable and produced an identifiable *nusaḥ* or rite of their own. These rites, generally referred to by the geographical areas in which they were practised, e.g. French, German, Italian, North African, Spanish, Yemenite and Romanian, differed from each other in detail but were all substantially based on the format and content earlier dictated by the Babylonian authorities of the late geonic period. Minor and vestigial elements of non-Babylonian provenance occasionally appeared but a great deal more of the non-standard was lost than was retained. When some further attention is given in the next chapter to the emergence and development of these rites it will become apparent how dominant the Babylonian tradition finally became and how extensively its influence was felt, long after its talmudic academies had ceased to occupy first place among Jewish intellectual endeavours.[18]

As far as the text of the major prayers is concerned, there was a reluctance to approve any subtractions or additions. Clear rules were laid down for how many benedictions, and of what form and content, were to accompany particular prayers and how much variation from the norm was to be permitted to take account of special occasions such as sabbaths, festivals and fasts, some allowances always being made for variety between rites.[19] When, in spite of a reluctance to sanction post-talmudic benedictions, the geonic authorities felt a polemical need (for whatever reason) to boost the status of a particular ceremony, as in the case of the lighting of sabbath lamps, they grudgingly approved the recitation of the blessing but were clearly ill at ease in justifying it on their own liturgical terms.[20] A concern for precise language, grammar, vocalisation and punctuation began to be expressed and was a factor in the liturgical editions from then until the modern period. Liturgical Hebrew emerged as the chosen medium of prayer and, at least in the major communities influenced by the authority of the Babylonian Talmud and the codification of its *halakhah*, Aramaic was used only when it had so long been associated with a particular prayer that it appeared to be an act of revolution to alter it. Once a *siddur* existed as a Jewish literary entity, it was not long before commentaries on its contents became a feature of rabbinic scholarship.[21]

An even more interesting feature of the late geonic and early mediaeval periods is the transfer of what had originally been domestic or academic liturgy into the synagogue and its incorporation into the standard prayer-book. Benedictions relating to morning activities such as rising, washing and dressing, ultimately entered the communal liturgy, as did the recitation of psalms by way of preparation for prayer proper. The *qaddish*, the *ʿaleynu*, the praises associated with the academy such as the *qedushah*, even the *qiddush* and *havdalah* which were still recited at home, became integral parts of the synagogal liturgy and reasons were advanced to justify their retention there, or sometimes, indeed, to challenge it. Whether the individual prayers of earlier geonic centuries had been the remnants of an original, fixed liturgy that had survived the onslaught of ḥazzanic and piyyuṭic activity, or had always represented valid variations, in one form or another, dating from talmudic times, what was now incorporated into the prayer-book became acceptable rite while the remainder was consigned to an oblivion from which only Genizah research has fortuitously rescued it. The synagogue itself became a more elaborate affair and a degree of ceremonial was introduced of which there is little mention in the talmudic sources. A regular cantor and choir, special seats for dignitaries, processions, use of the Torah scroll, *ṭallith* and *tefillin* as integral parts of the ritual, had all now become familiar elements, in one context or another, of communal worship in the synagogue.[22] As the institution grew in communal and liturgical significance, so it became necessary to provide it with a distinguished history. It is perhaps for this reason that the claim was made that the first synagogue was built in Nehardea in the sixth century BCE from stones brought from the Jerusalem Temple. When Sherira made such a statement, he was telling us more about tenth-century Babylonian attitudes to the synagogue than about its authentic historical origins.[23] Formal ceremonies associated with *rites de passage* were not yet inveigling themselves into the synagogue but the process of evolution had begun that would in the long term lead to such a development.

In the matter of the reading of the Pentateuch and the Prophets, a more clearly defined lectionary was now preferred and the annual cycle of the Babylonian Jews had virtually replaced all the others, particularly the triennial cycle of Palestinian Jewry, which some refugees from the Crusades apparently brought with them to Cairo and succeeded in preserving for at least a century or so. During his visit to Cairo in about 1170 the famous Jewish traveller, Benjamin of Tudela, noted that the Palestinian *émigrés* had no completion of the annual cycle to celebrate at the end of *Sukkoth* each year and therefore joined their Babylonian co-religionists on that festive occasion. Such exchanges of liturgical custom apparently left their mark on the Palestinian Jews since manuscript evidence from early in the thirteenth century indicates the existence among them of hybrid tendencies, evidently adopted as a compromise as they fought unsuccessfully to maintain their own liturgical traditions in a more pristine form. When read, the scroll was taken from the ark and returned to it with some accompanying verses and its presence among the worshippers was made the occasion for the recitation of special prayers. It may also have been at this time that the lectionary ceased to be distributed among various participants who read and expounded it but came to be performed by a competent and knowledgeable individual while the required number of participants made formal benedictions to begin and end each section. A set of benedictions had also by this time been attached to the reading from the Prophets at the outset and the conclusion.[24] As far as the use of blocks of psalm chapters is concerned, this too had come under control and a limited number were sanctioned for formal use in the synagogal context, with introductory and concluding doxologies.[25]

If stock is now taken of these developments, it will become apparent that significant changes have occurred during the centuries that extend from the talmudic period to the early Middle Ages and that they concern the theory, practice and location of Jewish prayer and prayer-customs. To begin with the first of these, it is no longer a matter of debate whether prayer has a central role in the theological priorities of rabbinic Judaism and the stress is rather on finding all manner of justifications – historical, philosophical and halakhic – for the central role that it has come to occupy. The inner contradictions inherent in a pluralistic approach to liturgical expression – whether that approach is to be traced, as is here being suggested, to the talmudic period, or to novel developments in a later era, as Fleischer has been seen to prefer – have given way to the consistencies of a system in which clear-cut definitions and applications iron such awkward creases out of the fabric of prayer. Instead of limited guidance and extensive creativity, the worshipper is faced with the prospect of extensive guidance and limited creativity. A standard, hitherto vague and adjustable, has taken on a stricter form, and makes demands for adherence. In sum, a text has emerged to replace what had for centuries been a predominantly, if not exclusively, oral medium and the authoritative, written version now has a major relevance to discussions in which the previous consideration had been one of options. Whether this assumption about the predominance of orality is a justified one, or may rightly be challenged by a view that postulates an earlier history for the written version, is a matter that will shortly receive attention in this chapter.

A close examination of the practice is also instructive. Differences of principle are no longer the major matter that they were for the talmudic rabbis. Variations now generally concern minor details and, explode in number as these details may, they will not constitute significant variation until the modern period, when different considerations are destined to apply. While neither the need nor the methodology for distinguishing a prayer from a benediction or for institutionalising popular forms of liturgical expression had been apparent to the amoraim, authorities are now laying down rules for the structure and content of prayer-texts and applying these in an increasing number of contexts. It is true that Aramaic still has a place in the newly produced texts of the *siddur* but not of the same nature as before. Once, the language of a prayer first depended on its original context and was then subject to change and exchange. Now, Hebrew is to be dominant and, as far as popular Aramaic prayers are concerned, matters are frozen as they stand and arguments are offered in favour of the *status quo*, not just as such but as a sanctified tradition, even with a profound cosmic significance. The evidence from the earlier period, around the ninth century, provides the first hints of a move from a widespread pluralism of detail, albeit within a fairly well controlled general context, towards an authoritative format; the sources from the latter period, around the twelfth century, indicate the existence of a pull, however limited by the clearly expressed regulations, away from centralisation towards regional autonomy of a sort. Given, however, the manner in which major elements of the liturgy had now become subject to standardisation and control by authority, the degree of that autonomy was destined to remain severely controlled in all circles until the modern period.

In matters of location, too, the theme is one of transformation. The variety of centres – domestic, academic and cultic – has given way to the dominance of the synagogue which has absorbed the forms originally associated with these alternative *loci*. Whatever had been seen to be of lasting significance among the prayers and supplications of the individual has been incorporated into the communal rites. While, at the earlier stage, part of the emerging liturgy modelled itself on the practices of various individuals or groups of individuals, the position is reversed at the later stage, the individual having to follow much of the communal pattern when he chooses to recite his prayers outside the synagogue. Ceremonial has also become an integral rather than an occasional element of synagogal worship, with the attendant adjustments in the physical and organisational structure. What is even more interesting is that the educational and exegetical significance of the scriptural reading has, to a considerable extent, given way to its ritual and ceremonial function. It would appear that it has become more important to read precisely the relevant section of the Hebrew Bible, with or without its standard translation of one sort or another, than to engage in the public exposition, whether in legal, aggadic or poetic form, of a suitable text. That latter exercise has acquired an existence independent of the formal biblical reading, though not necessarily of its detailed content, and has taken to including as much general, moral and religious guidance as it does direct interpretation of verse after verse. Similar considerations apply in the case of the recitation of passages taken from talmudic literature or inspired by comments therein, such as *'eyn ke'lohenu*, the daily psalm and the end of tractate *Berakhoth*. Originally intended to stress the centrality of the learning process, they have acquired an almost ceremonial function, and eventually come to be 'prayed' rather than 'perused'.[26]

Before an explanation is offered of what occurred in Jewish religious and literary history between the late talmudic and the immediate post-geonic periods that brought about such developments in the liturgy, it may clarify matters if some reference is made to the way in which previous generations, from as early as mediaeval times until recent works of scholarship, have viewed the relationship between these two periods and to the new evidence that calls into question many of their presuppositions.

As far as the text of the two Talmudim is concerned, it is assumed that this is an accurate reflection of talmudic rather than geonic practice and little attention is paid to the possibility that major editorial revision was undertaken at a time when liturgical customs had substantially altered. Where technical terminology is employed, whether with regard to the prayers and benedictions themselves or to the synagogue, its functionaries and ceremonies, the natural tendency is to equate the sense borne in one generation with that used in another, and if the abbreviated title or introductory phrase of a prayer is encountered it is taken for granted that the full text, though not given, is substantially the same as it later came to be known. Where the view of an amora does not accord with later custom, it is regarded as an individual quirk rather than the reflection of an existing practice, or it is somehow explained away. Sometimes it is forgotten that the talmudic system of presentation is not geared towards codification but is rather a dialectic method aimed at defining the issues and factors, and that when a decision is clearly recorded it may well be that of a post-talmudic redactor. Above all, it is commonly presupposed that Jewish liturgical development consistently moves in one direction, either from the original, pristine form to various corruptions of it or, indeed, from a variety of possibilities towards an authoritative version.

It is acknowledged that the *siddur* did not exist before about the ninth or tenth century but at the same time its contents are regarded as a written version of what had already existed for an extended period in oral form. The geonim are viewed as the continuators of the talmudic tradition and credited with no more than the finalisation of a textual, exegetical and codificatory process that was already well under way some centuries earlier. Wherever any suspicion of creativity on their part is encountered, it is explained as a response to a particular set of circumstances, be they catastrophic or restrictive. The emergence and/or development in talmudic and post-talmudic times of such genres as *midrash*, *targum* and *piyyuṭ* are seen as the gradual accretion to a basic form of liturgy or lectionary of creative expansions which actually come into conflict with the parent body. Differences in liturgical practice are attributed to geographical variation, such as the earliest one of Palestine and Babylon, and later rites are traced to one or other of these two original forms.[27] As in the case of general historians who once interpreted the darkness of the 'dark ages' as a reflection of the ignorance of those times rather than of their own lack of knowledge and understanding of that part of history, scholars of Judaic studies have supposed that the limited nature of their information about the geonic period may indicate that there was not much of significance to report and that the talmudic and mediaeval periods may conveniently be linked together without reference to any intermediate stage. The tendency to underestimate or virtually ignore the major geonic influence on the talmudic material itself and on the development of rabbinic liturgy is apparent not only in the relevant mediaeval works but also in Seligmann Baer's classical work and in many aspects of modern scientific treatments. Although questioned in the Hebrew edition, Elbogen's lead is followed by many scholarly and semi-scholarly works and the liturgical innovation and productivity of the talmudic and modern periods are viewed as vastly superior to what emerged in the geonic era. Elbogen's estimate of the post-talmudic period deserves to be quoted (which is done in the writer's own translation of the original): 'There then followed a period of inactivity during which further developments were prevented by severe persecution . . . There was insufficient stamina for individual creativity and they contented themselves with supplementing and developing those ideas and subjects that they had inherited . . . The era of individual, liturgical composition was over and the available stock of prayers came to be recognised as obligatory and unalterable.' Interestingly, Baron makes a much more favourable assessment of liturgical creativity at that time, describing how after the sixth and seventh centuries 'the synagogue emerged as the mainstay of Jewish life', noting the efforts of the saboraim and geonim 'to assemble and solidify the accumulated liturgical measures' and referring to the 'compilation of the great Jewish liturgical classics' from the ninth century onwards.[28]

Lest it be thought that, for their part, the most contemporary of historical theories make no assumptions based on their own attitudes rather than on the historical evidence, one may point out that we today sometimes choose to forget or ignore the fact that the rabbis of all post-talmudic generations viewed everything in terms of *halakhah*. They were not biblical critics, midrashic analysts or liturgical historians but religious leaders anxious to interpret God's original word and his current message and to follow procedures for communicating with him that could somehow be seen as authoritative and sanctioned by tradition. With our modern scientific approaches, we tend to overlook the fact that all Jewish religious developments had a practical, halakhic aspect to them, even if we are entitled to look beyond that and to theorise about their historical nature.[29]

That all these presuppositions may now be exposed as faulty, and that some light may currently be shed on the 'dark' geonic ages, are due to the discoveries made in the remarkable collection of documents from the Cairo Genizah. As is well known, some 200,000 fragmentary texts, a significant number of them at least a thousand years old, and comprising a total of perhaps as many as a million leaves, survived in the storeroom of the Ben-Ezra Synagogue in the old section of Cairo and are today housed in famous libraries around the world, about three-quarters of them at Cambridge University Library. It is beyond dispute that these Genizah fragments represent the most important discovery of new source-material for every aspect of scientific Hebrew and Jewish studies, ranging from the early mediaeval period until the age of emancipation. As they have been deciphered and identified, especially as a result of the work of the Cambridge Genizah Unit, previous ignorance has given way to detailed information and earlier theories have been drastically modified. Among the fields of research that are now benefiting most from these developments are the analysis of talmudic study in the geonic period, the history of Jewish Bible reading and exegesis at that time, and the emergence of post-talmudic Jewish liturgy. Although the majority of Genizah texts are generally dated from the tenth to the thirteenth centuries, it is clear that there are a number of earlier date and that in the nature of things the adoption of liturgical customs and rituals must anticipate their earliest recorded usage, even by some considerable time. What is more, the authoritative sources cited from these centuries refer to what their authors were clearly interested in establishing as the standard, while fragments from the Genizah provide evidence of practice at all levels, as much by the Jew in the pew as the rabbi in his code – 'counter-history' of a liturgical variety, as some scholars may please. The chronological range of material from the Cairo Genizah also makes it possible for the historian to obtain a more accurate overview of a great variety of activity rather than a narrow perspective based on the sight of a few specific landmarks.[30]

With regard to the Talmud, that overview is gradually indicating the major role played by the geonim in bringing all aspects of talmudic study, ideology and practical guidance to the centre of Jewish religious activity. It was they who transmitted, expounded and perfected the predominantly oral traditions and ultimately made it possible for actual copies of texts to be circulated and for commentaries to be composed. It was in their heyday that study circles became major academies. It was in these academies that decisions were made for appending to long talmudic discussions, that the first elementary codifications were drawn up, and that responsa were dispatched to far-flung communities who sought advice on Jewish religious procedure. They constituted the essential link between the mass of source-material available in the talmudic traditions and the exploitation of that material for the construction of a system of Jewish law that could be comprehensively codified by such later scholars as Maimonides. In addition, they functioned as institutions of Jewish communal and political authority.[31]

The Genizah evidence that relates to biblical matters is no less revealing although it may often have more to do with the Palestinian scholars than their Babylonian counterparts. Whatever the precise origins of the developments – whether inspired by the example of the Qur'an or the Syriac Christian tradition, or the result of the schism between the Rabbanites, who upheld the authority of the talmudic tradition, and the Karaites, who looked to a literal interpretation of the Hebrew Bible for their religious guidance – it was in the geonic period that various systems of Hebrew vocalisation and cantillation were attached to the biblical text and that schools of Masoretes laid the foundations for what was ultimately to become a standard text of the Hebrew Bible but was yet far from it. It was also at that time that regulations came to be written down, as in *Massekheth Soferim*, for the writing of a Torah scroll. Such a wealth of lectionary variation has been uncovered that it can no longer be suggested that the talmudic rabbis, let alone their predecessors in the time of Jesus, followed specific systems that can today be clearly identified. While it was once suggested that the bulk of known *midrashim* developed in the talmudic age and that an authoritative *targum* emerged at a similar time, the riches of the Genizah are now providing scholars with quite a different impression. All manner of midrashic and targumic creativity in the geonic centuries is now being recorded and the new discoveries have provided examples of selections, anthologies and expansions on the one hand, as well as alternative recensions and halakhic and aggadic commentaries on the other. It is only towards the end of that period, and perhaps in the century or two following it, that authoritative and standard versions may justifiably be recognised.[32]

And so to the numerous aspects of the synagogal liturgy that are preserved for us in thousands of Genizah fragments so impressively identified and analysed by Schechter, Elbogen, Mann, Assaf and Zulay in the earlier part of the century and by Wieder and Fleischer in our own day. Although there are fairly full versions of the prayers that can be located in the prayer-books of such leading geonim as Saadya and identified with what later became the norm, there are also previously unknown benedictions and prayer-texts for all manner of liturgical occasions, some of them in flagrant contradiction of instructions recorded in the talmudic texts. Among the most remarkable examples are benedictions for the recitation of the *shema*', the beginning and end of a collection of psalm-readings, the confession recited on the Day of Atonement, the public recitation of the second chapter of the tractate *Shabbath* on the subject of the kindling of lights on the eve of the sabbath, and the different kinds of hand-washing performed at the Passover *Seder*. Scholarly research is notably enriched by the discovery of a variety of alternative versions for the *qaddish*, daily, sabbath and festival '*amidoth*, morning benedictions, grace after meals and names of the festivals. There is also evidence of the wide use of numerous psalms, sets of psalms and biblical verses, the introduction of ceremonies involving the use of the Torah scroll, a diversity of pentateuchal and prophetic readings, and special prayers for dignitaries. As far as the recitation of the Ten Commandments is concerned, the controversial rabbinic decision, in both Eretz Yisrael and Babylon, to abandon its daily recitation, is now seen to have been ignored by some Palestinian communities who persisted in incorporating it in their central, formal liturgy. Its additional appearance in the sabbath service and, in some cases, with the psalm collections and other scriptural readings such as Exodus 15 rather than in the formal section of the liturgy introducing the *shema*' and continuing with the '*amidah*, may indicate some degree of compromise with the dominant view. Novel, messianic, pietistic and mystical 'expansions' associated with the trisagion, the benedictions surrounding the *shema*' and such domestic prayers as *qiddush*, *havdalah* and the Passover *Haggadah* have come to light. If it was once possible to state categorically that a certain type of text-form was exclusively of the Babylonian kind while another was its uniquely Palestinian equivalent, such a confidence is becoming progressively more misplaced. Having recently discovered significant variation within the liturgical practice of each of these major Jewish communities, scholars must now proceed with greater caution and, instead of referring to two distinct, original forms with later, hybrid adaptations, are obliged to acknowledge a variety of internal trends and tendencies in each case, perhaps leading later to an attempt at arriving at one standard in particular centres, as well as the possibility of other rites having once existed, say, for instance, in Egypt, which were gradually eliminated.[33]

It is not only in the realm of the messianic, the pietistic and the mystical that Genizah texts provide us with greater variety and more extensive content than is available from the standard sources and the later rites. The same situation applies with regard to the choice of language for some prayers and to the incorporation of *piyyuṭim* in others. It is no longer surprising to encounter an Aramaic version of a well-known Hebrew prayer or vice versa[34] and for the last half century it has been almost commonplace to discover new poems, unknown poets, novel uses of poetry and unfamiliar poetic versions of familiar prose texts within liturgical settings being revealed among these worn but distinguished fragments. The spread of the piyyuṭic genre was so successful that it invaded almost every aspect of Jewish liturgical expression, establishing its presence and threatening to dominate the whole environment of prayer. Poets and cantors innovated and improvised in a most extensive fashion and produced a vast variety of new forms of language and poetry. At the height of its influence it was on the point of strangling the more original and natural products of that environment and it was only the controls introduced by the halakhic codifiers, who were aware of its growing power and bewailed it, that eventually forced it to come to terms and accept a more limited role within the standard prayer-book. Indeed, according to the view of Fleischer, such a strangulation did in fact take place and many of the variant Genizah texts are not, as is being argued in this volume, remnants of earlier versions, otherwise lost, but the novel products of the writers and reciters of synagogal poetry.[35] Above all, the existence of so many texts convincingly demonstrates that whatever apprehensions still remained about the dangers of committing prayer-texts to writing have by this time either been allayed or have given way to greater fears of the consequences of not doing so.[36]

Having discussed the differences between Jewish liturgy as it was in the time of the talmudic rabbis and as it emerged in the post-geonic centuries, and having demonstrated the contrast between the assumptions made about the intervening, geonic period and the hard facts that have been revealed in the contents of the Cairo Genizah, it remains for this study to offer some explanation of what these facts indicate in terms of general liturgical development within the history of Jewish religious tradition.

The overall liturgical theme of the early geonic age was one of creativity and expansion. The basic foundations of rabbinic prayer, and Bible reading in its widest sense, having been laid down earlier, every opportunity was taken, perhaps especially in the tranquil periods of that age, to build all manner of structures. It is not clear whether at this stage *piyyuṭim*, *midrashim* and *targumim* were, as has often been claimed, an intrinsic part of liturgy as such or were rather, as seems more likely, developments out of the original centrality of the biblical lesson which eventually attempted to acquire a virtually independent status. Either way, the tolerance and, indeed, encouragement of diversity applied among these genres no less than in the area of prayers and benedictions and the earliest Genizah texts are a reflection of the extent of that unregulated productivity. To argue, however, as Fleischer does, that such productivity on the part of the *payyeṭanim* and *ḥazzanim* included the creation of the variant texts of the standard prayers found in the Genizah, is to exaggerate the case. One cannot at one and the same time argue that all the major texts were fully standardised (but, remarkably, not recorded in the sources) in the second century and then claim that they were rejected and replaced, apparently with ease, after a further five or six centuries of *increasing* rabbinic authority. The adoption of such arguments also presupposes a different interpretation of liturgical variants from all other kinds of non-standard literary forms found in the Genizah. Are we to imagine that those responsible for the transmission of *masorah*, *targum*, *midrash* and *halakhah* iconoclastically altered the inherited forms that had once been standard in order to create what has been found in Genizah texts, or is it more likely that their activities are the reflection of an earlier propensity towards variety which had come under attack from those who regarded the time as then ripe for more centralised and authoritative source material?[37]

The view here being championed is that in liturgy, as in other manifestations of the Jewish religious tradition, there are crests and troughs of creativity, and periods of innovation are followed by years of conservative retrenchment in which yesterday's novelty is retained only because it has become today's established tradition. There are also inbuilt tensions within the liturgy between spontaneity and rigidity, synagogue and home, law and mysticism, Hebrew and vernacular, and brevity and protraction, to cite but a few, and at times laxity about the choice gives way to a strong stand about what represents the preferable alternative in each case. Such changes appear to have occurred in the latter part of the geonic period and to have reached their peak in the century or two immediately afterwards. The theme then became one of standardisation and consistency and all the authority of *halakhah* was employed to ensure that variation from the established norm was kept to a minimum.[38]

This was not, however, the whole story. A process of ritualisation also took place in which those para-liturgical activities associated with the study and interpretation of the Hebrew Bible were virtually incorporated into the liturgy and given a ceremonial role. Particular parts of the poetic, exegetical and mystical traditions were digested by the standard liturgy and other parts diverted to different functions. The centralisation of Jewish worship according to the particular Babylonian rites acceptable to the late geonim was also undertaken and what has been called the 'canonization of the synagogue service', i.e. the acceptance of a written *siddur* as one of Judaism's authoritative sources, became a reality.[39]

The question yet to be answered is why this change took place. As with all historical developments, there were surely a number of factors. The new authority of the talmudic text and interpretation as laid down by the geonim; the emergence of the synagogue as the centre of Jewish communal life, just as the mosque and the church had become symbols of the significance of corporate worship to Muslims and Christians respectively; the success of the rabbinic leadership in spreading their religious ideas and practice to a wide body of the Jewish public; the need for a clearly defined response to the religious challenges of Christianity and Islam from without and Karaism from within; and the general intellectual atmosphere of the day which favoured authority and centralisation over variety and pluralism, reflecting as that did the power of Islamic caliphates, operating from their newly founded capital cities, to exercise political and religious influence over vast territories – there are strong grounds for regarding these influences as major in matters of liturgy, as they undoubtedly were in matters of theology and language.[40]

It is not, however, unlikely that the dominant theme is to be sought elsewhere. While the Jews had for many centuries attained high levels of literacy and had recorded various aspects of their religious teachings on papyrus and on leather scrolls, the rabbinic tradition had been a predominantly oral one and there is a singular lack of manuscript evidence of any sort from the second to the ninth century. Even if the occasional tradition had been committed to an inscription, a scroll or a piece of papyrus, wood or leather, the inefficient and awkward nature of such media made them singularly unsuitable for the transmission of such traditions in any wholesale manner, whether the attitude to orality here being presupposed is fully justified or not. The versatile nature of the bound codex had already been recognised by the Christian community a few centuries earlier and had been a factor in its prolific literary activity but it would appear not to have been adopted by the Jews for their major corpora of talmudic and related traditions until some time between the seventh and ninth centuries. During that time, what had previously been restricted to oral circulation was committed to codices and this produced precisely the effect that some rabbis feared and that others no doubt welcomed. The authority of the written word now spread from the biblical field to its rabbinic counterparts and the bound volume became the medium for the dissemination of authoritative texts. As a result, what had previously been the exclusive terrain of the scholar became familiar ground to the literate Jew and, by the same token, the attempts of the leading schools and champions of rabbinic Judaism to establish authoritative guidance for the populace could achieve success by the circulation of volumes newly composed and sanctioned by them.[41]

Some objection may be raised against a supposition that the rabbinic tradition had remained a predominantly oral one for a number of centuries. It may be argued that learning by rote is educationally inferior to committing to writing; that orality conveys only the gist of a message while literacy assures precision; that the processes of remembering and reading are quite different functions; and that complicated literary forms are evidence of a move from the spoken to the written word. If studies of oral transmission among ancient and primitive people and their application to biblical studies have not put paid to such notions, recent research into the nature of orality and literacy in the Middle Ages should certainly do so and it should no longer be possible to argue that because a 'text' was known to scholars in detail, it must surely have been disseminated in a written format. Mary Carruthers has produced a detailed history of memory in which she demonstrates convincingly that the phenomenon was highly regarded among intellectuals in the classical and mediaeval worlds and that mnemotechnical devices were developed to enable the recall of highly complicated compositions. For her, the oral and written media were complementary and she regards it as 'simply silly' to suppose that in the mediaeval period scholarship was conducted by 'frequent consultation of indices, thumbing books to pick up previously marked passages, writing citations on to parchment slips, even "scissors-and-paste" composition'. The spread of the codex is not therefore to be explained as a reflection of an intellectual and literary development which might just as well have produced an oral response, but as evidence of a concern for authorisation and institutionalisation. It is true that our discussion is of the situation in the Orient while she is concerned with the western world but recent research has pointed away from the supposition of two watertight cultural entities and the logic of much of her argument may be equally applied to the case in hand.[42]

The evidence from the Cairo Genizah leaves little room for doubt that many of the fragments from that source originally belonged to codices of various types of literature dating from as early as the ninth and tenth centuries and emanating primarily from oriental Jewish communities. While the eighth-century post-talmudic tractate *Massekheth Soferim* (a significant part of it originally of Palestinian provenance) was, with the exception of one problematic reference, primarily concerned with the writing of a biblical scroll, the position totally changed within two or three centuries by which time there were already standard practices for Jewish scribes copying all kinds of literature on to codices. With similar developments taking place among the Muslims, the Jews were gradually replacing papyrus with vellum as the primary material for the transcription of texts and would soon begin to adopt paper. Quires were composed, catchwords included, sections numerated, lines justified, folios pricked and ruled, and the *mastara* (ruling-board) was employed to facilitate the planning of the lines. Pride was taken in producing particularly beautiful codices of the Hebrew Bible. The different Jewish communities followed their own customs in these scribal practices but the codex was unique in offering versatility, ease of reference and substantial capacity. It was therefore widely adopted for the circulation of the literature created and expanded in the previous few centuries. It has indeed recently been demonstrated by M. Ben-Sasson that in the Jewish communities of North Africa in the ninth and tenth centuries texts were being widely copied and circulated and extensive libraries, both private and public, and covering various languages, were being amassed and sold. Such libraries included not only the classical Jewish sources but also the newest commentaries on the one hand and more general learning on the other. By creating, preserving and disseminating the contents of these libraries, the Maghrebi Jews of means introduced a wide variety of literary works to other communities and thereby exercised a powerful influence on the levels of Jewish cultural achievement. In addition, the Genizah manuscripts make it clear that the degree of literacy among the ordinary members of the Jewish community was such that the dissemination of the written word was bound to have a significant and extensive effect on their attitudes and practices.[43]

In the field of liturgy too, then, the codex became the medium for the transmission of authorised sets of prayers and a process was initiated which was ultimately to lead to the *siddur*'s acquiring what amounted to a form of popular canonisation. The existence of thousands of Genizah texts representing almost every area of the Jewish religious tradition provides ample evidence of the growing tendency to commit the relevant teachings to authoritative, written form and it is perhaps in the light of this development that the later literary history of *midrashim*, *piyyuṭim* and *targumim* should be viewed. Once the emerging prayer-book had chosen what it wished to include from these and other such fields, the remaining material gradually, or perhaps contemporaneously, formed itself into written corpora suitable for the codex and thereby moved from a para-liturgical function to a purely literary one. This may be a more controversial point; what is, however, beyond dispute is that the written prayer-book preserved much of the centralised liturgical tradition of the leading Babylonian geonim long after the authority of those leaders had waned and the centre of Jewish cultural activity had moved elsewhere.

That same centralised liturgical tradition remained at the heart of future developments but the gradual breakup of the once united Islamic empire brought with it the emergence of local autonomy and this political state of affairs also had some effect on its religious equivalent. Various Jewish communities around the Mediterranean and, indeed, further afield began to look to their own customs and authorities for liturgical guidance when composing their *siddurim* and there emerged a plethora of rites that incorporated some Palestinian as well as many Babylonian elements, each true to the basic recipe dictated by the geonim but also happy to lend it some local colour and flavour. These rites form the drive-shaft between the power house of geonic *halakhah* and the momentum transmitted to Jewish liturgical progress in the late mediaeval and early modern period. As such they deserve closer attention in the next chapter.

CHAPTER 6

Authorities, rites and texts in the Middle Ages

Moving as we now do to the period that ranges from the embryonic prayer-books of the geonim across some five or six centuries to the earliest printed *siddur* involves passage through the Middle Ages, an exercise that is always fraught with danger for the historian, whatever aspect of human endeavour he is attempting to chronicle. The sources are never extensive; their interpretation requires a judicious blend of critical detachment and sympathetic understanding; and distinctions must be drawn between their concepts of authority, attribution and transmission and our own. Whatever modern scholars may identify as the dominant idea or the intellectual theory that lies behind a particular development or group of developments, the contemporary practitioner was responding to an immediate and local need within his world of commitments and their motivating ideology. Sometimes the result of his activities was less of a factor in the ultimate turn of events than some more haphazard circumstance such as the survival of a particular volume. *Et habent sua fata libelli.* But the mediaeval period is no longer being seen by historians as the backward, disorderly and obscure hiatus between the classical world and modernity. However little such academic disciplines as theology, law and philosophy currently take account of the Middle Ages, it is becoming progressively clearer that major contributions were then made to these and other fields of intellectual development and that it is partly as a result of the biases of early modern scholarship that they have not been given their due attention. Recent research is, however, beginning to correct the balance and to demonstrate how much more can be learnt about the mediaeval period if scholarship is so minded. Culture did not then falter but even often flourished, not only in the Islamic and Jewish worlds, where this is certainly true, but also in countries under Christian hegemony. Attempts were made to impose order on various aspects of life and the roots of many a modern idea or institution, even where they sprouted from an original seed in earlier times, may be traced to the intellectual soil of a thousand rather than two thousand years ago. Naturally, one must avoid attributing modern motivations to pre-modern authorities but at the same time one should grant them a degree of sophistication that makes it less surprising when the sources are seen to indicate innovation, progress and adjustment on their part. It is against the background of such a less dismissive and patronising attitude that an examination may now be made of the major developments in Jewish liturgy from the tenth until the fifteenth century.[1]

It will be recalled that in the previous chapter part of this story was already told. A sufficient degree of pluralism on the part of the talmudic rabbis about the nature of prayer in general and the precise form of the major devotions in particular ultimately made possible the emergence of a plethora of text variation, poetic and mystical composition, innovation in benedictions, language choice, and Bible reading traditions in the immediate post-amoraic centuries. The synagogue and its activities grew into the educational and exegetical centre of Jewish communal life and the style and content of the formal services took on their own particular forms in the various Jewish locations of Babylon and Palestine. For a number of internal and external reasons, some of which were noted, the ninth to the twelfth centuries saw the imposition of controls on all these developments. More precise halakhic guidelines, in the forms of codes, responsa and rubrics, were drawn up for most aspects of the liturgy and the growing use of the codex by Jewish scholars made it possible to encompass the newly authorised versions issued by some of the geonim in the written text of the *siddur*, or order of prayers.[2] Lest it be thought that this process put paid to argument, variation, expansion and contradiction, it should immediately be stated that the evolutionary and innovatory elements simply found different ways of expressing themselves. Having been limited to the gains already made by them in the central parts of the statutory prayers, poetry and mysticism tended to expand on their periphery. Creativity concentrated more on the choice of biblical texts, the development of *rites de passage* and the elaboration of synagogal customs. The precise shape of each word, the number of such words per prayer and the order in which everything was recited became the major issues and each rite jealously sought to protect its characteristic elements in these respects from encroachment by competitors.[3] Persecution did of course play a part in the introduction of more eirenic prayer-texts on the one hand and the abolition of some established forms on the other but one must be wary of following a lachrymose interpretation of Jewish historical development. In spite of what some mediaeval authorities claim, there are few major changes that are directly attributable to manifestations of anti-Semitism and such explanations are more often than not offered in the absence of a more reasonable and sensible clarification of a puzzling liturgical phenomenon.[4]

If a comparison is made, or rather, a contrast is drawn between the overall liturgical situation that obtained during the late geonic period and its equivalent at the invention of printing, the nature of the major changes will immediately become apparent and will suggest the direction that needs to be taken in the course of this chapter. When Jewish communities in Spain in the ninth century wished to be instructed in the formulation, order and explanation of their prayers, they had no major rabbinic figures, no unified and established rite and no authoritative texts to guide them. Situated as they were at the outposts of the Muslim empire, they clearly felt the danger of drifting away from a more central form of practice. The variety of custom that the various pioneers and immigrants might have brought with them, and that had their origins in the talmudic traditions, lacked the binding force necessary to pull the communities together and the position in the Holy Land at the time was no more definitive than that in such provincial centres. The whole theme of Palestinian liturgy was one of extensive improvisation and there was no widely recognised authority there to lay down the law. Consequently, approaches were made to the spiritual leaders of the Babylonian communities and academies whom they saw in Spain as their halakhic and talmudic mentors and who, as part of their drive for the establishment of a normative *halakhah* in all aspects of Jewish religious activity, were only too happy to compile the required responsa and manuals and issue them in a much wider geographical context than the Iberian peninsula.[5] By the middle of the fifteenth century the power of the Babylonian geonate had waned to the point of decadence and the characteristic customs of Eretz Yisrael had either disappeared or were barely recognisable as such, so that these two once dominant communities and ritual adversaries no longer stood at the centre of discussions and practice.[6] The liturgical parvenus, so to speak, were now the Sefardi rites of Spain and Portugal and the Ashkenazi customs of central and eastern Europe, in both of which areas dwelt an extensive proportion of the world Jewry of the day. With demographical change and a degree of relative economic affluence had come greater independence and this had expressed itself in various manifestations of autonomy, in the synagogue as well as in the wider setting.[7] The Babylonian and Palestinian customs had left their mark, as will shortly be explained, but the stronger communities had maintained or evolved a liturgical identity of their own that combined communal customs with what had become the halakhic norms. Such customs and norms had found written expression in the prayer-book codices that were by that time no longer the rarities that they had once been and in the halakhic codes of various leading rabbis some of which were comprehensive, or at least extensive, while others concentrated on the liturgical ritual to be followed in a particular communal context. As the Hebrew codex developed so did it become better known and admired and so did it attract to itself the further contributions of glossators, rubric writers and illustrators. Having once been the specific *ad hoc* response of one authority to a particular problem, not always recorded in writing, liturgical authority had moved to the medium of the bound volume, the work of a professional scribe, with what often amounted to extensive text and commentary.[8] Simply to list the names of the authorities, rites and texts that characterised the various stages of Jewish liturgical development in the Middle Ages is not only a boring exercise; it also fails to place such contributions in their historical and religious setting. Having partly described the nature of that setting it will now be possible to offer an account of the personalities and the works on the one hand and to trace the brief history of the various rites on the other, always attempting to relate such details to the general context just outlined.

Perhaps the Jewish homeland is a suitable place to begin, particularly since there was so much liturgical innovation and expansion there in the centuries before the armies of the Crusaders virtually brought about a third destruction of the sanctuary at the end of the eleventh century. In spite of all this activity, perhaps even because of reactions against it, the remarkable fact is that the Palestinian rite in all its richness, as indeed virtually the whole history of that community in pre-Crusader times, disappeared from Jewish history as a recognisable entity and has only gradually been reconstructed through the fortuitous discovery and critical analysis of the manuscript fragments from the Cairo Genizah. From these torn, worn and delicate pieces of forgotten history, insights have been gained, particularly over the last four decades, into the social, political and intellectual development of the Jews in the Holy Land in general and into the characteristics of their prayer-forms and customs in particular, over a thousand years ago.[9] For them it was the colourful variety of traditions that remained predominant. The sabbath and festivals bore numerous titles and any or all of them could be employed in the relevant texts. The themes of particular compositions were not strictly adhered to and it was consequently not thought irrelevant to insert petitions for the future in passages about the past or to construct a concluding doxology that was beyond the topic in hand. Novel doxologies were coined almost with abandon and if one epithet was devout, a plurality of them was positively inspired. The use of the Hebrew Bible was not limited to illustrative verses but could extend to the ceremonial recitation of whole sets of psalms and the weekly pentateuchal lectionary ranged over three years and more and not over one. Above all, a positive delight was taken in the use of the medium of *piyyuṭ*, so that there was hardly an area of prayer that was not permeated with what were often the complicated, allusive and linguistically novel verses of the liturgical poet. Although it has sometimes been suggested that the mystical texts of the *hekhaloth* and *merkavah* literature influenced the Palestinian rite more than its Babylonian counterpart, no conclusions can yet be reached since there is no clear evidence to establish the original context of such texts. According to Swartz, elements of Palestinian mystical hymns ultimately found a place in the standard Babylonian liturgy but the relationship between the mystical and non-mystical circles was one of mutual rather than one-sided influence, the Palestinians having borrowed contents and patterns from what ultimately became centralised rabbinic liturgy.[10]

Other characteristics of the Palestinian synagogues will be noted when the Babylonian rite is described and contrasted with its great rival. While indulging their love of variegated and improvised liturgy the Jews of Eretz Yisrael apparently took little care to give it formal expression in a code or a prayer-book or to associate it with the name of some leading authority. Perhaps it was in the nature of their whole approach to avoid such rigid structure. There were lists made of the distinctive elements of Palestinian religious custom but from the fragments that have survived these appear to have been neither in the form of codes, nor consistent with one another, nor attributed to any major halakhic figure. Liturgy does not figure prominently in the *Sefer Ha-Ma'asim* traditions but there are references to the synagogal lectionary and to the qualifications required of one who would lead the congregation in prayer. There is also evidence of the prospective abrogation on *Rosh Ha-Shanah* of recklessly taken vows, a custom which, in the well-known *Kol Nidrey* form, was later transferred to *Yom Kippur*, met with the opposition of the Babylonian authorities, and was destined to be the subject of much discussion about its prospective and retrospective formulation.[11] Matters such as the structure of the Torah reading and the qualifications of the one acting as precentor are reminiscent of parts of *Massekheth Soferim* but do not always reflect the same tradition.

The one detailed list that has survived from geonic Palestine, *Sefer Ha-Ḥilluqim*, covers at least fifty-two differences between Babylon and Palestine, of which eighteen may be said to belong to the wider liturgical field. A number of examples may be cited that offer some guidance on the general nature of the Palestinian approach to such matters. The rules about the priestly benediction indicate a greater concern to maintain the special nature of this ceremony separately from the more general context of ordinary worship. The customs concerning the recitation of the *shema'* in a standing position and the seating of the congregation facing the ark containing the scrolls may be interpreted as reflecting a degree of respect for scripture that was perhaps slightly reduced in Babylon because of the livelier debate there with the Karaites. The public declamation of the whole *'amidah* by a cantor as against its silent recitation in Babylon may be related to the fact that the extensive variety of Palestinian wording prevented universal acquaintance even with the standard prayers. Also noteworthy are the use of the *lulav* on the sabbath and the counting of the *'omer* both morning and evening.[12] In at least one instance a list of Palestinian customs represents a final and forlorn attempt of the Palestinian *émigrés* in Cairo to maintain their separate synagogal identity.[13] Another Genizah manuscript, published by M. Margaliot, though incorporating Palestinian elements, is more concerned with pietistic prayer-customs and exudes the atmosphere of the later rather than the earlier part of the classical Genizah period.[14] But some of such customs may also have had their origin in the pietistic circles of pre-Crusader Palestine. Thousands of verses of liturgical poetry testify to Palestinian creativity in this sphere.[15] A variety of *targumim* or Aramaic renderings of the Pentateuch, representing different methods of approaching the word of God in the context of its public recitation and/or study, indicate a deep interest in the educational potential of such a medium.[16] Similarly, the numerous forms of Hebrew exegesis collected into *midrashim* demonstrate an enthusiasm for the dissemination of edifying material, of a largely homiletical nature, in Jewish gatherings.[17] Remarkably, however, there is only one work emanating, at least to a significant degree, from Eretz Yisrael in geonic times that may loosely be regarded as a guide to some of its authoritative liturgical practice, namely, *Massekheth Soferim.* In this post-talmudic tractate, dating from about the seventh or eighth century, are recorded not only the scribal customs required of those writing sacred scrolls, which accounts for the title of the work, but also a variety of liturgical instructions. The theme of biblical lectionaries looms large and covers all three parts of the Hebrew Bible with special attention to Psalms and Esther and to the benedictions, here in their earliest recorded form, introducing and concluding the prophetic passages recited on sabbaths and festivals. Whether or not it is originally related to the other sections, there is also a body of traditions briefly dealing with aspects of the liturgies of weekdays, sabbaths, festivals and fasts and with the context in which certain prayers such as the *qedushah* (built around Isaiah 6:3) may be read. A quorum of ten adult males is reported as the required number for public worship but a subsequent passage mentions the possibility of either six or seven in Eretz Yisrael, leaving open the question to later commentators and scholars whether this reference is to the actual number present or those who have not yet heard any of the prayers for which the quorum is required. Qualifications are also laid down for the one leading the congregation in prayer and only limited, public, liturgical functions are permitted to the youngster of between twelve and twenty.[18] Although the Palestinian content is manifest, there are enough exceptions to the rule to question the assumption of many scholars that everything in the tractate is from the Holy Land. It would be more accurate to describe it as betraying Palestinian provenance or influence, reflecting many but by no means all of the Palestinian traditions, with Babylonian additions and elements.[19] By its very definition, Palestinian practice was bound to make room for a variety of custom and one must therefore be cautious about claiming that a particular form of prayer is to be found only in Babylon or is consistently present in the rite of Eretz Yisrael. The question that must now be addressed is the matter of the fate of the variegated Palestinian liturgical tradition following the collapse of the communities that had owed allegiance to it after the conquest of the Holy Land by the Crusaders at the end of the eleventh century.

If the truth be told, that particular Palestinian tradition was destined never again to occupy a central place in the development of Jewish liturgy. By the time that the Crusaders put an end to its physical presence the Babylonian geonim had already ensured that the Palestinian community would leave only minor marks on the body of Jewish prayer and that all future rites would carry the genetic fingerprints of a Babylonian patrimony. Nevertheless, there were a few areas of Jewish settlement that had absorbed or retained a liturgical influence from the homeland before the Mesopotamian centres of talmudic study had dictated the direction of further progress and that were therefore able to preserve some elements of it, albeit as patriarchal rather than specifically Palestinian traditions, in spite of the new trend. The significance of that preservation was further enhanced by the sad fact that the rites once characteristic of these areas, having at least to a limited extent withstood the challenge of the Babylonian halakhic cohorts, were unable to summon the energy to re-defend themselves against the encroachments of the latter's Sefardi heirs. Though effectively disappearing from the scene, they nevertheless retained fossilised evidence of the old Palestinian tradition. The rites here being described were the original prayer-books of Aleppo (*'Aram Ṣova*), Romania and Persia. The geographical distribution itself is of interest. Close cultural links between the communities of Palestine and Syria were a characteristic feature of Jewish history throughout the first Christian millennium and it is hardly surprising that Aleppo should have looked to the motherland for liturgical guidance or inspiration.[20] In so far as Romania is concerned, what is being dealt with here is the area now comprising Greece, the Balkans and European Turkey and once forming part of the Byzantine Empire that championed Christianity. The Jews of this Empire also felt themselves close to Eretz Yisrael and maintained many of its customs.[21] The reasons for the presence of the Persian community among those with the closest identification with Palestinian customs are perhaps less obvious. Perhaps the arrival and influence of *émigrés* from the Holy Land during the talmudic and geonic periods left more of an effect on some parts of the diaspora than on others. Alternatively, the Babylonian rite was, as has previously been argued, far from monolithic in its early stage and certainly contained elements that were eventually dropped from its practice and retained only in what became the more characteristically Palestinian version of the prayer-book and by those who inherited it.[22] Whatever their original association with the Palestinian community, it is in these three rites that one can detect a number of its characteristic components. Poems composed by Palestinian *payyeṭanim* appear in large numbers and there is a tendency to versify what is elsewhere more prosaic. Psalm collections and individual verses occur in number and biblical verses in general are often employed to introduce and conclude sections of the prayers. Benedictions, formulae and phraseology preserved only in Genizah texts are to be found and there is a varied use of *qedushah* versions that clearly predates any serious attempt at standardisation. There are also examples of what may be called the futuristic prayer, a genre that had its essential origin in tannaitic times and constituted an appeal to God to effect in the future what he had done or promised to do in the past. This became popular among the Jews of Eretz Yisrael but was generally not to the liking of the halakhic authorities of the Babylonian academies in the late geonic period. In addition, there are features concerning the order of the prayers, the content of the biblical lectionaries and what was regarded as acceptable Hebrew language that tend to occur more commonly in one of the three than in the others but that require a more thorough treatment. Only the Persian rite has attracted a contemporary editor, Shelomo Tal having edited an important manuscript and supplied an introduction with detailed historical, liturgical, codicological and bibliographical information, but there are plans for Ezra Fleischer to write an introduction to the Aleppo rite, and there are at least early printed editions of that and *Maḥzor Romania*.[23]

If one defines 'Babylonian' and 'Palestinian' in terms of the kind of liturgical poetry originating in each of these two major centres rather than in accordance with the order and content of the statutory daily prayers, then one is entitled to trace the Palestinian even further, in both the geographical and chronological senses. It is predominantly for this reason that scholars have traditionally allowed themselves to include the Ashkenazi rite among those of Palestinian provenance although it retains only remnants of what were once the regular formulae of that centre. Before some explanation is offered of how and why this rite came into being, a few words are in order concerning other, more minor prayer-books that still contain evidence that they were once less dependent on the Babylonian–Sefardi trend than they later came to be. In view of what has previously been noted about the origins of the Romanian rite, it is hardly surprising that the original liturgical customs of Corfu and other 'Greek' centres have much in common with that rite.[24] More problematic is the existence within a number of North African prayer-books, such as those of Fez and Tripoli, of elements that predate the period when the influx of Sefardim dictated a new liturgical order to their liking and are reminiscent of aspects of the non-Babylonian tradition.[25] What is apparently being encountered here is an older, more authentically North African rite or a non-standard Sefardi rite and the question to be answered, if or when Jewish liturgical research uncovers the evidence, is what the nature was of such a rite. The same, or a similar problem exists with regard to the Egyptian rite before the immigration into Cairo, and other such centres, of persecuted Jews from the Maghreb and from Palestine. Do the Genizah fragments from the Ben-Ezra Synagogue of Fatimid Cairo reflect not only Palestinian variations from what was destined to become the dominant Babylonian–Sefardi ritual but also their North African, Sefardi and Egyptian equivalents? If so, what is claimed about the variety of Palestinian usage may have applied to a wide area of the Jewish liturgical world until the tenth century and it may have been the rite laid down by some (but not all) of the halakhic authorities of Babylon that is to be more accurately described as the exception rather than the rule. In that case, the achievements of the latter rite in not only coming to the fore after the tenth century but also in virtually eliminating so many of the alternatives is even more noteworthy than hitherto believed. Some further attention will be paid to this tricky subject when the history of the Babylonian and Sefardi traditions is traced.[26] In the mean time, it should be stressed that no clear-cut answers are yet available to these questions.

For remnants of the Palestinian rite, or variety of rites, to have made their way as far as the countries of western Europe, a channel of communication must have been in existence. If the link in the chain of transmission in Asia Minor and the Balkans was the Byzantine empire and its successors, so was it the unifying factor of Christendom that made possible the spread of a similar set of liturgical traditions through Italy, France, England and Germany. Although the history of the Jewish communities in these countries lacks any major, reliable documentation in the period that is of the greatest interest in this immediate context, namely, from the seventh to the tenth centuries, it may with some confidence be conjectured, and frequently is, that a connection between the Holy Land and Italy was made by way of the normal social and economic intercourse of the Mediterranean and the countries bordering it. Here again, if there was a North African–Sefardi tradition that preceded the one laid down by the Babylonian geonim, and consequently resembled what we tend to define as Palestinian, it is just as possible that the movement towards Italy was along that coast as along the northern coasts or through the various central islands such as Crete or Sicily. If not, the progress of Jewish liturgy in its various forms from Palestine to Italy may simply and somewhat ironically have been via the eastern to the western Roman Empire. Whatever the direction from which they arrived, a deep interest in liturgical poetry and midrashic compilations as well as a respect for the authority of the Palestinian centres are attested before the tenth century and allow us to characterise the Italian community as a spiritual heir of the homeland.[27] If, indeed, the earliest representative of the Italian rite, the *nusaḥ Roma* or *minhag ha-lo'azim*, is to be identified as the *Seder Ḥibbur Berakhoth* and this work is to be attributed to the twelfth century Italian homilist, Menaḥem ben Solomon, the exegetical and liturgical interests of the two major centres are seen here to have come together nicely. Not all the interpretations offered sixty years ago by the editor of the work, Abraham I. Schechter, remain valid but there are numerous similarities between the *piyyuṭim*, morning benedictions, aspects of the benedictions associated with the *shema'*, *qedushah*, recitation of the Song at the Red Sea, and general phraseology to be found in it, and those that are recorded in the manuscript evidence of the Palestinian traditions now available to us from the Genizah.[28] If one adds to this the evidence from Italian manuscripts of the Hebrew prayers that highlights *remnants* of Palestinian practice regarding the lectionary, the use of psalms, and special sabbath prayers and that has recently been noted by Ezra Fleischer,[29] and such well-known and long-established characteristics as the ubiquitous use of a double *le'eyla* in the *qaddish* and of *kether* in all *qedushoth*,[30] it becomes clear that Italy constituted the gateway through which the last few surviving stragglers of the once powerful liturgical customs of Eretz Yisrael found their way into the synagogal rituals of central and western Europe. Once the Babylonian customs took overall control, that liturgical route was firmly closed. Unlike other rites that had wholly disappeared by the time that the first Hebrew books were being set on the newly invented printing-presses of the last third of the fifteenth century, that originating in early mediaeval Rome was destined to grace one of the incunables of Soncino printed at Cassal Maggiore in 1485–6.[31] That it maintained an identity for so long is certainly due in part to the large number of codices on to which it was copied in the centuries immediately before printing. It is self-evident to anyone with a smattering of general history that Italy was one of the most literate countries of the period and the Jews more literate than most. Consequently, it is no surprise to find so many Italian prayer-books among the Hebrew manuscripts of the major collections. Such manuscripts are also rich in the *piyyuṭim* which were produced in large numbers in that Jewish community and which, by their close association with the original rite and consistent citation of parts of it, helped to ensure the survival of the traditional Roman *nusaḥ*. The rubrics to be found in those codices also stand testimony to an important liturgical development during the period under discussion in this chapter. Now that the trend towards systematic halakhic codification, initiated by the Babylonian geonim, had become well established, there were few who did not devote significant parts of their compendia to guidance in liturgical matters.[32] One of the most ancient and renowned of Italian Jewish families, the Anaus, not only distinguished themselves as talmudists and liturgical poets. They were also responsible for penning, in the latter part of the thirteenth century, two halakhic compendia that recorded and thereby protected the old Roman rite. Zedekiah ben Abraham Anau was the author of the *Shibboley Ha-Leqeṭ* and this work is closely related, in a manner yet to be convincingly demonstrated, to the *Tanya Rabbati* attributed to his second cousin, Yeḥiel ben Yequthiel, which appears to be either a digest of the other or an early transcription of it, later edited, or perhaps simply based on the same original source. The work concentrates on prayers, blessings, customs and rituals for daily, sabbath and festival use and makes much of its dependence on the traditions of earlier authorities.[33] In spite of all these fine efforts, however, the later history of the Italian Jewish prayer-book involves a departure from the 'purer' Roman source, as will later be explained.

In seeking the origins of the Ashkenazi rite, first in western Europe and then among the communities of that group as they moved steadily more eastwards, many students of Jewish liturgy presuppose one direct link between Italy, which inherited some remnants of the Palestinian traditions, on the one side and the Jewish centres of France, England and Germany on the other. Distinctions are blurred between the usages of these latter three and they are treated as effectively identical. Given that their selection of *piyyuṭim* is similar, it is supposed that their daily rites also tally. There are, however, a number of reasons why this categorisation will not do. First and foremost, there are certain characteristics which the 'Old French' or 'North French' and the German rites do not have in common. In the order of words, the use of biblical verses, the preferred vocabulary and phraseology and the degree of dependence on the standardised Babylonian formulae, a comparison of the numerous early manuscripts hailing from North France and the German communities reveals important distinctions.[34] Secondly, the ultimate disappearance of the French rite after the fourteenth century from all but the three small Piedmontese centres of Asti, Fossano and Moncalvo in North Italy tended to give the impression that the Ashkenazi ritual, as it came to dominate most of Europe, was the key to understanding all earlier western European traditions. Thirdly, what is generally overlooked is the early struggle of the Ashkenazi rite against the strong influence of its French equivalent and how often the authorities of the former criticised the liturgical customs of the latter in their struggle to establish their independent identity.[35] Granted that there then existed a North-East French rite, entitled *nusaḥ Ṣarefath*, from at least the eleventh to the fourteenth centuries, and that it had a form independent of its Ashkenazi equivalent, the question to be answered is what was its origin and why is it closer to the Babylonian–Sefardi heritage in some key respects. It is of course theoretically possible to argue that the Italian customs were imported into Germany and from there into France and that somehow the French were then infected by spores from the Babylonian–Sefardi tradition to the south. Chronology, geography and political history all militate against such a supposition and support the alternative hypothesis that all manner of influences from the Iberian peninsula and Provence with their close association with the Islamic world and the Babylonian tradition were an early element in the formation of the French rite. The customs recorded in the twelfth- and thirteenth-century works compiled by Abraham ben Isaac of Narbonne, Aaron ben Jacob Ha-Kohen of Lunel and Asher ben Saul of Lunel certainly support such a hypothesis.[36] The documented confusion that reigned among the Jewish settlements in Provence and that Abraham ben Nathan Ha-Yarḥi tried to clear up with his summary of the various rites and customs in his *Sefer Ha-Manhig* in the twelfth to thirteenth century is perhaps a remnant of early such south-western influences which were in competition with those of Italy from the south-east. As far as the fate of the Provençal rite of the Middle Ages is concerned, it survived in a fragmentary state in the customs of Carpentras and Avignon. The history of Provençal Jewry takes in periods of Gothic, Islamic and Carolingian dominance in the era now being discussed and it is consequently no wonder that various traditions are represented among its liturgical customs. In that case, it is possible that the French Jewish prayer-book of Rashi's day also owed at least as much to Spain and Provence as it did to Italy.[37]

What is beyond controversy is that such a prayer-book was of major significance in the eleventh, twelfth and thirteenth centuries in western Europe. Rashi himself no doubt played a central role in its preservation and promotion but, as with so many of the writings of that outstanding scholar, it is virtually impossible to isolate the original views and decisions of the master from the transmissions of these by his family and pupils for a century or two after he flourished. Great teacher that he was, he clearly inspired many glosses, notations and decisions but the process was a continuous and dynamic one. Consequently, it may be stated with some confidence that such works as *Siddur Rashi*, *Sefer Ha-Pardes* and *Sefer Ha-'Orah*, although they are not to be attributed directly to the master himself, all emanate from the school of Rashi and record the halakhic decisions reached there concerning Jewish ritual in general, with numerous references to liturgy in particular but little detail of the full texts followed in his day.[38] Scholarship is however fortunate in having at its disposal for this purpose manuscripts of the French rite that date from within two centuries of Rashi's time and may generally be relied upon to reflect the rite much as he knew it. On the French side of the English Channel, there is the rich collection of halakhic decisions relating to everyday Jewish life and worship composed by Simḥah ben Samuel of Vitry, a small town 70 kilometres south-east of Rheims, 160 kilometres east of Paris and in the department of Marne. Known as the *Maḥzor Vitry*, it provides important and fairly detailed textual documentation of the prayers of the French rite of the period together with commentaries and rubrics.[39] The work is a halakhic compilation rather than a prayer-book, the word *maḥzor* still here carrying the older sense of annual cycle or a composition relating to such a cycle, but it contains more liturgical text than the other works from Rashi's school mentioned above. When all the manuscripts of the work that have fortunately survived are critically analysed and composed, a fairly full picture will emerge of where it stands *vis-à-vis* the Ashkenazi rite.

The Norman Conquest having brought England under French influence from Rashi's day, there are also manuscripts emanating from that country that reflect the French rite. This is not to say that there are not variations between the texts followed in France and England but to point out that the manuscripts representing them clearly demonstrate that they belong to the same general rite and that this is French rather than German. The main representative of Norman Jewish liturgy in England is the *'Eṣ Ḥayyim* of Jacob ben Judah whose epithet *ḥazzan* at that period probably indicates an expertise in matters relating to the text and language of the prayers rather than or in addition to a synagogal function.[40] Now that a number of manuscripts have come to light or been identified from this early Anglo-Jewish provenance,[41] it has become clear that there was a considerable degree of Jewish literary activity there and that the *'Eṣ Ḥayyim* takes its place as the principal representative of the liturgical area. Again, interest in codifying daily *halakhah*, recording usage and citing authorities is paramount and the extensive work covers religious duties, including many of a liturgical character, in the first part, entitled *Sefer Ha-Torah* and a wide range of civil and communal law in the second part, entitled *Sefer Ha-Mishpaṭ*. As in *Maḥzor Vitry*, much of the actual text of the prayers and *piyyuṭim* (sometimes his own) is transcribed and there are clear indications that the author had personally experienced various customs that were specifically English rather than French or vice versa. Although in general halakhic matters he is much dependent on Alfasi, Moses of Coucy and the Tosafists and his major source is Maimonides, he is conscious of the need to record his community's own liturgical rite. A similar motive drove two thirteenth-century French rabbis, Nathan ben Judah and Judah ben Eliezer, to record the customs with which they were familiar, the former in a work known as *Sefer Ha-Maḥkim*[42] and the latter in a summary of the liturgical practices of the community of Troyes, as inherited from the authoritative prayer-leader, R. Menaḥem.[43] Neither work is, however, usually concerned to record the precise wording of each text. R. Nathan records the liturgical customs relating to the daily, sabbath, festival and fast-day offices and lectionaries, and offers a commentary which is a mixture of sources, explanations, *'aggadoth* and the significance of numbers. The treatment of R. Judah, although he utilises R. Nathan's work as one of his sources, is more thematic than chronological since he divides his treatment into ten subjects and explains the customs of Troyes with regard to each of them. Psalm readings, *qaddish*, regular *teḥinoth* such as those of Monday and Thursday, *seliḥoth* and *piyyuṭim* such as those recited on festivals, special entreaties, talmudic passages for study during prayer, and pentateuchal and prophetic lectionaries are among the topics with which he deals and his aim is clearly to make some sort of authoritative order out of such peripheral material that has not yet acquired the more fixed nature of the standard prayers. He compares sabbath and weekday prayers, gives special attention to all the festivals and fasts, and mentions the customs of local communities and rabbis in France, Germany and England. In both cases, the introductory section comments on the qualifications required by one who would lead the congregation in worship.

Having established that the mediaeval French rite had an existence of its own that was of significance until the thirteenth century and did not disappear until a century after that, it is now necessary to complete the Jewish liturgical picture in western Europe by providing some comments on the nascent Ashkenazi rite and its subsequent development. In view of its earliest documented history, there can be little doubt that the

Ashkenazi community brought with it into the Rhineland vestiges of those Palestinian traditions that were already built into the liturgical customs of Italian Jewry. This would account for the similarities that are to be found between the three rites as they are known from manuscript sources. It cannot, however, be stressed enough that the occurrence of such vestiges is limited to rare occasions, special circumstances, and the field of *piyyuṭ* rather than throughout the statutory prayers. Already by the latter part of the eleventh century the wider cultural influences on the few families of Jewish leaders that dominated such centres as Worms, Mainz, Regensburg and Speyer were owed as much, if not more, to the guidance emanating from talmudic centres permeated with the philosophy of the Babylonian geonim, a state of affairs that also seems to have applied in Italy by that time. The halakhic and talmudic methods that were destined to become dominant in and characteristic of the developing Ashkenazi communities were taking hold and inevitably had their effect on overall attitudes to the structure and content of prayer.[44] Nevertheless, in matters of custom, *midrash* and linguistic tradition, the older inheritance held its ground so that liturgy, which, as always, represented an amalgam of Jewish cultural elements, was drawing its inspiration from both Italian and Spanish sources by the time that the massacres perpetrated by the rampaging mobs that history has graced with the title of Crusaders put paid to the literary creativity of Ashkenazi Jewry in the older definition of the name.[45] Although the centre of western European Jewry then moved to the French rather than the German settlements, the process of the fusion of liturgical traditions continued.

What is intriguing is that within the next two centuries, the twelfth and thirteenth, a new western European liturgical identity emerged that was to leave behind some of the French elements and adopt various, fresh characteristics. The constant reference back to family customs and traditions became a dominant theme and was utilised to justify their retention and dissemination. The effort to record what was regarded as the authentic rite produced a corpus of authoritative works and numerous codices (unjustifiably underestimated by Elbogen with his modern prejudices),[46] while the acceptance of the prayer-book virtually as one of Judaism's canonical texts induced a concern for its accurate transmission, reliable exposition and linguistic authenticity. If Haym Soloveitchik is correct in his proposition that Ashkenazi Jewry of the twelfth and thirteenth centuries saw Jewish religious authority as a combination of the talmudic dialectic championed by the French Tosafists and the sanctity of popular practice, the merger of the overall Babylonian requirements with the detailed, communal traditions in the liturgical sphere would represent another example of where the Ashkenazim differed from their Spanish and Provençal neighbours.[47] Most of the relevant liturgical sources post-date the contribution made by the German Ḥasidim and their major teachers, a contribution that was to have a profound effect on all subsequent liturgy not only in Ashkenaz but also in areas further afield. Before their contribution receives its required attention, however, it should be acknowledged that even while the Ashkenazi centre was located in France, and had not yet moved back to the German cities, a major figure of German background was the first to compose a work that recorded the early Ashkenazi *halakhah* and custom and to write a commentary on the texts of the prayers. Rabbi Eliezer ben Nathan of Mainz who flourished in the first and middle parts of the twelfth century included in his most famous work (*Sefer Ha-Ravan* or *'Even Ha-'Ezer*) halakhic rulings and the exposition of talmudic topics that deal with liturgical customs and texts, such as the *qaddish*. His decision that, whatever their original format, biblical passages may be recited by heart in the liturgy is a clear indication that by that time their oral recitation was regarded as an integral part of the liturgy, and his argument that the individual follows the communal custom, even when that custom is based on purely communal considerations, demonstrates the degree to which personal prayers had come under the control of public usage. Also of interest are his comments on the permissibility of poetic insertions if they are somehow relatable to the subject, his reservations about the breaking of a glass at the wedding ceremony, and his explanation of *'el melekh ne'eman* as a form of *'amen*. He also left in manuscript, and incorporated into some prayer-book commentaries, comments on the prayers for the whole Jewish year that gave biblical and talmudic sources, references to the Babylonian authorities and demonstrated a keen sense of language, grammar and history. Whether or not this approach had been developed during his travels to the east, apparently as far as the Slavonic countries, or was a continuation of the earlier Italian tradition inherited by the Ashkenazim, is not clear but it certainly testifies to an acceptance of the *siddur* as worthy of treatment not dissimilar to that given to other authoritative pieces of Jewish literature.[48]

If Eliezer of Mainz laid the foundations of the Ashkenazi concern for the preservation of its independent liturgical traditions, whatever effect external influences were to have on its talmudic and halakhic study, it was the school of mystics led by Judah ben Samuel of Regensburg and his pupil, Eleazar ben Judah of Worms that was to give that concern additional structure and content. For them the recitation of the prayers was important not only as the fulfilment of one of the halakhic requirements incumbent upon the Jew but also as a powerful means of affecting those parts of God's essence such as the *sefiroth* that were not totally beyond man's reach. Prayer was indeed regarded by them as a mystical entity in its own right, even identifiable with part of the *Shekhinah*.[49] The problem of liturgy, then, was not just the halakhic or exegetical one but, as Joseph Dan has argued it, 'a theological one . . . closely connected with the developments in the concept of the divine world'.[50] In that case every word and letter, as well as their numerical combinations and associations, carry deep significance for the achievement of mystical harmony and any attempt to alter these or to recognise the equal validity of alternative versions runs the risk of upsetting the whole function and purpose of Jewish prayer for both the human and the celestial worlds. In a short thirteenth-century treatise called *Sodoth Ha-Tefillah* that incorporates some of Judah the Pious' otherwise lost commentary on the liturgy, the variations to be found in the English and French rites are therefore described as 'completely and utterly wrong . . . gross falsehood . . . lies . . . evil'.[51] In order to protect what they regarded as the authentic wording of the prayers and the *piyyuṭim*, such mystics wrote commentaries on their meaning and theological significance, recorded the precise number of letters and/or words that they contained and pointed out the special, religious significance of such numbers. This did not apparently inhibit them from a liturgical innovation that not only brought new poetry into the prayer-book but also sets of benedictions such as those concerning parts of the body recently published by Malachi Beit-Arié from an Oxford manuscript. Although most of Judah He-Ḥasid's work on liturgy, as on other subjects, has not survived, there are characteristic liturgical references in the *Sefer Ḥasidim*, for much of which he was responsible, and his pupil, Eleazar of Worms, exemplified the whole approach of the Ashkenazi mystics of the day in his *Roqeaḥ*.[52] As well as covering halakhic details, this work also records *minhagim*, evaluates the importance of prayer and justifies some prayer-texts by reference to their numerical value. The author also wrote many *piyyuṭim* and commented on others but his major contribution to the liturgical sphere was his commentary on the prayers which is extant in manuscript only. Here again not only is the aim exegesis and theology but the use of numerical devices in the promotion of his mystical ideas. If there had ever been any doubt that the Ashkenazi liturgical traditions would be capable of surviving their exposure to the dominant talmudic traditions of the French Tosafists, the powerful teachings of the German Ḥasidim established once and for all that the future direction to be taken by the western and, subsequently, eastern European rite would be dictated by the combination of an attachment to communal custom and a fascination with precise liturgical formulation. What is being encountered here, and not for the first or last time in the history of Jewish liturgy, is a harmonisation of the novel, actual and specific expression of the smaller group with the authoritative, general theory established by the dominant leadership in the wider Jewish world. Aspects of that harmonisation occur and recur in the texts and authorities that represent the Ashkenazi tradition from the thirteenth until the fifteenth century and witnessed its gradual move eastwards across Europe.

The length and breadth of the commentaries on the *piyyuṭim* of Abraham ben Azriel of thirteenth-century Bohemia stand testimony to a desire to use the exposition of liturgy as an outlet for all manner of scholarly and spiritual preoccupations and to see in it, at the same time, an important source for Jewish religious ideas.[53] In the translated words of the modern editor of the commentary, E. E. Urbach, the *'Arugath Ha-Bosem* 'constituted a kind of chrestomathy of mediaeval Hebrew literature, containing a wealth of information and tradition unknown from other sources'.[54] In that work the author cites, not always in agreement, numerous scholars from as far afield as Babylon and Egypt as well as from nearer to hand in Spain, France and Germany, including his teachers Judah He-Ḥasid, Eleazar of Worms and Barukh of Regensburg. R. Abraham traces sources, makes wide use of talmudic and midrashic literature, and includes philosophical ideas. More important in the present context, however, is the fact that he subjects the texts of the liturgical poetry to strict, linguistic analysis on grammatical and masoretic grounds, transmits the teachings of the German mystics and provides his successors with an influential mine of information, as well as an example of liturgical commentary worthy of emulation. The interesting fact is, however, that his prototype does not appear to have been followed by the leading authorities of Germany and central Europe over the next two centuries. Rather than compiling systematic commentaries on the actual text of the prayers and poetry, they included their views in the large number of halakhic guidebooks through which they introduced the Jewish populace to the results of the detailed study of talmudic law that had been championed and perfected by the Tosafists. Admittedly, they continued to defend and promote the characteristic customs of their community's liturgical practice but, operating as they did as codifiers, their views were included in the wider halakhic context. While one of the earliest of such sources, the *'Or Zaru'a* of Isaac ben Moses of Vienna still records the texts of some prayers here and there in the passing, and notes a variety of liturgical customs, his main concern is to trace the *halakhah* from the talmudic text through various authorities to his French and German predecessors, providing a halakhic commentary and a code in the process.[55] An interest in recording the liturgical text is even less prominent in his contemporary Eliezer ben Joel Ha-Levi (*Ravia*)[56] and wanes further in the case of such major figures as Meir of Rothenburg (*Maharam*) and Jacob ben Moses Molin (*Maharil*).[57] Although the proportion of halakhic decisions given by the latter two rabbis that relate to the detailed recitation and interpretation of liturgical texts is small in comparison with other areas of Jewish religious requirement, it should be acknowledged that they do exist. The *Maharam* rules in favour of a number of phrases within the prayers, limits the use of *piyyuṭim*, finds the source of the Ashkenazi rite in *Seder Rav Amram*, *Halakhoth Gedoloth* and *Massekheth Soferim*, and offers no objection to the illumination of *maḥzorim*. As a regular leader of communal prayer on *Rosh Ha-Shanah* and *Yom Kippur*, the *Maharil* has strong views on the melodies to be used, on congregational participation in the prayers and on the current vocalisation of various words in the texts. Similar comments could be made about the interests of those who formulated collections of *minhagim* such as Abraham Klausner and Isaac Tyrnau.[58] As well as a determination to maintain Ashkenazi custom, for reasons that have already been explained, there was, at the same time, an apparent reluctance or inertia about the composition of systematic commentaries on the text of the liturgy and a commitment to establish an accurate use of Hebrew in the prayers. Both these phenomena now require some further attempt at interpretation.

As far as the language of the Hebrew prayers is concerned, it should be recalled that the formulation of these was originally carried out in rabbinic Hebrew, as is to be expected of an authoritative composition emanating from rabbinic circles for popular use or perhaps even reflecting the spontaneous self-expression of such circles and their supporters. The grammar, syntax, vocabulary and pointing system consequently tended to be that of other rabbinic texts, as, indeed, they are now known to have existed in the early mediaeval period. In addition, the development of the *piyyuṭ* genre in that period brought with it daring departures from any Hebrew precedent and the creation of novel terminology, sentence structure and word formation.[59] A further complication that was to beset the Ashkenazi authorities was the survival of a special system of vocalisation now traced back by contemporary scholarship to a Tiberian-Palestinian system that predated the emergence of that of Ben-Asher in the tenth century. When a form of his system eventually became the dominant one, the 'Tiberian-Palestinian' or 'Ashkenazi' set of rules or their remnants were stubbornly retained in various contexts for a number of centuries.[60] The crisis with regard to the use of rabbinic Hebrew, payyeṭanic forms and alternative vocalisation in the Hebrew liturgy came to a head because of the ultimate success of the schools of Masoretes and *Naqdanim* (literally, 'pointers' of the texts) in establishing a standard form based on that of Ben-Asher for the transmission of texts of the Hebrew Bible. Between the eleventh century and the invention of printing this group of grammarians played a central role in ensuring the elimination from Hebrew Bible manuscripts of the variant forms that had once existed and vigorously encouraged the extension of this newly established biblical uniformity to the liturgical sphere. Although the problem of deciding the extent to which such uniformity should be applied to the non-biblical areas of Hebrew literature was a fairly ubiquitous one for those required to set their linguistic parameters and is encountered in Sefardi sources, it was more severely felt among the Ashkenazim for a number of reasons. First of all, there was an established system of 'Ashkenazi' pointing widely in use at variance with the standard being proposed; secondly, the concern to maintain communal customs hallowed by time was often a paramount consideration; thirdly, the drive for internal consistency that had become a feature of Jewish religious life as a result of Tosafist teachings called into question the maintenance of maverick traditions; and, finally, the inheritance of the particularly complex and recondite compositions of the Palestinian *payyeṭanim* complicated the matter of standardisation to a biblical Hebrew paradigm.[61] The outcome was the existence of a tension between 'correctors' of liturgical Hebrew and defenders of inherited forms that was destined to survive into the modern, even contemporary period. Whenever a halakhic authority points to a biblical Hebrew precedent in arriving at a decision about the acceptable form of a liturgical term he is expressing allegiance, albeit sometimes limited, to the linguistic ideology of the former group. His antagonist, on the other hand, defending as he does the independent nature of non-standard forms of Hebrew and their right to differ from the linguistic criteria authoritatively applied to the Hebrew Bible by the Masoretes, is demonstrating an attachment, at least in some instances, to the more conservative trend.[62] It is in the light of this ongoing controversy that some of the comments of the Ashkenazi halakhists should be seen and that further developments in the formulation of the Ashkenazi printed prayer-books of later periods will be explained in the next chapter.

If, as was earlier argued, the major Ashkenazi authorities between the thirteenth and the fifteenth centuries did not issue prayer-book versions with their own, sanctioned texts and systematic commentaries, preferring rather to offer halakhic guidance where it was requested or required, what were the basic texts that were in use, who wrote them and supervised their accuracy, which form did they take, and how did they reflect previous practice and affect contemporary and future ritual in the synagogue? The first comment to be offered in response to all these questions is that when Rashi and his school began to dominate the Ashkenazi scene the Hebrew book had been in existence, or at least in established use, for the relatively short period of some two centuries. If the theory propounded in the previous chapter is correct, this acceptance of the codex among Jews had effected revolutionary changes in attitudes to the authority of all Jewish literature and the *siddur* had emerged as a text with a sanction of its own. Aspects of this development will again be referred to when the history of the Babylonian–Sefardi tradition is considered below.[63] In the mean time it has to be stressed that the existence of this medium enabled the liturgy to acquire a more precise identity and, by the very nature of its physical form, to attract the further attention of emerging generations of glossators and commentators. The next point to be made is the very obvious one that prayer-books were not a common commodity, widely acquired and in use by individual worshippers. Codices written on vellum and on the progressively more available material of paper had to be commissioned at some considerable expense from a scribe and therefore came into the possession either of communities as a whole or a few wealthy members within them, some of whom might be generous enough to donate or bequeath them for communal use. A large such manuscript, sometimes well bound and richly illuminated (by Jewish if not Christian standards, and sometimes with rabbinic hesitation), might be used by the *ḥazzan* for leading the communal prayers and most of the congregants would have to recite by heart, repeat what they heard from the cantor, or simply recite *'amen* to his benedictions and invocations. Even the wealthy owners of their own volumes might choose a small format and prefer to keep it at home, sometimes indeed recording therein details of ownership or family history. The communal volumes naturally acquired an authority of their own and rabbis, cantors and scribes corrected, defended and expanded old and new texts by the use of glosses, both minor and major in extent.[64] Thus were born liturgical rubrics, glosses and commentaries. In addition, the thirteenth century saw the first examples of Christian expurgation with the result that parts of some texts disappeared while others were internally modified to ensure their survival.[65] Interestingly, the style of *Maḥzor Vitry*, *'Eṣ Ḥayyim* and *'Arugath Ha-Bosem*, combining as it did text and commentary, is not reflected in the Ashkenazi manuscripts of the period after the return of the Ashkenazi centre eastwards from France. The two dominant influences on the liturgy by that time were the trend towards halakhic consistency and systematisation originating in Babylon and the fascination with the ideology and the practical guidance emanating from the schools of German Jewish mystics. It would appear that during the two centuries before the invention of printing these two influences went their separate ways as far as the acquisition of literary forms is concerned. The method established by the Tosafists led to the composition of compendia of halakhic rulings, with references included to liturgical matters, while the *Ḥasidey Ashkenaz* left their firm imprint on the actual wording and glossing of the liturgical text.[66] Where commentaries were attached to the prayer-book texts they were generally of an anonymous kind and recorded the mystical traditions concerning the numerical significance of words and letters and the importance of utterances that meant what they said and said what they meant. The two compartments were not of course watertight. Currents from the one flowed into the other so that liturgical manuscripts carried halakhic decisions and collections of responsa noted what had to be recited in the prayers. The overall picture would, however, appear to support the idea that the victory achieved by the legal traditions and the standardised liturgy of the Babylonian geonim was not total among the Ashkenazim. They found ways of maintaining some of their proto-Ashkenazi communal customs in both areas and ensured that the distinctive flavours of western European religiosity remained identifiable among the medley of pungent dishes that they had adopted from the Orient. Before this latter, spiritual cuisine receives some further attention, it is necessary to note the bifurcation of the Ashkenazi custom itself into a number of sub-divisions as the major areas of Jewish settlement made their way towards Poland and Russia.[67] If one draws an imaginary line southwards from Hamburg on the Elbe to Saltzburg at the edge of the Alps, the communities to the west continued to refer to their rite as that of Ashkenaz or the Rhine (*Raynus*), while those to the east characterised their liturgical customs as those of *Ostraykh*, *Polin*, *Pihem*, *Merrn*, *Lita* and *Raysen*. Expressed in more contemporary political geographical terms, the former covered the territories of today's western Germany, Switzerland, Holland, Belgium and North France while the latter currently approximate to eastern Germany, Austria, Hungary, Rumania, Poland, Czechoslovakia, Lithuania, Ukraine and Belorussia. The differences between the two and within each of the two were minor and concerned which liturgical poetry was recited on what occasions, the particular order of the same prayers and synagogal custom. It is possible that such differences existed from an earlier period of eastern settlement but lack of any documentary evidence prevents their being dated earlier than the fourteenth century.[68] Whenever their origins, the distinctions were not meaningful in the period being covered in this chapter since the dominant rite became the more eastern one after the expulsions and persecutions of the German, French and English centres, in the course of the thirteenth, fourteenth and fifteenth centuries, considerably reduced the importance of these communities. It was only at a later date, as will be chronicled in the final chapters of this volume, that the two rites met on equal terms in free communities and had to vie for synagogal preference.

Throughout this chapter reference has continually been made to the fact that the heads of the Babylonian academies were successful in laying down the detailed structure of the statutory prayers in the latter part of the geonic period. The task will now be to spell out further this process by tracing the history of the Babylonian rite and demonstrating the effect it had on all the other Jewish communities that were blossoming in and around the Mediterranean area at that time, and in a number of which Babylonian immigrants were settling down. What the geonim did, of course, was to formulate principles and rulings on the basis of the talmudic views in matters of prohibition and apply these with equal stringency to the field of liturgy. For some three hundred years, beginning at least as early as the middle of the eighth century, one after another of the major authorities struggled to impose their interpretation of the nature of Jewish prayer on their far-ranging halakhic empire and by the time that their authority was on the wane after the death of Hai ben Sherira in 1038 their objective was well on the way to being met.[69] Part of the victory was achieved by the earlier compilation of halakhic rulings, some of which obviously made reference to liturgical matters, in such collections as the *Halakhoth Pesuqoth* attributed to Yehudai ben Naḥman and the *Halakhoth Gedoloth* now assumed to be the work of Simeon Qayyara.[70] Their major tool was however the legal responsum, in which they could base their decisions on selected talmudic passages, rail against any opposing views and dictate the course of future action to those who required guidance and in some cases had actually requested it. Given the prestige that the Palestinian Jewish community enjoyed, at least from time to time, it represented the first target in the Babylonian campaign to gain ascendancy for its own rite. In a well-known and sharply worded epistle of the early ninth century, Pirqoi ben Baboi, whose teacher was one of Yehudai's pupils, polemicises against his co-religionists in Eretz Yisrael for adding benedictions, petitions, extra words, mystical texts and poetry to the basic prayers and cites the authority of the Talmud and of Yehudai for claiming that a terrible fate awaits those who continue to do so. In the same letter there is also a most interesting reference to the fact that the Palestinian communities did not recite the pre-*shema'* *qedushah* every day until the Babylonian Jews living in Jerusalem and some other cities created such contention over its omission that it was adopted in these places in accordance with their home usage.[71] This is a clear indication that however at odds the general Palestinian usage was with that of Babylon there were still contexts even in the Holy Land in which the latter was followed. By the same token, not all of the geonim always took such a firm line as that reported by Pirqoi in the name of Yehudai and, as has already been established by Naphtali Wieder in recent years, there was no lack of variety in Babylon in respect of such liturgical texts, within the same academies as the generations moved on, or between each of them, Sura and Pumbeditha, at any given time.[72] Nevertheless, there is still a group of Babylonian characteristics that ultimately became dominant and left their mark on the future course of Jewish liturgy. This is not to say that there are no traces of them in material otherwise characterised as Palestinian; simply to point out that they were championed in the East rather than in the West. In addition to the daily *qedushah* just mentioned and the customs noted in the previous chapter and earlier in this chapter in the context of the description of the Palestinian rite, these characteristics include the annual cycle of Torah reading;

permission for the reading of the Torah by an officiant rather than by the one called to make the blessing; the nineteen-benediction *ʿamidah*; the inclusion of theological and talmudic matter rather than the more intensive use of biblical verses typical of Palestine; the recitation of the priestly benediction by the cantor whether a priest was present or not; the limitation of benedictions and their concluding doxologies to the immediate subject, preferably one that was sanctioned for such treatment by the talmudic rabbis; the extra day of the festival; the seven (and not three) blessings at the wedding and wedding-feast; the restricted inclusion of *piyyuṭ* and pietistic expansions; and the use of the prayer *Uvekhen ten paḥdekha* on the solemn days of *Rosh Ha-Shanah* and *Yom Kippur*.[73] It will not have gone unnoticed that while in the case of the Palestinian customs earlier listed scholarly efforts have had to be made in the modern period to trace and reconstruct their further history, virtually all these Babylonian rites, as well as the basic wording of much of the text that they presupposed, became standard practice in Jewish liturgy through all the communities. Equally significant is the fact that these customs convey a message of authority, centralisation, formality and consistency (brought first by emissaries and then by immigrants) and thereby play a major role in the institutionalisation of the synagogue and its attendant functions and functionaries.

As already noted, the medium for conveying this message was the halakhic responsum and it is through the most famous of these that the history of Babylonian influence on Jewish liturgy will shortly be traced. Before this is done, however, a few words about a very specific statement made in the name of Yehudai Gaon will be in order. Even assuming that the attribution to the eighth-century teacher is dubious, the ruling is hardly likely to be later than the ninth century because of the language and content and is therefore of significance for the picture here being built up of the Babylonian relationship with other centres. The responsum deals with an enquiry as to whether liturgical poetry for penitential and festive occasions should be recited by the cantor from a written text or not. In reply, the authority refers to the established practice of the academies whereby the cantor avoids errors in the recitation of such poems on *Yom Kippur* and communal fasts by using a written text but trusts entirely to memory on all other festivals.[74] Clearly, the issue of orality as against written transmission was a burning one in the eighth and ninth centuries, as also evidenced by Naṭronai's responsum about a blind synagogue reader,[75] and such a supposition would fit well with the theory propounded in the previous chapter about the emergence of the Hebrew codex in about the ninth century and its success in lending authority to much of the literature composed and transmitted at that time. The question to be raised here is whether the adoption and promotion of the codex for liturgical purposes is inseparable from the enthusiasm for authoritative liturgy and both trends are Babylonian in origin or whether the latter's success was dependent upon the former's development but did not necessarily share a common, original provenance. The issue has relevance for the subsequent few hundred years of Jewish liturgical history since it may be related to the preference in some areas and periods for an independent volume exclusively containing liturgical text and complemented by codes offering general liturgical guidance as against the alternative predilection for a fully comprehensive *maḥzor* or *siddur* that provides text, commentary and halakhic instruction at a stroke, as it were. What we may here be facing is simply another of the ubiquitous tensions that are so regularly encountered in the history of Jewish liturgy. The problem with such an explanation is that it would be satisfactory if one could directly link the written textual authority of Babylon with one of the later tendencies but the evidence is much more complicated than this, including as it does Babylonian orality and authority, Palestinian textuality and variety, the dissemination of codices in North Africa, French and Spanish comprehensiveness and the Ashkenazi dichotomy between halakhic compendium and mystical prayer-book. When all the evidence has been sifted in a more specialised context than the present one, a pattern may emerge but in the mean time one can do no more than offer a speculative reconstruction of one possibility. The Genizah documents certainly testify to an explosion of the written word in Palestinian circles and this may have originally applied to the *piyyuṭ* and later spread to the statutory prayers.[76] For the Babylonians on the other hand the rabbinic tradition was predominantly an oral one even if it had to be standardised and authorised.[77] Perhaps, then, the fusion of these two elements produced different results, dependent on the degree of input of each ingredient. Sometimes one authoritative text emerged for synagogal use, supported by separately composed, halakhic works for the expert; at others, the effect was the liturgical conglomerate, suitable for wider exploitation by the educated layman. This dual response will be met again as details are now provided about the authorities that stamped the characteristics of the Babylonian rite on all future Jewish prayer-books.

Somewhat paradoxically, it was the spread of Jewish communities to the farthest corners of the Islamic Empire that led in the first instance to the issuing of guidelines for their liturgical practices and, at a later date, to the consolidation of their own versions of the standardised format. It was the Spanish centre in particular that apparently felt isolated and confused since it was enquiries for instruction from there that inspired the ninth-century geonim Naṭronai ben Hilai and Amram ben Sheshna to compose the earliest known orders of Jewish prayer. There must have been some difference of opinion in the community of Lucena about how to give practical expression to R. Meir's talmudic statement that a hundred benedictions are to be recited each day that led them to request a definition of these from the head of the academy in Sura.[78] In reply, Naṭronai, who devoted many responsa to liturgical matters, defines the liturgical *berakhah* and, with due references to various talmudic passages, lists the possibilities from rising and commencing the day at home, through donning the *tefillin* and reciting the *barukh she'amar*, *shema'* and the *'amidah* of the morning, to the afternoon and evening services and retiring to bed. He also notes the blessings required when eating and points out that since the statutory, liturgical benedictions are less numerous on the sabbath, the number is to be made up by partaking of fruits and enjoying spices.[79]

In the case of the liturgical responsa of Naṭronai and several other geonic authorities contemporary scholarship is fortunate in having at its disposal a rich collection of Genizah fragments that have been little interfered with since their composition over a thousand years ago and may consequently be regarded as reliable testimonies to the period being discussed. Where some of these have been transmitted through the ages it immediately becomes apparent just how inferior the transmitted texts have become in comparison with those pristine manuscripts which, happily from today's academic viewpoint, were soon consigned to an oblivion lasting for a thousand years. Fortunately for the fate of Amram Gaon and for the Babylonian rite that he was championing, but sadly for critical students of Jewish history, the same cannot be said for the 'order of prayers and benedictions for the whole year' that Amram Gaon compiled for the communities of Spain (perhaps Barcelona in particular) with whom he was obviously in close contact and who provided financial support for him and his *yeshivah*. Whatever the original text and format of Amram's responsum – whether another simple account of the hundred benedictions or a comprehensive guide to the liturgy – the work became so popular in such a variety of centres that it virtually lost its identity as a discrete rite and became a concept, even an institution. There were French versions and Spanish versions; it exercised a formative influence on communities in Palestine, North Africa and Italy; halakhic authorities as far away as Germany cited it as the standard liturgical source *per se*; and it took on the detailed characteristics of local custom. It was used as much as a justification for a community's own customs as an authority against which to measure them and this was reflected in the manner in which scribes transmitted its text. It is not then surprising to find that the various manuscripts, editions and fragments are at odds with each other with regard to its text and to have to admit that while we can, on the basis of all the manuscript evidence and citations, perhaps reconstruct a text of 'Seder R. Amram' that may fairly be said to reflect its general content and structure within two or three centuries of its compilation, there is at the moment no prospect of recovering the liturgical text that Amram himself favoured. What cannot be denied, however, is that in the earliest years of its existence it ensured that the Babylonian rite became the halakhic yardstick against which everything liturgical was measured and, together with other geonic responsa, put paid to any major differentiation in the central, statutory prayers. Although there has been scholarly controversy even about its basic framework, and it is possible that such a chronology should be reversed, the current view is that the original version probably did contain text, halakhic rulings and sources, constituting the kind of compendium that became the model for some later liturgical commentators. The claim in the preface that the standard liturgy of the geonim was of biblical origin, had then been forgotten and was subsequently recovered by the talmudic rabbis, is certainly characteristic of those pressing for the total acceptance of a centralised and authoritative rite.[80]

The textual history of Saadya Gaon's major contribution to the development of the *siddur* is of quite different an order. The impressive quality of the fullest manuscript, the fairly consistent nature of the Genizah texts, and the linguistic evidence of the Judaeo-Arabic in which the commentary and rubrics are composed all point to an authentic and early version of the work. Having been transmitted in such a reliable form for the first half of its millennial existence and having since then virtually disappeared from the Jewish literary world, Saadya's *Kitāb Jāmiʿ al-Ṣalawāt w'al-Tasābīḥ* ('Collection of all Prayers and Praises'), composed early in the tenth century, has been capable of scholarly reconstruction and publication in a critical edition in our own century.[81] It is altogether a more rational and comprehensive treatment of the topic than any comparable contribution and reflects the independent spirit and discerning mind of an outstanding intellectual figure. The Egyptian-born Gaon set out not only to record the rite that he approved and the manner of its employment but to define the constituent parts of Jewish liturgy and thereby to introduce consistency as well as authority into its further development.

His exercise was an educational and exegetical one and as such was aimed at justifying rabbinic theory and practice in the face of Karaite opposition and criticism. His choice of Judaeo-Arabic and his tendency to eschew the provision of sources testify to his purpose of providing an immediately and clearly assimilable guide but these also became reasons why his text never achieved the fame or popularity of the *Seder Rav Amram*. The language limited its major impact to the Islamic countries and the self-confidence of the author created some suspicion in the minds of later authorities, while the unusually logical system of presentation was probably also a factor in its lesser degree of success. Nevertheless, as Mark Cohen and Sasson Somekh have recently demonstrated, Saadya's *Siddur* was so widely disseminated in these countries by the end of the tenth century that the Fatimid vizier, Ya'qub Ibn Killis, a convert from Judaism to Islam, was able to refer to it in order to heap ridicule on Jewish prayers. He did this during a theological discussion with Rabbanites and Karaites and thereby inspired a written defence of Rabbanite practice by one of the Jewish participants.[82] Saadya's work did succeed in influencing liturgical progress in Babylon, Syria, Eretz Yisrael, Egypt, North Africa, Spain and Yemen and was cited in other Jewish centres but the influence was in matters of detail rather than in overall authority. Another possible reason for this is that, in spite of his being the head of the Sura academy, his liturgical preferences, which may indeed have originally been expressed before his appointment, do not fully tally with those of Babylon or Eretz Yisrael but appear to represent an amalgam of each that may be traceable to his Egyptian background and/or to a particular Babylonian tradition that was less dogmatic about some of its characteristics. Although he specifically states that the purpose of his prayer-book is not to record liturgical poems, he does include his own more concise, popular and attractive compositions and, while he cites his objections to Palestinian liturgical laxity, he is not averse to nodding an occasional approval in the direction of alternatives to the Babylonian standard. Distinctions between the *shema'* benedictions for sabbath eve, the conclusion of sabbath and weekdays, and between the *barukh she'amar* prayer on sabbaths and weekdays; the inclusion of *ya'aleh we yavo'* in the *musaf* prayer for New Year; and the absence of *uvekhen ten paḥdekha* on New Year and *'ashamnu* on the Day of Atonement are reminiscent of similar 'Palestinian' tendencies. He sub-divides prayers and blessings under a variety of more specific headings, distinguishes weekdays, sabbaths, New Moon, festivals (including *Rosh Ha-Shanah*) and fast-days (including *Yom Kippur*) and, above all, offers alternatives for individual and communal worship so that, for instance, he omits the *qedushah* not only from the individual's *'amidah* but also from his pre-*shema'* benedictions and after *'ashrey*.[83] In spite of what is sometimes claimed on his behalf, he was, as Robert Brody has recently demonstrated, not averse to certain non-talmudic interpolations, as long as they were thematically compatible with the original benediction and strategically placed within it to achieve such an end.[84] All these finely drawn distinctions were possibly additional reasons why his particular version of the Babylonian rite did not become universally accepted when the campaign for its general adoption gradually met with success, the preference being rather for a commitment to the principle with reservations about the niceties.

In our efforts to document the growing influence of the most standard form of the Babylonian rite, as championed by many of its authorities, the case of Kairouan in Tunisia, so well analysed in recent years in the Genizah research of Menahem Ben-Sasson, proves highly instructive. What emerges from the evidence of this important centre is that in the tenth and eleventh centuries there was much concern on the part of that community to make the right decisions in connection with its liturgical behaviour. Immigrants were making suggestions that did not tally with local usage, the communal custom did not always coincide with what was being decreed by the Babylonian geonim and there was a fear that actions might be taken that would prejudice the Rabbanite position in its theological exchanges with the Karaites. It is noteworthy that the community turned to Babylon for guidance and thereby acknowledged its allegiance to the halakhic authority of that centre.[85] No less interesting, however, is the fact that a close examination of each of the issues reveals that in its earlier state the local liturgical custom certainly contained elements that had subsequently to be altered in order to give way to the trend towards Babylonian liturgical domination. Among such issues were the public release of congregants from religious oaths, the status of priests, the use of various *targumim*, the possible distinction between the one called to recite a benediction over the Torah and the one reading it, the order of prophetic readings and the sounding of the *shofar*. *Piyyuṭim* were also employed, despite the objection of some authorities, although it is not clear how closely they were attached to the statutory prayers.[86] There may have been more to Pirqoi ben Baboi's accusation of North African dependency on Palestine than the licence for exaggeration of the seasoned polemicist. Ben-Sasson stresses the point that when decisions had to be made about the future, nothing was done without Babylonian authorisation and this confirms the argument here being propounded that these centuries saw the conquest by the Babylonian rite of the communities around the Mediterranean.[87] At the same time the controversies documented in the Genizah sources stand testimony to the battles that had to be won in the process. Since another of the matters troubling the North African community was that of the status and qualifications of the *ḥazzan*, it may be noted in the passing that the more formal and authoritative the established liturgy became, the greater the need to ensure that the one reciting on behalf of the congregation could be relied upon for worthiness and efficiency. The absence of a prayer-book or of a fair degree of knowledge on the part of the congregant mattered a great deal more if he could no longer meet the halakhic requirements in the general statement of a theme but had to express himself in precisely worded formulations. Also significant for the history of the Babylonian rite is the evidence of a significant immigration to North Africa from among the intellectual elite of the Mesopotamian centres, an immigration that was bound to strengthen the move towards the adoption of geonic attitudes and practices.[88] As the Babylonian power waned, so the independence of the North African centre grew, but, in liturgical matters, only on the Babylonian base already firmly established, a process that was again destined to be reversed by Sefardi encroachments later to be discussed. The reputation acquired by the last of the major geonic figures, Hai ben Sherira Gaon, who died in 1038, meant that many works and decisions came to be spuriously ascribed to him. It is therefore difficult to judge precisely what he compiled in the liturgical sphere and whether quotations supposedly cited from a prayer-book by him are authentic. Groner, however, while recognising the spurious nature of some responsa, has concluded that the many that Hai provided for a wide range of communities around the Jewish world included a number of reliable texts on the subjects of sabbath, holidays, prayer and benedictions. He does appear to have been the author of noteworthy *piyyuṭim*, to have taken a less dogmatic approach to liturgical uniformity than his predecessors, especially where the Talmud offered no specific ruling, and to have adjusted the text of the *kol nidrey* recitation.[89]

The prayer-book compiled by Solomon ben Nathan of Sijilmasa in south-west Morocco in the twelfth century, again mainly in Judaeo-Arabic, tells a similar story about Babylonian influence. In this case the influence is not only on the prayer-texts themselves but also on the attitude to halakhic codification. 'Rabbenu Shelomo' is not content to record the text and rubrics but also offers detailed presentations of many areas of Jewish law, less than directly connected with prayer, as a self-styled improvement of the earlier liturgies. This fusion of the two areas of prayer and Jewish religious law, reminiscent of such works as *Maḥzor Vitry*, has been previously encountered and is always an indication of a major geonic influence that goes beyond the relatively moderate Babylonian commitments of Saadya Gaon. *Piyyuṭim* are mentioned, but not transcribed, only in connection with *Simḥath Torah* and *Tish'ah Be'Av* and the order of the prayers is in accordance with the calendar and not the dictates of reason. There are still, however, in the work, texts and customs relating to the *barukh she'amar*, first *'amidah* benediction, hand-washing and belt-wearing, as well as a philosophical, or perhaps more accurately, a theological orientation that all have their parallels in Saadya's *Siddur*. And from the other side there are customs that reflect a more ancient local tradition, possibly not without its link with the Holy Land, and related to the recitation of psalm-verses on the first evening of each festival, the manner of reading and translating the Torah, and the prophetic lectionary.[90] Fortunately, an impressive Oxford manuscript dated 1203 has preserved this early Moroccan rite that straddles the geonic and the Sefardi liturgies and considerably predates the period when the Jewish *émigrés* from Spain imposed their own liturgical customs on the North African communities. During Solomon of Sijilmasa's day the Almohadic dynasty did unite Spain and parts of North Africa, including Morocco, but both these areas of Jewish settlement, heavily influenced as they no doubt were by Babylon, still maintained a variety of local custom within the larger influence.[91]

This fact partly accounts for the difficulty in assigning the liturgy approved by Maimonides to one or other of the rites generally known from his day. The famous twelfth-century sage was reared and educated in Spain, escaped from persecution there to North Africa, travelled to Palestine and settled, with considerable success, in Cairo. Spiritual leader of the Jewish community there as he was, Rambam may have chosen to champion what was substantially the Egyptian rite as it had by then developed. On the other hand, given his independence of mind, one cannot rule out the possibility that his prayer-book, at least in parts, represents his own eclectic set of prayers.[92] The version of his prayer-book printed in standard editions of his code is so full of omissions, abbreviations and harmonisations with later rites that it simply cannot be relied upon. Once again, however, modern manuscript research comes to the aid of the researcher and an Oxford manuscript provides a text of the first two books of his code with his personal signature authenticating the copy, followed by a version of the prayers apparently added with his approval when it turned out that it would be useful.[93] Although Maimonides himself tells us nothing here about the nature of the rite he is recording, some of the language he uses may be interpreted as a guide to his sources and attitudes. When he wishes to express a clear preference for a particular text he states that 'the rite is as follows'. He is being similarly categorical when he adds to a particular rubric the word 'always' or the phrase 'whether individual or congregation' or, as on one occasion, the phrase 'without omission or addition'. Where there are local customs that he tolerates to a greater or lesser degree, he refers to them as such or as the custom of 'most of the people' or 'some of the people'. There are certainly common features between the Maimonidean version and those of the Babylonians and North Africans earlier mentioned and less evidence of any traces of Palestinian ritual than in those earlier sources. The presence in the Cairo community of his day of a sub-group with its origin in Eretz Yisrael and a commitment to the survival of at least some of its variegated customs was apparently a factor in goading Maimonides towards his preference for the standardised format of the geonim. If it is true, as has been suggested, that Saadya was perhaps one of those less wholeheartedly committed to the rite of the Babylonian establishment, it is not surprising that Maimonides' rite is at variance with his on no small number of occasions. Among examples may be cited the daily *qedushah*, the central benedictions of the sabbath *'amidoth*, and one of the penitential prayers used in the *'amidah* for *Yom Kippur* and other occasions when Maimonides expands on a basic Saadyanic text.[94] The best and most well-known example of his independence of mind was his abolition of the repetition of the *'amidah* because of the lack of decorum associated with it that led to the pointless recitation of benedictions and to Muslim criticism of the synagogue.[95] As with so much of his other work, Maimonides laid down more clearly than most authorities what he thought was right and, as a result, his influence among those looking for clear-cut guidance was that much more pronounced. His authority was accepted in numerous ways throughout the Jewish world but in the liturgical sphere it was particularly central in the development of the Yemenite rite, which will shortly be discussed. As a result of this centrality, that rite may serve and, indeed, before the discovery of the Oxford manuscript, did serve as an important witness to the original prayer-book of Maimonides. Loyal as they were to much of what Maimonides taught them, the Yemenite community preserved the liturgical traditions sanctioned by him and this contributed to their survival when the Sefardi tradition swept all before it after the Expulsion. It may again be noted that Maimonides chooses to treat the whole halakhic topic of *tefillah* in a systematic and comprehensive manner in his code, with what was to his mind a historical introduction, and separately provides a virtually independent text of the prayers, presumably for practical use.[96]

Whether as a reaction against his father's intellectual approach or an extension of his near-mystical drive towards achieving the spirituality of the prophets, the religious philosophy of Abraham Maimonides was a remarkable syncretism of Jewish and Muslim ideas.[97] Developing into a deeper relationship an earlier Jewish fascination with Neoplatonism and flirtations with aspects of Islamic and talmudic mysticism, the spiritual and lay leader of the Jewish community of Egypt in the first third of the thirteenth century fully committed himself to the piety or *ḥasiduth* of the 'way of the Lord' that was the hallmark of the Sufi ascetics who were flourishing in his day. For him the ideals of physical deprivation, isolation and weeping were the means of achieving the spiritual ecstasy of the Hebrew prophets and he envied the Sufis their mastery of what had once been a Jewish experience and wished to restore it to Judaism by emulating their example. Believing, or being incapable of not believing, that such a religious ideology was originally part of the Torah, Moses Maimonides' son and heir borrowed customs from Islam and devoted himself to demonstrating their authentic Jewish pedigree, particularly in his compendium of pietist theory and practice, *Kitāb Kifāyat al-ʿĀbidīn* ('Complete Guide for the Servants of God').[98] This is not to say that Abraham neglected his duties as leader of the community and, indeed, promoter and defender of his father's works and outlook; simply to explain why this was not sufficient for him and that he felt compelled to increase the regularity of Jewish prayer and to reform it in such a way as to bring at least a touch of religious elitism to the ordinary Jewish worshipper.

Clothing his reforms in the language of restoration and ancient tradition, Abraham Maimonides strengthened the preparations for prayer by insisting on feet-washing, ritual ablution after seminal discharge and, in special circumstances, the dusty sackcloth of the penitent. To ensure concentration during prayer he proposed as many as forty prostrations at all major junctures in the statutory prayers, standing in rows and kneeling instead of sitting, always towards the ark containing the scrolls, and the stretching out of hands with upturned palms. Only in the matter of the ritual ablutions and the abolition of the repeated *ʿamidah* did he have serious precedents in geonic or his father's practice; in all other matters, as already pointed out by Naphtali Wieder forty-five years ago, his initiatives were novel and inspired by the Islamic example. It is by no means surprising that they attracted opposition as well as enthusiastic endorsement and that he had to defend himself to the conservative administration of Sultan al-Malik al-ʿAdil (reigned 1200–18) to whom complaints about such innovations had been addressed by his fellow Jews.[99] A group of Jewish mystics led by Abraham and by his colleague, Shelomo He-Ḥasid or Abraham Ibn Abu'l-Rabīʿ, succeeded in establishing what may be called a Jewish pietist movement that had its influence in Egypt, Eretz Yisrael, Syria and Iraq and therefore deserves to be evaluated in the history of Jewish liturgy. Perhaps the most interesting point of immediate note is that there existed a group of such *ḥasidim* in the Near East at almost exactly the same period of Jewish history that saw the successful emergence of the mystics of mediaeval Ashkenaz. It is perfectly valid to see in both movements an attempt, partly inspired by Christian and Muslim example, partly by earlier Jewish trends, to return to prayer as a transcendental experience rather than a requirement of daily observance, with a renewed stress on the intensity of the individual devotion and its consequent efficacy, and to identify on the part of the establishment a suspicion about such esotericism that expressed itself in opposition that was at times violent. It is tempting to equate the effect of the two movements on the later history of the Jewish liturgy, particularly in relation to the emergence and successful encroachments of the

Spanish kabbalah, but one should avoid going beyond the current evidence.[100] Abraham Maimonides' group certainly left vestiges of its ideology on oriental Jewish life until the fifteenth century but only limited aspects of its particular form of pietism had significant backward or forward connection with any similar Jewish tradition. The most that one can say is that although the actual Judaeo-Arabic compositions of Abraham (as well as of his son Obadiah) virtually disappeared from Jewish literature, it had by then been demonstrated that the canonisation and standardisation of so much of the synagogal ritual were not irreversible processes. For the moment it remains an open question whether there was any direct link between the Egyptian Jewish Sufis' attitude to the liturgy and the Spanish and Safed kabbalists' effect on the structure of the Sefardi prayer-book. The German Ḥasidim, on the other hand, as has been demonstrated, left their mark on the Ashkenazi prayer-book in important respects. Their ideology and practices were apparently not so alien to the Jewish tradition as those of Abraham Maimonides and found ways of inveigling themselves into the more standard liturgical customs, particularly since the halakhists were primarily concerned with laying down the general rules in accordance with Tosafist philosophy. The absence of such a strong alternative philosophy in Egypt is perhaps the paradoxical reason why interest and opposition were concentrated on the revolutionary nature of the mystical reforms proposed for the established prayer-book.

While Rambam's son was seeking ways of improving upon his father's liturgical instructions there was apparently a whole community of Jews that regarded them as the ideal guide to the formulation of their prayers and who based their *Tiklal*, as they refer to their *siddur*, on his code and responsa. As with so many of their traditions, the liturgical practices and customs of the Yemenite Jews, surviving today only in Israel, are a fascinating topic for the ethnographer as well as the historian, so fascinating in fact that one must be wary of doing what some nineteenth- and twentieth-century scholars have done in romanticising instead of analysing them. Whatever the community itself says about its own social and cultural origins, whichever pre-modern ideals it appears to have embodied, and however close its Judaeo-Arabic linguistic traditions to those represented in the Genizah documents, theories about its contribution to the history of Jewish liturgy must not be allowed to go beyond the evidence.[101] The earliest prayer-books with the Yemenite rite that are known to us date from no earlier than the fifteenth century, when the majority of equivalent such texts in Europe were already being produced on printing-presses.[102] Within two hundred years of that date, two competing traditions were being promoted in Yemen, the *sha'mi* or Palestinian, influenced by the newly arriving prints and the adoption of the customs, particularly of mystical bent, of the Holy Land and the Spanish *émigrés*, and the *baladi* or local i.e. conservative, defending what its adherents regarded as the more authentic rite of the community.[103] Through the manuscripts of the Cairo Genizah there is the additional information about the close contacts enjoyed by the Jews of Yemen with their sister communities in the major centres of Babylon, Eretz Yisrael and Egypt from the tenth to the thirteenth centuries. The use of the South Arabian coast by traders to India and those prevented by the military and political situation from travelling overland from Egypt to Babylon, the financial support made available by Yemenite congregations to the major centres' talmudic academies, the lack of acquaintance with Palestinian *piyyuṭim*, the prestige enjoyed by the geonim and by Maimonides among the Jews of Yemen, and the punctilious preservation of linguistic traditions known to have flourished in the Babylonian Jewish communities of the Middle Ages – all these factors, taken together with the other evidence mentioned, permit a reconstruction, with a fair degree of accuracy, of the history of the Yemenite prayer-book between the geonic period and the invention of printing.[104] Since the earliest manuscripts are not yet influenced by the fifteenth- and sixteenth-century Sefardi and Palestinian customs, and there is little evidence of immediate pre-Crusader Palestinian input, they can be compared with the versions of Saadya and Maimonides to ascertain whether the common factors are sufficient in number to permit two basic assumptions. The first is that

Yemen not only succumbed to the dominant Babylonian tradition, as did so many other communities, but was closely associated with it rather than with its Palestinian equivalents from at least the time when the earliest prayer-books were formulated. This is not, of course, to say that before the rise of Islam the Yemenite Jewish community did not follow some Palestinian liturgical practices and thereby influence Muḥammad and the formation of early Islamic ideas about prayer. The second assumption is that the help extended by Maimonides to the confused community of Yemen in the matter of its false messiah, taken together with its adoption of his various works and its preference for the clear-cut guidance of a major authority, ensured that the community would see his prayer-book as the most authentic inheritor of the geonic tradition, suitable for substantial incorporation into their own rite.[105] According to Maimonides himself, Saadya exercised a powerful influence on the Yemenite community and this is confirmed by their use of his Judaeo-Arabic translation of the Pentateuch as a verse-by-verse rendering in the synagogue, by their acceptance of the *kol nidrey* formula in spite of Maimonides' omission of it, and by their adoption of a number of his poetic compositions. As pointed out by S. Assaf in his edition of Saadya's prayer-book, there are numerous examples of Saadyanic influence even where they had to survive an alternative view proposed by Maimonides himself. Among these are the recitation of *sefirath ha-ʿomer* in Aramaic, the text of the marriage benedictions and contract, and the expanded *qiddush* for the first night of Passover.[106] The most impressive parallels to the Yemenite rite are, however, found in the manuscript version of Maimonides' prayer-book and each, when taken together with other evidence, assists the scholar in the reconstruction of the other. Some thirty-two examples have been listed by Zion Madmuni in *Yahaduth Teman* and include one version only of *barukh sheʾamar*, the text of the *qedushah*, the method of reciting the priestly benediction, the text of *qaddish*, the removal of only one Torah scroll at a time even when reading is done from two, the structure of the *musaf* prayer, the system of declaiming the *hallel* and the form of the confessionary prayer on *Yom Kippur*.[107] Clearly the evidence is more than enough to warrant the two assumptions earlier made. In addition it should be noted that the removal of shoes, the washing of the hands and the kneeling on the floor are reminiscent of the Islamic influences already mentioned and the close association of the study of talmudic texts and traditions with periods of prayer is a custom that originated in the geonic circles of Babylon. These remarks about the Yemenite rite should not be concluded without mention of the fact that it retained an old custom long abandoned elsewhere. When, in geonic times, it could no longer be assumed that those called to the Torah could read from the scroll, it was permitted to arrange for an expert to read the Torah and those called to it to make the blessing. This became the widespread practice but in Yemen, possibly for serious theological reasons, no such division was made between the reading and the benediction.[108]

Turning now to the Sefardi liturgical tradition, one may be forgiven for making some immediate assumptions about its historical development. Given (as has been pointed out) that it was the Spanish communities of Lucena and Barcelona that sought and obtained the guidance of the geonim Naṭronai and Amram in the matter of prayer-book structure in the ninth and tenth centuries, that it was their Babylonian rite that came to dominate mediaeval Jewish prayer, and that it was the Jewish refugees from the Expulsion who imposed their liturgical customs on almost all the lands to which they were dispersed, it seems reasonable to presuppose that the Sefardi *siddur* acquired its structure in Babylon, maintained that format during the geonic period, the 'golden age' and the centuries of persecution, and was the same rite that was exported after 1492. This view of the Sefardi rite, which essentially characterises it as the most ancient and authentic of all such liturgical forms, is not only simplistic but fails to tally with the evidence of the sources. By way of explanation of these sources, it should first be recalled that the period being discussed is one of some six hundred years during which time Spain was at various stages, Muslim, Christian or divided between these two religious empires. Independent political units stubbornly resisted unification or standardisation, some of them taking pride in their separate identity, others looking southwards to North Africa or northwards to France for various cultural influences.[109] It is not therefore surprising to find these differences reflected in the variety of customs that can be traced among the Jewish communities of Spain during its heyday and much discussion among its authorities as to the correct way forward.[110] Following the Islamic conquest of Spain, contacts between its Jews and their co-religionists in the remainder of the empire naturally strengthened and a particular closeness was effected with the Babylonian academies, with scholars travelling in both directions. Typical is the case of Eleazar ben Samuel Ḥurga of Lucena who made an impact in Babylon in the ninth century.[111] The very fact that the Spanish communities sought guidance from the geonim would appear to indicate a degree of ambivalence about which customs to follow and it is not therefore unlikely, although documentary evidence is lacking, that at this early stage there was some input from the Palestinian community. Some ninety years ago, Moses Gaster already had a sense of such a Palestinian influence on Spain, even if his arguments and evidence do not quite tally with what is here being offered.[112]

Be that as it may, the influence from the ninth to the eleventh century was predominantly geonic and the responsa sent by Naṭronai and Amram set the tone for the adoption of the standard Babylonian formulae with regard to the statutory prayers. There was, of course, also a flourishing of religious Hebrew poetry which left its mark on the local prayer-book but took little account of the Palestinian precedent and its alternative variety in doing so.[113] Such developments were, however, not without their controversial aspects, as documented in the halakhic works of Isaac ben Judah Ibn Ghiyyat of Lucena and Judah ben Barzilai al-Bargeloni of Barcelona, *Halakhoth Ha-Keluloth* and *Ha-'Ittim* respectively. Although both scholars, and especially the former, are anxious generally to promote the Babylonian geonic standard, they nevertheless record the local *minhag* and not infrequently find, especially in the case of the latter, some justification or defence for it. A close reading of Ibn Ghiyyat's composition reveals that in liturgical as well as other matters there were a number of factors that were operating in shaping his decisions. These included the place of geonic instruction as against established local traditions emanating from various other centres, including Eretz Yisrael; the issue of individual versus communal practice; and the pressure from groups anxious to apply criteria of accuracy and consistency to the liturgical texts. The emphasis is on the recording of custom rather than of text but there is a concern to establish the parameters of sabbath and festival prayers, the correct synagogal lectionaries, the antiphonal recitation of *hallel*, the essential nature of benedictions recited over halakhic precepts, and the variety of forms taken on various occasions by the *qedushah desidra*.[114] R. Judah ben Barzilai exhibits a closer interest in the liturgical text itself and a more favourable evaluation of some Spanish customs in spite of his acceptance of an overall geonic domination. By way of examples, he takes a negative line, familiar from the geonim, regarding *piyyuṭim*, the introduction of sabbath elements into Friday afternoon prayers and their corollary on Saturday evenings, and the inclusion of the Song at the Sea (Exodus 15) within the morning psalms and not after their doxology. The abandonment of the public reading of the Aramaic *Targum* in Spanish synagogues elicits the sharp comment that such communities are disloyal to the Torah and that if their services are proving too tiresome they should rather omit their lengthy additions to the basic prayers and homiletical expansions of the biblical readings and reintroduce the more worthy and ancient custom. On the other hand, he recognises the strength of local custom regarding *qiddush* in synagogue on Friday evening, the special *hafṭarah* for a bridegroom, and the *yishtabaḥ* devotion to be recited during the cantorial *barekhu*, claiming that whatever the logic of one's own opinion 'one lacks the power to displace customs that have been adopted by a majority of Jewish communities'.[115]

Like the other rites that have already been discussed, then, the Sefardi rite took its general form from Babylon and left itself scope for the independent development of details. As the *reconqista* by the Christians chalked up its successes from the twelfth to the fifteenth century and the Babylonian centres declined into insignificance, so the numerous Spanish communities extended that development and many of them acquired their own liturgical identities, depending on the new influences that were then prevalent. Communities to the north east, such as those of Catalonia, were affected by religious and cultural developments in Provence and France while those of the south, in Granada and Andalusia, were closer to their North African cousins. The Jewish populations of Castile and Aragon, which had consisted of large numbers, had flourished culturally, and had enjoyed considerable influence, were particularly affected by the newly expanding Christian persecution and intolerance. Such an atmosphere of uncertainty and vulnerability to the latest trends, was bound to produce controversy, the blossoming of mystical traditions and the composition of new forms of literature. In the field of liturgy, it is unfortunate that Spanish manuscripts have generally not survived from earlier than the fourteenth century and that there is consequently a lack of prayer-book texts from the period of the Christian conquest that can clearly be identified as belonging to the rites of one of these geographical or intellectual groupings.[116] Given the later history of the Jews of Spain this is perhaps not surprising. It is, however, possible to be sure that such groups were taking account of various rites and were not united in their liturgical practice on the basis of the evidence preserved in a number of important thirteenth- and fourteenth-century works. Some of these emanated from Provence and have already been mentioned earlier in this chapter in the context of the Jewish cultural interplay between that area, France and Spain. The remainder, too, were clearly influenced by what was happening in other Jewish communities and their attempts to create order and offer guidance are proof of the contemporary confusion and varied input.

A leading figure in this connection was Judah ben Yaqar who was born in Provence in the middle of the twelfth century but studied in France and then raised disciples in Barcelona, among them the famous Naḥmanides. As his systematic liturgical commentary makes clear, he was acquainted with numerous customs in France, Germany and within various Spanish kingdoms and not only expressed views on such texts but also commented extensively on their biblical and rabbinic sources as well as their literal, philosophical and mystical sense.[117] What is here being viewed is a parallel development to that taking place in the Provençal, French and German communities to the north, especially significant with regard to the incorporation of kabbalistic ideas into Sefardi tradition and liturgy through the Gerona school of mystics and the efforts of Naḥmanides himself. The manner in which such ideas infiltrated the prayers at this early stage and the degree to which they did so before and after the dissemination of the Zohar is yet to be adequately researched but it may be stated with confidence that while in the Ashkenazi communities the halakhic took control of the mystical tradition, the situation in the Sefardi communities was a more delicately balanced affair until the Expulsion, and afterwards even reflected a reverse control.[118] Thirteenth-century liturgical and mystical progress in Spain may be charted in the halakhic responsa of Solomon ben Abraham Adret who, according to Scholem, 'although . . . very cautious in his dealings with kabbalistic matters . . . often alluded to them in his commentary to the *aggadot* . . . and . . . composed a long prayer in the kabbalistic way' and whose pupils, in Scholem's words 'assigned a central place to the Kabbalah'.[119] Adret takes a strong line against the attempted reintroduction of the recitation of the Ten Commandments in the morning prayers and is critical of gossiping and of gathering in the courtyard outside the synagogue during the services but demonstrates a fairly tolerant attitude to the variety of rites and customs that he has encountered around Spain, whether in the matter of the recitation of the *shema*ʿ quietly or aloud, the repetition of the ʿ*amidah* in the evening service or the addition of *piyyuṭim* in honour of a wedding or circumcision. He summarises his position as follows: 'As regards the customary order that you follow in liturgical matters, no two places follow precisely the same practice. Consequently, I cannot agree with the view expressed to you that the omission to which you refer is critical and constitutes a failure to adhere to the statutory format established by the talmudic rabbis.'[120]

Another halakhic work that devotes a substantial section to the prayers, their value, their sources, their form in his community and their interpretation is the *Menorath Ha-Ma'or* by Israel al-Nakawa of Toledo, who is content, at the end of the fourteenth century, to cite statements from the Zohar, albeit by a different title. As he himself indicates in the introduction, where he sets his own efforts in the context of historical attempts to solve similar problems, the inspiration for the work came from the contemporary lack of knowledge and religious guidance, and the persecution of the Jews was also no doubt a factor in creating a need for it.[121] Similar considerations must have played a part in inducing David ben Joseph Abudraham to write his full liturgical commentary in Seville in 1340 and thereby to influence the future direction of Sefardi liturgy as well as reflecting its contemporary confusion.[122] Abudraham pays close attention to the text and interpretation of all the daily, sabbath, monthly, festival and fast-day prayers as well as providing guidance on lectionaries and the calendar and an extensive treatise on the various kinds of benedictions. Taking his immediate lead from predecessors such as Judah ben Yaqar and making use of all the major liturgical authorities, Abudraham justifies his work by reference to the current liturgical situation. 'Lengthy exile and intensive persecution,' he writes, 'have led to a variety of customs in different kingdoms so that most ordinary folk, when they offer their prayers to God, are totally in the dark about their meaning and have no idea about the sense and structure of liturgical practices.'[123] Aware as he was of the rituals of Spain, France, Provence and Germany, he was able to evaluate these and provide an important textbook that was destined to be printed many times after its initial appearance in Lisbon in 1490.[124] Before attempting to summarise the final developments in Spanish Jewry's last century before the Expulsion, this chapter should also briefly note the halakhic authority, Isaac ben Shesheth Perfet (*Ribash*) of Barcelona and Algiers who resisted the growing influence of the kabbalah and whose responsa reflect the customs and controversies of Spain and North Africa. He mentions the practices of Catalonia, Aragon and Castile, for instance, on the matter of the repetition of the ʿ*amidah*, contrasts the new custom of reciting *barekhu* at the end of the prayers with the older custom in Barcelona not to do so, offers no objection to calling numerous congregants to the Torah on *Simḥath Torah* and in the case of the use of the verse in Leviticus 16:30 in the ʿ*avodah* service on the Day of Atonement sets out the 'biblicist' argument for citing all last three words of the verse, as in the text, as against the 'historicist' claim that the High Priest's original words in the Temple should be the paradigm.[125]

By way of summary, then, it may be stated that the two major influences on the Sefardi liturgical tradition were the geonic responsa in the early part of its history and the kabbalistic ideology and practice as the community reached the apogee of its misfortunes but that throughout their existence Sefardi Jews maintained a variety of rites and customs. It was only after they left the land that had been host to them for some six hundred years that they eventually opted for a more unified form of liturgy that allowed mysticism a more central role than ever before, not only for their own reconstituted communities but also for the many others which they came to dominate. An examination of prayer-books from the fourteenth and fifteenth centuries reveals the earliest effects of Spanish kabbalistic teachings on the Sefardi prayer-book and justifies the conclusion that wherever the earliest origins of these teachings, whether in the Palestinian or Byzantine communities, and however the ideas of the mystics of talmudic times had been preserved, whether among particular groups of rabbinic Jews or outside their immediate circles, they ultimately came to be championed by those who had to find new homes after the catastrophic events of the famous year of 1492. The liturgical history of the subsequent three and a half centuries was destined to be substantially affected by that and similar Jewish migrations, by the manner in which kabbalah came to be absorbed into the popular prayer-book, and by the invention and widespread adoption of the printing process. Such developments, which begin with the fifteenth-century texts of the Sefardi and Ashkenazi communities and end with hints of the earliest efforts to match the Jewish prayer-book with the social and intellectual ideologies of Europe after the French Revolution, form the subject of the next chapter.

CHAPTER 7

From printed prayers to the spread of pietistic ones

As with the remainder of the book, the purpose of this chapter is not to offer a detailed history of the individual prayers that make up the Jewish liturgy of today but to offer a general survey of liturgical developments that takes account of changing circumstances and outlooks, as well as of ongoing tensions, and thereby facilitates the process of understanding, more than has hitherto been possible, what is likely to have emerged when, and why. In order to be accurate and reliable, however, general surveys have to be based on particular details, however briefly presented, and it is with this in mind that the initial section of the current chapter offers some remarks about the specific accretions to the prayer-book that had occurred between the late geonic period and the first century of printing, without becoming involved in their intricate evolution. By examining such accretions and attempting to explain the overall theory behind the devotional practice, these remarks should clarify the nature of the starting-point from which the fifteenth- and sixteenth-century *siddurim* set out on their typographical odyssey and should thus set the tone for subsequent sections of the chapter in which demography, printing and mysticism dominate the description and analysis of developments before the Jewish emancipation and enlightenment.

A singularly intriguing set of prayers are those that came to function as introductory, concluding or parenthetical items during the period under discussion, and among them are to be counted *ʿaleynu* and *qaddish*, *mah ṭovu* and *wayehi binesoaʿ*, *ʾadon ʿolam* and *yigdal*, and *shir ha-yiḥud* and *shir ha-kavod*.[1] The first point to be made in connection with such additions is that the practice of surrounding the statutory prayers with what are originally optional extras is not a novel one and has been encountered in earlier periods. It will be recalled that the recitation of selections from Psalms as in *hallel* and *pesuqey dezimra*, the declaration *barekhu*, the reading of the Song at the Sea from Exodus 15 and the termination of the *'amidah* with specific personal requests, were all originally in the nature of liturgical material designed to prepare the worshipper for more central prayers and benedictions.[2] The process of their absorption into the standard liturgy had, however, apparently altered their erstwhile function and accorded them a more dignified status, leaving the secondary role vacant for a variety of newcomers to occupy. It would appear that there was always the need for groups of passages that could be regarded with a lesser degree of seriousness, perhaps so that closer and greater attention could be paid to what was regarded as of more major significance. The theory being propounded is that the bestowal of authority on the total structure of a rite created the need for the introduction of fresh compositions that would not disturb the essential liturgical requirements of the *halakhah* but would somehow protect it (much as the concept of *seyag la-torah* forbad peripheral activities to protect the essential religious law),[3] while at the same time setting the worshipper on the correct path towards devotion. An additional support for such a theory may be found in the fact that certain prayers were recruited for the secondary purpose even if their original function had been a more primary one, thus giving the impression of an authentic need that had to be fulfilled. Two such prayers are the *'aleynu* and the *qaddish*.

Much as its language, history and content have been carefully and consistently studied, no clear picture has yet emerged of the original provenance of the *'aleynu* prayer. Its earliest documented place in the Jewish liturgy is in the section dealing with God's kingship in the *musaf* service for the New Year and its style is such that it fits well with the numerous other Hebrew prayers, the simple, neatly balanced and direct expressions of which characterise them as belonging to the first centuries of the Christian era, if not to the end of the Second Temple period. Various traditions ascribe it to Joshua in biblical times, to the Men of the Great Assembly in the post-exilic era, and to the third-century Babylonian teacher, Rav, but the stress on God's universal dominion and Israel's special mission is not exclusively associated with one particular part of Jewish history and the problem of dating remains.[4] What concerns us here are its peregrinations in the history of Jewish prayer. First as a New Year prayer, then incorporated into the *Yom Kippur* liturgy, also to be found in the singular form *'alay leshabeaḥ* among the *hekhaloth* texts of the Jewish mystics, and ultimately in use as the concluding prayer *par excellence* of late mediaeval manuscripts and the earliest printed prayer-books, this poetic composition clearly moved from a highly specialised to a more general use. That its content makes it eminently suitable for such a purpose is beyond question; what remains to be explained is why such a change came about from about the twelfth to the fourteenth century, at precisely the time that most of the rites were acquiring their authoritative format. A common theory refers to the twelfth-century report of Ephraim of Bonn that mentions the use of *'aleynu* as the final prayer of the Jewish martyrs of the north-central French town of Blois massacred as a result of a blood libel in 1171 and its consequent adoption as a daily hymn,[5] but such tendencies to see all Jewish liturgical developments as the result of persecution are not historically convincing, especially since the more general usage seems to have predated the massacre. The censorship of the prayer, which will be discussed later in this chapter,[6] is also cited as a reason for its growing popularity but, again, there may in such explanations be a confusion of cause and effect. The impetus may have lain, as has been suggested, in the need for formal conclusions to match what had come to be regarded as the formal body of the liturgical text.

Such structuralisation would also require a recurrent theme, ideally of a doxological nature, that would set apart one section of the liturgy from another, particularly when the text had expanded from its original *shema'* and *'amidah* into a whole set of biblical and talmudic readings, *piyyuṭim* of various types, and special entreaties. The *qaddish* ultimately came to serve in such a capacity, being used in its various shorter and longer forms to mark pauses between sections as well as their final conclusions. Originally associated with the rabbinical academy and the study session, the *qaddish* was still being used in the early Middle Ages, even indeed as late as Maimonides, for calling down special blessings on leading rabbinic figures, by which time it had also acquired a synagogal function as a communal doxology to be recited only in the presence of ten males (*minyan*). With the addition of a variety of alternative verses, in both Hebrew and Aramaic, it could take on different forms and these were again ideal for overtures and finales, as well as for marking intermissions.[7] The point may here be made that the formalisation of each of the rites in the late mediaeval period left the problem of what to do with the variant texts of a number of the prayers that had, apparently, previously existed as valid alternatives. The solution to such a problem was to accord each of them a unique function in a specific set of liturgical circumstances. By way of example, each of the various textual forms of the *qedushah* used in the repetition of the *ʿamidah* tended to be assigned within each of the rites to a particular occasion, thus ensuring the survival of all or most of the versions. In the case in hand, the basic form of the original *qaddish* was set to mark pauses; a longer text was used to conclude the *ʿamidah*; one remained in association with study and another with the burial service; and, ultimately, a particular text was assigned to the mourner. It would appear that this usage, contrary to what is popularly thought, is the latest and least closely linked with the original nature of the prayer, as will be noted when texts relating to death are discussed below.[8] In the mean time, the point has again been made that a specific change of function for one prayer is indicative of an overall alteration in the nature and purpose of a formal set of prayers.

The use of biblical Hebrew chapters, passages, verses and expressions, is a trend that runs through the whole of Jewish liturgical history, at times amounting to an illustration of the nature of a special day or event by reference to its biblical precedent, at others involving the recitation of psalms or of sections for edification or study[9] and on occasion consisting of the introduction of no more than a few verses. It is this last-mentioned phenomenon that is of particular interest in the present context of a discussion of the supplements to the *siddur* that characterise the period up to and including the invention of printing. The first point to be made in this connection is that although there is little consistency in the precise choice of verses, there is a clear tendency towards the insertion of a number of Psalm verses at the beginning of the prayer-book, ostensibly for the worshipper to recite on his entry into the synagogue. Among these are to be found Numbers 24:5, Psalms 5:8, 26:8, 55:15, 69:14 and 95:6. Similarly, the removal and return of the scroll in connection with its formal reading, attracted to itself a growing number of biblical verses, some of which do not yet even appear in the early printed prayer-books. The most common of these on a weekday are Numbers 10:35, Isaiah 2:3 before the lectionary and Psalms 148:13–14 and Numbers 10:36 after it, and in this case it is interesting to note that there appear to have been verses attached (not without controversy) to this ceremony on the sabbath at an earlier stage than that during which a number of them began to be used on a weekday, and that the sabbath custom came to influence that of the weekday.[10] It should also perhaps be noted at this point that verses continued to be added to the scroll ceremony during the centuries following the invention of printing and that the conclusion of the morning service also attracted to itself the addition of such verses as Psalms 5:9 and, again at a later date, such passages as the Binding of Isaac (Genesis 22), Gift of the Manna (Exodus 16) and Decalogue (Exodus 20).[11]

Before assessing the significance of such developments, it will be necessary to take account of non-biblical additions too. The late manuscripts and the early printed prayer-books include in their introductory pages a selection of such poems as *'adon 'olam*, *yigdal*, and compositions by Solomon Ibn Gabirol.[12] The first of these, with no clearly established author, entered the Ashkenazi liturgy in about the fourteenth century and came to be used at the beginning and end of various prayer sessions among a variety of Jewish communities. It praises God's eternity and unity and expresses man's trust in Him and its contents vary in the different rites. There is also some doubt about the origins of the second poem, *yigdal*, a lyrical version of Maimonides' thirteen principles of faith, although the dominant view would now appear to be that it was composed in fourteenth-century Italy, probably by Daniel ben Judah of Rome. Once again, having entered into the liturgy, it became a popular hymn used to introduce and conclude the statutory prayers in the various rites. The most common introductory poems among the Sefardim of the fourteenth and fifteenth centuries would appear to have been those of Ibn Gabirol and frequent use was made of compositions that he created for specific liturgical occasions. While these poems may be described as having common factors with the Hebrew poetry of Spain as regards their language, content, metre and rhyme, two other poems that also entered the liturgy at about the same time are of a rather different nature. *Shir ha-kavod* and *shir ha-yiḥud* are both anonymous and appear to originate in the Ashkenazi mystical circles of the twelfth century, the former, a short alphabetical acrostic of thirty-one lines, possibly the work of Judah ben Samuel and the latter, a long poem of over 400 lines divided into double sets of rhyming couplets, perhaps from the pen of his father, Samuel ben Qalonymus. The shorter poem is designed to describe the nature of God's glory in highly figurative and allusive language while the longer piece, more closely related to the philosophical notions such as occur in Saadya's *Beliefs and Opinions*, sets out to express the inscrutability of God's power and the insignificance of man's praises.[13] Again, there is controversy among the authorities concerning the appropriateness of these poems for daily as well as sabbath use and some overall objections to their inclusion in the liturgy. Where they are included, they appear at the beginning or end of a service, in the case of the sabbath either early or late in *shaḥarith* or late in *musaf*. In spite of the spread of all these four poems into various liturgies, it should be noted that their acceptance was not without a struggle. Interestingly enough, one of Polish Jewry's leading rabbis in the sixteenth century, Solomon Luria, took an independent line in the matter of *shir ha-yiḥud*, as he did in so much else, and forbad its recitation when he held rabbinic office in Lwow and Lublin, arguing that it was composed by a heretic. He also objected to the verse from Numbers 24:5 on the strange basis that it was recited by the non-Jewish prophet Balaam![14] Ḥasidic groups rejected *shir ha-kavod* and *yigdal*, Sefardim did not incorporate the former in their standard prayer-books, and the *shir ha-yiḥud* tended to be too long for universal acceptance. B. S. Jacobson argues that the custom of inviting a young boy to lead the congregation in the singing of *shir ha-kavod* is not only pedagogically motivated but also demonstrates the spiritual purity of the poem by choosing a spiritually pure child to declaim it.[15] It is more likely that here, as in other cases such as the drinking of the *qiddush* wine in the synagogue on a Friday evening, a youngster substitutes for an adult because of an intrinsic difficulty about a custom and thereby mitigates any serious objection on the part of the congregation.

A short pause in this coverage of the liturgical newcomers is now in order so that stock can be taken of the various factors at work in their introduction and general acceptance into the prayer-book. While the need for what may perhaps be characterised as peripheral material has been acknowledged and discussed, this can in no way represent the whole story and, as with all texts that stand at the centre of religious usage, there are diverse reasons to be sought for dynamic developments. Even in the case of the peripheral material, the explanation for its being accorded a less than central place in the liturgy may lie as much in the desire for a control mechanism as in the need for the provision of such material. Differently expressed, what is happening is that such secondary compositions are indeed required but the reason why certain interlopers are given such a task is because some authorities are determined that they should never advance beyond this level of importance. Solomon Luria, however he may have argued, was probably not enamoured of kabbalistic insertions or of too many addenda and the ultimate compromise reached by other authorities was to limit their number and restrict their status. Not that they often say so in direct terms; their arguments are expressed positively and usually designed to demonstrate how particularly suitable the controversial prayer is for the specific purpose they are suggesting. Nevertheless, they amount in effect to the expression of doubts and the suggestion of compromise. At times, of course, a downright rejection is expressed and the attribution of authorship to one who is for one reason or another a religiously unsavoury character supports the critic's unfavourable evaluation.

What, then, may be other possible reasons for the innovations earlier listed? There is no doubt that the growing but still fairly unripe influence of kabbalah is to be taken into account in the matter of such poems of the type emanating from the Ashkenazi mystics, as has been indicated in the previous chapter, and the gradual maturing of this process will receive further attention later in this chapter.[16] There is, however, the additional point to be made that poems are entering the liturgy that are independent of the statutory texts and constitute self-contained compositions devoted to specific theological statements that could conceivably belong anywhere, or nowhere, in the fixed liturgy. Whether the treatment is a mystical one or of more philosophical bent, it seems to vary from that of the many *piyyuṭim* that had found their way into the very body of the liturgy during the geonic and early mediaeval periods. The history of Hebrew poetry and its special relationship with the liturgy is a topic that is dealt with elsewhere and by others. It is, however, necessary in this context to note that the poems of Ashkenazi, Sefardi and Italian circles of the thirteenth to the sixteenth centuries, as their equivalents in Greece, Turkey, Yemen and North Africa, often developed independently of synagogal prayer and only few of them ultimately won a place therein.[17] Those that did are consequently doubly interesting since they reflect what is essentially an external creation more likely to be subject to the dominant thought patterns of their day than the highly stylised *piyyuṭim* of earlier times. In the cases noted above, it is not only kabbalah that is represented. *Yigdal* and *'adon 'olam* may justifiably be regarded as hymns of an almost catechismal nature and, whatever their original provenance actually was, their growing popularity may not be unrelated to the intellectual and theological developments of the Reformation and the Renaissance. It remains to be proved that the expansion in the use of the Hebrew Bible is sufficiently different from earlier trends to warrant independent explanation. If it does indeed turn out to be so, it may also have links with the return to the text of the Old Testament that was an important theme in the dominant religious culture of the day, but the suggestion is at present no more than speculative.

Hardly speculative is the claim that the nature of Jewish prayer and the structure of the synagogue in which it was communally conducted have always exercised mutual influences. While in the early mediaeval period circumstances prevented any significant architectural developments and the Jewish place of worship remained a simple affair, the 'encounter between Jewish tradition and mediaeval architectural concepts, particularly the Romanesque and Gothic ideas of space distribution, did, however, produce a specific architecture in the restricted meaning of the term, in so far as it related to space-form'.[18] The builders who erected the Moorish structures of Spain and the grand cathedrals of more northerly parts that also ultimately influenced the Iberian peninsula were the same craftsmen employed to build synagogues and decorate them. As more latitude was offered by the gentile authorities and sanctioned by most of the rabbis, so the styles of synagogues became more elaborate and absorbed at least some limited aspects of the grandeur of their neighbours' houses of worship. Add to this physical development the institutional emergence of rabbis, cantors and other synagogue officials during this post-mediaeval and pre-modern period and you understand better the increasing stress on formality and ceremonial and the need for a more intricate set of prayers to accompany and embody them. This is not to say that there were not earlier representatives of Jewish liturgical formality, as certainly in the Temple, the Hellenistic synagogue and the stately rituals of the Babylonian geonate, but to argue that some epochs encouraged them more than others and that when they emerged they often did so hand-in-hand with changes in the form of communal expression. In the period being discussed, then, it is not surprising that the need for mosaics and murals, for double naves and for biblical motifs had its parallels in the encouragement of additional hymns, doxologies and scriptural quotations. It may not be coincidental that the externally modest, internally ornate and culturally symbiotic is as characteristic of Italian Renaissance prayer-books as it is of their synagogues.[19]

A brief word is here relevant about yet another swing in the Jewish liturgical pendulum from the locally exclusive to the globally standard. Just as the various rites had responded to the virtual disappearance of the two dominant traditions of Palestine and Babylon by evolving their own versions of Jewish standard prayer, so did the growing interchange of ideas, improved communications and dissemination of authoritative, halakhic tracts ensure that islands of liturgical uniqueness were soon colonised by champions of ritual conformity. Statements by Ashkenazi talmudists were taken seriously by Sefardi liturgists and the mystical traditions of each group influenced the other. The effects of demographical change, the printed book and the spread of kabbalah were also of a universal rather than parochial nature, as will shortly be argued, but a few remarks first have to be made about two other sets of prayers that stem from the period under discussion.

Bearing in mind that it was the fate of personal prayer of the biblical and talmudic type to become the basis for Jewish communal worship in the later periods, the researcher should not be surprised to find that new niches had to be found for the expression of immediate individual or local feelings in the now dominant synagogal context of the Middle Ages. Not that it was felt that private entreaty was inappropriate or likely to be ineffectual; simply that the stress on the importance of communal prayer left the distinct impression that the chances of success were best in that context. The presence of the Torah scroll among the worshippers came to be regarded as particularly auspicious, the reading process steadily moving out of its sphere of the educational and into the realm of the ceremonial. The post-geonic period thus saw the development of a number of prayers that were to be recited after the pentateuchal (and prophetic, where applicable) readings and before the return of the scroll to the ark and, at a later date and in some rites, even after each person was called to the reading. One class of such special entreaties called for the divine blessing on leading figures within the community or beyond it, on particular groups of Jews, on those with special problems or celebrations, or simply on individuals, and there is much scope for the socio-historical study of such texts, revealing as they do, at least when they were first introduced, the overriding concerns of the congregation that adopted and promoted them. Even a casual glance at their form immediately reveals that one of them, *yequm purqan*, composed in Aramaic, is for the benefit of the teachers, students and academies of Babylon and the Land of Israel, and the logical assumption to be made, as has indeed been made by many scholars, is that this goes back to the geonic period.[20] Since, however, it is preserved only in the Ashkenazi rite as inherited from its North French predecessor, cannot be traced before the twelfth century, and is not of the same type as the blessings referred to by the earlier sources, it is possible that it was initially composed as an expression of support for the ideals of Torah scholarship championed in the two great centres when they were already in a state of crisis and decline. The writer has argued elsewhere that the use of Aramaic may have been a device for identifying with and continuing that scholarship, as its use in unnecessary and unexpected contexts such as *'aqdamuth* and *'ilu finu* would appear to indicate.[21]

From about the same date, Hebrew benedictions, usually beginning *miy sheberakh*, made their appearance in liturgies of the various rites and in the discussion of them by halakhic authorities. Many of these have been collected in a most interesting study by A. Yaari and reflect the virtues that local synagogal leaders most wished to encourage. Hearty blessings are, as expected, invoked on those who attend synagogal prayer regularly and punctually, take upon themselves extra fast-days, participate in the study of Torah and support charitable causes. What is more fascinating is that the community also offers its prayers on behalf of those who undertake communal tasks, especially with regard to burial, congregants who do not disturb the services with idle chatter, women who donate their handiwork for religious purposes, and those who abstain from drinking non-Jewish wine.[22] Belonging to the same genre of liturgical composition are the prayers on behalf of the local non-Jewish rulers that are already to be found among Genizah material dating from the eleventh and twelfth centuries. It has become customary among those writing in general terms about such customs to point to the exhortation in Jeremiah 29:7 and to such talmudic passages as Mishnah *'Avoth* 3.2, Tosefta *Sukkah* 4 and BT *Yoma* f. 69a in support of the antiquity of Jewish respect for royalty and interest in its preservation. There is, however, more than an element of the apologetic in such claims, the evidence for such formal and regular prayers dating back no earlier than the Middle Ages, at first in general terms such as in the Genizah texts, subsequently in the *miy sheberakh* style found in manuscripts, and later, from the mid-sixteenth century, in a particular formulation commencing with the phrase from Psalms 144:10, *ha-nothen teshu'ah*.[23] There is no doubt that in the Middle Ages the Jews were heavily dependent on the king as controller of their destiny. Standing outside the church, nobility and serfdom, they were his *servi camerae*, the king's private property as it were, and they consequently had more than a passing interest in his survival and prosperity. As the modern period dawned in Europe, migrating Jews were still dependent on the goodwill of governments. This blessing is, then, a response to a special political need rather than the expression of a theological principle and there are indications in the wording of *ha-nothen teshu'ah* that the veiled emphasis is on God's supreme power and on the Davidic kingdom rather than on their temporal equivalents.[24] As with all the examples of the genre, the time of its recitation varies from rite to rite, with the most popular occasions being sabbaths and festivals, but it should be noted that the presence of a scroll on a Monday and Thursday was also made the occasion of a special prayer very much based on talmudic style and entitled *yehi raṣon*, requesting Temple restoration, an end to public disasters, successful Torah-study, and good news culminating in a return to the Holy Land.[25]

It is generally assumed that the central place given to

suffering, death and resurrection in the theology and consequently the liturgy of Christianity has no parallel in rabbinic Judaism. It is nevertheless an intriguing fact that however low-key the treatment of such subjects in the talmudic and geonic periods, there appears to have been an intensification of interest, at first in Franco-Germany, then in the remainder of Europe and later among the oriental communities, starting perhaps as early as the eleventh century. A responsum cited in the name of Hai Gaon declares that whatever entreaties are made and charity performed for the sake of the dead, it is only their own merits that stand to their credit, and the best possibility is that their punishment might be mitigated. This cautious expression of opinion on the part of Hai is also recorded in the name of the geonim Sherira and Nissim, thus indicating doubts on the part of such authorities that such customs should be sanctioned.[26] That they nevertheless developed into formal communal prayers is clear from the practice recorded as early as the thirteenth century to mention lists of the dead each sabbath (*hazkarath neshamoth* or *mazkir* or *yizkor*), an act of memorial that was probably linked initially to the martyrs of the Crusader massacres, subsequently took on a more individual reference, and ultimately came to be performed in Ashkenazi circles on the three pilgrim festivals and *Yom Kippur*, in Italian communities on the last day of Passover, and among the Sefardim on *Yom Kippur* eve (*hashkavah*). There was also a custom of pledging charitable support for the poor of Eretz Yisrael on such occasions and attempts have been made to link the two, either by arguing that the gifts were intended as a way of building merit for the dead who were being remembered or by suggesting the opposite chronology, namely, that these occasions were chosen for the memorial prayers because of their prior association with charity. The order of developments remains unclear but there is no doubt that a number of liturgical customs concerning the dead are to be traced back to the same period following the Crusades. The prayer *'av ha-raḥamim* was composed in memory of the Jewish victims of the Rhineland massacres during the First Crusade and seeks remembrance of the idealised martyrs and vengeance on their murderers. It naturally suffered considerably at the hands of the censors but survived in the Ashkenazi liturgy, variously recited every sabbath, on most sabbaths, on two sabbaths in the year, and together with *hazkarath neshamoth*.[27]

Whether such prayers, which certainly grew in importance among the ordinary worshippers over the centuries, whatever their formal status in Jewish theology, had their origin in earlier Jewish tradition or, as may be suspected, constituted a Jewish version of mourning practices performed in the more general Christian environment, as Petuchowski has briefly suggested, remains to be researched in a satisfactory way. The one custom that has received much attention from scholars and may fairly be described as the most successful of all the mediaeval innovations dealing with the liturgy of the living in connection with the dead is the recitation of the *qaddish* by the son of the deceased for eleven months after the bereavement and on its anniversary in the Jewish calendar each year thereafter. Granted that the idea of marking an annual day of memorial for at least a distinguished person goes back to earliest times, the use of *qaddish* as a mourner's prayer is no earlier than the first half of the twelfth century and post-dates the change of usage of the prayer earlier referred to in this chapter. There is no definitive explanation of how the custom arose but the latest thinking, as represented by the view of Israel Ta-Shema, is that it represents a weakened and more easily followed version of the original requirement for such a mourner to lead the congregation in prayer, especially on Saturday evening, when the end of the sabbath signalled the return of the soul to its purification process. Leading the prayers involved the recitation of *qaddish* before *barekhu* but those who were unable to undertake the whole task eventually recited only *qaddish* which was later moved to an independent place at the end of the service for the mourner as such. The attempts at explaining the phenomenon as a special prayer for the dead have no evidence in support, the growing mystical beliefs about the fate of the soul inspiring the interest in a special act of piety but not specifically in the recitation of what is essentially, as earlier explained, an unrelated doxology.[28]

It will now be necessary to make some general remarks about the change in the status of the prayer-book as it evolved from the composition that was offered to interested Jewish communities by individual geonic authorities to the printed texts that were widely circulated by many publishing houses in the century or two after the invention of printing. As has earlier been demonstrated, the *siddur* was a novelty for the period of its early existence with a standing that hardly compared with the authority of the Hebrew Bible, the talmudic corpus and the multiplying cells of tradition that they were propagating. It existed as a text suggested by an authority, sometimes with brief guidelines about the nature and purpose of prayer, and expressions of opinion about the alternative texts available or rejected.[29] Gradually, however, a whole set of secondary liturgical literature appears among the manuscripts of the late mediaeval period, and this goes beyond the halakhic dimension. Legal codes do deal with the general and detailed structure of the prayers but the *siddur* also attracts to itself the kind of attention previously reserved for what one might call the more central works of Jewish literature. Commentaries came to be written on the texts of the prayers and of the more standard liturgical poems that accompanied them, each of them tending to concentrate on a particular aspect of their significance. Some commentators were anxious to ensure that a text sanctioned by tradition survived while others felt that the yardstick for the formulation of its Hebrew vocabulary, grammar and vocalisation should be that of what was becoming, or had become, the standard form of the Hebrew Bible. A kind of *masorah* attached itself in the form of rubrics to some texts while the philosophers and theologians (if the two can genuinely be distinguished) took to supporting and promoting their ideas by reference to the contents of the Jewish communal worship and the mystics stressed the importance of every word and letter for their theosophical and cosmic notions. Benedictions that still belonged to the realm of individual duty and piety were given a place in the prayer-book and, once ensconced, enjoyed the same ritualisation as that undergone by more communally based liturgies. It even became possible for commentators on biblical and talmudic texts to cite words and phrases from the *siddur* as such by way of illustration of the point being made.[30] The conclusion is inescapable that what had begun its life as the oral expression of individuals in praise of God and had been given a formal, textual structure by the geonim, was at this later stage becoming transformed into an authoritative representative of classical Jewish writings, for some even a sacred text of sorts. How else can one explain the features of an increasing interest in translation within the community and in censorship from outside it? Those who went to the considerable trouble of utilising Jewish versions of the local French, German and Italian vernaculars to compose translations of the prayers clearly felt that their exercise was a worthwhile one for those, among them no doubt women, youngsters and less Hebraically educated men, who were linguistically denied access to what they must have regarded as one of Judaism's spiritual jewels. And, as in the nature of popularisation, translation in the fourteenth century gave way to paraphrase two centuries later.[31] Also for the gentiles anxious to mount attacks on Judaism, the prayer-book represented an important target and when censorship became one of the tools of suppression and persecution the liturgical texts suffered accordingly. Whether such aggressors were apostates from Judaism or priests well versed in the mother religion's rabbinic form, they looked upon the *siddur* as central enough to its theory and practice to merit their detrimental attention.[32]

Mention has just been made of the need to satisfy an interest and involvement on the part of women and, this point having been raised, the opportunity should here be taken of dealing briefly with Jewish liturgical developments regarding the female sex in the late mediaeval Ashkenazi world. After all, this is the world that produced the definitive tenth-century decree, attributed to Gershom ben Judah of Mainz, 'the Light of the Exile' (= *Me'or Ha-Golah*), that formally forbad Jewish polygyny and protected the Jewish wife from divorce against her will within the communities living under Christian hegemony. The question therefore may legitimately be raised whether there was a change in the role of women in Jewish communal worship from that played in earlier periods. It will be recalled that evidence exists for some participation by women in some aspects of the ancient Hebrew cult and in Jewish acts of public worship during the late Second Temple period, and for serious discussion by the talmudic rabbis about women's involvement in the public reading of Scripture and in the study of Torah. It was also suggested that the synagogal arrangements that applied in the diaspora may have encouraged a more active role on the part of women and that it can by no means be taken for granted that Jewish prayer meetings were always segregated.[33] The whole matter of the relative degrees of participation in Jewish worship by men and women through the ages is one that has only recently begun to receive the serious and detailed scholarly attention that it deserves.[34] Unfortunately the more general task here in hand is itself so vast that such topics can only be touched upon but even such a brief mention may be useful in pointing out the direction that future research should take.

As has just been noted, the talmudic rabbis were somewhat concerned about the formal status of women with regard to Torah in the public and communal contexts then being developed but their concern about their equivalent position in the matter of public prayer was considerably less. The reason for this may be that they recognised clearly and unequivocally the woman's obligation to pray but the whole process of formalisation and structuralisation of congregational prayer with its creation of an authoritative text and legally sanctioned means for its public recitation was a product of the geonic rather than the talmudic period. That period, as has been demonstrated, was dominated by the *yeshivoth* of Babylon more than by any other influence and in that environment, perhaps also because of the Islamic cultural context in which it flourished, there appears to have been a singularly male-dominated establishment that controlled the development of Jewish communal prayer. It is not then surprising to find limited interest on the part of the geonic authorities in the possibility of women performing the same liturgical functions as men either for themselves as individuals or in a congregational context. What concerns them is whether there is any objection to menstruant women attending synagogue, a matter that should be seen in the context of the gradual abandonment in non-mystical circles of the commitment to ritual purity during prayer. When one comes to the halakhic authorities of Ashkenaz and communities not far removed, however, there does seem to be a greater willingness to challenge the assumptions of the immediately earlier period and the views expressed appear, from their contexts, to be practically and not only theoretically orientated, in spite of their rather surprising nature. Rabbenu Tam, for instance, the grandson of Rashi, permits women not only to take upon themselves precepts from which they are exempt, such as *tefillin*, but also to recite a benediction when performing them.[35] A further sign of the kind of connections between France, Provence and parts of Spain mentioned in the previous chapter may be detected in the occurrence of a similar ruling about *tefillin* by Aaron ben Jacob Ha-Kohen of fourteenth-century Lunel and Narbonne and by Solomon ben Abraham Ibn Adret a few decades earlier in Barcelona.[36] On the matter of *minyan* and being called to the Torah, too, there are some unexpected expressions of halakhic opinion. Simḥah ben Samuel of Speyer (twelfth to thirteenth century) is willing to count a woman as the tenth member of the quorum necessary for formal, congregational prayer, while Menaḥem ben Solomon Meiri of Perpignan a hundred years later and Meir ben Barukh of Rothenburg, an earlier contemporary, finds circumstances in which it is possible to argue that the 'honour of the congregation' is not affected by a woman's *'aliyah la-torah* and the talmudic objection to it may therefore be set aside.[37] Similarly, Nissim ben Reuben of Gerona in the fourteenth century argued that women have an equal obligation to hear the Esther *megillah* being read publicly and that they may therefore be counted in the *minyan* required for such a reading.[38] While on the subject of what appears to be a greater leniency about female participation in worship, particularly in the early Ashkenazi communities, mention may also be made of the favourable attitude to Torah-study by women expressed in the *Sefer Ḥasidim*, of the mediaeval female cantors who apparently led their own sex in prayer, and of the *vorsugern* (*firzogerin*) of a later period who led the women around her in the synagogue in the recitation of the prayers.[39] This is not to say that these views became normative, nor to express an opinion about their relevance to the contemporary argument involving the status of women in *halakhah*, nor to suggest that they may legitimately be employed for justifying liturgical developments of a quite different motivation in the post-emancipation period. It is rather to point to a few individual halakhists in pre-Renaissance western Europe whose minds were exercised by what appears to have been a growing involvement in synagogal worship on the part of Jewish women. Whether this has to do, as no doubt the decrees attributed to Rabbenu Gershom do, with the attitude of the dominant Christian environment is not immediately clear; nor is it obvious whether the growth in importance of the women's gallery in the architectural history of the synagogue during the late mediaeval and early modern periods, inspired by precedents in the Jerusalem Temple and in some (but not all) early synagogues, is a cause or an effect of women's greater involvement. What is beyond doubt is that kabbalists, printers and translators had to take greater account of the female constituency when they considered the needs of the worshipper and the synagogue and that, at least in the western European context, the foundations were being laid for the more intense arguments about liturgical equality that will be discussed in the next chapter.

The current chapter may now move on to a discussion of the demographical changes that affected the Jewish world between the periods of the general Renaissance and the Jewish Enlightenment that was to a great extent its equivalent in the effect that it had on Jewish religious thought and practice. The four centuries beginning with the fifteenth and ending at the close of the eighteenth saw movements of Jewish population as significant as those from Babylon and Palestine to Spain, North Africa and western Europe in the latter part of the geonic period and their modern equivalents from the oriental countries and eastern Europe to Israel and the USA. Following these movements, there emerged strong new centres that were to see their Jewish communities into the modern world, albeit each in a different manner. The primary migrations were from Spain to North Africa and the Ottoman Empire, from western Europe to eastern Europe and from both these older centres to the Italian states. It is self-evident that these migrating communities had their own liturgical traditions and that they were destined to clash with existing rites where there already were established communities. Once the victorious tradition emerged, its chances of maintaining its position and becoming firmly fixed as standard practice were greatly increased by the historical development of the new Jewish centres. For socio-economic reasons as well as cultural ones, the Ottoman, Polish–Lithuanian, and Italian settlements exercised powerful influences on the direction to be taken by Jews and Judaism as they emerged into the modern world. The changes that took place in the prayer-book while this process was under way were no longer a matter of an inner dynamic shaping the emergence of a new ritual form by gradual degrees but of particular ideas and prayers attaching themselves to the practice of a rite in one area and then quickly spreading through the powerful new centres by virtue of their structure, influence and means of communication. In a sense this was the last time in the history of the halakhically bound liturgy that such innovations were, not of course without considerable controversy and acrimony, incorporated into the traditional prayer-book. The adjustments made in the nineteenth and twentieth centuries were of a different type, dictated either by the totally new factor of reformation in response to the dominant ideologies of the non-Jewish environment or by the need for minor and highly circumspect adjustments to take account of changes in the make-up of communities and the cataclysmic events that precipitated them. The earlier innovations are often presented as the result of a distraught community of Sefardi *émigrés* seeking solace in kabbalistic ideas and spreading such mystical notions to a Jewish world disillusioned, for one reason or another, with what is assumed to be a more balanced and conventional religious ideology. A closer examination of the emerging new centres and their cultural propensities will help to demonstrate the fallacies and oversimplifications that lie behind such a supposition and set the tone for a survey of the kabbalistic influences on the prayer-book from the Zohar until the successes of Polish Ḥasidism.[40]

As is well known, the expulsion from Spain in 1492 was only the climax of a long period of persecution during which a Jewish community that had developed considerable wealth, culture and pride in its own ritual traditions had suffered the grave disadvantages of living in a bigoted and intolerant Christian kingdom. It was not by accident that when they sought an alternative home they chose an empire that was expanding from the east into the continent of Europe, was non-Christian, and needing as it did the expertise that westerners could bring it, whether in the fields of medicine, commerce, or in the manufacture of firearms, was therefore happy to adopt a liberal attitude towards them. The spread of Ottoman power from the fifteenth to the seventeenth centuries had brought under its jurisdiction Byzantine or Romaniote Jewish communities that had also previously suffered the miseries of life under Christian rule and offered them a considerable improvement in conditions. As a result of this improvement, Jews from other communities made their way to the territories of the Ottoman Empire and it was their confirmation to their co-religionists of the attractions of the new centre that led to the mass influx after 1492. The existent community was not without its own Jewish cultural achievements and customs and it must not be imagined, as J. Hacker carefully points out, that it simply became a matter of a cultured community dictating change to a less educated one.[41] At first, indeed, as far as ritual is concerned, the great variety of immigrants brought about a situation in which there were many synagogues, each following its own inherited and/or imported rite. Zunz notes that even as late as 1540 there were at least fourteen different congregations operating more than twenty synagogues in Salonika and identifying themselves by their places of origin, among them Aragon, Catalonia, Portugal, Italy, Sicily, Provence and Greece.[42] Naturally, tensions were created, particularly if we accept the view that the existent communities were not without their own strong commitments, but it was ultimately the Sefardi immigrants who came to dominate the activities of the Ottoman communities, no less in liturgical than in other spheres. Their determination to maintain their Spanish inheritance, their sense of the superiority of their cultural traditions, their creation of an active and productive intellectual and literary society and their simple weight of numbers ultimately assured them of success. As Samuel ben Moses de Medina somewhat immodestly put it: 'It seems to me that those who abandon other liturgical rites and adopt that of Sefarad are not only undeserving of censure but should actually be praised since their ancestors might have done the same in similar circumstances.'[43] It should not, however, be supposed that such liturgical rites were already permeated with kabbalistic notions. As previously in Spain, mysticism had been the preoccupation of only a select group of scholars and although it had begun to leave its mark on a few items in the liturgy, as suggested earlier in this book, it was by no means the dominant factor. The majority of *émigrés* continued in Turkey what they had started in Spain and concentrated on the study of philosophy and *halakhah*. It was only in the seventeenth century that *midrash* and *aggadah*, halakhic *pilpul*, and, concurrently, kabbalah came to the fore.[44]

It should also be noted that the refugees from Spain found havens in the Portuguese colonies and the Muslim-controlled parts of North Africa as well as in Egypt and in most of these communities they imposed their liturgical customs much as they did in Turkey, although the challenge was somewhat less since the existent rites, as was noted in the previous chapter, already had much in common with at least those that had come from the southern parts of Spain.[45] Nevertheless, the assimilation to the Sefardi practice was such that it is difficult when examining manuscript material from the fifteenth and sixteenth centuries to establish confidently whether the handwriting, the rite and the halakhic tradition are from Spain or from North Africa. The influence on Egypt is apparent from the Genizah texts dating from the sixteenth century and written in Judaeo-Spanish and should make us cautious about pinpointing the date of each liturgical fragment before we jump to conclusions about the existence of a Sefardi-type custom in the 'classical' Genizah period of the tenth until the twelfth century. Until all the liturgical fragments have been identified, their contents classified and at least their approximate dates estimated, it will be a wise precaution to refrain from making too many assumptions about the precise liturgical relationship of Egypt and Spain in the late Jewish Middle Ages.[46]

The situation was significantly different in Eretz Yisrael. The communities that had re-established themselves there after Saladin's defeat of the Crusaders and in the subsequent three centuries were essentially offshoots of the Ashkenazi and Sefardi centres. There had been the occasional difference of opinion where the older pre-Crusader custom had been remembered but to all intents and purposes the new *'olim* brought their rites with them. The twelfth-century scholar Zeraḥiah ben Isaac Ha-Levi Gerondi, writing in Provence, reported that the Provençal immigrants had unjustifiably introduced the diaspora's second day of *Rosh Ha-Shanah* into Palestine and pleaded for a restoration of the former custom; but evidently to no avail. The few hundred families, both Ashkenazi and Sefardi, were in a state of decline at the end of the fifteenth century and were greatly strengthened by the arrival of the newcomers from the Iberian peninsula. Within a few decades there appear to have developed a number of new synagogues, in some cases continuing to follow their own rites and customs, but with the Sefardi traditions of the *émigrés* becoming all the time stronger.[47] Here is not the place to expatiate on the economic and social developments that changed the face of the Palestinian Jewish community but simply to state that they allowed the development of Safed as a centre of independent religious expression. The groups of pious Spanish Jews for whom such expression was highly motivated, creative and intense were able to cultivate an idealised form of mystical Judaism, argues H. H. Ben-Sasson, because they could afford to make light of the tensions that this created with the established communities in Jerusalem.[48] An additional consideration, and one that will again figure later in this chapter, was the weakening of the authority of the local rite. While this had been the major factor in liturgical decision-making in the earlier period, it was now under attack from what may be termed the itinerant rite. Such a development was possible because change was in the air and authority was widely being questioned, a state of affairs that also applied to the Polish community now to be discussed.

Although there had been a trickle of Jews into Poland from other areas, including the Byzantine areas to the south, and such immigration had already occurred for some three centuries, it was the arrival of numerous Jews from the west, escaping persecution and subjected to expulsion, that laid the foundations of the community that flourished there from the fifteenth to the seventeenth centuries. Just as the general cultural domination tended to come from the Germanic lands to the west, so the major influences on Polish Jewry were Ashkenazi and while there were differences in the precise liturgical arrangements, as was noted in the previous chapter, these were of minor significance and greatly outnumbered by the similarities.[49] With the expansion of the Polish kingdom and the spread of its nobility's power into the Ukrainian lands to the east, there was a need for Jewish merchants, exporters and importers, property-lessors and tax-farmers, especially to fill the gap between Polish nobles and Ukrainian serfs, and Jews exchanged the declining communities of Germany for the emerging and expanding settlements to the east. As a result, the centre of Jewish religious activity in Europe became the area of Poland, Lithuania, Bohemia and Moravia and the relative stability that it enjoyed until the 1648–9 massacres brought about a high degree of intellectual productivity. Centralisation of both rabbinic and communal authority through chief rabbinates and the 'Council of Lands' ('Three Lands' or 'Four Lands', referring to the various parts of Poland), the influx of the liberal ideas of the Reformation and the Italian states, and the intensification of Jewish learning all combined to effect what has been described as a 'cultural flowering and religious ferment'.[50]

The late sixteenth and early seventeenth centuries saw a

Jewish intellectual development at least on a par with that of Spanish Jewry in its heyday and with that of the modern world but without the iconoclastic elements that have tended to mar the internal efficacy of the latter. Although the study of the Talmud was actively promoted, particularly as a result of the introduction of the *pilpul* method, and halakhic codification was a product of the *yeshivoth*, these were by no means the only areas of learning to receive the close attention of the leading thinkers of the day. Hebrew Bible and grammar occupied the attention of some teachers and they strove to apply its standard form to all the Hebrew texts they knew, rabbinic as well as biblical. The educational methods of the day came under scrutiny and there was an intense discussion about the most systematic way of introducing youngsters to the classical works of Jewish literature. Such a discussion was not restricted to the theoretical but led to the production of elementary textbooks with sound pedagogical methodology. In this connection the name of the *Maharal*, Jacob Löw of Prague, figures most prominently but by no means exclusively. Solomon Luria, the *Maharshal*, also advocated educational reform in the direction of grammatical and linguistic accuracy and took exception to the interest of his contemporary, Moses Isserles, the *Rema*, in philosophy. There was also controversy about the merits of secular studies and of the increasing fascination with kabbalah and a growing use of Judaeo-German translation as a means of widening knowledge.[51]

All this had its effect on attitudes to the prayer-book. The previously mentioned commitment to the 'correction' of the non-standard Hebrew of the liturgy was championed, interest was expressed in the production of prayer-books that could confidently be used for educational purposes, the meaning of the prayers was of concern to both philosophers and kabbalists, even if for different reasons, and precise guidance on what was to be recited when was considered of importance. The culmination of such efforts in connection with the *siddur* came with the work of Shabbethai Sofer of Przemysl (*c.*1565 – *c.*1635) whose primary aim was to produce a text that would meet all these educational expectations. Meeting at the spring fair in

Lublin in 1610, the Council of Three Lands passed a resolution calling for the production of what effectively amounted to an 'authorised daily prayer-book' and the rabbis of Cracow and Przemysl were instrumental in persuading Shabbethai to undertake the task. The latter spent most of the decade working on a text and commentary and at its meeting on 9 March 1617 the Council was able to give its collective approbation to his work, the text alone of which was published in Prague later that year. No less remarkable than the project itself is the list of those who formally approved it, including as it does such major figures as Joel Sirkes, Samuel Edels, Joshua Falk, Joseph Delakrut, Nathan Spira and Isaiah Horowitz.[52] Shabbethai's work demonstrates a literary, historical and critical approach, a commitment to linguistic accuracy, and a desire to educate the public. He cites manuscripts and editions in the evaluation of versions, sometimes prefers Sefardi formulae to Ashkenazi ones and is at the same time not averse to the acceptance into his prayer-book of some of the better established kabbalistic insertions.[53] The future direction of the liturgy in the communities of Poland in the late seventeenth and through the eighteenth century was not quite as Shabbethai would have predicted or proposed it and the continuation of his approach is rather to be sought in nineteenth-century Germany. As the writer has suggested elsewhere: 'Partly because of the subsequent collapse of the Jewish communities of the area following the Khmelnitski massacres, and partly due to the advanced and premature nature of his ideas, Shabbethai's work . . . was not immediately successful, and Jewry preferred to wait until the age of the Haskalah proper, brought about externally through emancipation rather than internally through scholarship, and accept such opinions in a spirit of revolution rather than evolution'.[54] Nevertheless, it has again been demonstrated that, given the acceptance of a general commitment to an authoritative body of liturgical texts, there was scope for independent minds to propose adjustments in the detail of their structure.

Independent minds were also a feature of the Italian communities of the fifteenth and sixteenth centuries. It will be recalled that these were among the few that retained some significant vestiges of the pre-Crusader Palestinian rite and this situation certainly continued into the sixteenth century.[55] The earliest settlements had been to the south, centred in Rome, but from the fourteenth century there developed some large and active communities in the north and central parts of what is today known as Italy but was of course then a collection of papal territories, city-states and colonies of various sorts. Responding to the need for banking, and then remaining as merchants, the Jews moved in number into such cities as Venice, Mantua, Ferrara and Cremona and attracted to themselves fellow members of the faith from among the beleaguered Ashkenazi centres to the north. During the zenith of Italian Jewish prosperity, that is in the fifteenth and early sixteenth centuries, there was, in spite of regular bouts of persecution, a blossoming of culture, with a wide scholarly syllabus including Bible, grammar, philosophy and poetry, as well as the more traditional talmudic disciplines on the one side and more 'secular' pursuits, such as medicine and the arts, on the other. Italian printing-presses in the cities mentioned also produced large numbers of Hebrew books, not only for their own communities but also for such markets as Poland, with which their scholars maintained a lively contact. The prayer-books produced in Italy consequently catered for various liturgical rites.[56] With the arrival of the Sefardim after the Expulsion there was inevitably a tension between the older Italian rites and the liturgical customs of the newcomers and this ultimately led to the virtual disappearance of the former in many cities. Interesting evidence of the varied origin, for instance, of the immigrants to the newly developed free ports of Leghorn and Pisa is to be found in the charter issued in 1593 by Ferdinand I of Tuscany to the 'Spaniards, Portuguese, Greeks, Germans, Italians, Hebrews, Turks, Moors, Armenians, Persians and others' and it is noteworthy that in this area it was the 'Portuguese' Jews and not their Italian and German cousins that dictated ritual matters. As Baron puts it, they 'retained their uncontested supremacy and were even able to prevent the erection of synagogues of non-Sephardic rituals'.[57] In the older centres such as Venice, the struggle continued for the maintenance of the Italian rite in the face of the overwhelming numbers of Jewish arrivals from other communities. When the distinguished Venetian rabbi Leon da Modena and the communal elders issued a formal invitation to such newcomers to participate in their synagogal services, they took the precaution of pointing out that 'at the time our synagogue was founded the initiators intended not only to provide a place where *Italian residents* of our city would be able to pray *according to the rite of our forefathers* but also to satisfy the desire of transients from other *Italian regions* to have a synagogue *of their own rite*'.[58] It should be borne in mind that the likelihood of changes in attitudes to the nature of the prayers was increased not only by the mixture of groups with different liturgical allegiances but also by other factors. It is commonly presupposed that one of these was the increasing extent of persecution. Whatever their economic need for the Jews, the Italian states continued to subject them to mediaeval conditions. The creation of the ghetto, the censorship and burning of books and the onward march of counter-Reformation forces, had their effect throughout Italy and although Jewish life maintained high standards of cultural achievement there was also inevitably a greater yearning for redemption, messianic fulfilment and the expression of what may be characterised as a more nationalist religiosity.[59] Robert Bonfil stresses that this move in the sixteenth century away from philosophy and towards mysticism was primarily neither anti-halakhic nor a rejection of rationalism. It was rather a disillusionment with systematic, philosophical thought, perhaps similar to the anti-scholasticism that was currently in the intellectual air, and a reaffirmation of the more traditional Jewish notions of ethics, piety, repentance and worship.[60] With the spread of the Sefardi prayer-book, the presence of Spanish and Portuguese Jews who had brought with them the Zohar and some of the mystical traditions of Spain, and the preference for spirituality over intellectualism, the stage was set in Italy, as it was being set elsewhere, perhaps for varying reasons, for the spread in the sixteenth and seventeenth centuries of the ideas being cultivated by the pietist elite of Safed. The medium for the diffusion of an ideology that involved a fairly radical reassessmnent of what had become the dominant attitude to Jewish prayer was the printed word. It consequently becomes necessary to devote a few remarks to this new science before the progress of the ideology that it helped to promote is charted.

It should not be forgotten that the printing-press brought about as revolutionary a change in cultural developments in its day as the computer in our own. For those whose ideas it purveyed, it was a 'heavenly craft'; those who saw their conservatism or livelihood threatened by it regarded it as the 'work of the devil'.[61] No accurate examination of the cultural history of the last half millennium can afford to ignore its wide-ranging effects. These may be summarised under various general headings that may be related to the specific instance of the printed Hebrew prayer-book.[62] Data collection and preservation became an altogether less haphazard and difficult proposition. As long as one manuscript was available, it could be used by the printer and given a greater lease of life by production in numerous copies. Items that were or might have become rare were within a short time widely available. Thus the numerous incunables and sixteenth-century editions of the Ashkenazi, Sefardi and Italian prayer-books produced in the Iberian peninsula and Italy ensured that the future of such rites was no longer exclusively dependent on the employment of copyists, the memory of the *ḥazzan* in the synagogue or the whim of the censor or persecuter. Indeed, it may fairly be argued that the mass destruction of Spanish and Portuguese Jewish communities and their cultural inheritance, including copies of their literature, might have been even more disastrous for the survival of their traditions, had a small proportion of their printed editions not succeeded in escaping destruction. The amplification and reinforcement of knowledge was another feature to benefit considerably from the emergence of the printed volume. Previously, a view or a piece of information was likely to be known in a limited circle and only rarely became widespread enough to win universal acceptance or to attract extensive comment, whereas now the reverse was possible. As the content of the printed *siddurim* became more sophisticated, so they came to record not only the rites themselves but rubrics about their use, reasons for their suitability, and justifications of their inclusion by reference to major figures who suggested or approved them.

The compositor, faced with the task of setting up a collection of writings in print, was also forced to make decisions about the organisation of the text, and such decisions were bound to have an effect on the reader of the material. The order of topics, the juxtaposition of individual items within given topics, and the relative print size of all the constituent parts said a great deal about the priorities and values of the various contents, as the compositor saw them. Printers of Hebrew liturgies produced a more common set of texts for daily and sabbath use in larger format for the cantor and of less imposing size for the individual, with separate volumes for festivals and booklets for special contexts and occasions such as grace after meals, Passover *Haggadah* and fast-days. The precise division between the volumes ultimately became a matter of distinction between Sefardi and Ashkenazi prints. At first there was little to distinguish one part of the prayer-book from another, few headings, rubrics or incipits, a fairly primitive line justification, precious little commentary and text repetition as seldom as possible. Gradually, however, all these features were significantly improved and some of them marked by the use of varied founts. Pagination was added and the precise make-up of each set of prayers was made clear to the worshipper.[63] Not only the format of the text but also its precise wording was also of major concern to the editor of a new publication: whose version was to be followed, which linguistic conventions were to be adopted, and what were the criteria for the preferences ultimately to be expressed. Once such decisions were made, they obviously had a major impact on the future history of any given text, so that for years, even centuries, the choice of an early printer was regarded as the standard edition. There were particular Jewish rites that fell at this first hurdle. Provençal liturgies did not receive typographical attention until the eighteenth century because of their junior status compared with the 'heavyweights' while the geographical and cultural isolation of Yemenite Jewry denied them printed prayer-books until a century later than that.[64] No doubt a wide variety of local traditions once followed in the hundreds of synagogues of Spain and their equivalents further north in Europe simply disappeared for want of a printer's interest and a bookseller's market.

More positively expressed, these developments meant a standardisation of each of the rites and even of elements common to each of them and those with a commitment to the adoption of one standard Hebrew in the Jewish liturgy, with a 'biblicised' vocabulary and vocalisation, saw the printing-press as a weapon with the potential for assuring their campaign of success. The group previously referred to as 'correctors' of liturgical Hebrew (*methaqqeney ha-tefilloth*) had existed for a number of centuries before the invention of printing but the debate naturally became more heated when this new device became available but did not respond sufficiently well for their liking.[65] A whole group of Polish rabbis of the sixteenth and seventeenth centuries call the printers to task for insufficient effort and liturgical standardisation of the sort approved by them. Poland had followed Italy as a centre of Jewish printing in the second half of the sixteenth century and many editions of the prayer-book were available to these authorities. In assessing the significance of their remarks it is important to bear in mind that the 'errors' they bewailed were not simply printers' mistakes, of which there are obviously many examples, but the preservation of any linguistic traditions that did not match what they had come to regard as 'standard'. Nathan ben Samson Spira, Meshullam Faivush of Cracow, Jacob Koppel and Shabbethai Sofer of Przemysl variously censure the printers for inconsistency, unnecessary abbreviation, and the inclusion of inveterate errors, leading to popular ignorance of correct Hebrew and havoc in its pronunciation. As a result, they claim, Jewish prayer is rendered ineffective, the exile is prolonged and the messianic redemption prevented. A standardisation had taken place but in their view the wrong versions had been given permanence. In league, as it were, with the printers were the *ḥazzanim* and they therefore came under attack from the same quarter. Through their conceited concern with showing off their voices, their lack of the proper virtues required by their profession and their ignorance of 'correct' Hebrew grammar, vocalisation and punctuation, they were a party to the perpetuation of errors and therefore responsible, in the view of the 'correctors', for blasphemy, communal misfortunes and the failure of Jewish prayer.[66]

Wide and prompt dissemination of literature became the order of the day, bringing new knowledge within the grasp of anyone who could afford or had access to the new publications. While only a very wealthy patron could have engaged a scribe to transcribe a text for him, multiple copies made it feasible for the growing numbers of the merchant class to purchase a greater stake in learning and thereby increase their degree of involvement in decisions about its future direction. In the Jewish liturgical sphere the congregation had relied on the rabbi for the theory, on the *ḥazzan* for the practice and sometimes on an authoritative exemplar held at the synagogue for checking a text. Now there was a partial transformation of their involvement from doing little more than listening to actually reading a text. The artistic representations of earlier synagogues and Jewish worshippers show few prayer-books; the later they are the more common become examples of their presence.[67] The 'authorised daily prayer-book' that the Polish Jewish Council commissioned from Shabbethai Sofer was intended 'to benefit the public', as it was expressed in the relevant resolution. What these leaders had in mind was the dissemination of a popular edition that would serve as a model text for both *ḥazzanim* and congregants and the volume that was evidently printed in Prague in 1617 was protected by decrees that forbad any new edition either until it was sold or until six years had elapsed from its first appearance.[68] It should be added that the wide dissemination of printed prayer-books in Poland and the surrounding areas was matched by a similar activity in Turkey in the sixteenth century and subsequently in Germany and Holland.[69]

For the Jewish world, as for its gentile counterpart to an even greater degree, the published word attained the status of what

Elizabeth Eisenstein has called 'a new estate', with a power and authority that could not easily be matched by other estates of the realm.[70] This led to a process of codification by publication and usage and it required a brave rabbi to challenge a text with which Jews had become familiar from an early age, whatever the rights and wrongs from the linguistic, theological or ritual viewpoint. Thus it was, for instance, that those *piyyuṭim* that had survived the decline of this genre in the late mediaeval Jewish world, and had the good fortune to be included in printed texts, stood a greatly increased chance of being accepted and others that were early set aside by the printers were easily consigned to oblivion. If the fate of Jewish communal worship had in earlier periods been dictated in turn by personal relevance, theological status, halakhic centralisation and ritual dominance, so was it now in large measure subject to the supremacy of the printing-press and those who could or would exercise control over it. This supremacy was recognised not only by the representatives of Judaism but also by its enemies. Expurgation had been a fact of Jewish literary life for at least two centuries before the invention of printing as the omissions, deletions, alterations and messy obliterations to be found particularly in liturgical manuscripts clearly testify. With the extensive publication of such 'heresies' now possible, and the wheels of active persecution powerfully driven anew by the fuel of Counter-Reformation zeal, objections to traditional Jewish prayer-texts were more strongly expressed and their effect felt by way of both internal self-censorship and external interference. It was not as in other cases, the total Hebrew work that was seen as dangerous or offensive (although the *Index Librorum Prohibitorum* did list any *translations* of the Hebrew prayer-book) but particular words and phrases, and these relevant parts of the Jewish liturgy therefore underwent alteration and abbreviation in the editions being produced and circulated. References to non-Jews that might be construed as referring to Christians in particular had to be removed so that *goy* ('gentile') and *'arel* ('uncircumcised') were replaced by *nokhri* ('heathen') *'akum* (abbreviation for 'worshipper of stars and planets') and *kuthi* (Samaritan) or a paraphrase was substituted (e.g. 'who has made me a Jew' for 'who has not made me a *goy*'). Prayers that called for revenge for Jewish suffering or martyrdom had the wording adjusted or removed and anger against *minim* ('heretics') or *meshumadim* ('apostates') or indeed *noṣerim* ('Christians'), where such indiscretions still existed, was diverted to a more general group such as *malshinim* ('slanderers'). If a prayer looked forward to the end of the 'wicked kingdom', the arrival of the true messiah, or the end of pretensions to this claim, it rarely remained intact and some prayers such as *'aleynu* and *kol nidrey* were particular victims of expurgation. The sentence in the former describing other peoples as 'kneeling and prostrating themselves to pointless folly and praying to an ineffectual god' was, whatever its origin, regarded as anti-Christian and the nullification of religious vows was seen as a licence to Jews to go back on their word to Christians. Various means were found to overcome the objection and in some of these cases a tell-tale blank in the body of a printed liturgical text is all that remains of a prayer that incurred or was likely to incur Christian wrath.[71]

In dealing with the development of the mystical approach to prayer in the period under discussion, scholars of today no longer adopt the unfavourable value judgement that was once characteristic of scientific Jewish studies and is to be found in textbooks on the history of Jewish liturgy that are still widely used. To regard such an approach as a 'negation of life, an escape from its realities' and to link it with 'misery and . . . cultural decline', as Idelsohn did, is to fail to do justice to the independently valid part it played in the religious traditions of Judaism.[72] Elbogen, of course, went even further in the negation of the Jewish mystical inheritance for the sake of modern theological polemic. He compared the influence of Isaac Luria's kabbalistic ideas on the liturgy with an 'infectious disease' that spread widely and swiftly and he lamented 'the unparallelled esteem that it still enjoys among Jews who remain untouched by the spirit of modern religious movements'.[73] It is now widely recognised that mysticism has had an effect on Jewish attitudes to worship from earliest times, that it deserves a fair and balanced assessment in that and other contexts, and that it simply is not historically accurate to dismiss the Jewish mystic as marginal to the normative practice. At the same time, the success achieved by Scholem and his school of students in putting Jewish mysticism back on the map has encouraged an unfortunate tendency to present kabbalah as in some way antithetical to *halakhah*. To argue such a case, except in a small minority of instances through Jewish history, is to deny the evidence of the vast majority of sources. Those who espoused the kabbalistic cause certainly applied it to the details of their daily lives but in the context of an adherence to the precepts of the halakhic system as they understood it. The authorities who favoured an overall approach that was somewhat drier or inclined towards the rational and philosophical nevertheless engaged in personal prayers that were not, as they were often aware, without their pietistic leanings. The truth is surely that in Jewish liturgical matters there has always been a tension between the mystical and the halakhic that sometimes succeeded in pulling in one direction, sometimes the other, and often brought about a compromise in the resultant practice. The *merkava* traditions of the talmudic period and their subsequent development in the *hekhaloth* literature of the geonic period centred on the angels, the celestial world, and the use of the ecstatic hymn and left their mark through such praises as the *qedushah*.[74] It was, however, by no means the same set of factors that led each generation to express its preferences and before an account is given of the successful impact the Safed mystics had on the prayer-book it may be useful to recall the mystical teachings that they had imported with them from Spain and some of the general developments in the intellectual history of the Jews in the sixteenth and seventeenth centuries that contributed to their success.

As has previously been pointed out, the manuscript liturgies of the fifteenth century already begin to show some small influence of the kabbalistic teachings that had been developed in Spain but it was never more than a small elite that applied them intensively to their lives. Following the example set by the schools in Provence and Gerona, and to an extent publicised by Naḥmanides, the ideas of the thirteenth-century kabbalist, Abraham Abulafia, had laid the foundations with their expansion of the German Ḥasidic doctrine of the numerical value of words and letters into the special importance of their particular combination, their use of the doctrine of the ten *sefiroth* and their 'practical' ideal of communion with God. Although it is not easy to draw direct parallels between his concepts and those of the Muslim Sufis, some points of contact have been established between Egypt, Spain and Safed that may ultimately demonstrate more of a dependence than can yet be adjudged. The more theosophical and meditative aspect was represented by Moses de Leon and the Zohar, with the emphasis on biblical exegesis, myth, mystery and sexual imagery. Common to all Spanish kabbalists was the central aim of *devequth* (= 'cohesion'), the blissful communion with God, at least some stages of which could be achieved by prayer with the required degree of devotion. Much, then, of what the Spanish kabbalists took with them at the Expulsion had been adumbrated in the teachings of earlier generations of mystics but it was to be a unique combination of circumstances that gave them the opportunity of incorporating many more of these teachings into the prayer-book than it had previously been able to absorb.[75]

It is probably fair to say that there are rarely developments within any religious ideology and practice that are not motivated by a variety of factors rather than by one cataclysmic event and that it is a misguided pursuit of the latter that often sends scholars off in wrong directions. It has been a central thesis of much of this volume that the history of Jewish liturgy may best be understood by a reference not to one area of scholarship but to an analysis of the interplay of various influences at given periods in Jewish history. It should already have become apparent from earlier parts of this chapter that there were various reasons for the widespread acceptance by what may be called ordinary congregations of worshipping Jews of many aspects of what was at heart an elitist, ascetic and pietist expression of Judaism and this is one of the best examples of the kind of complicated historical phenomenon that is being proposed. In the realm of ideas, the Jews of Poland, Italy and Turkey were ready, as many of the non-Jewish circles around them, for a move away from the purely scholastic and philosophically systematic to the more religiously personal and romantic. If Maimonides had previously represented the intellectual ideal, the less universal notions of such thinkers as Judah Ha-Levi came back into the limelight and current historians of ideas have traced the same tendency in all three major centres of Jewish population. If one may narrow down the more broadly philosophical to the more immediately theological, note has also been taken of the renewed interest in the soul, the after-life and the cosmic spheres and the growing belief that human prayer could have a direct effect on all these. Whether or not a concern for the dead constituted the more popular expression of such lofty ideas, it came to play a greater part in liturgical formulation. As far as such formulation is concerned, a new mixture of Jewish populations brought an awareness that what had previously been viewed as the rite sanctioned by authority and tradition and exclusively applied in one area might be challenged by its equally valid alternative from another. There were even those who detected in alternative rites examples of texts that they regarded as worthy of emulation and the apparently increasing desire for introductory and concluding items also gave scope for the absorption of previously unfamiliar prayers. The development of trade, the consolidation of Jewish communities in greater numbers in major centres, the emergence of the Sefardi rite as the standard in most such centres, and the consequent contraction in the size of the Jewish world from the viewpoints of travel, accessibility and individuality, were the result of significant demographical change and the reason for remarkable liturgical adjustment. A new means of widely marketing such adjustment was available in the technical process of printing and the 'canonicity' of the *siddur* had been long enough established to encourage the acceptance of its printed form as an important element in decisions about future ritual. The success of the special community of Safed in establishing its social, economic and religious independence led to the production of a spiritual commodity that came to be neatly encompassed in the new volumes and easily made available to those who, for all the above-noted reasons, were hungry for its consumption.

It has even been suggested by Elliott Horowitz that such a humble matter as the drinking of coffee had an influence on the acceptance of one of the practices of the Safed school of mystics and the convincing case that he has made indicates that the wider social sphere, what he calls the 'social history of piety', is another one that has to be taken into account in arriving at explanations of liturgical developments. Although there were precedents in the land of Israel and in Italy for prayer vigils at night and in the early morning, the fact is that it was the midnight *tiqqun ḥaṣoth* championed in Luria's Safed, that succeeded in becoming the popular form of such piety in the late sixteenth and early seventeenth centuries. Although on such occasions as *Shavu'oth* and *Hosha'na Rabbah* it became customary to spend the whole night in prayer and study, the *tiqqun ḥaṣoth* was generally adopted as a lengthening of the evening and it is Horowitz's thesis that the increase in the drinking of coffee and the opening of coffee-houses in the Holy Land and in Italy were major factors in the preference for staying up at night over rising at dawn. The introduction of this stimulant brought with it 'the emergence of a new perception of the night in which the hours of darkness could be shaped and manipulated by human initiative rather than condemn men to passive repose'. Thus it was that laments for the destruction of the Temple, prayers for the restoration of the Jews to their land, and the recitation of certain psalms, centred around the midnight hour, became a popular addition to the catalogue of Jewish acts of worship in the form chosen by the *Ari* (the 'lion', i.e. *'Elohi Rabbi Yiṣḥaq*, R. Isaac the 'divine').[76]

There were, however, numerous other additions to the standard liturgy, many of them more popular than the *tiqqun*, that were bequeathed by these mystics and their later emulators and a brief survey of the major figures and the compositions their circles produced will demonstrate clearly the major impact that they made on the prayer-book. The impetus for the practical adoption of kabbalistic teachings in the Egyptian, Syrian and Palestinian areas had come primarily from such outstanding leaders as David ben Solomon Ibn Avi Zimra (= *Radbaz*) and Jacob Berab, although it should immediately be stated that the former was antagonistic to the latter's messianistically inspired idea of reintroducing the ancient rabbinic ordination (*semikhah*). By the time that they settled in Safed as mature men around the middle of the sixteenth century, it already had a lively community of Ashkenazi, Sefardi and Italian Jews and had been growing for over half a century. Both Joseph Karo and Solomon Alkabetz had joined the community in the thirties of that century and the former's inspiration as a mystical visionary and the latter's poetry and mystical interpretations of the prayers exercised a profound influence on their pupil, Moses Cordovero, who married a sister of Alkabetz. Isaac Luria, of mixed Ashkenazi–Sefardi parentage, had already studied with the *Radbaz* in Egypt, mastered the Zohar, adopted an intensely pietistic lifestyle and developed his own system of kabbalistic thought, but he took advantage of the few years that he had in Safed towards the end of his life to sit at the feet of Cordovero who, incidentally, was also the author of a commentary on the prayers. Luria also attracted to himself a whole circle of scholars and mystics and inspired them through direct contact with his personality and religiosity to study his system and spread his ideas. The most famous and active of his disciples, his 'Boswell' in fact, was Ḥayyim Vital whose *'Eṣ Ha-Ḥayyim* is a vast collection of Luria's teachings parts of which, when taken together with his *Sha'ar Ha-Kawwanoth*, provide a record of the Lurianic school's liturgical compositions and practices. Other leading figures in the remarkable community of that day were Moses Alsheikh, homilist and halakhic authority, and Eleazar Azikri whose daily life was devoted to cultivating the highest ideals of communion with God. As Alkabetz before him, he particularly favoured the recitation of prayers at the graves of the righteous. In addition, the community was probably visited by Israel ben Moses Najara of Damascus, entitled by Schechter 'the mystical bard', during the period that his father was resident in Safed and no doubt had the benefit of hearing some of the poems he eventually published in the collection *Zemiroth Yisrael* that was one of the books printed in the kabbalistic centre itself, appearing there in 1587.[77]

In attempting to establish the precise date and place for the incorporation into the prayer-book of each of the compositions that was either produced by the Safed mystics and their followers or at least given an increased significance by them, the researcher is in some difficulty. Although the general trend is clear and the specific items are fairly easily identified, if only from a comparison of prayer-books of the early sixteenth century with their counterparts of the mid-seventeenth, it soon becomes apparent that the basic analysis of all the various rites during this period has yet to be done. Consequently, current scholarship may note the overall developments and hope that later research will fill in the details for the various communities. What is certain is that Scholem's claim that the Lurianic kabbalah was 'the last religious movement in Judaism, the influence of which became preponderant among all sections of the Jewish people in every country of the diaspora, without exception' is fully borne out by the liturgical sources.[78]

The idea of introducing one's prayers with a suitable formula was, as demonstrated earlier, not new, but there was a considerable degree of novelty about the composition of kabbalistic devotions attuned to the ideas of the sixteenth-century mystics for recitation before the benedictions attached to the performance of particular religious rites or during the acts themselves. Such devotions, usually beginning with the words *hineni* ('here I am'), *leshem* ('for the sake of'), *keshem* ('just as') or *yehi raṣon* ('may it be the will') are intended to create the correct frame of mind (*kawwanah*) in the reciter so that his use of the Divine Name will contribute to the restoration of its disturbed unity (*yiḥud*) and thereby to the 'correction' (*tiqqun*) of the process of creation, thus also effecting the personal and national redemption of the Jewish people. With this aim in mind, the four letters of the Divine Name were introduced into prayers and supplications in various forms. There were other passages too that had long been in existence but were now inserted at strategic points in the established liturgy because of the deep religiosity they expressed either through their formulation or, more mystically, through the special numerical significance of their content or number of words. Examples are *berikh shemeh* ('blessed be the name') from the Zohar, the thirteen divine attributes included in Exodus 34:6–7, and *'ana bekhoaḥ* ('we pray that by your might') attributed to the first-century teacher Neḥuniah ben Ha-Qanna but first appearing among the thirteenth-century Spanish kabbalists. The most sustained, composite and popular import into the prayer-book from the Safed mystics was the set of prayers known as *qabbalath shabbath* ('the reception of the Sabbath'). These included the recitation of some psalms and Alkabetz's *lekhah dodi* poem before the prayers proper in synagogue and the addition of the poem *shalom 'aleykhem*, the blessing of the children (Numbers 6:24–7) and Proverbs 31:10–31 at home. According to the different rites, *'ana bakhoaḥ*, *yedid nefesh*, composed by Eleazar Azikri, and Song of Songs also achieved a place at some stage in what soon became one of the Jewish people's most favourite liturgical practices. The creation of an atmosphere of joy, even religious ecstasy, was also the aim of the hymns (*zemiroth*) sung at the sabbath table, some of which are the work of Israel Najara and probably of Isaac Luria himself. Special verses, poems and supplications, often with the subject of repentance as their main theme, came to be used on such major occasions for the kabbalists as the dawn vigil, the seven days of *Sukkoth* and *Pesaḥ*, and the fast-days introduced on Mondays and Thursdays, immediately after these two festivals (*behab*), between *Ḥanukkah* and *Purim* (*shovevim tat*) and on the day before the New Moon, known as *Yom Kippur Qaṭan*, 'the minor day of atonement'. Even Torah-study was mobilised in support of the mystics' religious campaigns, the recitation of sections of *mishnah* being regarded as especially efficacious for the soul (*neshamah*) of the departed, because of the use of the same four Hebrew letters in the two words.[79]

In order to understand how it was that the bitter controversies surrounding the Sabbatean movement in the seventeenth century did not prevent the spread of many of the liturgical usages of the kabbalists of the previous two centuries, it is necessary to draw a distinction between the philosophy and lifestyle of the pietists who promoted these usages and the more mundane existence of the everyday Jews, whether rabbis or simply worshippers, who adopted them in their synagogues. While the texts and practices were attractive and won a place in the prayer-book, the more intense and systematic approach to kabbalah remained a matter for the few. Consequently, when the 'profound upheaval' brought about by Shabbethai Ṣevi and his followers rocked the Jewish mystical world and led to strong reactions against the mystical approach, those who tried to discredit all the kabbalistic additions to the prayer-book achieved only a very limited success.[80] Popular liturgical practice held its ground in the oriental communities through to the modern period and the liturgical paths of Ashkenazi Jewry ultimately split, one remaining the choice of those more committed to the rational, legal and grammatical, while the other broadened into the popular road of eastern European Ḥasidism. A brief account of these two approaches, as they developed from the sixteenth to the eighteenth centuries, will prepare the ground for the novel developments of the nineteenth and twentieth centuries and so bring the current chapter to its close.

A continuation of the more text-critical and linguistic treatment of the prayer-book that was, as has been demonstrated, the hallmark of the work of Shabbethai Sofer of Przemysl may be traced in the Ashkenazi prayer-book texts and commentaries of the seventeenth and eighteenth centuries and his work is often cited in these publications as the ideal to follow. Although Ḥayyim ben Benjamin Ze'ev Bochner (d.1684) wrote on the halakhic and kabbalistic aspects of the prayers, he was also most concerned to eliminate what he saw as mistakes in Hebrew liturgical language and content and refers approvingly to Shabbethai's prayer-book text, which had been claimed as the prototype for a number of seventeenth-century editions. A similar line was taken by the famous Jewish bibliographer, Shabbethai ben Joseph Bass, who published a *siddur* in Dyhernfurth in 1690, again with a claim, but with only limited justification, that the grammatical accuracy of Shabbethai Sofer had been followed. Indeed, in this case the publisher reported that he had been fortunate enough to have obtained manuscript notes on the prayers penned by Shabbethai himself from an elderly notable called Naḥum, who confirms this in the introduction.[81] And at this point the opportunity may be taken of eliminating the name 'Naḥman Lieballer' from Jewish bibliographical and liturgical history. The elderly Naḥum is described in the introduction to the *siddur* as *ha-lablar* and, whether this is a pseudonym or an accurate reference to his profession, it is not a surname. That error originates in a misreading of the forename and of Steinschneider's 'Libellario' in the *Jewish Encyclopaedia*, subsequently copied by Goldschmidt into the *Encyclopaedia Judaica*.[82]

The next relevant publication in the textual history of the Ashkenazi prayer-book is one produced in Frankfurt-am-Main in 1704 by Azriel ben Moses Meshel of Vilna and entitled *Derekh Siaḥ Ha-Sadeh*. Included in the edition was a short work on the grammar and vocalisation of liturgical Hebrew entitled *Miqra Qodesh* by Azriel and an introduction to this work, entitled *Ma'aneh 'Eliyahu* by his son, Elijah. Again, support for the edition is claimed from a manuscript source containing notes by Shabbethai Sofer but there was some controversy between Azriel and Bass as to whose edition was the more authentic successor to the work of the Przemysl grammarian. Indeed, the outstanding grammarian and controversialist Solomon 'Zalman' Katz Hanau directly questioned the reliability of the edition produced by Azriel and Elijah in this respect, in spite of its growing popularity. The argument about what constituted linguistic accuracy in the Hebrew of the prayers was conducted between the two sides in Hanau's *Binyan Shelomo* and *Sha'arey Tefillah* on the one side and the second and third editions of *Derekh Siaḥ Ha-Sadeh* on the other. It may be added that Hanau was something of a purist in linguistic matters and naively believed that an honest pursuit of the truth entitled him to attack earlier authorities and question their linguistic competence. Grammatical considerations alone should decide the matter of liturgical text and vocalisation. Such an approach invited the criticism of no less a figure than Jacob Emden, no opponent of grammar himself but a defender of traditional liturgical language and of the maintenance of a distinction between biblical Hebrew and its rabbinic equivalent. In his *Luaḥ 'Ereṣ*, published in Altona in 1769, Emden acknowledged Hanau's grammatical expertise but challenged his peremptory and disrespectful dismissal and alteration of well-established readings, arguing the need for a defence of time-honoured practices. Mordecai Düsseldorf also took exception to Hanau's suggestions, arguing that the prayers were originally oral and therefore reflect the non-biblical form of the Hebrew language.[83] It will not be forgotten that Emden was a leading anti-Sabbatean, suspicious of the influence of the Zohar and of kabbalah and the author of his own text and commentary on the prayers. It was not the grammatical approach he derided but its biblical precedent being followed to an extreme in a traditional rabbinic text. He was in his whole *Weltanschauung* attempting to marry rational, historical and liberal ideas with the best of the rabbinic tradition and his approach to the prayer-book is a fine example of this philosophy. The former part of the equation obviously has close affinities with the Haskalah movement beginning to emerge at the end of his life but the Maskilim were less inclined to be sympathetic to the latter part. They consequently preferred the purist attitude favoured by Hanau and their similarly iconoclastic tendencies had much in common with the revolutionary religious ideology of the nineteenth century. As such, they will be discussed in the next chapter.

In the mean time it will be recalled that even in these more 'grammatical' prayer-books much of the content had originally infiltrated from kabbalistic circles and was not eliminated until the Haskalah had its effect in the nineteenth century. The split referred to earlier, however, was the point at which the limited kabbalistic content was no longer sufficient for some circles in eighteenth-century Poland. That content had begun to appear in the Ashkenazi prayer-book in the sixteenth century. The kabbalistic commentary on the prayers compiled by Naftali Hirṣ Treves (Drifzan) and printed in Thiengen in 1560 had made an impact and the work of Mattathias Delakrut and his pupil, the halakhic codifier, Mordecai Jaffe, had introduced mystical ideas from Italy to the Jewish community. Shabbethai Sofer had corresponded with the kabbalist Menaḥem Azariah de Fano, even if on grammatical and liturgical rather than purely kabbalistic matters, and had cited in his prayer-book the views of Menaḥem Recanati, Moses Cordovero, Isaac Luria, Elijah de Vidas and Moses Ibn Makhir and personal communications between Poland and Safed that had come to his attention. He had also, while stressing his major interest in grammar, admitted the kabbalistic significance of certain liturgical readings. The next stage of kabbalistic progress had been ensured by Nathan Nata ben Solomon Spira and Isaiah ben Abraham Horowitz who had introduced elements of Lurianic teaching and a more direct influence on the prayer-book had been achieved by the liturgical edition *Sha'arey Ṣiyon* of Nathan Nata Hanover, first published in Prague in 1662 and reprinted many times all over Europe. The specific items that had entered the liturgy as a result of these more general developments have already been noted. While the scholars of more central Europe were concerning themselves with the grammatical accuracy of all the prayers, the communities of eastern Europe were making more radical demands of their prayers and changes in their format.[84]

The history and significance of eastern European Ḥasidism is a vast subject that receives considerable attention in current scholarship and is greatly beyond the scope of this study. What must, however, be explained here is the development among the Ḥasidim of an alternative set of Ashkenazi rites and customs that were to have a major effect on Jewish liturgical history not only in the eighteenth century, when they emerged, but up to and including the present. To that end, it will be necessary to make a few historical and theological remarks about that form of Ḥasidism in general and then to move on to summaries of its attitude to worship and of the characteristic elements of its prayers. It is of primary importance to bear in mind that Ḥasidism, like so many Jewish religious movements before it, was a combination of the inherited and the innovative. The inspiration provided for all mystics by the Lurianic kabbalah was already available to such pre-Ḥasidic groups as the ascetics of the *kloyz* ('conventicle') in Brody nearby and the followers of the Yemenite kabbalist, Shalom Sharabi, in faraway Jerusalem. Notions of ecstasy and of messianism were very much in the air and challenges to authority, within the halakhic tradition as well as in the excesses of the Sabbatean movement, were no longer a rare feature. The standard Ashkenazi prayer-book had adopted prayers popularised by those with leanings towards the teachings of the Safed school but the mysticism of early Ḥasidism was still an elitist occupation. At a later date there were new trends and renewed emphasis on elements of religiosity that had tended to be neglected. The parts to be played by emotion and social conscience, the importance of *hithlahavuth* ('enthusiasm'), the possibility of communal ecstasy, and the roles of the ordinary individual as well as of the special *ṣaddiq* all then came to the fore in Ḥasidism. The tendency towards the spontaneous, the interest in transforming such acts as eating, drinking and sex into spiritual functions, and the evident laxity about such matters as the precise timing of prayers and the centrality of Torah-study, all combined to create a strain on the established halakhic framework but also gave the emerging group its own identity and set of priorities. Less than a hundred years after the activity of the founder of the movement, the *Baʿal Shem Tov*, Israel ben Eliezer of Medzibozh, it had taken hold in the majority of communities in eastern Europe and, far from being threatened by the previously dominant Ashkenazi scholastic tradition, had begun to exercise a distinct influence on it.[85] As far as prayer is concerned, this was to be motivated by love and joy rather than by dry duty and by passing through various stages of speech and thought was to strive for the annihilation of the ego (*biṭṭul ha-yesh*) and the attainment of *devequth*, cohesion with the Divine. As Rivka Schatz has explained it, lips produce only lip-service, and words themselves do not exercise an influence on the Divine. Effective prayer becomes invasion *by* rather than *of* the Divine. What has then occurred, in the words of Joseph Weiss, is that 'an originally intellectual effort of meditation and contemplation has become an intensely emotional and highly enthusiastic act'. Such an approach does of course create tensions, firstly, between an attachment to the traditional words and a desire for the spiritual ideal and, secondly, between the individual's expression of need and the total removal of the self from the picture. The tensions tend to remain but are somewhat resolved by the beliefs that the letters have a spiritual importance in themselves regardless of their literal meaning and that the need being expressed by the individual is that of God for celestial harmony. It should also be noted that in some Ḥasidic groups such as Ḥabad (or Lubavitch) there is always a tendency to stress, and to return to, the intellectual dimension.[86]

The practice of prayer is naturally a reflection of the theory. Communally chanted melodies, physical movement, loud singing and shouting (even sometimes in Yiddish) infused the atmosphere of what was usually a *kloyz* or a *shtiebel* ('conventicle' or, more simply, 'a meeting-room'). Formality and decorum of the conventional ecclesiastical type are absent and the prayers are led by congregants and not by cantors and choirs. Although each individual's efforts in the sphere of prayer, however meagre, are applauded, the specially devout individual or the leader of the group may achieve particular success. At times, therefore, the Zaddik composes his own personal devotions for recitation before or after the regular prayers and the style may be confrontational, as in the cases of the famous challenge to God reported in the name of Levi Yitschak of Berditchev, or simply expressed but deeply spiritual as with Elimelekh of Lyzhansk and Naḥman of Bratslav. Apparently from the very earliest days of the movement, the Sefardi rite adopted by Isaac Luria (the *Ari*) for his *kawwanoth* and later followed by many of the mystics, contained kabbalistic elements that were attractive to the Ḥasidim. They therefore developed a liturgy which they called the *nusaḥ Ha-Ari* ('rite of Isaac Luria') or *nusaḥ Sefarad* but was in effect a combination of his version of the Sefardi rite with the Polish Ashkenazi version of their own day, including some of its own *piyyuṭim*. A number of liturgical editions were published by them in the second half of the eighteenth century, some of them with the Lurianic *kawwanoth*. There was never a uniform Ḥasidic rite and *nusaḥ Ha-Ari* consequently meant a variety of liturgical contents to a large number of worshippers. There were indeed instances in which the printers tried to capture both markets, that of the Ḥasidim and that of their opponents (*Mithnaggedim*) by producing *siddurim* with both versions and the use of brackets to distinguish them. As may be imagined, this led to chaos and the emergence of some conflated liturgical readings. The founder of the Ḥabad group, Shneur Zalman of Liady, produced an apparently better organised and less confusing Lurianic text without *kawwanoth* that was published in Shklov in 1803 and his son, Dov Baer, combined his father's contemplative teachings with halakhic material in the prayer-book he published in Kopys in 1816. There were also popular editions that had been produced by Koppel of Meseritch and Shabbethai Rashkover, but it never became universally clear exactly which Sefardi elements were *not* to be adopted. What are instantly recognisable as Ḥasidic traits in a non-Sefardi environment are, for example, the recitation of *hodu* before *barukh she'amar*; the inclusion of the phrase *we-yaṣmaḥ purqaney wiqarev meshiḥeh* in the *qaddish*; numerous small variations in the wording of the *'amidah*; the completion of the service including *qaddish tithqabel* before the return of the scroll to the ark; the inclusion of *'eyn ke'lohenu* and related talmudic passages in daily as well as sabbath services; the use of different *qedushoth* at the repetition of the *shaḥarith* and *musaf 'amidoth* on the sabbath; and the introduction of the ceremony to remove the scroll from the ark on the sabbath with various Psalm verses beginning with 86:8 and not with Deuteronomy 4:35. There are also obvious differences on the festivals such as the recitation of *hallel* in the synagogue on the first night of Passover and the custom not to put on *tefillin* on the intermediate days. Such customs led to major controversies in eastern Europe and fuelled the fires of the dispute between Ḥasidim and Mithnaggedim. As Louis Jacobs describes in his book on *Hasidic Prayer*, there were exchanges of conflicting halakhic rulings on the matter of the inclusion in the prayers of the kabbalistic formula *leshem yiḥud* between the distinguished authority, Ezekiel Landau of Prague (1713–93), on the one side, and the Ḥasidic leader, Ḥayyim ben Solomon of Czernowitz, with support from the renowned Sefardi rabbi, Ḥayyim Joseph David Azulai (= *Ḥida*), on the other. Landau's objections were certainly motivated by his fear of such religious innovations whether for modernists in Germany or mystics in Poland. Also of interest is the defence of the *nusaḥ Ha-Ari* by the Ḥasidic master, Ḥayyim Halberstam of Zans against the attack by the leader of Hungarian orthodoxy, Moses ('Chatham') Sofer, on its use by Ḥasidim. Similarly indicative of the issues of the day are the same Ḥasid's objections to the use of synagogues, cantors and choirs in a way that appears to him to be motivated by a desire to ape Christian worship because of embarrassment about traditional Jewish forms. It is these various tendencies towards a modernist philosophy that stand at the centre of much of the next chapter of this book.[87]

CHAPTER 8

The challenge of the modern world

In an overall treatment of any aspect of Jewish religious activity through its inevitably chequered history, the survey of the modern period ought on the surface to be the easiest to complete and the least problematic to analyse. The original sources are numerous and varied, the events are not chronologically distant and previous scholarly attention is rarely lacking. Paradoxically, however, these same considerations may bring with them the danger of misrepresenting the nature and significance of developments. Because of the documentary *embarras de richesse* one is easily tempted to treat both sources and earlier assessments at face value and to overlook the fact that the modern period is no more free of tendentiousness than any other.[1] Indeed, the very variety of views and freedom of opinion that are among its hallmarks may intoxicate the enquirer with a surfeit of information and precipitate a failure to distinguish adequately between historical criticism and theological bias. As with the early Christian era, scholars approaching the nineteenth and twentieth centuries are rarely without their preconceived notions and personal religious biases and while this state of affairs may not necessarily invalidate their evidence, one is well advised to take it into consideration in assessing the validity of their evaluations. Grandchildren and great-grandchildren that we are of those who created much of modern history, it is no mean challenge to have to stand back from personal biographies and family commitments and offer as near a scholarly interpretation of their historical background and development as human propensities make possible. Of substantial assistance in doing so may be the conviction that the only answer to the request for a view for the present on the basis of one's foraging in the past is a form of the somewhat hackneyed one, namely, that all that one may learn from Jewish liturgical history for today's decisions is that Jewish liturgical history does not necessarily teach us anything for that purpose. One of the reasons for this is that there are unique factors at play in the contemporary world that invalidate the nineteenth-century assumption that the 'truth' uncovered by historians is so reliable and pure that it may aspire to serve as the basis for building the future. It therefore remains the scholar's duty to report and analyse but at the same time to retain more than a modicum of humility in applying his findings to the search for the way forward, be it political, social or religious.[2] To understand in depth what has just been stated and wherein the modern Jewish world constitutes a unique amalgam of inherited tradition and the totally unprecedented, it will be necessary to preface this chapter with a few remarks about the nature of Jewish modernity.

It has often been claimed that while modern European history for the Christian world dates from the fifteenth century and is characterised by Renaissance culture and Reformation ideology, its equivalent among the Jews cannot be dated before the end of the eighteenth century when the ghetto walls began to crumble and the Haskalah or intellectual enlightenment dawned on the Jewish mind. Arising out of such a claim, it has been presupposed that all 'modern' ideas to do with Hebrew language, Bible exegesis, Jewish education and the philosophy of Judaism, to take only some examples, were successfully promoted in the nineteenth century and that earlier generations of Jews were to all intents and purposes mediaeval in their cultural outlook. Recent research on the history of Jewish culture has exploded such a myth by uncovering numerous forerunners for such ideas and made it clear that while the earlier context was evolutionary rather than revolutionary and by no means universally traceable, the notions were often as 'modern' as those of the Christian world, whether they emerged by direct influence or through parallel development.[3] If Jewish modernity is not then entirely the product of the nineteenth century, it becomes necessary to redefine which aspects of it may genuinely be attributed to that period and to explain why what had existed previously on the periphery of most communities was able to become of central significance at that later date.

The essential difference between 'proto-modern' and 'modern' ideas in the Jewish world lies in the distinction between, on the one hand, the theories propounded by Jews within their own communities and subject to practical application only when the authorities of those communities deigned to permit it and, on the other, the novel plans of action proposed and more freely adopted by Jews when they found a place in the wider non-Jewish world. There were a number of reasons why such a place was eventually granted to them and why the authority of the Jewish community was no longer able to control the ideas and behaviour of its members. The commercial success of Jews brought them into the non-Jewish world and gave them a new and improved status there, as well as a desire to justify and maintain it. Modern political and social thought, as generally associated with the ideas of the American and French Revolutions, inspired a movement to grant Jews emancipation and a conviction on their part to prove themselves worthy of it, often in non-Jewish terms. The European vernacular was seen as a means of expression superior to the Yiddish of the *shtetl* and was either imposed or adopted, depending on the circumstances of the recipient community. The new power of the European nation-state deprived the alleged Jewish 'state-within-a-state' of much of its autonomy and particularly of its sanction to use the *ḥerem*, or power of excommunication from the religious group.[4] This historical change meant that Spinoza's excommunication could be effective in suppressing the spread of his ideas among Jews in the seventeenth century while any similar attempt at censorship in the nineteenth led at best to no more than a redefinition of the Jewishness of the victim. Not that the authority of the conventional community and its rabbinate had experienced no serious challenge before the Haskalah. The spread of both kabbalah and of Ḥassidism had already meant the development of alternative leadership, both rabbinic and communal, and had thereby contributed to a breakdown in the traditional *kehillah* structure that had served so well in the pre-modern period.[5] Now, however, it was not only possible to suggest individual interpretations of aspects of Judaism or an alternative relationship between religious law and mysticism within the faith; the new option was to offer a faith for Jews that was shaped by current patterns of thought or at least not inimical to their basic guidelines. These have been described by Alexander Altmann as 'the unmistakable shibboleths of the *Aufklärung*' and neatly summarised as 'the denunciation of "false accretions" (viz. "superstitions") to the pristine truth of natural religion, the ultimate supremacy of reason, the stress on human happiness as the be-all and end-all of philosophising'.[6] Whatever the prevous basis of Judaism's authority, it had now become axiomatic for many emancipated Jews that they should adhere to these principles and any religious act that was not self-evidently natural and rational, or left modern man somewhat ill at ease, was bound to be called into question by one thinker or another. Thus it was that the theory and practice of Jewish liturgical expression came to be questioned in a manner hitherto unknown, with a consequent effect, as will shortly be demonstrated, not only on the more novel forms of the religion but also on substantial sections of its traditional and orthodox manifestations.

Although the intellectual developments just described have had their effect through the modern period, the nature and degree of that effect have not been standard among all the communities of the Jewish world, nor in every period of modern Jewish history. In addition to the differences between the responses of the liberally minded and the traditionally inclined in central/Western Europe and the American continent, there are also to be taken into account the varying circumstances and outlooks that obtained in Eastern Europe and the oriental communities, and the changes that came about as a result of momentous events in the late nineteenth and mid-twentieth centuries. The Jewish communities of the Islamic world were virtually isolated from modern intellectual developments until the Imperial powers began to encroach upon the Ottoman territories and eventually replaced that Turkish hegemony by the establishment of their own spheres of political influence. By that time rational thought had begun to lose some of its burnish and was destined to be replaced by more modern versions of national and ethnic expression. Consequently, there is little to parallel European Jewry's early nineteenth-century developments in the intellectual history of oriental Jewry, particularly not among the communities divorced from the centres of European domination.[7] Most of the Jews of Russia and Poland, too, remained little affected at that time by liberal thought since it was inexorably linked in the minds of the masses with assimilation, forced conversion and state anti-Semitism. Attempts were made by Jews as well as non-Jews to introduce such thought into the religious, social and educational institutions of the Jewish world and, in spite of earlier scholarly claims to the contrary, some evidence of success can be documented. Since, however, even a liberalised Judaism stood little chance of approval or, indeed, tolerance among the Eastern European establishment, the flavour of Haskalah in Poland and Russia tended towards the secular or the national rather than the theological or the social.[8]

If geographical and political considerations alter the liturgical picture in different parts of the Jewish world, chronological factors are of no less significance for any attempt at arriving at an overall view of the fate of the Jewish prayer-book in the modern world. While the *Aufklärung* dominated the central and Western European scene in the nineteenth century, the situation altered when masses of persecuted Jews from Eastern Europe fled their dismal homes and lifestyle and resettled in the various countries of the West and in Turkish and, later, British Palestine. A tragically high percentage of such immigrants were completely lost to the Jewish world within a generation or two but those who retained a Jewish religious identity gradually came to dominate the communities where they had found refuge and to question, and ultimately to reject, much of the nineteenth-century philosophy that had hitherto characterised the outlook of their hosts, be it, for example, that of Turkish Palestine or of Victorian Britain. Like their oriental brothers, they tended to be less embarrassed than their German, French, British and American co-religionists about their rituals and, if they rejected them, it was for secularist and not for liberal reasons. No less of an impact on attitudes resulted from the *Sho'ah*, commonly called the Holocaust, that destroyed at least a third of world Jewry, degrading and abusing many of those who lived to relate their experiences either as the inmates of concentration camps or as refugees fleeing the Nazi terror and finding few havens prepared to accept them.[9] This terrible event, and the establishment of the State of Israel that followed close upon it, left their imprint on the prayer-book, as they did on most, if not all other elements of Jewishness. Together with other developments in the last half-century, they have brought about a revival of strong commitment, public identification and group pride that have made their mark on the content, appearance and purpose of the *siddur*, whatever the rite or variety of Jewish religious expression.

It will not have gone unnoticed how often it has been necessary to state in this volume that the required research remains to be done in a particular area of Jewish liturgical study. Here too, many aspects of what has just been claimed in a rather general way require to be followed up in detail and accurately assessed. The first step is, however, to attempt a general survey that marks out the territory and indicates which parts of it would repay closer scrutiny. Such an attempt will be made here as it has been in earlier chapters and will cover the major points of reference. Among the themes that will prove dominant will be the continued history of textual 'correction', translation and commentary; the effects of scientific research and liberal thought on attitudes to prayer; the theological issues that arose from the prayer-book and the variety of responses to their airing; the characteristic developments in a number of areas with extensive Jewish population; and the impact of evolving social and political ideas on the contents of the *siddur*.

As indicated in previous chapters, there had already been a

tradition of textual and linguistic treatment of the prayer-book from as early as the Middle Ages and this had grown in the course of the seventeenth and eighteenth centuries. The champions of this approach were interested in establishing what was to their mind an accurate version that accorded with the rules of Hebrew language and grammar. Their aim was not primarily liturgical reform and in that sense they belong to those whose ideas were 'modern' in the evolutionary rather than revolutionary sense, at least as far as the liturgical text was concerned.[10] Nevertheless, they were associated, at times rather closely, with the circles of the Haskalah and its ideology proved one of the motivations for their work. The earliest representative of the type is Isaac ben Moses Ḥa-Levi Satanow, a native of Podolia who was educated in Berlin and made his mark there as a prolific author and the director of the printing-press of the Jewish Free School established by David Friedländer in 1781. Though knowledgeable in such fields as philosophy, natural sciences and kabbalah, Satanow's distinction was as a Hebraist with a deep understanding of the development of the language and an ability to classify its various forms.[11] Maintaining as he did that rabbinic Hebrew was a linguistic hybrid of Hebrew, Aramaic and Arabic, he proposed the use of only biblical Hebrew in the prayers. In his various liturgical editions and in his grammatical comments on the prayer-book, in the promotion of which he did not shrink from employing dubious methods, he put his theory into practice.[12] When Friedländer produced an annotated German translation of the prayer-book *in Hebrew characters* in 1786 it served as a companion volume to an edition of the prayers containing Satanow's grammatical notes.[13]

Satanow's Polish background, involvement in the printing world and devotion to the study of the Hebrew language were shared by a younger contemporary, Judah Leib Ben-Ze'ev whose love of his Jewishness was matched by a passion for Hebrew, as a modern as well as a classical language. Justifiably regarded as the father of modern Hebrew linguistics, Ben Ze'ev penned a large number of works on grammar, syntax, phonetics and lexicography, as well as participating in the production of the Haskalah periodical *Ha-Meassef*. The language of the prayer-book also attracted his attention and he applied his methodical approach to the production of a corrected text and commentary, not only dealing with the forms of the words but also taking the revolutionary step of discussing their meaning.[14] His edition of the prayer-book *Tefillah Zakah* was posthumously published in 1816 by Anton von Schmid in Vienna, the establishment where he had been employed, under the supervision of his successor, Solomon Löwisohn, who also provided an introduction. Löwisohn's intellectual background was also a combination of the traditional and the 'enlightened' but he came to Vienna by way of Hungary and Prague. As a literary critic and poet he had a deep appreciation of Hebrew language and a profound sympathy with the ideas of Satanow and Ben-Ze'ev with regard to the language and text of the prayers. In addition to his introduction to Ben-Ze'ev's edition he also edited and annotated Hebrew liturgical poetry. In that introduction, Löwisohn extols the beauty of the Hebrew prayers and laments the fact that the purity of their language has been sullied over the centuries. He proposes to retrieve the situation with the same 'biblicising' campaign as that reported by him in the names of Hanau, Emden, Düsseldorf and Satanow and through the publication of the liturgical text of Ben-Ze'ev which, in his view, complements the work of these earlier scholars. Jewish worshippers will thus receive the clear guidance they require and will no longer run the risk of offering prayers in a form of language that is corrupt and contemptible.[15]

For anyone with even a basic knowledge of modern editions of the standard Hebrew prayer-book, the names Heidenheim and Rödelheim, more than any other, stand for typographical accuracy and style. It was Wolf Benjamin Ze'ev ben Samson of Heidenheim (= Wolf Heidenheim) who succeeded in establishing a tradition for the publication of quality editions of the daily and festival prayers in the first quarter of the nineteenth century at the German and Hebrew printing-presses that he founded in Rödelheim. The familiar imprint of books printed there was so much a guarantee of commercial success that it was often pirated through the nineteenth century. Heidenheim's interests were in biblical exegesis, masoretic studies and grammar but it was for his work in the liturgical sphere that he became best noted. Making extensive use of manuscripts, early editions and liturgical authorities, he produced texts, German translations, commentaries and studies, not only for the daily and festival prayers but also for the *piyyuṭim*, thus setting an example for the later efforts of the *Wissenschaft des Judentums*.[16] Although his earlier work obtained the approval of the rabbis of his day, who attempted to protect its copyright, his association with one of the fervent proponents of 'enlightened' education and theological reform, Michael D. Creizenach, towards the end of his life led to serious criticism on the part of the religious establishment. Creizenach was a teacher and preacher at the Philanthropic High School in Frankfurt and an early Reformer, and Heidenheim's *Siddur Liveney Yisra'el* (Rödelheim, 1831) not only included a German translation in German characters (previously restricted to Hebrew characters) but also omitted some items and prefaced the work with Creizenach's historical and critical analysis of the prayers with his suggestion for their gradual reform in the light of changing circumstances.[17] It is remarkable that such a prolific, influential and controversial scholar as Heidenheim has yet to attract a scholarly biographer, especially since there is a rich collection of his unpublished work that remains to be exploited.

A similar regret may be expressed about the lack of scientific analysis of the life and work of Heidenheim's pupil and successor in the textual study of biblical, masoretic and liturgical sources, Seligmann (Isaac ben Aryeh Joseph Dov) Baer (1825–97). As well as writing on the cantillation of the poetic books of the Hebrew Bible and preparing an edition of the *Diqduqey Ha-Te'amim* of the tenth-century masorete, Aaron ben Moses Ben Asher, Baer worked with his Christian mentor, the Protestant theologian, Judaeophile and missionary, Franz Delitzsch, on a masoretic Bible edition based on extensive manuscript evidence. His edition was even reproduced in the standard rabbinic Bible first published in Vilna and reprinted many times thereafter.[18] Even more successful was his comprehensive edition of the Ashkenazi prayer-book published in Rödelheim in 1868 under the title *Seder ʿAvodath Yisraʾel* since it became the text exemplar for the majority of editions subsequently printed in Western Europe. The texts of all the daily, sabbath and festival prayers are included but the contents also range widely over the more occasional liturgical items and thereby provide reliable texts of a whole host of brief prayers, benedictions and synagogal poetry as well as complete sets of weekday Torah readings, Psalms and the mishnaic tractate *ʾAvoth*. The text is generally clear and bold and is supplemented with a large number of helpful rubrics in Hebrew and German (in Hebrew characters). Perhaps of even greater value, at least to those with a wish to understand the sources, textual history and linguistic forms of the prayers, is his running commentary on the whole text, entitled *Yakhin Lashon*. Baer was clearly anxious not only to encourage what he regarded as the 'correct' form of the Hebrew but also to guide the worshippers towards a decorous, organised and standardised ritual. Towards this latter end he devotes the first part of his introduction to a summary of the halakhic requirements regarding rising for prayer, hand-washing, the wearing of *ṣiṣith* and *tefillin*, and synagogal behaviour, providing a number of the relevant Hebrew texts, in pointed form, and the special rules that apply to the recitation of the *qaddish* and the use of the word *ʾamen*.[19] The second part of the introduction constitutes an explanation and justification of his methodology. He indicates to the reader just how much effort he has invested in his edition and how his use of manuscripts dating back to the fourteenth century and printed works from the early fifteenth have helped him to produce a unique publication. As Heidenheim's literary heir he has been able to complete the work that his teacher commenced. He is anxious to point out that he has not only cited views on the language, sources and meaning of the prayers from his scholarly contemporaries but has also drawn material from authoritative sources of earlier periods. The publications of Leopold Zunz and correspondence with him have been of major assistance but he has also benefited from the advice of the Orthodox rabbi, Salomon Wolf Klein, leader of French communities in the Haut-Rhin, who provides a rabbinic approbation for the *siddur*. It is no accident that Baer cites a scholar of the *Wissenschaft des Judentums* and an Orthodox rabbi as his major contemporary mentors. As is clear from the last part of his introduction he is anxious to pre-empt criticism of his work as a rejection of traditional views. If change has been proposed and earlier views questioned, he argues, the motivation has not been disrespect, rebellion or arrogance but the pursuit of clarity, accuracy and truth. Baer declares that he will welcome fair and honest criticism but will ignore the foolish abuse of those driven by religious hypocrisy and malice to fault his work.[20] Before we leave Baer, it should be noted that in addition to his *'Avodath Yisra'el* he produced a number of popular handbooks for a variety of liturgical purposes, most of them with German translations.[21]

That Baer's work on a Jewish literary classic should have been substantially influenced by the researchers of a leading exponent of *Wissenschaft des Judentums* is no surprising phenomenon, given the impact that such scholarship was having by the middle of the nineteenth century on attitudes to Hebrew language and literature as well as Jewish historiography and theology. The field of liturgy was one of those most immediately and significantly affected and it will therefore be appropriate to say something about the method of study and its application to the Jewish prayer-book. The *Wissenschaft des Judentums*, literally 'science of Judaism', was an offshoot of the German Haskalah, or enlightenment, that began to flourish in the second and third decades of the nineteenth century and received a boost in the middle of the century when reactionary tendencies among non-Jews led to a pause in the drive towards emancipation and assimilation. Conscious as they were that the dominant culture was attracting Jews and leading to assimilation on the one hand and making its Jewish equivalent appear inferior in the eyes of the gentile world on the other, the young Jewish intellectuals of Berlin set themselves the task of countering these effects with the development of a new system of learning. Taking their lead from such predecessors as Solomon Löwisohn, they promoted a historical, critical and literary study of the Jewish sources that demonstrated their impressive, intellectual value and the importance of their contribution to civilisation. In this way they restored the pride of at least a proportion of the emancipated Jews of the day and presented the wider world with an image of Judaism ostensibly less likely to attract non-Jewish derision and animosity. Programmes laying down coverage, methods and aims were drawn up and the mechanisms for their implementation were scientific periodicals, learned societies, the discovery and study of early manuscripts, publication series, and rabbinical seminaries for the training of rabbis who would be modern academics as well as experts in Talmud and *halakhah*. The progress of the movement was of course limited to those countries where Jews could enjoy a wide general education as well as an intensive Jewish one and where political and social emancipation was at least on the agenda. In addition, it did not always represent an attempt to stem the tide of assimilation but sometimes amounted to what Moritz Steinschneider, for example, regarded as giving the moribund religious traditions of the Jews a decent burial. Nevertheless, it laid the foundations for much of the academic Jewish studies of the twentieth century and the researches of its major figures remain the starting-point for much contemporary scholarship.[22]

Leopold Zunz is generally regarded as the outstanding representative of such figures and it was his promotion of the ideals of the *Wissenschaft* and his prolific publication of the kind of research to which it was devoted that did more than anything else to establish its central position in nineteenth-century Jewish scholarship. Nevertheless, Zunz did not by any means operate in a vacuum and there is no doubt that he was influenced by such contemporaries as Solomon Judah Rapoport in the critical study of mediaeval rabbinic personalities and scholarship, Isaac Marcus Jost, the pioneer of modern Jewish historiography, and by those with special interests in scholarly treatment of the daily prayers and liturgical poetry. Michael Sachs, with whom Zunz was engaged on the German translation of the Hebrew Bible, was particularly interested in the Spanish Hebrew poets and produced annotated editions and German translations of the daily and festival prayers, while the Italian rabbi, Samuel David Luzzatto, regular correspondent of many critical scholars, translated the Ashkenazi and Italian prayer-books, composed an anthology of mediaeval Hebrew poetry and edited, with an introduction, the standard modern edition of the old Italian rite.[23] The earlier attempt of Eliezer (Leser) Landshuth to produce a dictionary of Hebrew liturgical poets was significantly improved upon by Zunz but Landshuth, for his part, felt that Zunz's historical analysis of the prayer-book paid insufficient attention to individual prayers. Some years earlier, in response to some urging by Hirsch Edelman to provide a commentary for the daily prayer-book that he was about to publish entitled *Hegyon Lev*, Landshuth had applied his critical acumen to establishing the source, authorship and date of many of the prayers, also touching on rites other than the Ashkenazi by way of comparison and on matters of literary style.[24] Appreciating, as he did, the centrality of the synagogue for modern Judaism itself as well as for non-Jewish assessments of it, Zunz had practical reasons for writing a history of its various constituents and his own contribution to the scientific analysis of Jewish liturgical developments over the centuries was massive. In one of his earliest works, *Die gottesdienstlichen Vorträge der Juden* (= *History of the Jewish Sermon*), the origins and development of the synagogal lectionaries, Bible translations and homilies are carefully traced not for scientific reasons alone but also to justify the view that preaching had always been a part of Jewish religious expression and the importance attached to it by religious reformers of synagogal activities.[25] It should immediately be added, however, that as Zunz grew older, his sympathy for the reformers was replaced by a greater faith in tradition and he busied himself with scholarship rather than religious politics.[26] Perhaps as the result of a move towards a more introverted Jewishness in the middle of the century, he concentrated on the history of liturgical rites and poetry and produced three seminal publications. *Die synagogale Poesie des Mittelalters* is the first attempt to describe the development of Jewish religious poetry from the biblical to the mediaeval period and to demonstrate clearly that the Jewish historical experience has left a sharp imprint on its liturgical expression. This theme is also present in his briefer study of the evolution of the various liturgical rites *Die Ritus des synagogalen Gottesdienstes* and is documented by reference to the influences of major historical events, be they social, religious or intellectual, on the contents of the prayer-book. Liturgical poetry is again the subject in *Literaturgeschichte der synagogalen Poesie* in which Zunz combs hundreds of manuscripts to identify and list the composers of *piyyuṭim* up to the sixteenth century.[27] It will not have gone unnoticed that poetry was a major preoccupation of these pioneers of scientific Jewish learning and in all fairness it should be acknowledged that because of the religious and intellectual trends of their day such literature, as well as homilies, grammar and religious philosophy came to be regarded by many of them as somehow more authentic than the more Jewishly mundane topics of talmudic study and halakhic guidance and more rational than the rich mystical traditions of Judaism. Their studies therefore reflect such a bias both in content and in approach. As a result, the critical study of Hebrew poetry has been making excellent progress for a century and a half while an equivalent examination of the daily prayers themselves has tended to receive little priority because of its more internal relevance. The central prayers of the talmudic tradition were original and therefore admirable, while later accretions were regarded as of a lower standard. Although *piyyuṭim* were dated after the fixed liturgy, they were forgiven their lateness if they matched the ethos of the nineteenth century and were aesthetically pleasing. Otherwise, like the Ashkenazi festival *piyyuṭim*, they were regarded as an awkward intrusion. By the same token, modern Jewish scholarship often concentrated on the Sefardi contribution to mediaeval Jewish culture, believing the 'golden age' to be a kind of proto-*Wissenschaftliche* period, while it neglected and downplayed the importance of Ashkenazi developments which were very much linked in the minds of nineteenth-century German scholars with the *Ostjuden* whose immigration into their cities from Poland and Russia caused them acute embarrassment.[28]

Current scholarship is gradually rectifying these biased assessments and they are mentioned here not to invalidate the scholarship of *Wissenschaft des Judentums*, much of which remains basic and sound, but to sound a note of caution about the dangers of uncritical acceptance of any theories, particularly when they date from over a century and a half ago when the Jews in the countries of emancipation were engaged in new theological battles about tradition, progress and change in the modern world.

For political, social and educational reasons already touched upon, such battles were fought in and around the German communities of the nineteenth century and led to the emergence there of three basic forms of modern Judaism, neo-orthodox, positive-historical and liberal, equivalent in more modern terminology to Orthodox, Conservative and Reform. From their German launching pad, such interpretations of Judaism were fired into Jewish religious space and have continued to orbit the world of Judaism for almost two centuries, sending their messages to a much wider body of Jewry than was ever envisaged at the time of their creation. Since it is difficult to understand liturgical developments in the twentieth century, even as far as the traditional text of the *siddur* is concerned, without reference to the emergence of such novel philosophies, some attention will now be paid to the liturgical issues that lay behind their tripartite division.[29]

From the aesthetic point of view it was important to the German Jew of the early nineteenth century that the sights, sounds and general atmosphere of the synagogue be a matter of pride rather than embarrassment, that is to say, more akin to ecclesiastical formality than to what had become the more improvised expression of Jewish worship. To that end, the maturity, clothing, singing and movement of congregants had to meet certain standards and the activities conducted in the synagogue had to be restricted to those that were thought worthy of a house of prayer. If egalitarianism was the order of the day, consideration had to be given to the matter of the place and role of women in the communal service and to the references to non-Jews and to Jewish election in the prayers.

Given that congregants should have a perfect understanding of the words and sentences being recited, a limitation on the use of Aramaic and, to a lesser extent, Hebrew, seemed rational and a greater use of the vernacular only sensible. Now that it had been widely accepted, as proposed at the Paris Sanhedrin of 1807, that Jews would be loyal to the modern nation-states in which they resided, there arose the problem of the meaning of the Jewish hankering after a return to Zion, a restoration of a kingdom of Israel, and a messianic redemption. Equally problematic from the contemporary theological vantage-point was the stress on physical resurrection and the restoration of animal sacrifice that stood at the heart of so much of the prayer-book. In an age that prided itself on reason, science and the rejection of superstition, the presence of mystical formulations, the use of passages from the Zohar, and the reference to angels were all a source of some embarrassment.[30]

It was inevitable that such considerations should begin to affect the traditional Jewish prayers and their synagogal recitation and the first signs of an attempt to reform the practice may be detected in the liturgical procedures laid down by the Adath Yeshurun congregation of Amsterdam, established in 1796. Limitations on the length of the liturgy, the omission of liturgical poems and kabbalistic prayers, and the introduction of orderly singing and recitation were among the changes that were adopted by that community and that led to the beginning of a bitter debate destined to continue through the modern period.[31] In the early years of the nineteenth century such personalities as Israel Jacobson, and his fellow Maskil, David Friedländer, introduced private changes in the prayers for the social and educational circles in which they operated, replacing traditional texts with German hymns and catechisms and borrowing such characteristic elements of local Protestant worship as the organ and canonical robes.[32] A more formal, communal dimension was given to such innovative trends by the establishment of the first Reform temple in 1818 and the publication of its prayer-book *Nach dem Gebrauche des Neuen-Tempel-Vereins* edited by S. J. Fränkel and M. J. Bresselau in 1819. In addition to choral singing with organ accompaniment, a vernacular sermon and the adoption of the Sefardi pronunciation, there were significant omissions and innovations that reflect the character of the reforms being championed. It is neither possible nor necessary in the present context to detail all the editions of the Reform communities any more than those of the Orthodox and Conservative. It will, however, be useful to summarise the Hamburg reforms in the liturgy for the sabbath in order to establish a yardstick against which to measure subsequent attempts at greater radicalism or returns to tradition. Collections of psalms and other scriptural passages, *piyyuṭim*, biblical and rabbinic texts dealing with sacrifices, and morning benedictions are generally omitted, although some individual items are replaced with German hymns or versions. The use of the *qaddish* is limited; the evening *shema*ʿ benedictions are rendered in a German version but those of the morning are retained in Hebrew with alterations, German choral parts and an adoption of a Sefardi version; the *shema*ʿ and the ʿ*amidah* are retained in Hebrew in the morning with changes or omissions regarding gentiles and sacrifices; the Torah is read in an abbreviated rite and followed not by a *hafṭarah* but by a psalm, German hymns and a prayer for the government.[33] The choice of what to retain, alter and omit was not, then, as consistent or systematic as it might have been and the Reform philosophy did not attract major support for almost twenty years. At that point, a new generation of scholarly rabbis took on important communal posts and a fresh historical and theological basis was provided for the Reform position on liturgical matters by the 'spiritual father of the Reform movement', Abraham Geiger.

Geiger was one of the leading scholars of the *Wissenschaft des Judentums* but, unlike many of his colleagues, he took a leading role in Jewish communal as well as academic matters. He was convinced that the essential nature of Judaism was universalist and rational, and that its theology was more important than the law and ritual that had historically become attached to it. At the same time he recognised the importance of analysing the historical developments so that a modern Judaism could be reconstructed on the basis of objective scientific criteria.[34] As far as the liturgy was concerned, he was theoretically unhappy with the second edition of the Hamburg temple's prayer-book for its return to tradition in certain respects. For example, he regretted the retention of so much Hebrew, any positive hints about sacrifice, however historical rather than devotional, and the inclusion of rabbinic benedictions for the *megillah*, *hallel* and lighting the *Ḥanukkah* lights. He looked for more systematic but historically based reform while at the same time rejecting what he regarded as the revolutionary stance of such reformers as Samuel Holdheim who replaced shabbat with Sunday worship and traditional Torah cantillation with modern declamation, and abolished head-covering, *ṭallithoth* and the sounding of the *shofar*. Geiger's theory, however, as has been pointed out by Michael Meyer, was not matched by his practice because he had too much respect for the concepts of 'community' and 'spirit' in Judaism to ignore them when drawing up his own version of the prayer-book. Most of the Reform communities in Germany were part of the larger *Kultusgemeinde* and had to take account of the response that their innovations would elicit there, if they were not to find themselves outside the established system *vis-à-vis* the Jewish and general public. Geiger was no exception to this and the prayer-book that he himself published in 1854 and 1870, in spite of much of his theory 'followed the structure and rubrics of the traditional *siddur* very closely', to the extent of mentioning Zion and Jerusalem (in spite of his characterisation of the latter as 'the present heap of ruins'). He did, however, excise passages dealing with the sacrificial cult and the ingathering of the exiles, adopted the triennial lectionary cycle and evinced his strongly Reform tendencies in the German text accompanying the Hebrew prayers. Interestingly enough, while Geiger was preparing a more radical version of his 1854 edition for publication in Berlin in 1870, his successor as rabbi in Breslau, Manuel Joël, was revising the same edition in the direction of greater traditionalism.[35] This fact demonstrates two points that are worthy of note in the nineteenth-century history of liturgy. The first is that Geiger exercised an influence on Reform liturgies, positively and negatively, throughout the middle part of the nineteenth century and beyond, and the second that the Reform rite was by no means a static one but appeared in various guises during the first hundred years of its existence, no less than during the second.

Since this volume is primarily concerned with the fate of the traditional text of the prayers as it evolved over the centuries, the detailed history of the various Reform versions is beyond its terms of reference. It is, however, important to dwell a little on the nature of the changes proposed because of the general Jewish attitudes to liturgy that they betray and the effect that they ultimately had on Orthodox texts and practice too. At the earliest stages of Reform it was still thought necessary to seek justification for change in the halakhic sources and much of the argument was centred on the use and interpretation of the classical texts.[36] There thus developed a fairly moderate 'historical' approach that set out to combine more acceptable minority views that could be gleaned from the tradition with ideas that were more directly modern in origin and motivation. As some of the already cited examples of alteration demonstrate, prayers were abbreviated, sections were omitted, peripheral material was replaced and vernacular items were introduced but in spite of these changes the basic structure of the traditional liturgy often remained recognisable. When Steinschneider made suggestions for the adoption of such a policy in the new synagogue planned for the Oranienburgerstrasse in Berlin, he used *Wissenschaft des Judentums* as much as *halakhah* as his inspiration but still aimed at what he described as 'Conservative Reform'. As far as the Jewish community of Vienna is concerned, mild reforms were fairly swiftly sanctioned but the conservative nature of the population and the Kultusgemeinde's desire for unity prevented more radical changes.[37] As Reform grew in strength, however, and felt less inclined to justify itself in traditional terms, more radical surgery was applied to the prayer-book by some groups and the result had much less in common with the traditional versions. Even such basic items as the *shema'* and the *'amidah* were severely truncated in some congregations; the *musaf* service, because of its association with sacrifices, was abolished; and novel prayer-texts were composed to replace such familiar but no longer favourably regarded items as *kol nidrey*, *qaddish*, memorial services and benedictions. Complex poetry was rejected because of its obscure sense; kabbalistic, national and particularist elements were rejected as no longer in keeping with modern thinking; and customs that involved individual rather than communal or choral declamation, movement from one's place, or spontaneous expressions of personal religiosity, were forbidden. Synagogal rites had to be conducted by those specifically appointed for the purpose, such as the rabbi, cantor and choir, and even their participation was most strictly controlled by sets of regulations. Petuchowski dubs these kinds of radical reform as 'Independent Reform' rather than 'Reform from Within' and other forms of nomenclature were in fact employed in different countries and contexts to distinguish the less abashed revisers from their more moderate counterparts. While in Germany, as has already been noted, there sometimes were communal reasons for adopting a more moderate reforming stance, and the epithet 'liberal' came to be more widely used than 'reform' in describing such a stance, in other countries such as England, France, Holland and the United States, there was ultimately less compunction about introducing more radical measures and the departure from the traditional prayer-book became a more pronounced one among certain groups.[38] Demarcation lines between one group and another were not, however, always clearly drawn and not every congregant who belonged to a particular congregation was there because he fully identified with the liturgical policy adopted by its founders and/or leaders. Be that as it may, a radical tendency on the part of some reformers towards the middle of the nineteenth century was regarded in some modern and 'enlightened' circles as the result of a negative approach to the historical development of Jewish religious custom and consequently led to the emergence of a more 'positive-historical' interpretation of Judaism that was ultimately to attempt what it regarded as a more balanced synthesis of tradition and modernity.

The name most closely associated with this attempted synthesis is that of Zacharias Frankel, a Prague-born rabbi with a traditional talmudic training as well as an extensive secular education, who, by founding the scientific Jewish periodical *Monatsschrift für Geschichte und Wissenschaft des Judentums* in 1851 and the rabbinical seminary in Breslau in 1853, ensured that his ideas left their direct mark on European Judaism for almost a century. Frankel and his positive-historical Judaism are important to this discussion of modern Jewish liturgy because of the stand they took on the nature of liturgical reform. Frankel had regarded himself as a member of the reforming group of rabbis and scholars and had taken part in the rabbinical conferences called on the initiative of Ludwig Phillipson and Abraham Geiger and convened at Brunswick in 1844 and at Frankfurt in 1845. He had apparently sat through the proposal of radical measures regarding marriage laws, sabbath and circumcision without feeling the need to withdraw but when the gradual abolition of Hebrew from the liturgy was about to become the policy of the conference by a majority vote, he and his fellow conservatives removed themselves from the proceedings. His reasons for this simultaneous act of defiance and defence lie at the core of his whole philosophy of Judaism. Frankel was perfectly aware, and was on record as maintaining, that there was no halakhic objection to the use of the vernacular, that Jewish practice underwent historical changes and that the prayer-book could in principle be subject to revision. The nature of that change was not, however, to be arbitrary, personal or factional but had to be part of an organic process in the dynamic development of living Judaism. If the historical Jewish genius had lent deep significance to a language, a text or a practice, neither the discovery of its origins nor a disenchantment with its contemporary application was an adequate reason for its alteration. That could be effected only when it no longer had significance for the Jewish people as a whole. Traditions that were still vibrant and conducive to further development in the religious body of Judaism should therefore be given a new interpretation that would justify their retention. Basic to Frankel's theology was the notion that unresolved historical questions, however scientifically analysed and discussed, could not provide the rationale for disturbing established and vital elements of Jewish expression but had to await an ultimate decision by the authentic spirit of historical Judaism.[39] The problem, in liturgical no less than in other areas, was how to arrive at criteria for ascertaining when such a decision had been made. In practical terms it meant that for well over a century Frankel's form of Judaism, which was favoured by many representatives of *Wissenschaft des Judentums*, remained devoted to both scientific enquiry and traditional practice and opted not to grasp the nettle of when to allow a radical, as distinct from a minor adjustment, to be sanctioned. The result was that supporters of his philosophy in Germany might be at home with any particular variety of the traditional prayer-book ranging from mildly reformed to neo-Orthodox.

Where the situation was quite different, and each of the three main varieties of Jewish practice eventually strove to establish for itself a liturgical standard that would to a large extent reflect its character and its divergence from the others, was of course in the United States of America. To understand the liturgical developments in that country and how they responded to the immigration of millions of European Jews, particularly from Eastern Europe, some brief attention must first be paid to what may be termed the inner development of the *siddur* in Eastern Europe and among the Sefardi communities in the nineteenth century as well as to the effect on the traditional prayer-book of the development of 'modern', 'neo' or 'enlightened' Orthodoxy in the communities of Western Europe at the same time.

The first point to be made about the situation among the Eastern Europeans and the Sefardim is that there is no clear trend towards a standard, orderly and dominant structure for the prayer-book. Printing-presses did not of course restrict their output to the production of texts that followed only the rite that prevailed in their own communities and it was consequently inevitable that what had become the norm among one group might be reproduced by the printer for another. At times, indeed, there was a confusion of Ḥasidic and Mithnaggedic elements in the same edition and there are also examples of notes from such modern German scholars as Heidenheim being incorporated in more traditional texts.[40] By the same token, the desire for a handsome overall appearance on the part of a printer in, say, Vienna, was bound to influence the typographical style that he adopted even when meeting his orders from further east. That having been said, however, what strikes the researcher who sets himself the task of examining the numerous prayer-books of the nineteenth-century traditional communities is the great variety of form and content. There is little consistency in the matters of size, order, rubrics, kabbalistic influence, sensitivity to censorship, the inclusion of halakhic guidance and the provision of such biblical texts as Psalms. Commentaries too are of considerable variety but a specific few of these gradually through the nineteenth century became the favourites of particular communities. Some publishers chose to include rarer forms of explanation or a selection of abbreviated comments from various sources but it was always easier, once a certain commentary had made a successful impact, whether Ḥasidic or Mithnaggedic, to reproduce it in edition after edition and thereby further to increase its prestige and popularity.[41] A few examples will illustrate the point. The *Derekh Ha-Ḥayyim* of Jacob ben Jacob Moses Lorberbaum of Lissa, halakhic authority and rabbi in various Polish communities, provided the reader with a guide to the rules that were appropriate for the different parts of the Ashkenazi liturgy throughout the year while the various works of Aaron ben Yeḥiel Michael Ha-Levi of Mikhailisnek graced that liturgy with philological and etymological comments, with contextual explanations and with variants in text and vocalisation.[42] The distinguished Sefardi rabbi, Ḥayyim Joseph David Azulai contributed the *Qesher Godel* to the Sefardi prayer-book. That form of the liturgy incorporated an anonymous commentary entitled *Shelemuth Ha-Lev* and was indebted to Abraham ben Joseph Alnaqar for functioning as editor and commentator for various North African rites.[43] The influence of the 'enlightened' Italian rabbi, Solomon David Luzzatto, was not only felt in the Italian rite but also widely in the publication of the traditional *siddur*.[44] It should also not be forgotten that by this time the Sefardi prayer-book, with its enthusiastic incorporation of much that the mystical tradition could provide, had spread to the many parts of the globe where there were communities who had either once fled the Iberian peninsula or had been heavily influenced by the customs of those who had. Those in the oriental communities that were spread from Morocco to India (and once even to China) retained their allegiance to what was essentially a Sefardi prayer-book with the variations of local custom while those in the western countries of Europe and the Americas were obviously open to at least some of the influences of the 'enlightened' tendencies that were there regarded, with no real degree of justification, as has already been explained, as religiously superior.[45] While the communities of Eastern Europe and the Orient were not averse to using their own communal languages of Yiddish and Judaeo-Arabic to clarify the text of the liturgy, it was only in the West that it became customary to provide dual language editions of the prayers, with the Hebrew on one side and the dominant non-Jewish vernacular on the other.

In dealing with translations it has to be acknowledged that they did have a pedigree of sorts, from the earliest period of the rabbinic liturgy, even if the nature and use of an alternative language to Hebrew varied from period to period. In the mishnaic and talmudic eras, as will be recalled, Greek and Aramaic could function as liturgical languages in their own right, not merely as alternatives to Hebrew, primarily because the degree of standardisation was insufficient to impose formulae in one language only. When the activities of the Babylonian geonim led to an emergence of a more canonised Hebrew text, Aramaic and Judaeo-Arabic versions of known prayers maintained an existence as valid variants in certain contexts but gradually became curiosities rather than equally valid alternatives. The dominant form of the vernacular in Jewish liturgy in the Middle Ages was as a Jewish version used to ensure understanding on the part of the less educated. Thus it was that Judaeo-Arabic, Judaeo-Spanish, Judaeo-Italian, Yiddish and even Judaeo-Provençal, to give only some examples of languages written in Hebrew characters with some Hebrew linguistic elements, were used for the translation of liturgical passages, although apparently not in any extended synagogal application by the adult male congregation.[46] Complete editions, with or without the original Hebrew, were printed in such languages, in either Hebrew or Latin characters, in the sixteenth and seventeenth centuries and the Judaeo-Italian text published in Bologna in 1538 specifically mentions its suitability for women and children.[47] It was only in the modern world, if we may define this in the non-Jewish sense of post-Renaissance and Reformation, that totally secular languages, that is, those not specifically associated by their script, vocabulary or dialect with the Jewish community, began to find a place in the Jewish prayer-book. Translations of the *siddur* into Spanish appear to have been the first, in the sixteenth century, and were followed in the subsequent two centuries by editions in Italian, English, French, German and Dutch, and in the nineteenth century by a variety of other languages. While the earlier texts did not necessarily offer the Hebrew *and* European texts, such an arrangement had become the norm in Western Europe by the nineteenth century. It was there too that the vernacular came to be used not only for the occasional public prayer, for the purposes of Jewish advocacy in the general world, and for educational purposes, but also as an alternative means of liturgical expression, of equal validity with Hebrew.[48] The wheel had, in a sense, come full circle and the Reform congregations of the nineteenth century saw themselves as continuing a halakhic tradition but only substituting German for Greek. The issue was, however, not merely linguistic but also theological and, as has already been noted, new vernacular prayers were used to replace Hebrew ones. Given the developments described above in matters of text, translation, commentary, decorum and other responses to the pressures of the modern world, the question to be answered is whether the prayer-books of the Orthodox communities of central and Western Europe were affected more by the Eastern European model or came under an increasing influence from modernist movements. It will naturally not be possible in the present context to examine and present all the evidence but some remarks about the approach of Samson Raphael Hirsch in Frankfurt and the Chief Rabbinate in England as the leaders of late nineteenth-century German and English Orthodoxy will exemplify the position.

Before detailing his response to the liturgical challenges of his day, one is bound to stress the degree to which Hirsch was a doughty champion of Orthodoxy who made every effort to justify traditional practices in modern philosophical terms and generally preferred the theological reinterpretation of established custom to its adjustment or abandonment. Though much influenced by the historical and rational approaches of his day and committed to an enlightened Orthodoxy in his general outlook ('erleuchtet religiös'), he unashamedly traced synagogal prayer to the 'Men of the Great Synagogue', credited by the rabbinic tradition with the religious leadership of the early Second Temple period, and argued strongly for the liturgical retention of Hebrew, the priesthood, *piyyuṭim* and the recitation of passages concerning sacrificial rituals. There were, however, innovative and, dare one say, assimilationist aspects to his approach to Jewish liturgy and a better understanding of these is dependent upon a prior word about how he interpreted Jewish worship as a whole. He was clearly unsympathetic to any attempt to distinguish between the cultic functions of animal sacrifice on the one hand and prayer formulae on the other, maintaining that the two had always gone hand-in-hand and offering exegesis of the latter that made it wholly dependent for its meaning on the former and on the former's ultimate restoration. Synagogal prayer was of central significance to Jewish religious life but its purpose was in no way to affect or influence God but to achieve the spiritual edification of humanity.[49] Jewish redemption could not come through the banalities of human action or effort but only when the theological time was right.[50] Such attitudes meant that he agreed with his more religiously radical contemporaries that the dignity and formality of communal worship were essential to its efficacy, that mystical and theurgical practices were to be discouraged and that man's ultimate salvation was by way of political acquiescence rather than the promotion of any radical alternatives. In his early days in the rabbinate, beginning in Oldenburg, as well as in his later and more conservative period in Frankfurt-am-Main, Hirsch imported into the Orthodox synagogue various elements of liturgical reform. At one time or another he introduced a choir and a German sermon, preferred to give expression to his rabbinic dignity by way of clerical gown and white bands rather than a full beard, and approved of a whole set of rules designed to impose decorum on the synagogue. There was to be no noise, conversation or disturbance before, during or after services; the congregational reader was not to be accompanied by the chants of individuals or corrected by anyone other than the rabbi; and felicitations on the performance of a major ritual act such as the priestly benediction were to be offered exclusively by wardens appointed for the purpose.[51] The prayer for the royal family was given authoritative sources in his commentary on the prayer-book while any references to political change or dissatisfaction with Jewish feelings about their fate at the hands of gentiles were gently or sensitively explained away. Interestingly, the actual text of the *siddur* generally attracted only minor modification although his abolition of the *kol nidrey* at the *Yom Kippur* evening service was the subject of considerable controversy and pre-empted the later action of the reformers.[52] Although the prayer-book to which his liturgical commentary is attached follows the style of Heidenheim and the 'correctors' as far as the Hebrew text, vocalisation, rubrics and layout are concerned, this was chosen after Hirsch's death and the inclusion of prayers in his commentary is a better guide to his attitude to them. Significantly, there are no comments or translations for any of the additions promoted by the mystics nor for the ceremonies of *tashlikh* on the first day of *Rosh Ha-Shanah*, *kapparoth* on the eve of *Yom Kippur* or *ḥibbuṭ ha-ʿaravoth* on *Hoshaʿna Rabbah*. Where angelology is an embedded part of the established liturgy rather than a late mediaeval or early modern mystical addition, Hirsch explains the 'ministering hosts' as part of 'the heavenly household that is the world' and gives the whole passage a cosmic rather than a mystical significance.[53]

As in so many other respects throughout history, England was associated with European developments but at the same time made a unique contribution of its own, playing a part, as it did, in the emergence of the modern Orthodox prayer-book at the end of the nineteenth century. Although in the last two decades of that century the immigration from Eastern Europe that was to increase the Jewish population of the British Isles tenfold and ultimately to have a major effect on all its institutions was already under way, the nature of Jewish religious theory and practice was still shaped by the Victorian establishment figures whether in the Sefardi or Ashkenazi sections of the community. The liturgical rite of the former was that of the Western European Sefardim who had settled, often firstly as Marranos, in Holland, Germany and England, while that of the latter was that of the German congregations which had produced the bulk of the Ashkenazi immigration in the eighteenth and nineteenth centuries. Both parts of the Anglo-Jewry of the day were conservative in their official and formal outlook while allowing and even encouraging the individual to make his own private compromises with his traditions, as he saw fit. This elasticity meant that the Reform congregation established in 1840 as the West London Synagogue of British Jews was unable to make any more than a marginal impact on the wider community and that the incoming Eastern European variety of Judaism took over half a century before it could make its presence felt in any significant way in the standard form of British Judaism. It goes therefore almost without saying that the Jewish religious variations that were characteristic of Germany, the radical and novel approach that dominated American Jewry, and the intense but insular observance of Eastern Europe made little headway in the United Kingdom of the Empress Victoria. It may not even be unfair to suggest that the English penchant for centralisation, moderation and conformity had no less an effect on the Anglo-Jewish synagogues than it had on the Anglican Church. The creation of the United Synagogue in 1870 as the legally recognised body of Orthodox synagogues in London, and the emergence of the Chief Rabbi, first Nathan Marcus Adler and later his son

Hermann, as its sole religious authority, provided the Ashkenazi congregations with an almost Anglican ecclesiastical structure. For its part, the Sefardi position was that, however many synagogues and prayer-gatherings there might be, there could be only one official congregation, the one that came into existence as Kehillath Sha'ar Ha-Shamayim and built the Bevis Marks place of worship in 1701, with its *haham* as its spiritual leader.[54] Although both Ashkenazim and Sefardim produced English translations of the *siddur* through the nineteenth century,[55] it was not until the publication of the 'Singer's Prayer-Book' in 1890 that the growing tendency towards a minor adjustment of the German Orthodox ritual acquired a more formal liturgical textuality. As in Germany, the concern for decorum, the use of the vernacular, westernised music (with mixed voice choirs), adjustments in synagogal layout, abbreviation, the restriction of individual congregational involvement in the service, and a family involvement at a later hour had led to something of a synagogal syncretism of English and Jewish spirituality already in the period of office of Nathan Marcus Adler but under the leadership of his son, Hermann, the process was greatly intensified, to the extent that the latter saw himself as a kind of Jewish bishop or archbishop, complete with the required clerical garb. Though his father had given the new prayer-book his sanction before his death in 1890, it was Hermann who had functioned as 'delegate Chief Rabbi' from 1879 because of his father's illness (and perhaps because of his reticence about agreeing to liturgical reform) and had consequently presided over its production. Similarly important is the fact that the editor, Simeon Singer, though ministering to an Orthodox congregation and loyal to the Chief Rabbinate, was liberal in outlook, thoroughly Anglo-Jewish in temperament, and consequently not averse to anglicisation, mild change and influence from the political and religious Jewish 'left of centre'. It is against such a general background that the creation, adoption and spread of 'The Authorised Daily Prayer Book of the United Hebrew Congregations of the British Empire' should be seen.[56]

Before note is taken of the degree to which the 'Singer's'

introduced some modifications to the Orthodox prayer-book, it should be acknowledged that, as in the general running of the religious life of the United Synagogue and the Chief Rabbinate at that time, a shift of the central institutions towards the left ensured that they retained the loyalty of the majority of the community, withstood significant encroachment from Reform and Eastern European Orthodox and remained the 'umbrella' organisation for traditional Judaism that was a unique feature of Anglo-Jewry. The new prayer-book's adjustments were more discreet and moderate than some United Synagogue members would have wished them and, as the lack of any discussion or justification of them in the preface makes clear, it is not unfair to say that they were smuggled into the text rather than being trumpeted as a major improvement. At the same time the intention was to make an impact on many members of the wider community by having the edition adopted, as a kind of Jewish hybrid of the Anglican 'King James Version' and its 'Book of Common Prayer' (both of which had come to be known as the 'authorised' texts), not only in synagogues but also in homes and in schools, as specifically declared in the preface.[57] One of the ways of doing this was to introduce new prayers relevant to the everyday activities of a variety of congregants and thereby to lend a novel, liturgical dimension to aspects of life not already touched upon in the statutory texts. It is perhaps true to say that the *rites de passage* had a more central role in Christian worship and that the pious Victorian Jew therefore felt the need for something equivalent.[58] To meet that need Nathan Marcus Adler had composed a thanksgiving prayer for women on their return to the synagogue after childbirth, a special service on the occasion of making collections for hospitals, and a memorial prayer for recitation, with suitable psalms and *qaddish*, at the home of a mourner.[59] His son and successor, Hermann, now added to these his own versions of prayers to be said at the consecration of a new home, during illness and on a death bed, and all these, as well as prayers for young children and the marriage service, were incorporated into the new prayer-book.[60] Although the paradigm for the basic text is, as claimed in the preface, that of

Baer's *ʿAvodath Yisraʾel*, and the *nusaḥ* and vocalisation are most closely modelled on that edition, much can be learnt about Anglo-Jewish attitudes of the time from what quietly, and without explanation and justification, disappears, appears in abbreviated form, is given a second-class format, or is translated somewhat less than literally. Among items that make no appearance are most of the *piyyuṭim* for special sabbaths, festivals and fasts, very much a part of the standard Ashkenazi rite supposedly followed; kabbalistic, mystical and folkloristic items such as *shalom ʿaleykhem* and *zemiroth* on Friday evening, *hoshaʿanoth* and *ʾushpizin* on *Sukkoth* and *kapparoth* on the eve of the Day of Atonement; and the *ʿeruv* benediction, the memorial prayer for departed relatives, the ceremonial recitation of the priestly benediction by the priests themselves, most of the *qiddush ha-levanah*, and the special *miy sheberakh* entreaties. Also missing are *qiddush* for the mornings of the pilgrim festivals and New Year and the blessing on searching for leaven before Passover.[61] The doubts about sacrifices were sufficient to reduce the number of passages included for recitation and the sensitivity about references to non-Jews led to the omission of sections of the *piyyuṭim maʿoz ṣur* for *Ḥanukkah* and *shoshanath yaʿaqov* for *Purim*.[62] *Tashlikh* suffered abbreviation and the two kabbalistic introductions to the performance of the *sukkah* and *lulav* rituals were subjected to a form of demythologisation. In the case of the latter, Singer rushed in where Baer had, despite his stated preference for alteration, feared to tread. As for the abbreviated grace after meals composed by Naftali ben David Zechariah Mendel and intended for children, and for adults only in emergency, a conflation of the original text and that of Baer was adopted by Singer to suit his editorial purpose and was headed, simply, 'Shorter Form of Grace'.[63] The typography, the rubrics and the instructions to find required prayers elsewhere also provide theological clues for the analytical reader. A small spidery text is sometimes employed for items which were not recited in various United Hebrew congregations,[64] the afternoon and evening services have hardly any typographical existence of their own, the statement that a text is recited 'in some congregations' is tantamount to a theological health warning about its dangerous use, and the absence of anything but the *ʿamidoth* for the High Holidays presupposes that there were those whose presence on these occasions did not warrant further provision.[65] If, after all, the use of a *maḥzor* for the festivals was being presupposed, why trouble with the *ʿamidoth* at all? As for the translation, the aim was a 'simplicity of style and diction which befits the language of prayer' and this statement, the use of the Revised Version for biblical passages, and the assistance offered by non-Orthodox figures such as C. G. Montefiore and Israel Abrahams would explain the somewhat ecumenical flavour of the result.[66] Where there is a choice of universalist or particularist versions, as with the morning benediction about non-Jews and the *ʿaleynu*, there is no surprise in Singer's preference and where references to such human functions as urination or menstruation threaten to disturb the spiritual atmosphere, they are omitted from the translation or rendered euphemistically.[67]

If the situation in nineteenth-century America may now engage our attention, the most immediate impression is that such concepts as 'Gemeinde' and 'authorisation' were simply not possible in the socio-political climate that prevailed there after the American and French Revolutions. The rights of individual groups to express themselves after their own religious fashion and the absence of an established church ensured that the Jews ultimately followed the Christians in sanctioning, and even championing, a pluralistic rather than centrist or united position. This is not to say that the whole American community was committed to a pluralism that regarded non-Christian faiths as equally valid and respected. Such a development, and various others, did not take place until well into the twentieth century. It is, however, true to say that within the various religious groups that waves of immigration brought to the shores of the United States there was soon created that voluntaristic philosophy and preference for individual expression that was to became the hallmark of the American way of life. As their parallel communities in much of Western Europe, Jewish America began the nineteenth century with fairly low numbers and those that did not opt out of their inherited identity through conversion or assimilation maintained traditional Ashkenazi and Sefardi synagogues and liturgies. There were attempts at establishing a Reform movement along German lines as early as 1824 (in Charleston, South Carolina) but it was not until the thirty-year period beginning about 1840 that the progressive ideology and modernised practices of that movement made an impact on the expanding Jewish communities and took the lead in representing the kind of affluent, liberal Americanism that was endearing itself to them.[68] Given the social and political background, this was not surprising. As H. M. Sachar has expressed it, 'It was hardly an accident . . . that the Jewish Reform movement was to reach its fullest development in countries that were predominantly Low Church: Germany and then the United States.'[69] Unlike Europe, the first Jewish congregations to demonstrate strength, to move towards institutionalisation and to produce significant leadership were those that ultimately identified with Reform Judaism and it was their initial power that goaded traditionalists, first in the 'historical' school that became the Conservative movement, and finally among the Orthodox, both modernist and strict, into producing their own brands of American Judaism with which to attract the growing numbers in the 'goldene medineh'.[70] The creation of these distinct American interpretations and practices of Judaism, each with their own religious and communal infrastructures, was, however, a product of the twentieth rather than the nineteenth century, even if the foundations were laid in the decades that saw the increase of the American Jewish population, mainly by immigration from Eastern Europe, from about 150,000 during the Civil War to approximately three million in 1914. Indeed, that very influx strengthened the defence of tradition that became the hallmark of non-Reform Judaism in the last third of the nineteenth century and, as will be noted in the next chapter, ultimately found a place, even an honoured one, among the Reform ranks themselves half a century later.

As is so often the case, Jewish liturgical history in America is but a reflection of the broader Jewish experience, both social and religious. The emergence of truly American forms of

Jewish liturgy did not commence until the late nineteenth century and even then only among the Reform congregations. Forms of Conservative or Orthodox prayer-books that are instantly recognisable as products of the United States did not make their appearance until the middle of the twentieth century, as will later be noted. Basically, the European model dictated the format from before the rise of the Reform movement until the challenges made to its supremacy. What this means in bibliographical terms is that the vast majority of prayer-books used in nineteenth-century America were either European products or copies of such editions, whether with regard to typography or in connection with content.[71] As far as the Orthodox Eastern European editions are concerned, the point is self-evident and the mass immigration into such areas as New York's Lower East Side only served to strengthen such loyalties. But the same is true of the Sefardi and Ashkenazi editions and translations of the traditional *siddur* issued by the likes of Isaac Leeser, whose liberal outlook and observant practice could be little distinguished from what came to be promoted as neo-Orthodoxy in the Western European communities.[72] The Reformers too followed the lead of the German Jewish congregations in which most of them had been born or reared, although the American penchant for individualism and freedom led to greater variety and more radical change. The same type of omissions, adjustments and insertions that have already been described as characteristic of German Reform and expressive of its rational, liberal and universalist theology, are to be found in the prayer-books published for its American counterpart in the mid-nineteenth century and the language of translation, or indeed of recitation, was as likely to be German as English. The Hamburg *Gebetbuch* was the basic exemplar and out of a great variety of forms the ones that finally emerged as the most popular were the *Seder Tefillah* (*Order of Prayer*) of Leo Merzbacher (New York, 1855), the *ʿOlath Tamid: Gebetbuch für israelitische Reform-Gemeinden* by David Einorn (Baltimore, 1856 – New York, 1858) and the *Minhag Amerika* of Isaac Mayer Wise (Cincinnati, 1856–7).[73] Though obviously committed to such innovations as mixed seating, choir, sermon and confirmation, Wise hailed from an Orthodox background and education in Bohemia and, dedicated as he was to the idea of Jewish communal unity, sought to produce a liturgy for all American Jews. A similar motivation lay behind his initiatives in the creation of the Union of American Hebrew Congregations, the Hebrew Union College, and the Central Conference of American Rabbis, in none of whose titles the controversial word 'Reform' is incorporated.[74] His *Minhag Amerika* represented moderate Reform, with the usual universalist message, was primarily based on the traditional text and retained Hebrew as the dominant language. Although Wise's edition proved popular in many circles, the trends of the next thirty years were towards more radical forms, a lesser degree of identification with traditional circles and, ultimately, in 1894–5 to a definition of American Jewish liturgy in which the Jewish element represented only a third part of the equation. The *Union Prayer Book* published in those years was closer to the radical format preferred by Einhorn. English predominated; messianic, national, mystical and sacrificial texts made no appearance; no time was available for *piyyuṭim* or repetition but a sermon was obligatory; scriptural readings were abbreviated and the messages of universalism and Israel's mission were given prominence. The book even opened from left to right and the services were labelled in Gothic print.[75]

An understanding of 'historical' Judaism's response to these developments necessitates a return to the 1860s. Those who saw themselves as the intellectual heirs of Zunz, Krochmal and Frankel were in the same predicament in the USA as their colleagues were in Germany. While Orthodoxy had its traditional institutions and Reform was creating what it saw as their modern equivalents, those with a scientific approach to Jewish scholarship and tradition were by no means of one mind with regard to the nature of religious observance and, partly as a consequence, had given little communal structure to their ideology. There were among the leaders not only traditionalists such as Isaac Leeser and Sabato Morais but also moderate reformers such as Benjamin Szold and Marcus Jastrow. An Orthodox German rabbi who was unsympathetic to reform but who saw the need for new translations and editions of the prayer-book for American Jewry, an English sermon and a Jewish Publication Society, Leeser ministered to Sefardi congregations and has been described by Moshe Davis as 'one of the master builders of American Judaism'.[76] Morais was born and educated in Livorno and used his rabbinical training for the benefit of the Spanish and Portuguese Synagogue in London before succeeding Leeser at Mikveh Israel in Philadelphia. He, like Leeser, devoted himself to public defence of Judaism and the translation of Jewish classics and functioned as a central plank in the platform of counter-Reform.[77] Counter-Orthodoxy, on the other hand, was as much an article of the Hungarian-born Szold's faith as counter-Reform and, though he apparently later regretted it, Jastrow prevented his congregation from becoming Reform by being permissive in matters of practice and making concessions in matters of ritual.[78] Some students of Sefardi religious history might argue that it was the strong Sefardi connection that kept Leeser and Morais on the same traditional side in the face of the central European trend towards change.[79] Be that as it may, Szold and Jastrow, supported by Henry Hochheimer, were anxious to demonstrate their dissatisfaction with the traditional prayer-book so beloved of such supporters of Leeser as Morris Raphall by introducing into a new version of the *siddur* the essential elements of progressive theology concerning God, the Torah, Israel and mankind and an acceptance of halakhic adjustment. The result was that the prayer-book produced by Szold as *Abodat Israel*, printed a number of times in the 1860s, first in a Hebrew–German edition and then in a Hebrew–English version, and revised by Jastrow in 1871, omitted all reference to sacrifices, resurrection, and God's special love for Israel. As far as synagogal ritual is concerned, he and Jastrow encouraged changes. In their communities such features as the organ, mixed choirs, family pews, and abbreviated Torah readings were introduced and the diaspora's second day of a festival, fast-days, daily services and *tefillin* were abolished. In theory, both scholars were historically in favour of the retention of such religious precepts and of the traditional sabbath but in practice they acknowledged the need to retain communal allegiance by allowing what they regarded as moderate reforms. The fact is that in many senses their approach to the text of the prayer-book was, despite their preference for Hebrew texts, a more radical one than that of I. M. Wise and just as the latter's hesitation about major textual adjustment left his ideas behind when the Reform movement preferred American innovation to immigrant caution at the end of the century, so their radicalism was deemed to be a burden to the newly emerging Conservative movement of that period as it strove to win adherents among the hundreds of thousands of Jews newly settling in America from their Eastern European *shtetlech*.[80] In 1891 another moderate reformer on the left wing of the historical school, Aaron Wise, the father of the famous Zionist leader Stephen S. Wise, attempted to produce a prayer-book for a congregation whose policy was Reform but its practice Conservative, his own Rodeph Shalom in New York; but his *Shalhevethyah: The Temple Service* (New York, 1891) was soon barely remembered.[81] Once again, then, the 'historical' school recoiled from throwing in its liturgical lot with the progressive movement and preferred to leave the matter of the prayer-book to the individual rabbi, who was often himself Orthodox, and the congregation, many of whom were comfortable with a familiar text. Consequently, whatever the scholars said about its development and the theologians regretted about its unenlightened religious ideology, the traditional *siddur* was still often to be found at the centre of communal usage.

As the nineteenth century came to an end, then, modernity of one sort or another was the dominant liturgical theme in the Central and Western European communities and in that of the United States of America and it seemed only a matter of time before the campaign for grammatical accuracy, widely understood content, decorous ritual and amended texts would also carry the day among the other major centres of Judaism, particularly as they began to move away from their contemporary environments into what was at the time seen as the more 'cultured' atmosphere of the West. That the major demographical and other upheavals of the twentieth century produced results of an altogether different and somewhat unexpected nature for Jews and Judaism will be the theme of the final chapter of this book.

CHAPTER 9

A background to current developments

Since most of the major studies of Jewish liturgical history were written in the first half of the twentieth century and later treatments very much based themselves on these and even nineteenth-century sources, much remains to be done in analysing developments in the middle and latter parts of the century now drawing to a close. It would totally unbalance both this chapter and the book of which it is a part to offer a fully detailed examination of such developments and such a piece of research will have to be undertaken, like so much else in this field, independently, at a later date, and in a different context. It is, however, essential to break the earlier habit of seeing the twentieth century simply as a continuation of the nineteenth and to point out the need for students of Jewish liturgy to follow general Jewish historians and sociologists in stressing the unique features of both the first and second halves of the century and how they deserve to be independently assessed.[1] To that end, a summary of the liturgical situation of the last eight or nine decades, with an occasional background glance at the nineteenth century when necessary, will be a suitable way of bringing this volume to a close.

Since the Jewish religious world now tends to be regarded as pluralistic, with three main forms of expression – Orthodoxy, Conservatism and Reform – dominating at least the most powerful centre of Jewish communal life outside Israel, namely, the United States of America, it will help us to identify changing trends in Jewish attitudes to worship if we pay brief attention to what has occurred in each of these three groupings. If one takes the view that each of these is an equally valid form of Jewish belief and practice, it is consequently necessary to trace the history of its overall liturgical attitudes. If, on the other hand, one favours the idea that authenticity lies with only one of them, as do many Orthodox Jews, there can still be little doubt that what one large group of Jews thinks or does will often influence their fellows across much of the religious spectrum. Such an influence can of course be both negative and positive but its undoubted existence necessitates a preference on the part of the scholar for an approach that takes account of a wide variety of ideas and customs even when the central topic is the fate of the traditional prayer-book itself. Because of these considerations twentieth-century changes and developments will be summarised according to their occurrence in the Orthodox, Conservative and Reform communities but for a number of reasons closer attention will be paid to Orthodoxy. The historical continuation of the traditional *siddur* is most easily traced and identified there; the common factor is easier to single out when worldwide trends are sought; there has recently been a resurgence of strict practice; and the writer's expertise and interest are more pronounced in the Orthodox liturgical area. Jewish demographical history having been what it was, it will make sense to deal with North American, central and Western European, and Israeli characteristics within each religious division. Given that the community of North America has become the world's most numerous and powerful representative of modern Judaism, it will not be surprising to find that much of what applies there has also a substantial degree of relevance in other centres of Jewish population, even to a limited extent in the State of Israel.[2]

The first point to be made about the influx of Jews from Eastern Europe at the beginning of the twentieth century is certainly valid with regard not only to America but also to other countries that offered them refuge. Contrary to what is often thought, such immigrants did not represent a bastion of Orthodoxy in their new domiciles. By definition, those that had the determination to flee the *shtetlech* and the major communities of Russia and Poland (the latter then of course lacking an independent political existence) were those who were dissatisfied with various aspects of life there and this dissatisfaction did not necessarily limit itself to relations with non-Jews and anti-Semitic governments. Many of them were therefore not entirely averse to the process of assimilation that immediately confronted them and it was generally destined to take at least two generations before their origins became a matter of pride rather than embarrassment. It was, however, assimilation, and not the attractions of progressive Judaism, that was the main motivation for their change in lifestyle. Unlike their central European co-religionists they had never needed to adopt a Judaism that was acceptable to the gentile world in return for a promise of emancipation and their concept of Jewish prayer, as of all other aspects of Judaism, remained a traditional one, even when it ceased to have any meaningful, practical effect on most of their day-to-day activities. It is thus possible, at one and the same time, to explain the desire of the Conservative movement to present a traditional front to such masses of immigrants but at the same time to argue that the impact made on local Orthodoxy by the relatively small number of committed Orthodox who survived the challenge of integration into the American lifestyle was not sufficient to effect a change in its overall nature from a central European to an Eastern European form, at least not yet.[3]

In the first half of the twentieth century, then, *American* Orthodoxy continued to be dominated, at the level of major congregations in their cathedral-like synagogues, if not among the small and struggling 'chevras' of such centres of Jewish life as New York's Lower East Side, by the kind of Judaism and Jewish worship that has already been explained as the 'established' variety typical of Germany, England, France and other centres on that side of Europe. In liturgical terms, this meant the acceptance even by the unimpeachably Orthodox of mild adjustments in both prayer-books and synagogal ritual, such as were noted in the previous chapter. That this kind of liturgy was not far removed from what was regarded by the right-wingers of the 'historical' movement as acceptable or even desirable was one of the reasons why the early institutions of the Conservative movement that were established at the end of the last century and the beginning of our own still hoped to represent Orthodoxy as well as the 'historical' school.[4] When this proved unacceptable and the schism finally came, it left moderately Orthodox rabbis and congregants on both sides of the fence, a fact that has created continuing tensions in both the Conservative and Orthodox movements throughout this century. It also, however, had a creative influence on moderate Orthodoxy since it led the leaders of that movement to break with the somewhat chaotic structure, or lack of structure, that characterised most Orthodox *kehilloth* of that time and to follow the Reform and Conservative synagogues in creating an American variety of rabbi, synagogue, communal administration and, ultimately, prayer-book edition. Although there remained the more *yeshivah*-orientated groups and an almost anarchistic tendency on the part of small *shtieblech*, where all the various rites of their Eastern European home communities were assiduously maintained, the centralisation process that had begun at the end of the nineteenth century saw the establishment of the Rabbi Isaac Elchanan Theological Seminary and the Union of Orthodox Jewish Congregations of America and, in the spring of 1919, the ordination of the first group of Orthodox rabbis specifically trained, under the tutelage of Bernard Revel, for the professional American rabbinate. In the years leading up to the Second World War it became possible, for the first time, for American-trained rabbis to receive an Orthodox institutional ordination and to take up posts in modern congregations. Their secular education, speech, clothing, interests, congregational centrality, concern for decorum and formality in the synagogue and tolerance of lax observance among their congregants (even of such dubious practices as mixed seating in a few cases) gradually became the standard in the larger Orthodox communities and the new spirit that they represented was given tangible institutional form by the founding of the Rabbinical Council of America in 1935. Major and influential figures in this new American rabbinate were such successful and popular rabbis as Joseph Lookstein of Kehilath Jeshurun and Leo Jung, spiritual leader of the Jewish Center on 86th Street, both in New York City.

Such distinguished personalities made it respectable, among all but the most right-wing circles, for the rabbis of an Orthodox congregation to take on many of the pastoral functions that had previously been associated with Christian churches or with progressive Jewish congregations. As a result, the synagogal functions of such Orthodox rabbis also gradually came to tally more and more with the ecclesiastical duties of the non-Jewish clergy. Not only did he teach the rabbinical sources and religious law, as traditionally required, but he also now read certain prayers, gave a sermon in English at the centre of the service, played a pivotal role in the *rites de passage* of his congregants and even became a kind of 'master of ceremonies' at the sabbath and festival services.[5] Although modern American Orthodoxy was thus gradually institutionalised, there was nothing that could be called the standard prayer-book of that movement until after the Second World War. Such publishers as the Hebrew Publishing Company of New York reproduced what were essentially European *siddurim*, with Yiddish or poor English translations, perhaps a prayer for the President and some Americanisms. The fact that both that Company and the Bloch Publishing Company, which had been founded by I. M. Wise and E. Bloch in Cincinnati in 1854 and moved to New York in 1901, issued editions of the 'Singer's Prayer-Book' created by Anglo-Jewry, is in itself an obvious indication that there was no clear liturgical identity worthy of being committed to print in the USA.[6] Interestingly, the nearest the modern Orthodox community in that country came to this was with the publication of the *siddurim* and *maḥzorim* edited by Philip Birnbaum and David de Sola Pool in the middle decades of the century. Birnbaum, scholar of Hebrew language and literature, editor and writer, produced his *Ha-Siddur Ha-Shalem* in 1949 and attempted to combine a contemporary translation, what he as a scholar regarded as a 'correct text', and historical notes on the one hand with a very full version of the traditional prayers on the other. Unlike Singer, he engaged in little theological 'censorship', happily including such items as *kapparoth*, *'ushpizin* and *hosha'anoth*.[7] This more comprehensive approach was also characteristic of the

Traditional Prayer Book edited and translated by de Sola Pool, published by Behrman House in New York in 1960 and 'authorised' by the Rabbinical Council of America, the grouping of Orthodox rabbis closely associated with Yeshiva University and looking to Rabbi Joseph Dov Soloveitchik as its halakhic authority. The format of this latter *siddur* makes it particularly suitable for use by the *ḥazzan* but it is also clearly intended for individual and domestic purposes. The commentary does not disturb the continuity of the text but is limited to the beginning of each service and there are English rubrics throughout the text. Not only does the text restore what Singer omitted but it also prefers the original wording in those cases where Singer modified it. On the other hand, the special needs of the American Orthodox congregation of modernist leanings are catered for by the inclusion of a prayer for the American government and the State of Israel ('the first flower of the promised redemption'), a '*bar mitzvah* prayer', a lengthy memorial service for departed relatives with 'meditations' in English, and a selection at the end of the volume of readings on Jewish theological themes from biblical and rabbinic sources.[8] The editor's activities as Sefardi congregational rabbi, as communal leader and as leading Zionist are clearly reflected in the fact that, despite its scrupulous adherence to a pre-Singer model, the authorised text takes account of the contemporary congregational requirements. Whatever their efforts to meet such requirements, perhaps indeed because of such efforts, these two editions never achieved the status of the official and widely acknowledged liturgies of modern American Orthodoxy.

Somewhat paradoxically, by the time that such prayer-books were emerging from the dominant modern Orthodox community of the United States, there was beginning to be a challenge from the right to the degree of authenticity of such a form of Orthodoxy. A number of factors lie behind this development of the last quarter of a century. The general acceptance of a pluralistic approach to religion, the increased respect for ethnicity and the religious rebellion against the permissive society lent a new confidence to a form of Orthodoxy that was less affected by and answerable to the external modern world and that had also been strengthened by the influx of *yeshivah*-centred groups between the two World Wars and after the Holocaust. The destruction of so many centres of such Jewish religious fervour in that European catastrophe had weakened that variety of Judaism numerically but had inspired the remnant to adhere to all the rigours of its faith and practice and to eschew what it regarded as compromises with the non-Jewish environment.[9] The presence of an increasing population in the Jewish State of what their opponents called the 'ultra-Orthodox', whether tolerant of political Zionism, suspicious of it, or downright opposed to its ideology, has also begun to have its effect on the Israeli political scene. It is hardly therefore surprising that it should be making its presence felt in liturgical matters too. American Jewish sociologists differ in their interpretation of the relationship between these two kinds of Orthodoxy. Samuel Heilman detects a distinct feeling of guilt on the part of the modern Orthodox about their moves towards accommodation with the dominant Western culture for the last century and a half and an acknowledgement that authenticity lies within the *yeshivah* world while C. S. Liebman sees two ends of the Orthodox spectrum here being represented, that of the 'sect' and that of the 'church'.[10] Whatever the analysis, there can be little doubt that while Judaism as a whole continues to lose between a third and a half of its adherents to the attractions of social and cultural assimilation through intermarriage, there is a new vibrancy among the right-wing Orthodox who, unlike their predecessors of a generation or two ago, can now be counted among the young professional and intellectual members of the affluent society proportionately no less than their Conservative and Reform fellows.[11] Such social, economic and cultural status no longer rules out identification with Ḥasidic sects and although few of these can match the success of Ḥabad and its leader, the Lubavitcher Rebbe, in reaching out to Jews of all types, operating in all sorts of environments and winning 'converts' by their missionary zeal, and that of Satmar in championing the anti-Zionist cause, there are a whole gamut of such groups that are no longer content to keep a low profile but make their views heard in the wider Orthodox community. Among the Sefardim too, what was previously no more than a respect for elders, a reverence for tradition and a desire for stability has been strengthened by immigration into America from Arabic-speaking countries of Jews who are dismissive of the ways of the Spanish and Portuguese congregations of the last two centuries and anxious to inject new life into their communities.[12]

The liturgical consequences of such remarkable developments deserve to be identified and explained, and the first point to be made is an ideological one. On the assumption that what has been claimed throughout this volume about rabbinic prayer's ambivalence with regard to any trend towards cultic ceremonial and liturgical formality is justified, it is by no means astonishing that recent moves on the part of many modern Orthodox to return to tradition should question, if not reject, Orthodoxy's flirtations with cathedral-synagogues, orchestrated congregational liturgy and authorised prayer-books. For Lawrence Hoffman it is clearly an indication of theological failure that Orthodoxy 'has generated no single prayer book' and a further sign that it 'has suffered chronically from a lack of institutional unity'. For the 'Torah-true' Orthodox, commitment to the *halakhoth* of prayer rather than to the formalities of its congregational presentation is the all-important matter and there is no need to develop one American liturgy when so many more traditional rites, created in communities that are alleged to have been less open to external influences, are available for continued use. As Hoffman himself notes, 'many of the groupings subsumed under the general title of "Orthodox" oppose the very idea of Americanization'.[13] It may be argued that they also oppose the very idea of seeing the synagogue as the main, or even the only, focus of Jewish religious activity when there are so many other *miṣwoth* to which they are at least equally devoted and which pervade all other aspects of their lives. This ideology finds practical expression in the return of the rabbi (or 'rebbe') to educational rather than liturgical functions, the substitution of a learned layman for a professional cantor as the prayer-leader, and the preference for the smaller, more intimate *shtiebel* or mini-synagogue over the grander buildings. Congregational prayer constitutes a medley of individuals at their own devotions who coalesce with the leader from time to time, spontaneous singing without choral rehearsal, direction or effect, and an apparent anarchy (but actually more of an anarchism) about dress, movement and decorum. For some groups of the religious Zionist type, the archetype is an Israeli one while for others who identify the secular Zionist state as a threat to Orthodoxy hardly less dangerous that Americanisation there is a conscious attempt to free members from its influences. Hence the tensions and divisions in many modern Orthodox groups about the prayer for the State of Israel, the celebration of Israeli Independence Day, and the adoption of customs practised in the Jewish homeland. It is not by accident that some choose to cover their heads with a large black *kipa* rather than a small crocheted one. A noteworthy phenomenon is the matter of the status of Sefardi pronunciation of Hebrew as generally followed in Israel. In the fifties, congregants in Orthodox synagogues who were particularly *avant-garde* could be heard struggling to overcome their native Ashkenazi pronunciation and to enunciate their Hebrew like their Israeli friends and family as a means of identifying with a Zionist Judaism. Today what are heard are the desperate attempts of youngsters brought up with Israeli Hebrew to demonstrate their allegiance to the *yeshivah*-world above everything else, whether in Israel or elsewhere, by cultivating what they fondly imagine is an Eastern European set of Hebrew vowels.[14] There has been a distinct disillusionment with Western European and American prayer-books and since all-Hebrew editions are regarded as more authentic, Israeli publications, later to be discussed, find acceptance in some circles. Others such as Ḥabad produce their own texts while there are those who photographically reprint, with American bibliographical details superimposed, older European editions, often following the Ḥasidic *nusaḥ Sefarad*, discussed in a previous chapter, rather than the Polish or German Ashkenazi rite.[15] Where for the less educated Jew a parallel English text is required, as in the case of the burgeoning *ba'aley teshuvah* movement (those 'returning' to Orthodox Judaism),[16] the preference is for the ArtScroll series. Here the technical production and overall layout are excellent and the stress is on the total adoption by the worshipper of all the detailed rubrics included by the editor, whether they are customary or statutory. On principle only religiously approved Jewish writers are cited and the English title 'God' being regarded as insufficiently reverential, the word *Hashem* (i.e. 'the (Divine) Name') is used throughout. The stress is on literalness rather than polish with the consequent adoption of some unusual English constructions. Sources are cited and there is no hesitation about the inclusion of kabbalistic material. Traditional rather than historical explanations are offered and transliterations of Hebrew are done in what appears to be an inconsistent combination of the Eastern European Ashkenazi version with its Israeli Sefardi counterpart.[17] Another noteworthy development in Orthodox liturgical matters is the degree to which even the communities that are the spiritual descendants of those who followed S. R. Hirsch in Frankfurt in his modern German orthodoxy and those who maintained for so long the traditions of the Lithuanian *Mithnaggedim*, both once staunch opponents of Ḥasidism, have had their rites infiltrated by ḥasidic practices.[18] Now that the main threat is perceived to be from the external world, there is again a tendency towards a degree of harmonisation on the part of the strictly Orthodox, at least in matters of minor detail. A detailed analysis of such developments would certainly pay scholarly dividends.

Much of what has just been written about general developments in twentieth-century Orthodoxy and their influences on liturgical practice is equally applicable in the surviving centres of active Judaism in Europe, such as the United Kingdom, but some brief remarks are called for about that community's particular history this century and its effect on liturgical change, both away from tradition and in return to it. As far as Anglo-Jewry is concerned, the Friday evening prayer-book printed for its intellectual elite studying at Oxford in 1914 still reads like a compromise between Orthodoxy and moderate

Reform. In addition to a slightly abbreviated, traditional service, there are Bible readings, English prayers, Hebrew poems, a prayer for the Royal Family and a slot for a sermon.[19] Between the two World Wars, however, children and grandchildren of the late nineteenth- and early twentieth-century immigrants began to make a serious impact on the religious community and, once strengthened by the arrival of additional groups of the committed Orthodox just before the Second World War, were able to take over the institutions in the two decades after the Holocaust and the creation of the State of Israel. Unlike America, of course, the 'establishment' variety of Judaism was undoubtedly Orthodoxy even if the adherence to that tradition on the part of the majority of the community was nominal rather than active and practical. The Chief Rabbinate, Jews' College and the 'Singer's Prayer-Book' continued to dominate the scene but each of these institutions went through a metamorphosis that reflected the drift in the wider community towards greater respectability, independence and assertiveness on the part of the Reform community on the one side and towards a less apologetic, more personally demanding and bolder form of Orthodoxy on the other. Given the developments in the USA and the wider Jewish world, it is hardly likely that Anglo-Jewry's former religious style, now hankered after by some of its erstwhile patrons, would have been able to maintain its virtually unique 'Anglican' identity, whatever its achievements and attractions, and the transfer of power to the alternative philosophy more familiar and acceptable to the immigrants, their children and their supporters, merely quickened the process. The Chief Rabbinate strengthened its links and thereby improved its status among the communities to the right of the United Synagogue and its increasing concern for halakhic propriety throughout the religious empire over which it ruled gave additional power to its Beth Din and the decidedly Eastern European Orthodoxy that its *dayyanim* promoted and applied. Jews' College set about training rabbis who could at least understand the halakhic process rather than 'reverend gentlemen' and 'ministers' who were more devoted to their pastoral duties, and weakened its links with the University of

London (before later attempting to strengthen them again) in order to establish its own scholarly priorities and to adopt a syllabus that created less theological strain on its students. In the synagogues themselves, mixed choirs were gradually phased out, the *bimah* was moved back to the centre from the 'eastern' end and therefore ceased to resemble an altar, and the times of services came again to be controlled by halakhic considerations rather than by congregational convenience. The abbreviation of services and the use of English were no longer among liturgical desiderata and rabbis who did not wear canonicals or preach in polished, native English once again became acceptable in Anglo-Jewish pulpits.[20] Of major significance are the revisions in the 'Singer's Prayer-Book' that can be detected in the years between the first edition of 1890 and its centenary successor's appearance in 1990 and that deserve closer attention.

Soon after its first publication it became apparent to regular users that the inclusion of a prayer only once when it was in fact used in a number of different contexts led to irritation and confusion and subsequent editions of the 'Singer's' have attempted to remedy this by offering such duplicated texts in full. The spidery print of parts of the original was also gradually replaced and eventually disappeared with the use of a totally new fount in 1962. Needless to say, given the generally patriotic nature of the community, care was also taken to update the prayer for the Royal Family as and when necessary. None of these changes are, however, liturgically significant while a number of others certainly are. Even before Joseph Hertz, who was appointed Chief Rabbi in 1913, had had time to influence matters, the omission of the *zemiroth* from the Friday evening table, the ceremonial priestly blessing intoned by the priests themselves, and the memorial prayer recited on festivals, had been regretted and rectified. Singer himself had lamented the absence of *zemiroth* but the restoration of the other two items probably represents a response to the growing band of traditionalists in the wider community. For the observant, the practice of the United Synagogue to omit the priestly blessing would have been found strange while for those many from Eastern Europe then fast assimilating into a non-observant lifestyle, the memorial prayer provided the opportunity for a nostalgic recollection of people and practices that had once been.[21] Although a staunch and outspoken traditionalist, Hertz on the whole remained loyal to the nineteenth-century flavour of the 'Singer's' and the changes he introduced in his thirty-three years in office demonstrate a concern with further increasing the prayer-book's relevance to contemporary needs and ideas rather than with the restoration of abandoned texts. His additions included a novel meditation for women before kindling the sabbath lights and he followed the earlier penchant for composing prayers associated with *rites de passage* (a tombstone consecration service had been introduced into the 1912 edition) by formulating suitable collections of texts for recitation on recovery from illness, before a funeral, and by a boy at the age of *bar-miṣwah*. He also made further adjustments to the abbreviated grace after meals which, admittedly, restored part of Baer's text but at the same time made a further abbreviation and introduced a halakhically questionable reference to sabbath or festival. Hertz was in his element when doughtily defending Orthodoxy's way of life against Jewish theological opponents and in the face of secular challenges and the annotated prayer-book that he produced during the Second World War offered lively essays on Jewish prayers and holidays as well as selected readings and historical notes.[22] It was his successor, Israel Brodie, whose new edition of 1962 began seriously to reflect the changing priorities of Anglo-Jewry. In addition to some minor revisions of the English, the introduction of a prayer for the State of Israel and the updating of the prayer for the traveller and the *bar-miṣwah* boy, Brodie presided over the re-introduction of *shalom ʿaleykhem* for Friday evening, *zemiroth* for the sabbath lunch table, *qiddush* for festival mornings, and the benedictions recited over *bediqath hameṣ* and *ʿeruv tavshilin*. This represented not only an awareness that practising Jews were again making the home, as well as the synagogue, a centre for their religious activities, but also a move towards the expectation of higher standards of observance on the part of many United Synagogue worshippers. The conviction that in religious matters one's practical observance is more important than one's scholarly achievements was clearly exemplified in the way in which the Brodie edition preferred a version of the original preface in which the name of C. G. Montefiore was replaced by an anonymous reference to 'an accomplished scholar'![23] The process of restoring missing texts is continued in the thoroughly revised *Authorised Daily Prayer Book of the United Hebrew Congregations of the Commonwealth* edited by Lord (Immanuel) Jakobovits, translated by Eli Cashdan and published in 1990. *Hoshaʿanoth* reappear; the rehabilitation of the *qiddush levanah*, which had been emasculated by Singer and partially restored by Hertz, is completed; the sixth stanza of *maʿoz ṣur* is again found acceptable; and the *piyyuṭim* constituting the prayers for rain and dew are included.[24] Although some kabbalistic items such as *yedid nefesh* on Friday evening and Saturday afternoon and *ribono shel ʿolam* after the counting of the *ʿomer* are apparently approved, others are not and the 'censored' versions of the meditations before the blessings over the *lulav* and the *sukkah* are retained.[25] The erstwhile Anglo-Jewish need for special prayers relating to a new home (Singer's version is considerably reduced), *bar-miṣwah* and collections for hospitals is apparently adjudged to have disappeared and it is assumed that *maḥzorim* will be available on *Rosh Ha-Shanah* and *Yom Kippur* and special booklets at a cemetery for burial services and tombstone consecrations. The weekday Torah readings are provided in full, as in many Israeli editions, and as far as Zionist ideology is concerned, the prayer for the State is shorter and less grand than that of Brodie but does include a reference to the Israeli Defence Forces and there is a note before *taḥanun* to indicate that many congregations omit it on the Israeli holidays of Independence Day and Jerusalem Day.[26] Strangely, however, no liturgical instructions are offered for these two days and the *naḥem* prayer on the Ninth of Av still refers to a Jerusalem that is 'mourning, laid waste, despised and desolate . . . all her glory gone . . . without inhabitant'. Jakobovits restores some of Hertz's omissions in the abbreviated grace, abandons the halakhically questionable reference to sabbath or festival, and limits its recitation to 'emergencies and special cases of urgency'.[27] As far as the order and content is concerned, the principle seems to be a general acceptance of the dominant current practice and there seems to be little compunction about the retention of a number of Singer's innovations. But the overall intention of the Jakobovits edition is not to be sought in matters of addition and subtraction but in the physical presentation, the pedagogical content and the devotional guidance. Aspects of the style of other popular prayer-books such as the ArtScroll are adopted (albeit in a more modest fashion), there are a variety of Hebrew and English typefaces, alphabetical acrostics are marked, each of the morning *'amidah* benedictions is named and there are fuller rubrics and helpful source citations. The editor's commentary eschews historical and scientific treatment of the prayers and services in favour of a summary of content, an explanation of meaning and an indication of contextual relevance and devotional value. The edition is available in three sizes: a large one to match Hertz's annotated edition; a medium one to match earlier editions; and a small one to match popular Israeli editions. The new Ashkenazi prayer-book is thus being employed to promote Jewish religious education in this generation as it was to encourage synagogal decorum and propriety a century ago.[28]

As far as the British Sefardi rite is concerned, the standard Spanish and Portuguese rite of the Western European communities, as canonised by David de Sola in his edition of 1836–8 and by Moses Gaster in his edition of 1901 (and claimed by him as the ancient Castilian rite), remained the dominant form until the arrival in the UK of Sefardim from more oriental countries after the Second World War.[29] Their preference for their own liturgical customs, whether Egyptian, Iraqi, Persian, Adeni or Indian, was one of the reasons why tensions arose within a community that had previously owed a fairly widespread allegiance to the Spanish and Portuguese custom and ultimately led to the development of a greater degree of synagogal autonomy on the part of the recent immigrants. Unlike the older community, which continued to use the Gaster edition, the newcomers preferred their own prayer-books or versions of them such as *Tefillath Yesharim* and *Sukkath Dawid* produced for the *'edoth ha-mizraḥ* in Israel in recent years but it seemed unlikely that they would be strong enough, or indeed inclined, to produce an Anglo-Jewish oriental Sefardi *siddur* of their own.[30] A further liturgical complication involving the immigration of Sefardim from elsewhere into the communities of Western Europe may be identified within the context of the influx of over a quarter of a million Egyptian, Moroccan, Tunisian and Algerian Jews into a French Jewish community that had amounted to only 180,000 after the Holocaust. Although there had already been congregations that followed Sefardi rites in the years before this influx, the moderately Orthodox Consistoire Central Israélite de France et d'Algérie had dominated the community and had generally followed the Ashkenazi custom. The new immigrants began to outnumber the existing Jewish population in the 1960s and not only to form their own communities and institutions but also to take over many of the established ones. The liturgical results deserve detailed independent analysis but in the present context it will be sufficient to point to the current existence of numerous hybrid practices in the French congregations that owe their origin to the fusion of Ashkenazi, Western Sefardi and North African Sefardi traditions.[31]

Demographical change was of course also the reason for the emergence of Jewish Palestine and the State of Israel as a major influence on the development of the Orthodox rite in the twentieth century. While the Jewish community of the Holy Land had at the beginning of the nineteenth century amounted to no more than a few thousand, living mainly off the charity of their brethren elsewhere, the situation changed significantly in the second half of the century and Jerusalem already had a Jewish majority in the last quarter of that century.[32] One of the industries that attempted to turn the Jews into a self-sufficient group was that of printing and the pioneer in this field was Israel Bek of Berdichev in the Ukraine who opened a printing-press in Safed, the first for 250 years, between 1830 and 1837 and then moved it to Jerusalem where he and his son produced some 130 titles before the business was sold off in 1883, by which time there were about another ten fairly substantial companies in the same business. A Sefardi prayer-book was published in Safed in 1832 and others of that rite followed in Jerusalem in the middle and latter parts of the century but the interesting fact is that with the exception of a few Sefardi prayer-books it was not the comprehensive prayer-book that was produced in number but the more limited publication specialising in prayers for specific places and occasions, especially of the mystical variety, and relating particularly to the land of Israel. Of forty-five liturgies published between 1841 and 1891 less than a quarter dealt with daily prayers and it was only towards the end of the century that the situation began to change, with the appearance of a number of prayer-books catering for various oriental rites.[33] This no doubt reflected the fact that the Sefardi community, which had previously been dominant and united, was beginning to split into groups according to origin. The degree of division was even greater among the Ashkenazim where all manner of Eastern European Jews, both Ḥasidim and Perushim, as the opponents of Ḥasidism were then dubbed, were emerging but, with a very few exceptions, it was not until the early twentieth century that they began to produce their own prayer-books in number rather than looking to the publishing houses of Eastern Europe (as the Sefardim did to Livorno) for copies.[34] The major waves of aliyah of the first few decades of the current century did not, as is well known, bring large numbers of Jews who were anxious to purchase prayer-books but between the two World Wars the situation changed when the bourgeois element settled in large numbers from central Europe and Poland and included a fair proportion of Orthodox families. By that time too, the institutions of the religious forms of political Zionism had taken root, a Chief Rabbinate for both Sefardim and Ashkenazim had been established, and the observant Jews of Eretz Yisrael were more inclined, as well as obligated by political circumstances, to look to their own resources rather than to those of their countries of birth in matters of educational and religious publications. Tel Aviv joined and then surpassed Jerusalem as a centre of Jewish printing already in the early days of its existence and prayer-books were produced in greater number, thus reversing the situation of the previous century in which most of such items had been imported. The nature of the Palestinian *siddurim* differed, however, but little from the diaspora archetypes on which they were based. Essentially, they represented the Eastern European Ashkenazi and the Leghorn Sefardi types, offering a wide variety of liturgical content suitable for use in many aspects of religious life rather than primarily in the synagogue. While the central and Western European, neo-Orthodox prayer-book was, as has been demonstrated, fashioned on the assumption that it would be used for formal congregational prayer in a dignified place of worship, its equivalent in Palestine, and later in Israel, was more of a liturgical vade-mecum for the observant Jew relevant to the performance of numerous religious duties.[35] With the establishment of the State of Israel in 1948 and, subsequently, in the 1960s, the confident emergence of a truly 'Israeli' religious identity to match the secular one that had previously held sway, there was a move in the direction of a contemporary Orthodoxy in certain circles. That Orthodoxy was not of the European neo-Orthodox variety or its strictly Orthodox competitor, both of which maintained a role in Israeli religious society, but reflective of a religio-political identity that was in its early manifestation based on the Mizraḥi concept of Orthodox Zionism as a religious adjunct to Socialist Zionism but later moved towards a politically conservative ideology, more acceptable to the growing Sefardi majority and a less religiously moderate European and American aliyah.[36] The *siddurim* printed in Israel for such groups over the last quarter of a century contain evidence of these theological and political developments. First of all, obvious account is taken in such publications of the fact that most of their users are resident in Israel and the tendency of their predecessors to ignore the custom relevant to the homeland is thus reversed. The norm is often taken to be one day of a festival and a note is made, or may be made, about the diaspora practice of observing a second day. The same preference for the Israeli custom occurs with regard to such rites as Torah readings, pleas for rain, prayers for the Israeli government and army, and of course in connection with such national holidays as Independence Day and Jerusalem Day. In these latter cases, the insertion of additional material identifying these days as minor festivals, though still controversial among even neo-Orthodox circles in both Israel and the diaspora, is becoming more common.[37] Until very recently the general style of print, layout and rubrics was still borrowed from the older European publications but this too has now changed. *Siddurim* such as *Rinath Yisrael* and that produced by Koren, as well as the scientific editions of the *maḥzor* produced by E. D. Goldschmidt, have taken on a totally new look, achieved by contemporary typography, educationally superior presentation and explanation, and the provision of instructions in current Hebrew, although it should be stressed that the content is still a reflection of Sefardi and Eastern European comprehensiveness rather than Western European synagogal centrality.[38] One simple example of this is in the absence of the growing ritualisation of the congregational response to the cantorial declaration such as is found in the 'Singer's' and is an attempt at creating a more extensive degree of formal response in the synagogue. Although the congregation follows or leads the *ḥazzan* on various occasions in Israel no less than outside it, there is rarely anything statutory about this and the individual's responsibilities may be met either by his own prayer or by that of the cantor without any formal exchange between them. There are established responses in the case of *barekhu* and the *qedushah* and some precedents for responsive chant in the talmudic and geonic periods as well as among the western Ashkenazim of the late mediaeval period. It was, however, only in the early modern and Haskalah periods that stress again came to be laid on such a practice and its decorous effect. Furthermore, texts such as the *ʿaleynu*, the censored versions of which had become the norm among the socially and politically abashed Jews of Western Europe and America, have regained their missing parts.[39] Another interesting development is the emergence of a *nusaḥ ʾaḥid*, or unified Israeli rite, based on that suggested by Rabbi Shelomo Goren when he was Chief Rabbi of the Israeli

Defence Forces. It is in essence a combination of Sefardi, Ashkenazi and Ḥasidic customs which has not yet become dominant but may have more prospect of doing so as the different communities intermarry and achieve higher degrees of mutual religious tolerance.[40] Where Sefardi and Ḥasidic customs tally, as they often do, the Ashkenazi tradition becomes a minority practice in Israel, as with the issues of donning *tefillin* on the intermediate days of a festival, which is now a sure sign of the *mithnagged*. Other developments that should not go unnoticed are the role of the media in protecting the traditional rite of each religious group by recording it for the public, especially on appropriate holidays; the acquisition by such days as *Lag Be-ʿOmer* and *Tu Bishevaṭ* of novel Israeli characteristics; and the adoption in secular circles of quasi-religious rites such as a Passover *Haggadah* that meets their own requirements and tallies with their particular ideology.[41]

Before leave is taken of the world of Orthodox prayer, one further issue that is currently occupying some congregations, particularly in the USA, should be noted. While women in the Reform and Conservative movements have now reached the level of synagogal rabbi and are to all intents and purposes liturgically indistinguishable from men, that is certainly not the state of affairs among the Orthodox. The same influences, arising out of the drive for sexual egalitarianism and women's liberation in the outside world, have begun to make themselves felt but are bound to take more central account of traditional *halakhah* among the Orthodox than they do among the Progressive movements. Questions are now being raised in neo-Orthodox circles about the basic nature of the contemporary rabbinate and whether such a position has primarily to do with making decisions in Jewish law, functioning as a teacher and communal leader, or performing the tasks of a religious functionary. On the basis of the answer proffered, rulings will be made about the halakhic possibility of expanding the role of the woman in the Orthodox congregation but it is not yet clear what the ultimate decisions will be. Is the move towards an alleged egalitarianism an aberration and no more than a current fad which will be abandoned when a return is made to the values of the traditional family unit? Alternatively, will the view that men and women have equally valid roles that are complementary but not identical in the long run give way to a more radical position that finds *halakhah* to be more in concert with what has become socially and politically fashionable?[42] In the mean time there are women, albeit still a minority, who find that their participation in the male-dominated Orthodox service, however justified on halakhic grounds by the different liturgical requirements made of the two sexes, is not providing them with the spiritual inspiration and the outlet for their religiosity that they crave. By pressing for women's prayer groups conducted within the 'four cubits of the *halakhah*', they have created an acrimonious debate among Orthodox authorities, some of whom argue that whatever is legally permitted should be granted and even encouraged while others claim that their motivation is separatist and religiously misguided and any leniency will only encourage the importation of strident feminism and other non-Jewish values into the synagogue. Where sanctioned, Orthodox women's prayer groups have scrupulously adhered to halakhic requirements and as a result have developed what is effectively a novel liturgy that removes those relatively few elements that require a quorum (*minyan*) of ten males but retained such major elements as the *pesuqey de-zimra*, *shema'*, *'amidah* and the Torah reading on a weekday or sabbath, and the recitation of the Scroll of Esther, the *haqafoth* of *Simḥath Torah* and the *bath-miṣwah* ceremony on more specialised occasions. Should such services ultimately win universal acceptance in Orthodox synagogues rather than remain substantially restricted to a few American centres, it will be interesting to see whether or how they are given written expression in a suitable female *siddur* and whether this leads to a greater separation of the sexes at Orthodox Jewish worship than is now practised.[43]

The question now to be briefly addressed is whether the direction of the Conservative movement that established itself early in the twentieth century, especially in the USA, with the strengthening of the Jewish Theological Seminary, and the establishment of the Rabbinical Assembly and the United

Synagogue of America, has also been a unified and consistent one since that time in matters of a liturgical nature. The overall picture in the first half of the current century is one of success and achievement on the part of the congregations that were part of the Conservative movement. They grew in size and number and, just as had happened in Germany in the previous century, their members became so much a part of the general social and cultural milieu, as they moved into affluent suburbs, that they wished their religious life to reflect something at least akin to the American Protestant faith and practice even if it also expressed a nostalgia towards traditional Jewish custom. Thus it was that the Eastern European style gave way to the American equivalent of the central and Western European mode but as it did so it no longer had to opt for the high class aspirations of the Reform communities; it could choose rather to maintain one foot in each camp and even argue that such a stance reflected the liberal values of compromise and moderation so much admired and promoted in Western culture. It was expected that as the second and third generations of immigrants made their way into the upper income brackets so would they tend to abandon certain embarrassing elements of their parents' and grandparents' 'Yiddish' culture while maintaining an overall commitment to the preservation of the more acceptable aspects of its religious traditions.[44] The story that unfolds as far as worship is concerned is one that is already fairly familiar to us from earlier contexts, particularly those of neo-Orthodoxy and mild Reform. Liturgical activity moves from Jewish life in general to the synagogue in particular and visits there become weekly on the part of the communal leaders, restricted to High Holidays and *rites de passage* on the part of most congregants, and a daily feature only for the 'old guard' who were brought up in an Orthodox environment. In order to combat this apathy, the Friday evening service is expanded at its edges and by the introduction of a sermon. The decorous nature of the service becomes of major significance and is controlled by 'ushers'; appeals, auctions and pledges are eliminated; while the rabbi functions as a master of ceremonies, as well as a synagogal manager. The growing trend towards sexual egalitarianism and the significant part played by women in the American Protestant churches has its influence on Jewish middle class suburbia and the absence of an increasing proportion of males is compensated for by the increased attendance of females at sabbath worship with the consequent acceptance of mixed seating or 'family pews' and a limited degree of female participation in the services of most Conservative congregations.[45] Until virtually the middle of the century, however, the text of the prayer-book being used in such congregations remained the one developed by the 'centrist' Orthodoxy of Anglo-Jewry and represented by the publications of Singer and of H. M. Adler (the 'Routledge' *maḥzor*) reproduced in New York.[46] The older congregants were more familiar and comfortable with it and it could be used as a base even when local variations, by way of introductions, omissions and abbreviations, were introduced. This Conservative liturgical trend was inspired by a number of factors in addition to the presence of the 'old-timers'. Solomon Schechter had made a determined effort to introduce the centrist philosophy of Anglo-Jewish Orthodoxy into the Jewish Theological Seminary and the United Synagogue of America and the aim of these institutions in their early years was therefore to represent not just another modern form of Judaism but to offer an umbrella under which a wide range of traditional Jewish opinion in America could shelter. A break with accepted *halakhah*, the creation of an independent religious movement, and the compilation of a new Conservative *siddur* were therefore resisted for a number of decades. It thus remained possible, especially early in the century, for Orthodox rabbis to be trained at the Seminary and to take up posts in either modern Orthodox or Conservative congregations and for the Seminary's largely traditional and halakhically observant faculty to feel that they could train those kinds of rabbis without any prick of conscience.[47] The only prayer-book 'authorised' by the United Synagogue of America was that published in 1927 for the festivals and those who wished to see the alteration there of the petition for the restoration of sacrifices to a recollection of its historical occurrence had to be satisfied with the restriction of such a change only to an 'unofficial' edition of that publication issued by individual rabbis. A satisfactory English translation, a correct Hebrew text and an appropriate prayer for the government were all innovations that might just as well have come from a neo-Orthodox source.[48] But of course the obvious contrast between the types of ideology and practice espoused by most of its congregants on the one hand and represented by the text of the traditional *siddur* on the other was felt by many and there were accusations of inconsistency and pressure for the creation of a liturgy that gave the movement its own identity.

It was in the late thirties and in the forties that more serious changes came and, in retrospect, they may be characterised as the first manifestations of a liturgical self-assertion that was now unapologetically progressive and American and would ultimately lead to a cleaner break from Orthodoxy and traditional *halakhah*. Part of the impetus came from the creation of the Reconstructionist form of Conservative Judaism under the influence of the ideas of Seminary teacher Mordecai Kaplan and its promotion of the idea of an evolving religious civilisation in which group survival and individual expression controlled ritual and not vice versa. The Reconstructionists produced their own *Haggadah* in 1941 and prayer-books for the sabbath in 1945, for the High Holidays in 1948, for festivals in 1958 and for daily prayer in 1963. It is not without significance that daily prayer, once the initial need of the Jewish congregation, was among the latest liturgies to receive communal attention in the progressive movements, given that for a long time congregational worship was almost by ideology but certainly in practice absent as a daily phenomenon. Concepts such as the superhuman God, the chosen people, the divine revelation and the personal messiah were omitted but traditional texts and melodies were retained, even if their meanings had to be explained in a novel fashion by the editors. The text might be doctored but remained recognisable while the nostalgic tune might be strummed on a guitar.[49] The early attempts of the Reconstructionists to express themselves independently in the liturgical sphere were matched by the composition by

Rabbi Morris Silverman of a prayer-book for the sabbath and festivals in 1937 and of one for the High Holidays in 1939. The moderate adjustments suggested by him and by other rabbis such as Solomon Goldman were carefully considered by a committee of the Rabbinical Assembly, chaired by Robert Gordis, and the result was the publication in 1946 of a sabbath and festival prayer-book, well laid out and retranslated, that adopted some of the adjustments and set out to represent the uniqueness of the Conservative position. The basic text remained the Hebrew version of modern Ashkenazi Orthodoxy but novel changes were made even in the statutory prayers, in addition to the change of tense regarding Temple sacrifices. The traditional Jewish prayer for peace was universalised and three of the early morning benedictions were altered from a negative to a positive formulation. Zionism and the revival of Hebrew were seen as justifications for the retention of the traditional allusions to the ingathering of the exiles and of the original language of the prayers while the omission of *piyyuṭim* and of the accretions of more recent centuries, especially in the area of the mystical, were seen as part of an organic change that was not in itself revolutionary. The desire for intellectual integrity that stood behind the textual adjustments was not, however, strong enough to overcome an antipathy to Reform and Reconstructionist innovations of a more extensive variety and there was a preference for the retention of the traditional text but with English supplements, consisting of modern prayers and readings, for inspirational use, and non-literal translations that permitted reinterpretation by means of paraphrase.[50] As Marshall Sklare describes it, 'By holding a service at which the traditional text is used, by glossing over objectionable portions or having them read or chanted in Hebrew, and by stressing English readings whose content is definitely modern in emphasis, it is possible to satisfy a wide audience.'[51] Although there was undoubtedly dissatisfaction on the more traditional right as well as on the more radical left, the synthesis was generally seen as a happy one and formed the basis for the gradually more radical editions of the daily, High Holiday, and *seliḥoth* services and Passover *Haggadah* produced by the

Conservative movement in the subsequent forty years. In these volumes, more extensive additions and alterations were made, reflecting Conservative ideology as well as contemporary developments, and the idea of providing alternative passages, to be chosen by the rabbi and congregation, was adopted from the Reform liturgy.[52] The Reconstructionists too saw the need for further change in the 1980s and published a new edition of the Friday evening service *Kol Haneshamah* in 1989 to take account not only of the Holocaust, the State of Israel and the new informality, but also of the search for Jewish roots, the return to lay leadership in worship, and the movement's commitment to pluralism and feminism.[53]

As the American Conservative movement became more independent and self-confident and the synagogue more distinct from its Orthodox and Reform equivalents, the pressures to evolve its own form of *halakhah*, as exemplifed in the decisions to permit driving to the synagogue on the sabbath, and to produce its own documentation for religious ceremonies such as marriage, could no longer be withstood and it was not long before individual congregations were permitted to abandon the second day of the festival observed in the diaspora in favour of the Israeli custom. The first women rabbis were being ordained at the Jewish Theological Seminary in the mid-1980s, although it was not every congregation that was happy to offer them appointments.[54] As a result, the tendency for that academic institution to represent enlightened Orthodoxy as much as right-wing Conservatism weakened and the moderate control it once exercised over the more radically minded United Synagogue of America was gradually reversed. The traditionalists, particularly well represented in the larger Jewish centres and in Canada, fought back and founded their own Union for Traditional Judaism which looked back to Schechter's ideals for its inspiration and to Professor David Weiss-Halivni of Columbia University, formerly of the Seminary, for religious guidance.[55] The strong presence of such modern traditionalists in Israel, where they made a major contribution to education at all levels, led to the adoption of the Masorti (= 'traditional') label by those who preferred a traditional Hebrew liturgy, with a degree of female participation in the services, but did not wish to depart greatly from the style of their enlightened Orthodox friends in, say, the Mizraḥi movement. The Jerusalem campus of the Seminary was therefore still a place where one could find a fully traditional *minyan* in the 1980s and the atmosphere there was similar to what it had been in earlier days at the Seminary in New York. The *siddur* predominantly in use in Israeli Masorti congregations was the Orthodox *Rinath Yisrael*. Naturally, the determination of the Orthodox political parties to prevent the recognition of any Jewish religious tradition but their own in so far as personal status and marriage laws were concerned made it difficult for even such Masorti traditionalists to feel part of the religiously observant camp in Israel and it remained to be seen whether their liturgical conservatism, with a small 'c', would ultimately survive the drive from both right and left to force them fully into the progressive grouping.[56] A similar situation has existed in the United Kingdom over the last quarter of a century. Rabbi Dr Louis Jacobs' congregation, founded when he was rejected on theological grounds for the principalship of Jews' College and later for the United Synagogue rabbinate, returned to the Anglo-Jewish Orthodoxy of Chief Rabbi Adler's day, as then practised by such synagogues as Hampstead and the New West End, and adopted a matching synagogal service with men and women seated on opposite sides of the synagogue, a mixed choir, no repetition of the sabbath *musaf ʿamidah* but a text that substantially followed the 'Singer's Prayer Book'. As pressure from within and without mounted, newer congregations of the British Masorti movement, though small in number, grew in confidence and made their own moves towards a more radical liturgical programme (including mixed seating and women's participation in Torah reading) but, at the time of writing, there were none that had yet adopted the American Conservative prayer-book in preference to a modern Orthodox one. Certainly they were not strong enough to produce their own and in practice would probably continue to use a congregationally adjusted form of the traditional text, as the

American Conservatives had done in the earlier part of the current century.[57]

It will be recalled that American Jewry's most powerful religious movement in the latter half of the nineteenth century was that of Reform Judaism and that it had by the end of the century produced the *Union Prayer Book* which added an American flavour to its German ingredients, replaced the great variety of radical liturgies with which it had experimented, and reflected the basic theology of classic Reform. That volume was therefore ready to do service in the twentieth century and it is a tribute to its remarkable suitability for the radical wing of American Jewish religiosity that it continued to do so for over three-quarters of a century. That radical wing did not, however, come through two World Wars, the Depression, the Holocaust and the establishment of the State of Israel without many times being challenged as to its theology in general and the nature of its liturgy in particular. The same factors that affected Orthodoxy and Conservatism, not the least of them the growing confidence of Jews from Eastern Europe and from other areas that the Reformers had earlier characterised as primitive and in need of Western acculturation, brought about two major revisions of the *Union Prayer Book* and ultimately its demise.[58] The changing attitudes are easily identified if a comparison is made of the manifestos issued by the leaders of American Reform Judaism at Pittsburgh in 1885, Columbus in 1937 and San Francisco in 1976 and how the topic of liturgy is treated in each. At Pittsburgh the overriding concern was with a modern Jewish theology 'in accord with the postulates of reason' and traditional synagogal rituals were given no attention, apparently being classified as worthy of maintenance only if they 'elevate and sanctify our lives'. As far as the text of the prayers was concerned, there was an explicit rejection of 'a return to Palestine', 'a sacrificial worship under the sons of Aaron' and 'beliefs both in bodily resurrection and in . . . Hell and Paradise'. By 1937 there was greater hesitation about assuming that scientific ideas conflicted with traditional religion and a place was found for the preservation of sabbath, festivals and ceremonies because of their inspirational value. The 'rehabilitation of Palestine' was regarded as holding 'the promise of renewed life for many of our brethren' and it was agreed that Judaism required 'the use of Hebrew, together with the vernacular, in our worship and instruction'. Specific mention was made of the synagogue as Jewish life's 'oldest and most democratic institution', of God as 'Lord of the universe and . . . merciful Father', and of a need to 'cultivate the traditional habit of . . . prayer in both home and synagog' (*sic*). The San Francisco platform stresses and encourages diversity while perceiving 'a certain unity' and 'what binds us together'. It regards it as self-evident that 'tradition should interact with modern culture' and widely accepted 'that women should have full rights to practice Judaism'. It is now acknowledged that Jews are bound to the State of Israel 'by innumerable religious and ethnic ties' and personal aliyah is even encouraged. Although 'the foundation of Jewish community life is the synagogue', claims on Jews also include 'creating a Jewish home'; 'private prayer and public worship; daily religious observance; keeping the sabbath and the holy days'.[59]

That the American Reform movement was able to make adjustments in the ideology and practice of its founding fathers is to the credit of a number of major figures that left their mark on its whole philosophy. Such leading Zionists in its rabbinate as Stephen Wise and Abba Hillel Silver succeeded in altering the status of anti-Zionism from the classical Reform norm into no more than the preoccupation of a splinter group such as the American Council for Judaism.[60] In the educational field, Emanuel Gamoran pioneered more intensive and modern methods and produced a large number of textbooks and curricula for the Union of American Hebrew Congregations and forced them to take the matter of Jewish knowledge more seriously than they had ever done before.[61] For Samuel S. Cohon, who taught theology at the Hebrew Union College and was the inspiration behind much of the Columbus platform, the *Union Prayer Book* reflected 'the present apathy and scepticism towards prayer' and amounted to 'a vague meditation on an ethical theme' and he spearheaded the struggle for serious modification.[62] The halakhic proficiency of J. Z. Lauterbach and Solomon Freehof and the deep knowledge of traditional liturgy on the part of A. Z. Idelsohn made possible the use of the classical rabbinic sources in the pursuit of the modern alternative and thus inevitably helped to effect a return to beliefs and practices once frowned upon in the movement.[63] As a result of all their efforts, the staid and defensive approach of the first two decades of the century that had virtually meant an acceptance of an inferior role to that of Conservatism gave way to a more dynamic outlook that permitted the eventual integration of significant elements of both tradition and change within the options open to the contemporary Reform Jews. While the adjustments made in previous years had been limited to the adoption of the Jewish Publication Society's translation of biblical passages, the greater involvement of the congregation, and the introduction of additional Hebrew, the revisions produced for the sabbaths, festivals and weekdays in 1940 and for the High Holidays in 1945 included distinctly Zionist prayers, the restoration of some mediaeval Hebrew poetry, a more important role for Hebrew, and references to the performance of such rituals as *qiddush*, *shofar*, *lulav* and *megillah*, none of them among earlier Reform's favourite activities.[64] The first evidence of the impact of the Holocaust on Reform liturgy even occurs shortly after the Second World War. Lest it be thought that these changes denoted a return to the traditional *siddur* or an acceptance of established halakhic procedures, it should be stressed that they represented only one aspect of the revision, namely, that intended to provide for those with a greater degree of nostalgia or those committed to a return to their roots. It was not unusual for the introduction of older traditions to clash with some principles of Reform theology, and some means had to be found of harmonising these conflicting interests.[65] In order to meet the differing needs of the wider Reform community, the idea of uniform, sanctioned liturgy was abandoned in favour of a number of options that were offered for each liturgical occasion and could be adopted as the rabbi and congregation saw fit.[66] In that respect, the 'progressive' nature of reform was not only maintained but enhanced and the desire for innovation, relevance and modernity was catered for, at least temporarily. The word 'temporarily' is apt in the context since by the 1960s and 1970s new pressures were mounting for further demonstrations of liturgical creativity.

The media were bringing an awareness of other people's customs into every home and what had once appeared strange and belonging to 'the other' suddenly became attractive as a potential experiment. The machinery of communication and education also stood at hand ready to record, transfer and copy information and the whole penchant of Western civilisation was in favour of the novel and the instantly achievable. By the same token, what had already been used was by definition disposable and had to be replaced by an alternative at a future occasion. The American Reform movement had to respond to these developments throughout its religious experience and no less in the liturgical sphere than in any others. Contemporary events and opinion, current music and daily language had to find their expression in the prayer sessions of a youth most of whom had little knowledge or understanding of the European past or the traditional *siddur*. Modern views on the need for egalitarianism in worship not only gave the Reform Jewish woman an equal role in the services; it also went the whole way and, in 1972, called her rabbi and gave her a pulpit – a lead followed by the Reconstructionists a year later. The allegedly 'sexist' language of the prayer-book also became a topic for serious criticism and suggestions were made for its amendment, including the use of words of common gender and the introduction of female as well as male figures and epithets.[67] And if liturgical renewal was the order of the day for many Christian groups, why should enlightened Jews lag behind? Larry Hoffman has described the phenomenon in vivid and pointed terms, indicating how American democracy allowed anyone to write a religious service and how almost everyone did: 'American technology, with its ubiquitous duplication machines and cheap sources of paper, enabled many congregations to write a service on Thursday, pray from it Friday evening or Saturday, and throw it out on Sunday. Though many of the services leave something to be desired in terms of Jewish sophistication and even English style, they also, nevertheless, provide unmistakable attempts to develop Jewish liturgies that reflect American Jewish consciousness.'[68] In response to such iconoclastic trends, the leaders of the movement concluded that the time was ripe for the creation of authorised liturgies that would replace the *Union Prayer Book* and its offshoots of the previous few decades. To move only in the direction of novelty and relevance was, however, no longer possible in the 1970s because there was among many Reform Jews a growing conviction that much religious inspiration could still be drawn from traditional sources, ancient customs and nostalgic feelings associated with the practices of one's immediate ancestors, within the family or in the more general sense. The solution adopted by the Liturgy Committee of the Central Conference of American Rabbis (Reform) was to follow a system introduced half a century earlier and provide something for everyone. When *Gates of Prayer* appeared in 1975 it contained 779 pages and offered a choice of most of the traditional prayers in Hebrew and in Aramaic, some Sefardi material, a role for a cantor as well as a choir, and a host of experimental English texts as well as readings from American writers and poets, in such a form and order that it could only with difficulty be seen as a descendant of the *siddur* that the Babylonian geonim had once vouchsafed to the widespread communities of the Jewish world. This style was also followed in the American Reform prayer-books issued for the Passover *Seder* (1974), the home (*Gates of the House*, 1977) and the High Holidays (*Gates of Repentance*, 1978) and ensured that at least for one large group of Jews liturgical, as halakhic, diversity had become the contemporary norm.[69]

For reasons already made clear it is not among the objects of this chapter to cover in detail the history of the liturgy of Reform Judaism in the twentieth century and that task has in any case already been performed in a more than satisfactory fashion by Jakob Petuchowski as far as the European congregations in the first half of the century are concerned.[70] It will, however, be useful for the overall picture being drawn of Jewish attitudes to prayer and prayer-texts in the current century if a summary is offered of developments towards and away from tradition on the part of the Reform communities in Europe and Israel, beginning with the West London Synagogue of British Jews whose first edition of *Forms of Prayer*, prepared by D. W. Marks, had appeared in 1841–2. As has already been noted, those who founded that synagogue were unable to make a major impact on the wider community, primarily because many of the milder degrees of liturgical reform that they were proposing were adopted by the United Synagogue and its 'Singer's Prayer Book' and there was not a large enough constituency for the more radical changes. These latter included the abolition of the second day of the festival, the removal of prayers that demonstrated an interest in angelology or might be construed as reflecting an antipathy towards non-Jews, and the abandonment of rabbinic benedictions for *hallel* and the reading of the Esther Scroll, and were most unlikely to attract the support of the new waves of Eastern European immigrants at the end of the century. By that time an organ and a mixed choir had also been introduced, English was more dominant in the service and the references to sacrifices, originally retained, had been excised although it is noteworthy that there seemed to be no objection to the continued appearance of a restored Zion and Jerusalem and a personal messiah.[71] This more conservative approach seems to have been challenged between the two World Wars with the strengthening of a middle European Reform presence in England, the development of a more radical alternative in the form of the Union of Liberal and Progressive Synagogues, and an awareness of the degree of support for the tenets of classical German Reform in the United States. The sixth edition of *Forms of Prayer* (1931) thus removed the restoration of Zion and Jerusalem from its liturgical entreaties and reduced the size of the *'amidah* from eighteen to twelve benedictions in the sabbath and weekday prayers, 'modifying and omitting where this has been deemed advisable, by reintroducing some ancient prayers, and by adding others entirely new'.[72] Unlike in Germany, the term 'liberal' in England was used to denote the more radical wing of reform and the Union of Liberal and Progressive Synagogues grew out of the Jewish Religious Union founded by Lily Montagu and Claude Montefiore in 1902, to the title of which the words 'for the advancement of Liberal Judaism' were added ten years later. This movement's liturgy preferred English to Hebrew, emphasised the universalist over the Jewish and opted for instrumental music and novel hymns. The *Liberal Jewish Prayer Book* edited by Israel Mattuck reflected the fact that he had been trained for the American Reform rabbinate but also offered a choice of prayers for the same occasion, a technique certainly absent from the *Union Prayer Book* but one that was to become more widely popular at a later date among 'progressive' Jews. It was Mattuck who was the spiritual leader of the British Liberal movement in a period covering both World Wars and most of the liturgies produced at that time were directly or indirectly his work.[73] Although there was a gradual tendency towards a greater use of traditional materials and away from 'freelance' liturgical innovation, items borrowed from the established Ashkenazi rite were pressed into service in a novel sequence and pattern in what Petuchowski has dubbed 'a wilful and arbitrary departure'.[74] The Holocaust and the establishment of a Jewish State left their impact on the whole of the British Progressive movement and ultimately led to the emergence of new editions of liturgies for both groups in the sixties and seventies. By that time, the six Reform and Liberal congregations of 1940 had multiplied by a factor of about seven, the Leo Baeck College had been established for training its rabbis and non-Orthodox Judaism was spreading to new suburbs and provincial areas as centrist Orthodoxy gave way to a more intense and less compromising commitment to traditional halakhic observance.[75] Non-Orthodoxy was confident enough to make greater use of the age-old contents of the *siddur* and to restore mystical, national and talmudic themes that had spelt anathema to its nineteenth-century promoters but at the same time abandoned little of its modern theological principles. As a result, the same prayer-book could include ancient Hebrew prayers (with updated translations), often in an adapted form, alongside contemporary English prayers and poems recently composed by Jews and non-Jews, and edifying readings from a vast variety of sources. In addition, sundry options could be offered for the same liturgical occasion as a way of meeting the requirements of different congregations and maintaining a degree of novelty. The Liberals' *Service of the Heart*, and its High Holiday equivalent *Gates of Repentance*, still have more English than Hebrew, open from left to right, and are only in parts recognisably related to the traditional *siddur*. As the editors put it, 'we have made ample use of the traditional liturgy . . . but we have also modified the text . . . in order to make it acceptable to Progressive Jews'.[76] Significantly, these volumes were produced in time to influence the creation of the new set of American Reform prayer-books already discussed. *Forms of Prayer*, now produced by and for the Reform Synagogues of Great Britain rather than simply for the West London Synagogue, stands closer to the traditional *siddur*, perhaps now representing 'Reform from Within' rather than 'Independent Reform'. In a move reminiscent of the American Conservative practice, the editors have often tried to marry the old-fashioned Hebrew with the new-fangled English. 'Traditional formulations have been retained wherever possible', claims the Introduction, but it adds that 'occasionally our modern understanding of them has been expressed by a freer translation rather than by a change in the original'.[77] Both Liberal and Reform liturgies include items relating to the modern State of Israel but neither goes as far as Zionist modern Orthodoxy and the Liberals are distinctly more hesitant than the Reform.[78] As Hoffman and Wiener have honestly expressed it, 'As with the *Shoah*, we progressive Jews have yet to settle on Israel's theological status among us.'[79] As far as what remains of Jewish communal life in the remainder of Europe is concerned, the story is also one of a return to the more unashamed use of tradition but without abandoning a basic adherence to the principles of classical Reform.[80] It is interesting to note finally that the founding community of Reform Judaism, that of Germany, had, in spite of a long tradition of individual congregational composition with a varied degree of traditional content, ultimately opted in the last decade of its pre-Holocaust existence for a unified liturgy that to an extent adumbrated the liturgical ideology of the Reform movement of almost half a century later. Under the editorship of the liturgical scholar, Ismar Elbogen, the sometime editor of *Liberales Judentum* Caesar Seligmann, and the Breslau rabbi Hermann Vogelstein, the *Einheitsgebetbuch*, as it came to be called (perhaps under the influence of the *Union Prayer Book*), provided complete Hebrew and German texts for all prayers, reintroduced classical prayers earlier removed, couched any new prayers in suitably lyrical style, and offered a wealth of German hymns and meditations in an appendix. Repetition, extravagance of expression and dogmatically unacceptable ideas were avoided but a wide enough compendium of the ancient and the modern was included to enable each congregation to make its choice, and thus to follow the example set by the *Liberal Jewish Prayer Book* in England.[81]

Given what has already been said about the predominantly Eastern European and Sefardi background of most Israelis, both secular and religious, it is hardly surprising that Reform Judaism, as founded in Germany and further developed in the United States, has found it difficult to play anything approximating to a major role in Israeli society and to produce a significant liturgical challenge to the Orthodox *siddurim* earlier discussed. With the influx into Mandatory Palestine of the bourgeois Jews of central Europe in the 1930s, 'Liberal' congregations were established in Haifa, Jerusalem and Tel Aviv. They followed what was for them the moderate path of German and Hebrew sermons, separate seating without a partition, and a traditional liturgy from which some items had been omitted. Familiar Lewandowski melodies were sung and there were no musical instruments. Nevertheless, the phenomenon was a strange one in Palestinian Jewish eyes and identified by the locals as characteristic of assimilationist *galuth* attitudes. The Haifa synagogue became Orthodox, the Jerusalem one joined the Conservative World Council of Synagogues and the Tel Aviv congregation simply petered out. One of the major figures in the earliest efforts to establish Progressive Judaism in the Holy Land was Max Elk, a Liberal rabbi from Stettin, and it was he who saw that an influence on society as a whole rather than the building of synagogues was what was required in the new Zionist environment. He therefore established a school for children of all manner of backgrounds which offered a syllabus that integrated Progressive Judaism with high standards of secular education and promoted closer ties between Jews and Arabs. It was that school, called after Leo Baeck and situated in Haifa, that later provided some of the first Sabra students for the Reform rabbinate.[82] In spite of the fact that it had been Reform rabbis such as Stephen Wise, Abba Hillel Silver and Judah L. Magnes who had struggled hard for the international Zionist movement and for the establishment of many of the institutions of the Yishuv, the creation of the State brought no improvement in the situation of non-Orthodox Judaism and the status of the individual as far as *rites de passage* were concerned became that defined by traditional halakhic practice.[83] In spite of these difficulties, the Reform movement made a new start in 1958 and eventually succeeded in founding small congregations throughout Israel, building a campus of the Hebrew Union College in Jerusalem and transferring the centre of the World Union for Progressive Judaism to Jerusalem. It also established kibbutzim of its own at Yahel and Lotan in the Aravah and made an impact on critical Jewish scholarship and campaigns for social justice. Such successes notwithstanding, those attracted to the movement remained predominantly Americans or central/Western Europeans, intellectually and socially advantaged, and at least ambivalent about the observance of most traditional religious precepts.[84] In the matter of liturgy, the developments once again demonstrated the growing importance of such issues as the relevance of the Jewish State to modern Jewish religiosity, the effect of the Holocaust on Jewish thinking and the role of women in the communal observances of Judaism. While the prayer-book of Palestinian Reform in the thirties had been that of its German parent, and the Israeli *Siddur* of the Har-El congregation in 1962 had made an effort to fuse the ideas of living in the modern Jewish nation-state and following the ideology of Progressive Judaism, the unified liturgy produced in 1982 by the Israeli Council of Progressive Rabbis was unashamedly Zionist and post-Holocaust. After much controversy it followed classical Reform in omitting references to rebuilding the Temple, resurrection and the re-establishment of the House of David, in abbreviating traditional texts, in offering a choice of versions, and in including selections by contemporary Jewish writers. At the same time, however, large sections related to the Return to Zion and to the Holocaust, a traditional structure was retained, many domestic rituals were included, and biblical and later Jewish sources were noted. This new Reform prayer-book and its later equivalent *Kawwanath Ha-Lev* demonstrated that the movement that produced them had come a long way, in every sense, from Berlin in 1819 to Jerusalem almost a century and three-quarters later.[85]

Notes

1 ON JEWISH LITURGICAL RESEARCH

1 See the articles cited in nn. 6 and 14 below; chapter 8, pp. 267–70 below; the evaluations offered in the standard Jewish encyclopaedias; and E. I. J. Rosenthal, 'A Remarkable Friendship: L. Zunz and A. Geiger' in *Tradition, Transition and Transmission. Jubilee Volume . . . I. O. Lehman*, ed. B. D. Fox (Cincinnati, 1983), pp. 79–92.

2 *Der jüdische Gottesdienst in seiner geschichtlichen Entwicklung* was published in Frankfurt-am-Main and was the culmination and revision of three decades of research in the field. Goldschmidt, Sarason (nn. 6 and 14 below) and the standard encyclopaedias again give evaluations but see also the introduction to the Hebrew edition of the work (n. 3 below) and E. I. J. Rosenthal, 'Ismar Elbogen and the New Jewish Learning' in *Year Book VIII* of the Leo Baeck Institute, London (1963), pp. 3–28, reprinted in his *Studia Semitica*, vol. I (Cambridge, 1971), pp. 327–52.

3 *Ha-Tefillah Beyisra'el Behithpatḥuthah Ha-Hisṭorith* translated from the third German edition (1931) by J. Amir, edited and updated by J. Heinemann, with the co-operation of I. Adler, A. Negev, J. J. Petuchowski and J. (Ḥ.) Schirmann (Tel Aviv, 1972).

4 See, for example, Heinemann's comments on pp. 204 and 211 of the Hebrew edition of Elbogen, *Ha-Tefillah Beyisra'el*, as well as chapter 5, p. 140 and chapter 6, n. 46 below.

5 For details see the bibliography of J. Heinemann's Hebrew volume (n. 9 below), pp. 196–7 (English edition, pp. 302–4).

6 See the list of publications that appears in his collected essays *On Jewish Liturgy. Essays on Prayer and Religious Poetry* (Hebrew; Jerusalem, 1978), pp. 445–51, and especially his article 'Studies on Jewish Liturgy by German-Jewish Scholars' in *Year Book II* of the Leo Baeck Institute, London (1957), pp. 119–35, translated into Hebrew and included in the collected essays, pp. 429–44.

7 *Islamic Influences on the Jewish Worship* (Hebrew; Oxford, 1947); 'Fourteen New Genizah Fragments of Saadya's *Siddur* together with a Reproduction of a Missing Part' in *Saadya Studies*, ed. E. I. J. Rosenthal (Manchester, 1943), pp. 245–83; and various articles in *Tarbiẓ* 37, 53 and 54; in *Sinai* 77, 78, 81, 82, 89, 96 and 98; in the memorial volumes for D. Ochs (Ramat Gan, 1978), N. Ben-Menahem (Jerusalem, 1981) and J. Heinemann (see n. 9 below); and in the *Festschrift* for E. Z. Melamed (Ramat Gan, 1982).

8 Among treatments of a more general, devotional and educational kind may be mentioned E. Levi, *Yesodoth Ha-Tefillah* (Tel Aviv, 1961, 5th edn); A. Millgram, *Jewish Worship* (Philadelphia, 1971); R. Posner, U. Kaploun and S. Cohen (eds.), *Jewish Liturgy: Prayer and Synagogue Service Through the Ages* (Jerusalem, 1975); H. Hamiel (ed.), *Me'assef Le'inyaney Ḥinnukh Wehora'ah* VIII. *Tefillah* (Jerusalem, 1964); and G. H. Cohn (ed.), *Ha-Tefillah Ha-Yehudith. Hemshekh Weḥiddush* (Ramat Gan, 1978). Both A. Z. Idelsohn, *Jewish Liturgy and its Development* (New York, 1932) and B. S. Jacobson, *Nethiv Binah*, vols. I–V (Tel Aviv, 1968–83), are more scientific in approach but still tend to oversimplify the historical process. The most recent works belonging to the educational category are J. M. Cohen, *Horizons of Jewish Prayer* (London, 1986) and E. Klein, *Jewish Prayer. Concepts and Customs* (Columbus, 1986).

9 Reference to Goldschmidt's *On Jewish Liturgy* has been made above (n. 6). Heinemann's major contribution was his *Prayer in the Period of the Tanna'im and the Amora'im. Its Nature and its Patterns* (Hebrew; Jerusalem, 1964; updated English version, *Prayer in the Talmud*, Berlin, 1977) and his other publications are listed in *Studies in Aggadah, Targum and Jewish Liturgy in Memory of Joseph Heinemann*, eds. J. J. Petuchowski and Ezra Fleischer (Hebrew; Jerusalem, 1981) pp. 185–92; cf. also his *Studies in Jewish Liturgy*, ed. Avigdor Shinan (Hebrew; Jerusalem, 1981). For details of Spanier's articles in *MGWJ* see Heinemann's bibliography in *Prayer in the Talmud*.

10 *Tarbiẓ* 59 (1990), pp. 397–441.

11 *Eretz-Israel Prayer and Prayer Rituals as Portrayed in the Geniza Documents* (Hebrew; Jerusalem, 1988). His major works on Hebrew liturgical poetry include *The Poems of Shelomo Ha-Bavli. Critical Edition with Introduction and Commentary* (Hebrew; Jerusalem, 1973); *Hebrew Liturgical Poetry in the Middle Ages* (Hebrew; Jerusalem, 1975); *The Yozer. Its Emergence and Development* (Hebrew; Jerusalem, 1974).

12 For a response to Fleischer, see S. C. Reif, 'On the Earliest Development of Jewish Prayer', *Tarbiz* 60 (1991), pp. 677–81.

13 E.g. *Contributions to the Scientific Study of the Jewish Liturgy* (New York, 1970); *Understanding Jewish Prayer* (New York, 1972); *Literature of the Synagogue* (with J. Heinemann; New York, 1975); and 'The Liturgy of the Synagogue. History, Structure and Contents' in *Approaches to Ancient Judaism*, vol. IV, ed. W. S. Green (Chico, 1983), pp. 1–53. See also his *Prayer-book Reform in Europe: The Liturgy of Liberal and Reform Judaism* (New York, 1968).

14 'On the Use of Method in the Modern Study of Jewish Liturgy' in *Approaches to Ancient Judaism: Theory and Practice*, ed. W. S. Green (Missoula, Montana, 1978), pp. 97–172.

15 'Recent Developments in the Study of Jewish Liturgy' in *The Study of Ancient Judaism. I. Mishnah, Midrash, Siddur*, ed. J. Neusner (New York, 1982), pp. 180–7; 'Religion and Worship: The Case of Judaism' in *Take Judaism, For Example: Studies Toward the Comparison of Religions*, ed. J. Neusner (Chicago, 1983), pp. 49–65.

16 S. C. Reif, 'Some Issues in Jewish Liturgical Research', *Proceedings of the Eighth World Congress of Jewish Studies, Jerusalem, 1981*, Division C (Hebrew; Jerusalem, 1982), pp. 175–82, published in an updated and revised English version in 'Jewish Liturgical Research. Past, Present and Future', *JJS* 34 (1983), pp. 161–70, on which most of this introductory chapter is based; 'Some Liturgical Issues in the Talmudic Sources', *Studia Liturgica* 15 (1982–3), pp. 188–206, now the basis of chapter 4 below.

17 *The Canonization of the Synagogue Service* (Notre Dame, 1979).

18 'Recent Developments', pp. 181–3.

19 L. A. Hoffman, *Beyond the Text. A Holistic Approach to Liturgy* (Bloomington and Indianapolis, 1987).

20 T. Zahavy, 'A New Approach to Early Jewish Prayer' in *History of Judaism: The Next Ten Years*, ed. B. M. Bokser (Chico, 1980), pp. 45–60.

21 'Some Liturgical Issues in the Talmudic Sources' divides the material into three sections: (i) The theological status of prayer; (ii) The essential nature of prayer; (iii) The mechanics of prayer. See also chapter 4 below.

22 T. Zahavy, *The Mishnaic Law of Blessings and Prayers. Tractate Berakhot* (Atlanta, 1987); 'Three Stages in the Development of Early Rabbinic Prayer' in *From Ancient Israel to Modern Judaism. Intellect in Quest of Understanding. Essays in Honor of Marvin Fox*, vol. I (Atlanta, 1989), pp. 233–65; and 'The Politics of Piety. Social Conflict and the Emergence of Rabbinic Liturgy' in *The Making*

of Jewish and Christian Worship, eds. P. F. Bradshaw and L. A. Hoffman (Notre Dame and London, 1991) pp. 42–68.

23 Vol. XXXII (Jerusalem and Tel Aviv, 1981), cols. 1008–23, substantially the work of J. Heinemann.

24 P. B. Bradshaw, *Daily Prayer in the Early Church* (London, 1981) p. ix.

25 The overall title of the two volumes is *Two Liturgical Traditions*. The first volume is *The Making of Jewish and Christian Worship* and the second is *The Changing Face of Jewish and Christian Worship in North America* (Notre Dame and London, 1991).

26 This impression may be confirmed by reference to S. Z. Fishman and J. Robbins, *Jewish Studies at American and Canadian Universities* (Washington, 1979), regular issues of the *Index of Articles on Jewish Studies* (Jerusalem, 1969 and continuing) and N. Marsden, *Register of Research in Jewish Studies in Great Britain* (Oxford, 1975).

27 Douglas Sturm, 'The Learned Society and Scholarly Research: Models of Interaction', *Bulletin of the Council on the Study of Religion* vol. 12 no. 2 (April, 1981), pp. 37–41.

28 Reported by D. H. Tripp in 'Worship and the Pastoral Office' in *The Study of Liturgy* eds. Cheslyn Jones, Geoffrey Wainwright and Edward Yarnold (London, 1978), pp. 510–32. See also A. Fox, *Dean Inge* (London, 1960), p. 115.

29 Some of the issues are touched upon in B. T. Viviano, *Study as Worship: Aboth and the New Testament* (Leiden, 1978), and, more specifically, in *The Lord's Prayer and the Jewish Liturgy* (London, 1978), eds. J. J. Petuchowski and M. Brocke; W. Horbury, 'The Benediction of the *Minim* and Early Jewish–Christian Controversy', *JTS* NS 33 (1982), pp. 19–61; D. A. Fiensy, *Prayers Alleged to be Jewish* (Chico, 1985); and Bradshaw and Hoffman (eds.) *The Making of Jewish and Christian Worship*. See also Sarason, 'Religion and Worship' and chapter 5, pp. 122–4 below.

30 A. M. Goldberg, 'Service of the Heart: Liturgical Aspects of Synagogue Worship' in *Standing Before God: Studies on Prayer in Scriptures and in Tradition with Essays in Honor of John M. Oesterreicher*, eds. Asher Finkel and Lawrence Frizzell (New York, 1981), pp. 195–211, especially p. 208.

31 M. Greenberg, *Biblical Prose Prayer as a Window to the Popular Religion of Ancient Israel* (Berkeley, 1983); M. Haran, *Temples and Temple-Service in Ancient Israel* (Oxford, 1978).

32 L. I. Levine (ed.), *Ancient Synagogues Revealed* (Jerusalem, 1981) and *The Synagogue in Late Antiquity* (Philadelphia, 1987); J. G. Griffiths, 'Egypt and the Rise of the Synagogue', *JTS* NS 38

(1987), pp. 1–15; L. L. Grabbe, 'Synagogues in Pre-70 Palestine. A Re-assessment', *JTS* NS 39 (1988), pp. 401–10.

33 J. H. Charlesworth, 'A Prolegomenon to a New Study of the Jewish Background of the Hymns and Prayers in the New Testament', *JJS* 33 (1982), pp. 265–85; D. Flusser, 'Psalms, Hymns and Prayers' in *Jewish Writings of the Second Temple Period*, ed. M. E. Stone (Assen and Philadelphia, 1984), pp. 551–77; M. Weinfeld, *Tarbiz* 45 (1975), pp. 15–26, *Tarbiz* 48 (1978–9), pp. 186–200 and *Sinai* 105 (1989), pp. 72–82.

34 J. Dan and F. Talmage (eds.), *Studies in Jewish Mysticism* (Cambridge, Mass., 1982); M. Bar-Ilan, *The Mysteries of Jewish Prayer and Hekhalot* (Hebrew; Ramat Gan, 1987); P. Alexander, 'Prayer in the Heikhalōt Literature' and the other articles in *Prière, mystique et judaïsme*, ed. R. Goetschel (Paris, 1987); P. B. Fenton, *The Treatise of the Pool* (London, 1981) and *Deux traités de mystique juive* (Lagrasse, 1987).

35 I. Ta-Shema, 'Some Notes on the Origins of the "*Kaddish Yathom*"', *Tarbiz* 53 (1984), pp. 559–68.

36 S. Schechter, 'Woman in Temple and Synagogue', *Studies in Judaism*, First Series (London and Philadelphia, 1896), pp. 313–25; B. Brooten, *Women Leaders in the Ancient Synagogue. Inscriptional Evidence and Background Issues* (Chico, 1982); A. Weiss, *Women at Prayer* (Hoboken, N.J., 1990); J. R. Baskin (ed.), *Jewish Women in Historical Perspective* (Detroit, 1991); see now also S. Grossman and R. Haut, *Daughters of the King. Women and the Synagogue* (Philadelphia, New York, Jerusalem, 1992); and W. Horbury, 'Women in the Synagogue' in the third volume (forthcoming) of the *Cambridge History of Judaism.*

37 S. C. Heilman, *Synagogue Life* (Chicago, 1976) and *The People of the Book. Drama, Fellowship and Religion* (Chicago and London, 1983).

38 S. C. Reif, *Shabbethai Sofer and his Prayer-book* (Cambridge, 1979); 'A Disputed Liturgical Vocalisation', *JJS* 20 (1969), pp. 5–24; 'A Defense of David Qimḥi', *HUCA* 44 (1973), pp. 211–26; 'Liturgical Difficulties and Geniza Manuscripts' in *Studies in Judaism and Islam*, eds. S. Morag, I. Ben-Ami and N. A. Stillman (Jerusalem, 1981), pp. 99–122; 'Festive Titles in Liturgical Terminology' (Hebrew), *Proceedings of the Ninth World Congress of Jewish Studies, Jerusalem, 1985*, Division C (Jerusalem, 1986), pp. 63–70. For additional Jewish liturgical bibliography, see Y. Tavory, 'Selected Chapters from a Bibliography of the World of Prayer', *Alei Sefer* 15 (1988–9), pp. 105–21 and his fuller treatment promised in a forthcoming issue of *Kiryat Sefer*.

39 These considerations of physical transmission were addressed at a conference entitled 'Artefact and Text' held at the John Rylands Research Institute of the University of Manchester in April, 1992. The papers, including one by the writer entitled 'Codicological Aspects of Jewish Liturgical History', are scheduled to appear in 1993 in vol. 75 of the *Bulletin of the John Rylands University Library of Manchester*.

2 THE BIBLICAL INSPIRATION

1 Samuel Sandmel was the first scholar to apply the term 'parallelomania' to the indiscriminate search for parallels without concern for their cautious and accurate assessment and has been followed by many others in more recent years; see his 'Parallelomania' in *Journal of Biblical Literature* 81 (1962), pp. 1–13.

2 The talmudic and mediaeval liturgical sources are dealt with in chapters 4 and 6 below. No less an authority than Maimonides explains the presence of the sacrificial cult in the Torah as a sop to the Israelites' need for a form of worship that was standard in their day; see his *Guide* III, 32, pp. 525–7 and D. Hartman, *Maimonides. Torah and Philosophic Quest* (Philadelphia, 1976), pp. 160–6 and 182–3.

3 This becomes clear from histories of Christian liturgy such as Dom Gregory Dix's *The Shape of the Liturgy* (London, 1945), L. Bouyer's *Life and Liturgy* (London, 1956) and J. A. Jungmann's *The Early Liturgy* (London, 1959) and has recently been stressed by P. F. Bradshaw, *Daily Prayer in the Early Church* (London, 1981). Cf. also G. D. Kilpatrick, *The Eucharist in Bible and Liturgy* (Cambridge, 1983), and chapter 5 below, pp. 122–4.

4 James G. Frazer published his *Folklore in the Old Testament* in three volumes in London in 1918 and his methodology has often been questioned in recent years. For a balanced assessment see T. H. Gaster, *Myth, Legend and Custom in the Old Testament. A Comparative Study with Chapters from Sir James G. Frazer's Folklore in the Old Testament* (London, 1969), preface. Howard Eilberg-Schwartz has recently made an attempt in his *The Savage in Judaism* (Bloomington and Indianapolis, 1990) to return to comparative anthropology in a more modern form but, even if no account is taken of the controversial nature of his views, such an approach is too general and speculative to be helpful in this treatment. For the methodology underlying the present book, see chapter 1 above, pp. 13–21.

5 The summaries here offered are particularly indebted to J. B.

Pritchard, *Ancient Near Eastern Texts relating to the Old Testament* (Princeton, 1969, 3rd edn); H. Schmökel, *Near Eastern Religious Texts relating to the Old Testament* (ed. W. Beyerlin; ET, London, 1978); M. Lichtheim, *Ancient Egyptian Literature* (three volumes; Berkeley, 1973–8); O. R. Gurney, *Some Aspects of Hittite Religion* (Oxford, 1977); H. W. F. Saggs, *Everyday Life in Babylonia and Assyria* (London and New York, 1965); J. Gray, *The Legacy of Canaan. The Ras Shamra Texts and their Relevance to the Old Testament* (Leiden, 1965, 2nd edn).

6 See Pritchard, *Ancient Near Eastern Texts*, pp. 325, 331 and 346.

7 *Ibid.*, pp. 370, 391–2 and 396–7.

8 Lichtheim, *Ancient Egyptian Literature*, vol. II, p. 6.

9 Schmökel, *Near Eastern Religious Texts*, p. 112.

10 The criticism here implied of theologically motivated approaches, particularly as represented by earlier generations of Christian scholars, is often now expressed by current specialists in the history of biblical theology and its study. See, for instance, the helpful article 'Theology (Old Testament)' by John Goldingay in *A Dictionary of Biblical Interpretation*, ed. R. J. Coggins and J. L. Houlden (London, 1990), pp. 691–4, and H.-J. Kraus, *Worship in Israel. A Cultic History of the Old Testament* (ET, Oxford, 1966), chapter 1, pp. 1–25.

11 Useful summaries, though from different perspectives from the one offered here and from each other's, are to be found in Kraus, *Worship in Israel*, pp. 93–188; H. H. Rowley, *Worship in Ancient Israel. Its Form and Meaning* (London, 1967), pp. 1–110; and M. Haran, *Temples and Temple-Service in Ancient Israel* (Oxford, 1978), pp. 13–83, 260–75. See also M. Haran, 'Priesthood, Temple, Divine Service', *Hebrew Annual Review* 7 (1983), pp. 121–35 and 'Priest, Temple and Worship' (Hebrew) in *Tarbiz* 48 (1979), pp. 175–85; G. A. Anderson, *Sacrifices and Offerings in Ancient Israel. Studies in their Social and Political Importance* (Atlanta, 1987); M. I. Gruber, 'Women in the Cult according to the Priestly Code', in *Judaic Perspectives on Ancient Israel*, eds. J. Neusner, B. A. Levine and E. Frerichs (Philadelphia, 1987), pp. 35–48; and see also chapter 1, n. 36 above.

12 See Kraus, *Worship in Israel*, pp. 26–92; Rowley, *Worship in Ancient Israel*, pp. 111–43; Haran, *Temples*, pp. 189–348; and M. S. Smith, 'The Near Eastern Background of Solar Language for Yahweh', *Journal of Biblical Literature* 109 (1990), pp. 29–39. On the matter of the sabbath, cf. N.-E. A. Andreasen, *The Old Testament Sabbath. A Tradition–Historical Investigation* (Missoula, 1972).

13 See Rowley, *Worship in Ancient Israel*, pp. 176–212.

14 G. Barkay, *Ketef Hinnom. A Treasure Facing Jerusalem's Walls* (Israel Museum, catalogue no. 274, Jerusalem, 1986), especially pp. 29–31.

15 See below, chapter 3, p. 85.

16 It is discussed by M. Weinfeld, *Deuteronomy and the Deuteronomic School* (Oxford, 1972), pp. 42, 213 and 221 although it should be noted that he associates the formula directly with prayer and the cult, a view that is being questioned in the present chapter. See also E. W. Nicholson, *Deuteronomy and Tradition* (Oxford, 1967), pp. 40 and 60.

17 Exodus 12:25–7, 13:8 and 13:14; Deuteronomy 6:20 and 31: 9–13.

18 E.g. Leviticus 5:5 and 16:21; Numbers 5:7 where the 'confession' is required in order to ensure the associated 'atonement' for the sin committed. See also Kilpatrick, *The Eucharist*, pp. 48–50.

19 Isaiah 6:1–7. For a summary of the treatment of this chapter in recent scholarship and detailed critical analysis, see J. N. Oswalt, *The Book of Isaiah, Chapters 1–39* (Grand Rapids, 1986), pp. 170–85. Note in particular his comment (p. 176) that 'attempts to prove that the vision took place in either the earthly temple or a heavenly one are generally of no consequence. They are frequently based upon overly literal interpretations of an imagery whose primary purpose is to convey theological truth.' The article by V. Hurowitz, 'Isaiah's Impure Lips and their Purification in Light of Akkadian Sources', is in *HUCA* 60 (1989), pp. 39–89.

20 For all the references see S. Mandelkern, *Veteris Testamenti Concordantiae Hebraicae atque Chaldaicae* (revised edition, Tel Aviv, 1971), pp. 950–2. On the idea of debating with God, see A. Laytner, *Arguing with God. A Jewish Tradition* (Northvale, N.J., 1990), pp. xiii–xxii, 3–39.

21 *Berakhoth* f.31a–b.

22 See p. 34 below.

23 The case of Solomon is particularly instructive in that verses 5–14 relate exclusively to the king's petition and God's favourable response while the verse immediately following reports a quite separate act of Temple sacrifice and a festive meal.

24 See, for example, A. Weiser, *The Psalms. A Commentary* (ET, London, 1962), pp. 19–52 which presupposes a direct link between the original use of Psalms in the Israelite cult and their later incorporation into the synagogal liturgy. See also *A Dictionary of Biblical Interpretation*, eds. R. J. Coggins and L. Houlden (London and Philadelphia, 1990), pp. 482–3 and 564; J. Day,

Psalms (Sheffield, 1990), pp. 14–16; and G. A. Anderson, 'The Praise of God as a Cultic Event' in *Priesthood and Cult in Ancient Israel*, eds. G. A. Anderson and S. M. Olyan (Sheffield, 1991), pp. 15–33.

25 This is made clear by A. A. Anderson in his *The Book of Psalms. Volume 1. Introduction and Psalms 1–72* (London, 1972), pp. 29–31 although he does come down firmly on the side of the cultic association of the majority of the compositions. Perhaps Dahood's demonstration of the dependence of so much of the language of the book on Canaanite paradigms (*Psalms*, three volumes, New York, 1966, 1968 and 1970) suggests a reason why the centralised sacrificial cult may originally have preferred not to make direct use of these hymns in their acts of worship. This consideration no longer applied in the post-exilic period and led to their closer association with activities on the Temple Mount.

26 Kraus, *Worship in Israel*, p. 124; contrast Haran, 'Priesthood, Temple, Divine Service', p. 131. Other examples of the two opposing views are cited by R. Hammer, 'What did they Bless? A Study of Mishnah Tamid 5.1', *JQR* 81 (1991), pp. 306–7.

27 Rowley, *Worship in Ancient Israel*, pp. 103–4; S. R. Hirsch, *Horeb. A Philosophy of Jewish Laws and Observances* (ET, I. Grunfeld, London, 1962), para. 624, p. 477, and on p. 640 of the original German edition *Versuche über Jissroels pflichten in der Zerstreuung* (Altona, 1837).

28 Moshe Greenberg, *Biblical Prose Prayer as a Window to the Popular Religion of Ancient Israel* (Berkeley, 1983), p. 17.

29 The material in the first three of these books is dated from about 400 BCE to 300 BCE while the last-mentioned was probably not edited until the second pre-Christian century but contains much older traditions. See H. G. M. Williamson, *Word Biblical Commentary 16. Ezra Nehemiah* (Waco, 1985), pp. xxxv–xxxvi; R. Braun, *Word Biblical Commentary 14. I Chronicles* (Waco, 1986), pp. xxv–xxix; L. F. Hartman and A. A. Di Lella, *The Book of Daniel* (New York, 1977), pp. 9–18.

30 The importance of this passage was also recognised in the talmudic tradition according to which (BT, *Megillah* f.3a and *Nedarim* f.37b) it represents the *locus classicus* not only for public reading but also for the targumic interpretation and masoretic punctuation, vocalisation and cantillation of the text that such a reading necessitated.

31 It is interesting that according to Mishnah, *Berakhoth* 9.5, such a phrase was adopted in the liturgy of the Temple to replace the simpler 'from everlasting' because it could be used in support of

the theory of two worlds, this and the next, and could thus challenge what was regarded as the heresy of those who believed in only one. Were such phrases already being used in a regular way on the Temple Mount in the middle of the Second Temple period? See also BT, *Berakhoth* f.63a and Nehemiah 9:5.

32 See the full discussions in J. A. Montgomery and H. S. Gehman, *A Critical and Exegetical Commentary on the Books of Kings* (Edinburgh, 1951), pp. 192–5; J. Gray, *I and II Kings. A Commentary* (London, 1970, 2nd edn), pp. 218–30; and S. J. DeVries, *Word Biblical Commentary 12. I Kings* (Waco, 1985), pp. 121–3. A book by Eep Talstra entitled *Solomon's Prayer* is scheduled for publication by Kok Pharos (Kampen, Netherlands) in 1992.

33 See J. L. McKenzie, *The Anchor Bible. Second Isaiah* (New York, 1968), pp. xx–xxi and 150–2; R. N. Whybray, *New Century Bible. Isaiah 40–66* (London, 1975), pp. 196–9.

34 See J. Bright, *The Anchor Bible. Jeremiah* (New York, 1965), pp. 288–98; J. A. Thompson, *The Book of Jeremiah* (Grand Rapids, 1980), pp. 590–4; W. L. Holladay, *Jeremiah 2. A Commentary on the book of the Prophet Jeremiah Chapters 26–52*, (Minneapolis, 1989), pp. 206–12.

35 For a useful selection and analysis of prayers other than psalms in the Bible, see R. E. Clements, *The Prayers of the Bible* (London, 1986).

36 See, in particular, pp. 25–7 above.

37 B. Porten, *Archives from Elephantine. The Life of an Ancient Jewish Military Colony* (Berkeley and Los Angeles, 1968), pp. 105–50, especially pp. 146–7.

38 For the relevant texts and their significance see R. H. Charles, *The Apocrypha and Pseudepigrapha of the Old Testament in English* (Oxford, 1913); J. H. Charlesworth, 'A Prolegomenon to a New Study of the Jewish Background of the Hymns and Prayers in the New Testament' in *Essays in Honour of Yigael Yadin*, eds. G. Vermes and J. Neusner (= *Journal of Jewish Studies* 33, 1982), pp. 265–85; D. Flusser, 'Psalms, Hymns and Prayers' in *Jewish Writings of the Second Temple Period*, ed. M. E. Stone (Assen, Philadelphia, 1984), pp. 551–77; N. B. Johnson, *Prayer in the Apocrypha and Pseudepigrapha* (Philadelphia, 1948); G. Vermes, F. Millar and M. Goodman (eds.), *The History of the Jewish People in the Age of Jesus Christ 175 BC – AD 135* by Emil Schürer, III parts 1–2 (Edinburgh, 1986–7).

39 See M. E. Stone, 'Apocalyptic Literature' in *Jewish Writings*, pp. 406–14 and Vermes *et al.*, *The History of the Jewish People*, pp. 294–303, 746–56.

40 Flusser, 'Psalms, Hymns and Prayers', pp. 563–5; cf. also Vermes *et al.*, *The History of the Jewish People*, pp. 288–94 and 546–55.

41 Y. Kaufmann argues strongly for a strict separation in ancient Israel between psalms and Temple activities but is very much aware of the change that took place in the post-exilic and later periods; see the English abridgment of his classic *Toledoth Ha-'Emunah Ha-Yisra'elith* (Tel Aviv, 1937–56) by M. Greenberg, *The Religion of Israel* (London, 1960), pp. 109–10, 205–6 and 309–11 and the translation by C. W. Efroymson of the fourth book, entitled *History of the Religion of Israel* (New York and Jerusalem and Dallas, 1977), pp. 30–5. See also Haran, 'Priesthood, Temple, Divine Service' (n. 11).

42 This point is firmly made by E. Fleischer although he has exaggerated aspects of the rabbinic situation and underplayed the influences of the wider world; see his article in *Tarbiz* 59 (1990), pp. 397–441 and the writer's response in *Tarbiz* 60 (1991), pp. 677–81. Compare the views of E. Bickerman, *The Jews in the Greek Age* (Cambridge, Mass., and London, 1988), pp. 241–3 and 279–81.

43 A useful summary of the evidence from Philo and Josephus is offered by E. P. Sanders, *Jewish Law from Jesus to the Mishnah* (London and Philadelphia, 1990), pp. 67–81.

44 In addition to Charlesworth, 'A Prolegomenon' and Flusser, 'Psalms, Hymns and Prayers' see also Vermes *et al.*, *A History of the Jewish People* III, part 1, pp. 440–69; D. Dimant, 'Qumran Sectarian Literature' in Stone (ed.), *Jewish Writings*, pp. 522–5; J. J. Petuchowski, 'The Liturgy of the Synagogue: History, Structure and Contents' in *Approaches to Ancient Judaism*, vol. IV, ed. W. S. Green (Chico, 1983), pp. 9–12; R. Hammer, 'What did they Bless?', pp. 305–24; B. Z. Wacholder, 'David's Eschatological Psalter 11Q Psalms[a]', *HUCA* 59 (1988), pp. 23–72; and M. D. Swartz, *Mystical Prayer in Ancient Judaism. An Analysis of* Ma'aseh Merkavah (Tübingen, 1992).

45 The principal edited texts are to be found in M. Baillet, *Discoveries in the Judaean Desert VII. Qumran Grotte 4 III (4Q482–4Q520)* (Oxford, 1982), pp. 73–286, especially pp. 106, 108–9, 137–75, 176–9, 185–6, 201, and in C. Newsom, *Songs of the Sabbath Sacrifice. A Critical Edition* (Atlanta, 1985). Cf. also D. Barthélemy and J. T. Milik, *Discoveries in the Judaean Desert I. Qumran Cave I* (Oxford, 1955), pp. 120, 153–4; J. Licht, *The Thanksgiving Scroll. A Scroll from the Wilderness of Judaea* (Jerusalem, 1957), pp. 128–35; and E. Qimron, 'Times for Praising God: A Fragment of a Scroll from Qumran (4Q409)', *JQR* 80 (1990), pp. 341–7.

46 See Flusser, 'Psalms, Hymns and Prayers' and the views of M. Weinfeld and R. Brody in *Tarbiẓ* 45 (1975–76), pp. 15–26; 48 (1979), pp. 186–200; 51 (1982), pp. 493–6.

47 See his article 'Ueber die Ursprünge und Grundformen der Synagogalen Liturgie' in *MGWJ* 37 (1893), pp. 441–51 and 489–97. Cf. also his further comments in his articles on 'Didascalia', 'Essenes' and 'Liturgy' in *Jewish Encyclopaedia* (New York, 1906) and on 'The Origin and Composition of the Eighteen Benedictions' in *HUCA* 1 (1924), pp. 387–425, reprinted in J. J. Petuchowski (ed.), *Contributions to the Scientific Study of Jewish Liturgy* (New York, 1970), pp. 52–90.

3 THE EARLY LITURGY OF THE SYNAGOGUE

1 See, for example, the attempt of D. Hedegård to reconstruct the first-century liturgy on the basis of the prayer-book of Amram ben Sheshna in ninth-century Babylon, *Seder R. Amram Gaon. Part 1. Hebrew Text with Critical Apparatus. Translation with Notes and Introduction* (Lund, 1951) and the unfavourable comment that this attracted from E. D. Goldschmidt, *Kiryat Sefer* 29 (1953–4), pp. 71–5, and K. Hruby, *Cahiers Sinoniens* 9 (1955), pp. 303ff.; see also the writer's review of T. Kronholm's edition of the second part of the same work (Lund, 1974), *JSS* 23 (1978), pp. 119–22, M. Bar-Ilan's article on the concept of the chosen in Jewish liturgy in *Ra'yon Ha-Beḥira Be-Yisra'el Uva-'amim*, eds. S. Almog and M. Heyd (Jerusalem, 1991), pp. 121–45, and R. S. Sarason's review of F. Manns, *La Prière d'Israël à l'heure de Jésus* (Jerusalem, 1986) in *JQR* 81 (1990), pp. 203–5.

2 See Fleischer's article in *Tarbiẓ* 59 (1990), pp. 397–441 and the writer's response in the same journal, 60 (1991), pp. 677–81. An argument has already been offered in chapter 1 above in favour of a comprehensive approach to the study of Jewish liturgy and in chapter 4 below preference will be expressed for a synchronic rather than a diachronic analysis of the rabbinic sources on liturgical matters, at least at the present state of research.

3 The third and fourth volumes of *The Cambridge History of Judaism* are scheduled to contain articles by Shaye Cohen, Louis Finkelstein, Froward Hüttenmeister, Steven Katz, William Horbury and Jacob Neusner that have a direct bearing on various aspects of the subject.

4 'The History of *Halakha* and the Dead Sea Scrolls – Preliminary Observations on *Miqṣat Ma'ase Ha-Torah* (4QMMT)', *Tarbiẓ* 59 (1990), pp. 11–76.

5 The argument about methodology in the study of rabbinic literature is well exemplified in the exchanges between Peter Schäfer and Chaim Milikowsky in *JJS* 37 (1986), pp. 139–52; 39 (1988), pp. 201–11; and 40 (1989), pp. 89–94.

6 One calls to mind the strange tendency of some scholars to ascribe a prima-facie degree of veracity to Philo and Josephus that they would grudge the talmudic sources, not to speak of the theologically tendentious reasons for looking upon the Qumran corpus and the New Testament as self-evidently more reliable than even the earliest rabbinic traditions.

7 As has been pointed out in the previous chapter, such a situation is widely presupposed in the latest books of the Hebrew Bible, in Philo and Josephus, in the Apocrypha and Pseudepigrapha, in the New Testament and in the early rabbinic traditions preserved in such tractates as *Yoma*, *Tamid* and *Middoth*. See, in particular, R. de Vaux, *Ancient Israel, Its Life and Institutions* (ET, London, 1961), pp. 322–9, 343–4, 388–405 and 457–9; H.-J. Kraus, *Worship in Israel* (ET, Oxford, 1966), pp. 229–36; S. Japhet, *The Ideology of the Book of Chronicles and its Place in Biblical Thought* (Hebrew; Jerusalem, 1977), pp. 187–212; N. B. Johnson, *Prayer in the Apocrypha and Pseudepigrapha* (Philadelphia, 1948); D. Flusser, 'Psalms, Hymns and Prayers' in *Jewish Writings of the Second Temple Period*, ed. M. E. Stone (Assen and Philadelphia, 1984), pp. 551–77; J. H. Charlesworth in *JJS* 33 (1982), pp. 265–85; S. Safrai, 'The Temple and the Divine Service' in *The World History of the Jewish People, First Series, VII. The Herodian Period* (ed. M. Avi-Yonah; New Brunswick, 1975), pp. 282–337; J. J. Petuchowski, 'The Liturgy of the Synagogue: History, Structure and Contents' in *Approaches to Ancient Judaism*, vol. IV, ed. W. S. Green (Chico, 1983), pp. 1–50; P. F. Bradshaw, *Daily Prayer in the Early Church* (London, 1981), pp. 1–46; and E. P. Sanders, *Judaism. Practice and Belief. 63 BCE–66 CE* (London and Philadelphia, 1992), pp. 47–118.

8 Contrast the ascriptions of Psalms to Adam (*Bereshith Rabbah* 22, end, ed. Theodor-Albeck, p. 220); 'blessed be the name of his glorious kingdom for ever and ever' to Jacob (BT, *Pesaḥim* f.56a); grace after meals to Moses, Joshua, David and Solomon (BT, *Berakhoth* f.48b); and the thrice daily recitation of an *'amidah* to the patriarchs (BT, *Berakhoth* f.26b) which are clearly in the realm of the fanciful, with casual references to known prayers included in Tosefta, *Berakhoth* 3.13 (Zuckermandel, p. 7), Mishnah, *Yoma* 7.1 and *Rosh Ha-Shanah* 4.5. See the Hammer article 'What did they Bless? A Study of Mishnah Tamid 5.1' in *JQR* 81 (1991), pp. 305–24.

9 Fleischer (*Tarbiẓ* 59 (1990) p. 416) follows Zeitlin (*JQR* 53 (1962), pp. 168–9) and Hoenig (*JQR* 54 (1963), pp. 115–31) in questioning the historical accuracy of the tradition about such a temple synagogue. See p. 74 below and I. Knohl, 'Participation of the People in the Temple Worship', *Tarbiẓ* 60 (1991), pp. 139–46.

10 The *locus classicus* for the existence and function of the *ma'amad* is in Mishnah, *Ta'anith* 4.2 and Urbach's treatment of the subject as a historical reality with later liturgical remnants (*Tarbiẓ* 42 (1973), pp. 304–27) is more convincing than Grabbe's scepticism (*JTS* NS 39 (1988), pp. 401–10). See also S. Zeitlin, 'The Origin of the Synagogue', *Proceedings of the American Academy of Jewish Research* 2 (1931), pp. 69–81. Fleischer (in *Tarbiẓ* 59 (1990), p. 422) assumes that their religious exercises excluded prayer.

11 See Mishnah, *Pesaḥim* 5 and B. M. Bokser's analysis of the pre-rabbinic sources in *The Origins of the Seder: The Passover Rite and Early Rabbinic Judaism* (Berkeley, 1984), pp. 14–28. See also Mishnah, *Sukkah* 3, for the association of *hallel* with Temple and, subsequently, synagogal rites.

12 Typical are 1 Samuel 7:5–9, 2 Samuel 12:16, Joel 1:14 and 2:15–18, Psalms 35:13 and 69:11–14, Nehemiah 9:1–3. Cf. also Mark 2:18–22 and parallels and chapter 2 above, pp. 38–9, regarding fasting.

13 Although the text has clearly been edited and redacted at a later stage, the second and third chapters of the mishnaic tractate *Ta'anith* contain the earliest rabbinic traditions about such customs.

14 See the passages discussed in G. Vermes, *Jesus the Jew. A Historian's Reading of the Gospels* (London, 1973), pp. 58–82.

15 The evidence is well presented by J. Lindblom, *Prophecy in Ancient Israel* (London, 1962).

16 See C. Rowland, *The Open Heaven. A Study of Apocalyptic in Judaism and Early Christianity* (London, 1982), particularly pp. 113–20 and 208–13; G. G. Scholem, *Jewish Gnosticism, Merkabah Mysticism and Talmudic Tradition* (New York, 1965), especially pp. 20–30 and 56–64; E. E. Urbach, 'The Traditions about Merkabah Mysticism in the Tannaitic Period' in *Studies in Mysticism and Religion presented to Gershom G. Scholem*, eds. E. E. Urbach, R. J. Z. Werblowsky and C. Wirszubski (Jerusalem, 1967), Hebrew section, pp. 1–28. M. Bar-Ilan in *The Mysteries of Jewish Prayer and Hekhalot* (Hebrew; Ramat Gan, 1987) draws insufficient distinction between the dates of the liturgical texts themselves and their ideological foundations. P. S. Alexander rightly points to the difficulties of establishing the precise relationship between stan-

dard rabbinic prayer and the *hekhaloth* variety in 'Prayer in the Heikhalot literature', in *Prière, mystique et judaïsme*, ed. R. Goetschel (Paris, 1987), pp. 43–64. See also M. Bar-Ilan, 'Major Trends in the Formation and Crystallization of the *Qedusha*' (Hebrew), *Daat* 25 (1990), pp. 5–20.

17 See *Theological Dictionary of the Old Testament*, ed. G. J. Botterweck and H. Ringgren, vol. II (ET, Grand Rapids, Michigan, 1975), the entry by J. Scharbert, pp. 279–308; the entry 'Prayers and Blessings', substantially the work of J. Heinemann in *Encyclopedia Hebraica*, XXXII (Jerusalem and Tel Aviv 1981), cols. 1008–23 (Hebrew); and Petuchowski, 'The Liturgy of the Synagogue', pp. 9–12.

18 There are clear indications of such graces or reminiscences of their later aspects in Jubilees 22.6, Letter of Aristeas 184f., 1QS 6.3–7, 1QSa 2.17, CD 13.1, Sira 36.12–14, Josephus, War 2.8.5.131, Didascalia 10 and Mishnah, *Berakhoth* 6–7. For detailed analysis see J. Heinemann, *Prayer in the Talmud. Forms and Patterns* (an updated and modified English version of the original Hebrew book, Berlin, 1976), pp. 118–22. See also Tzvee Zahavy, 'Three Stages in the Development of Early Rabbinic Prayer' in *From Ancient Israel to Modern Judaism. Intellect in Quest of Understanding. Essays in Honor of Marvin Fox*, eds. J. Neusner, E.S. Frerichs and N. M. Sarna, vol. I (Atlanta, 1989), pp. 233–65.

19 See Sira 36.1–17 and 51.21–35 (Hebrew), 1QH 16.8–20, 1QS 9–11 where concepts and terms occur that have their parallels in the '*amidah* and adumbrate the later developments. This is not, however, to say that either a formal '*amidah* or a set of specific daily benedictions are to be traced to the pre-Christian centuries. See A. Z. Idelsohn, *Jewish Liturgy and its Development* (New York, 1932), pp. 20–3; Heinemann, *Prayer in the Talmud*, pp. 218–24; S. Talmon, *Tarbiẓ* 29 (1959), pp. 1–20; M. Weinfeld, *Tarbiẓ* 48 (1978–9), pp. 186–200 and the discussion between the last-mentioned and R. Brody, *Tarbiẓ* 51 (1981–2), pp. 493–6; Fleischer, *Tarbiẓ* 59 (1990), p. 434. Cf. also Weinfeld in *Tarbiẓ* 45 (1975), pp. 15–26 and in *Sinai* 105 (1989), pp. 72–82.

20 See the monograph of M. Greenberg, *Biblical Prose Prayer as a Window to the Popular Religion of Ancient Israel* (Berkeley, Los Angeles and London, 1983) and the works cited there, especially in 'Lecture 3'.

21 This point is well argued and illustrated by L. A. Hoffman in his 'Censoring In and Censoring Out. A Function of Liturgical Language' in *Ancient Synagogues. The State of Research*, ed. J. Gutmann (Chico, 1981), pp. 19–37.

22 See the contributions of S. Talmon and M. Weinfeld on the biblical period and those of D. Flusser, A. Shohat and H. Mantel on the later period in *Educational Encyclopedia*, IV (Hebrew; Jerusalem, 1964), cols. 52–72 and 136–57, and e.g. Exodus 13:14, 24:4, 7; Deuteronomy 6:7, 31:9–13, 26; 2 Kings 23:1–3; 2 Chronicles 17:7–9; and Nehemiah 8:8–9, 13–15. Cf. also J. L. Crenshaw, 'Education in Ancient Israel', *JBL* 104 (1985), pp. 601–15.

23 For a useful summary of the processes of transmission and translation see E. Würthwein, *The Text of the Old Testament. An Introduction to the Biblia Hebraica* (ET of the fourth edition, London, 1980). For midrash there is a helpful introduction by B. W. Holtz in the third chapter of the volume he edited, *Back to the Sources* (New York, 1984). On the physical nature of scrolls see M. Haran's articles in *Eretz Yisrael* 16 (1982), pp. 86–92; *JJS* 33 (1982), pp. 161–73 and 35 (1984), pp. 84–5; *HUCA* 54 (1983), pp. 111–22 and 56 (1985), pp. 21–62; *Tarbiz* 57 (1988), pp. 151–64 and 58 (1989), pp. 523–4. For scripture as liturgy see A. Kavanagh, 'Scripture and Worship in Synagogue and Church', *Michigan Quarterly Review* 22 (1983), pp. 480–94.

24 M. Fishbane, *Text and Texture* (New York, 1979), pp. 79–83, 121–40; *Biblical Interpretation in Ancient Israel* (Oxford, 1985), pp. 107–13, 265, 270, 384–5 and 407; *The Garments of Torah* (Bloomington and Indianapolis, 1989), pp. 64–78.

25 The whole of Martin Hengel's *Judaism and Hellenism* (ET, London, 1974) is here relevant but see in particular Excursus I, pp. 78–83.

26 *Mezuzoth* and *tefillin* have been discovered among the Qumran, Murabba'at and Nahal Se'elim scrolls and designated XQPhyl 1–4, 8QPhyl, 8QMez, 4QPhyl a–d and I, MurPhyl, MurMez(?) and 34 SePhyl; see Y. Yadin, *Tefillin from Qumran* (Jerusalem, 1969), and J. A. Fitzmyer, *The Dead Sea Scrolls. Major Publications and Tools for Study* (Missoula, 1975), pp. 22, 25–6, 39, 41 and 50. Note also the existence of the Nash Papyrus, the contents and significance of which are discussed by the writer in a brief article in *Cambridge* 15 (1984), pp. 41–5, and see E. E. Urbach, 'The Place of the Ten Commandments in Ritual and Prayer' in *The Ten Commandments as reflected in Tradition and Literature throughout the Ages*, ed. B.-Z. Segal (Hebrew; Jerusalem, 1985), pp. 127–45.

27 Philo, 2 De Somniis 18.127 and De Opificio Mundi 43.128; Josephus, Contra Apionem 2.17.175; Acts 15:21; Mishnah, *Megillah* 3.4; BT, *Megillah* f.31b and *Bava Qamma* f.82a; I. Elbogen, *Der jüdische Gottesdienst in seiner geschichtlichen Entwicklung* (Frankfurt-am-Main, 1931), III, para. 25,3 (pp. 157–9 in the

pagination of the original German edition and pp. 118–20 in the revised Hebrew edition of Tel Aviv, 1972).

28 The attempts began with Adolph Büchler's two articles on the Palestinian triennial cycle in *JQR* (OS) 5 (1892–3), pp. 420–68 and 6 (1893–4), pp. 1–73, and continued up to and including the work of Eric Werner, *The Sacred Bridge* (London, 1959) and Aileen Guilding, *The Fourth Gospel and Jewish Worship* (Oxford, 1960). Jacob Mann exploited the mediaeval fragments from the Cairo Genizah to demonstrate how different the Palestinian customs were from the standard Babylonian practice in his *The Bible as Read and Preached in the Old Synagogue*, I (Cincinnati, 1940), II (with Isaiah Sonne, Cincinnati, 1966). See also Petuchowski, 'The Liturgy of the Synagogue', pp. 27–33.

29 The convincing objections raised by L. Crocket, W. D. Davies and J. Heinemann to the detailed aspects of the work of Büchler, Mann and such followers as Werner and Guilding have been neatly summarised by J. J. Petuchowski in the introduction to his *Contributions to the Scientific Study of Jewish Liturgy* (New York, 1970), pp. xvii–xxi. Fleischer now promises to argue the case for the originality of the annual cycle in a Hebrew article in a forthcoming issue of *HUCA*.

30 See Greenberg, *Biblical Prose Prayer*; the whole monograph is germane to this chapter and to chapter 2 above but the third lecture is worthy of special attention. See also M. Haran, 'Priesthood, Temple, Divine Service', *Hebrew Annual Review* 7 (1983), pp. 121–35.

31 See the previous chapter above, pp. 48–50 and, for the relationship between the Qumran and other sects, see the important article by Sussmann, 'The History of *Halakha*'.

32 Chapter 4 below briefly discusses methodology and historical background before treating the subject under the tripartite division of 'The theological status of prayer', 'The essential nature of prayer' and 'The mechanics of prayer'. Full documentation is there provided for the conclusions here summarised. For Fleischer's view see *Tarbiz* 59 (1990), especially pp. 426–37.

33 A start has been made by L. A. Hoffman in his useful study *The Canonization of the Synagogue Service* (Notre Dame and London, 1979) and chapters 5 and 6 below are devoted to a treatment of such developments.

34 See the remarks of F. M. Cross about Essene and Qumran objections to the contemporary Jerusalem cult in *The Ancient Library of Qumran and Modern Biblical Studies* (New York, 1961, 2nd edn), pp. 100–3. The references in tannaitic literature to the ritual

activities of the *ḥasidim* and the *'anshey ma'aseh* may also indicate a popular equivalent to the Temple priesthood. See also Josephus, Antiquities 20.7.8.180–1, 20.9.2.205–7. Furthermore, although the priests did not fully lose their status with the destruction of the Temple, the levites appear to have moved out of the centre of the cult from the Hellenistic era; cf. S. Safrai, 'The Temple and the Divine Service', pp. 293–4. For the overall historical development of alternative temple sites see M. Haran, *Temples and Temple-service in Ancient Israel. An inquiry into the character of cult phenomena and the historical setting of the priestly school* (Oxford, 1978), pp. 13–57. On the matter of cultic tension regarding the status of Jerusalem and other centres in the Second Temple period, see J. Schwartz, 'Jubilees, Bethel and the Temple of Jacob', *HUCA* 56 (1985), pp. 63–85, and the strange reference (and related textual confusion) concerning Shiloh, Nob and Gideon in BT, *Soṭah* f.16a.

35 The substantial alterations to the Temple made by Herod in order to bring it 'closer to the grandiose ideal of the great Hellenistic–Oriental sanctuaries' are described by M. Avi-Yonah in 'Jewish Art and Architecture in the Hasmonean and Herodian Periods', in volume VII of *The World History of the Jewish People*, pp. 254–6. The tensions between Herod and the people arising out of his ambition to construct what amounted to a third Temple are also documented there.

36 See n. 11 above and on the antiquity of family rituals see M. Haran, *Temples and Temple-Service*, pp. 289–323. On non-Temple worship in general see also Sanders, *Judaism. Practice and Belief*, pp. 190–212.

37 Matthew 21:12–16 and Mark 11:15–18.

38 See chapter 4 below, pp. 95–102.

39 See S. Krauss, *Synagogale Altertümer* (Berlin, 1927), pp. 52–88; L. Finkelstein, *PAAJR* 1928–30 (1930), pp. 49–59; J. Weingreen, *Hermathena* 98 (1964), pp. 68–84; I. Levy, *The Synagogue. Its History and Function* (London, 1963), pp. 5–27.

40 See G. F. Moore, *Judaism in the First Centuries of the Christian Era. The Age of the Tannaim*, I (Cambridge, Mass., 1927), pp. 283–307; S. W. Baron, *A Social and Religious History of the Jews* (New York and London, 1952, 2nd edn), II, pp. 121–9. For a geonic precedent for such views see chapter 5 below, p. 135.

41 Ezekiel 11:16, explained by R. Isaac in BT, *Megillah* f.29a as a reference to the synagogues and academies of Babylon and, even more fancifully, by R. Eleazar as a reference to Rav's academy in Sura. See also Jeremiah 39:8.

42 See the extensive and latest evidence cited in *Ancient Synagogues*

Revealed, ed. L. I. Levine (Jerusalem, 1981); *The Synagogue in Late Antiquity*, ed. L. I. Levine (Philadelphia, 1987); Gutmann, *Ancient Synagogues*; *Synagogues in Antiquity*, eds A. Kasher, A. Oppenheimer and U. Rappaport (Jerusalem, 1987), especially the articles by L. I. Levine on pp. 11–29 and A. Kasher on pp. 119–32; M. Meyers and J. F. Strange, *Archaeology, the Rabbis and Early Christianity* (London, 1981), pp. 140–54 and L. L. Grabbe, 'Synagogues in Pre-70 Palestine. A Re-assessment', *JTS* NS 39 (1988), pp. 401–10. See also Haran, 'Priesthood, Temple, Divine Service', pp. 127–8, and D. Noy, 'A Jewish Place of Prayer in Roman Egypt', *JTS* NS 43 (1992), pp. 118–22.

43 See M. Friedländer, *Synagoge und Kirche in ihren Anfangen* (Berlin, 1908), pp. 53–78; Hengel, *Judaism and Hellenism*, Index, s.v. 'Synagogue'; E. Rivkin, 'Ben Sira and the Nonexistence of the Synagogue' in *In the Time of Harvest. Essays in Honor of Abba Hillel Silver on the Occasion of his 70th Birthday*, ed. D. J. Silver (New York, 1963), pp. 320–54; J. Schwartz, 'Jubilees, Bethel and the Temple of Jacob', p. 80; E. Schürer, *The History of the Jewish People in the Age of Jesus Christ 175 BC–AD 135*, eds. Vermes *et al.*, II, p. 425; L. Roth-Gerson, *The Greek Inscriptions from the Synagogues in Eretz-Israel* (Hebrew; Jerusalem, 1987), pp. 76–86; J. G. Griffiths, 'Egypt and the Rise of the Synagogue', *JTS* NS 38 (1987), pp. 1–15 and Fleischer, *Tarbiz* 59 (1990), pp. 402–14.

44 See the various designs illustrated in the volumes cited in n. 42 above.

45 For more detailed discussions of these elements of controversy, see Heinemann, *Prayer in the Talmud*; J. J. Petuchowski, *Understanding Jewish Prayer* (New York, 1972); and chapter 4 below. Fleischer (see *Tarbiz* 59 (1990)) is clearly unsympathetic to such a presupposition of continuity.

46 It should be recalled that these were not restricted to the home, the academy and the desert but apparently included temples used for a continuation of the sacrificial cult after the destruction of the Jerusalem Temple; see BT, *Megillah* f.10a and the references given in n. 34 above.

47 See S. Lieberman, *Greek in Jewish Palestine* (New York, 1942); Hengel, *Judaism and Hellenism*, especially pp. 58–65 and 103–6; V. Tcherikower, *Hellenistic Civilization and the Jews* (ET, Philadelphia, 1959), especially pp. 344–77; E. Bickerman, *From Ezra to the Last of the Maccabees. Foundations of Post-Biblical Judaism* (New York, 1962, 2nd edn), pp. 72–90. For Jewish liturgical Greek, see Mishnah, *Megillah* 1.8 and *Soṭah* 7.1; PT, *Soṭah* f.21bc and BT, *Soṭah* ff.32a–33a and 49b.

48 See the references given in n. 42 above as well as M. J. S. Chait, *Handbook of Synagogue Architecture* (Chico, 1982) and B. Brooten, *Women Leaders in the Ancient Synagogue. Inscriptional Evidence and Background Issues* (Chico, 1982).

49 The discussion is taken further in the next two chapters; see also the exchange of views between the writer and Fleischer cited in n. 2 above.

50 See B. P. Kittel, *The Hymns of Qumran. Translation and Commentary* (Chico, 1981) and J. Licht, *The Rule Scroll. A Scroll from the Wilderness of Judaea. 1QS, 1QSa and 1QSb. Translation, Introduction and Commentary* (Jerusalem, 1965). See also chapter 2 above, pp. 48–50.

51 Those who write down benedictions are likened to those who consign the Torah to flames in BT, *Shabbath* f.115b. See chapter 4, below, p. 105 and chapter 5 below, pp. 124 and 149.

52 See P. S. Goldberg, *Karaite Liturgy and its Relation to Synagogue Worship* (Manchester, 1957) and the various controversies between Rabbanites and Karaites discussed by L. A. Hoffman in *The Canonization of the Synagogue Service.*

53 Apart from the general work of G. G. Scholem, see also S. Safrai, 'The Teachings of the Pietists in Mishnaic Literature', *JJS* 16 (1965), pp. 15–33; N. Wieder, *Islamic Influences on the Jewish Worship* (Hebrew; Oxford, 1947); P. B. Fenton, *The Treatise of the Pool* (London, 1981); J. Dan and F. Talmage (eds.), *Studies in Jewish Mysticism* (Cambridge, Mass., 1982); and Bar-Ilan, *The Mysteries of Jewish Prayer.* See also n. 16 above and ch. 7 below, nn. 74–5.

54 See Pliny the Elder, Naturalis Historia 5.15.73; the other sources cited by Cross, *The Ancient Library of Qumran*, pp. 96–100, and G. Vermes, *The Dead Sea Scrolls. Qumran in Perspective* (London, 1977) pp. 96–109; and Mishnah, *Sukkah* 5.2–4. See also chapter 2 above, pp. 45–6 and S. Schechter, *Studies in Judaism*, First Series (London and Philadelphia, 1896), pp. 313–25.

55 Brooten, *Women Leaders*; R. S. Kraemer, 'Jewish Women in the Diaspora World of Late Antiquity' in *Jewish Women in Historical Perspective*, ed. J. R. Baskin (Detroit, 1991), pp. 43–67. See also '*Women like This*'. *New Perspectives on Jewish Women in the Graeco-Roman World*, ed. A.-J. Levine (Atlanta, 1991).

56 The relevant talmudic references are Mishnah, *Ḥagigah* 3.1, *Nedarim* 4.3, *Soṭah* 3.4 and *Qiddushin* 1.7; PT, *Shevu'oth* 4.1, f.35b and *Soṭah* 3.4, f.19a; BT, *Berakhoth* ff.20ab, 45b, *Rosh Ha-Shanah* f.29a, *Megillah* f.23ab, *Soṭah* ff.20a–22a, *Qiddushin* f.29b, *Sanhedrin* f.94b, *Menaḥoth* f.43a and *Niddah* f.45b. For discussion of the issues

see J. Z. Lauterbach's responsum from *CCARYB* 32 (1922) reprinted in his *Studies in Jewish Law, Custom and Folklore*, ed. B. J. Bamberger (New York, 1970), 240–6; M. Meiselman, *Jewish Woman in Jewish Law* (New York, 1978), pp. 34–42 and 130–46; and the relevant sections of R. Biale, *Women and Jewish Law* (New York, 1984); A. Weiss, *Women at Prayer* (Hoboken, N.J., 1990); Baskin (ed.), *Jewish Women in Historical Perspective*; S. Grossman and R. Haut (eds.), *Daughters of the King. Women and the Synagogue* (Philadelphia and New York and Jerusalem, 1992).

57 See E. Ullendorff, 'Is Biblical Hebrew a Language?' in *BSOAS* 34 (1971), pp. 241–55, reprinted in the volume of his essays bearing the same title (Wiesbaden, 1977), pp. 3–17; S. C. Reif, *VT* 31 (1981), pp. 123–5; and E. Y. Kutscher, *A History of the Hebrew Language* (Jerusalem and Leiden, 1982), pp. 115–47.

58 See Lieberman, *Greek in Jewish Palestine*, pp. 29–67.

59 See Heinemann, *Prayer in the Talmud*, pp. 190–2, 265–6 and 287. Cf. also J. J. Petuchowski and M. Brocke, *The Lord's Prayer and Jewish Liturgy* (London, 1978), pp. 1–117, and Bradshaw, *Daily Prayer in the Early Church*, pp. 1–46.

60 E.g. BT, *Ḥullin* f.137b and *'Avodah Zarah* f.58b.

61 Heinemann, *Prayer in the Talmud*, pp. 123–38.

62 See S. C. Reif, *Shabbethai Sofer and his Prayer-book* (Cambridge, 1979), pp. 29–38.

63 Heinemann, *Prayer in the Talmud*, pp. 139–55; cf. also E. Fleischer, *Hebrew Liturgical Poetry in the Middle Ages* (Hebrew; Jerusalem, 1975), pp. 41–6. See also chapter 5 below, p. 129.

64 Heinemann, *Prayer in the Talmud*, pp. 77–122.

65 Kutscher, *A History of the Hebrew Language*, pp. 93–106, especially pp. 102–3. When Rabban Gamliel tried to standardise the liturgy in the second century (and, according to Fleischer's article in *Tarbiẓ* 59 (1990) succeeded in doing so), his linguistic commitment was undoubtedly to tannaitic Hebrew.

66 See n. 26 above and Josephus, Antiquities, 4.8.13.212.

67 See Mishnah, *Yoma* 4.1–2 and BT, *Ta'anith* f.16b.

68 See Mishnah *Berakhoth* 1.5 and 2.2 and the expansion of these comments in Tosefta, *Berakhoth* 1.10 (Zuckermandel, p. 2) and PT, *Berakhoth* 1.9, f.3d; cf. L. Ginzberg, *A Commentary on the Palestinian Talmud* (New York, 1941), 1, pp. 209–12.

69 Heinemann, *Prayer in the Talmud*, pp. 129 and 230. See also Petuchowski, 'The Liturgy of the Synagogue', pp. 18–24, and Hammer, 'What did they Bless?', p. 310.

70 See 2 Maccabees 1:1–6 and Heinemann, *Prayer in the Talmud*, pp. 130–1.

71 Heinemann, *Prayer in the Talmud*, pp. 124–9.

72 See n. 68 above and PT, *Berakhoth* 1.1, f.2d, BT, *Berakhoth* ff.4b, 9b and 42a, *Shabbat* f.119b. See Petuchowski, 'The Liturgy of the Synagogue', pp. 12–17 and 24–7.

73 That the same religious legislation is not applied to these two principal parts of the tannaitic liturgy is clear from the first five chapters of Mishnah *Berakhoth*.

74 'The Politics of Piety, Social Conflict and the Emergence of Rabbinic Liturgy' in *The Making of Jewish and Christian Worship*, eds. P. F. Bradshaw and L. A. Hoffman (Notre Dame and London, 1991), pp. 42–68. Zahavy is, however, correct (see 'Three Stages', p. 245) in stressing the second- to third-century efforts to amalgamate the *shema'* and the *'amidah* into a compound liturgy.

75 Heinemann, *Prayer in the Talmud*, pp. 113–22, and Petuchowski, 'The Liturgy of the Synagogue', p. 26.

76 Compare the later controversy between the Babylonian and Palestinian authorities as to whether the cantor or the priest should recite this benediction, an interesting reflection of the ambivalence towards the continuation of Temple practices in the synagogue; see Hoffman, *The Canonization*, pp. 53–5, and chapter 4, p. 99 below.

77 See chapter 2 above, n. 14.

78 See J. Mann, *HUCA* 2 (1925), pp. 282–4; G. Vermes, *BZAW* 103 (1968), pp. 232–40 reprinted in his *Post-Biblical Jewish Studies* (Leiden, 1975), pp. 169–77; and J. Blau, *R. Moses ben Maimon Responsa*, II (Jerusalem, 1960), pp. 495–9. See also various more general treatments of early Jewish liturgy by Solomon Zeitlin in *JQR* 36 (1946), pp. 211–29; 38 (1948), pp. 289–316 and 431–60; 53 (1962), pp. 22–9; 54 (1964), pp. 208–49.

79 E.g. Mishnah, *Yoma* 6.2 and 7.1.

80 To this controversy is to be attributed the tendency in such cases to reach a compromise whereby such rituals were at least abandoned in the synagogue on the Sabbath; see chapter 4 below, p. 100.

81 See e.g. Mishnah, *Megillah* 3.4–6, 4.10, *Ḥagigah* 2.1 and BT, *Megillah* ff.29a–30b. See also the reference to a forthcoming article by Fleischer at the end of n. 29 above.

82 See the references and comments in n. 16 above and P. Schäfer, *Geniza-Fragmente zur Hekhalot-literatur* (Tübingen, 1984), as well as M. D. Swartz, *Mystical Prayer in Ancient Judaism. An Analysis of* Ma'aseh Merkavah (Tübingen, 1992).

83 Heinemann, *Prayer in the Talmud*, p. 218.

4 SOME LITURGICAL ISSUES IN THE TALMUDIC SOURCES

1 For the background to the development of rabbinic Judaism and a variety of interpretations of its emergence, see S. Safrai (ed.), *The Literature of the Sages. First Part: Oral Tora, Halakha, Mishna, Tosefta, Talmud, External Tractates* (Assen/Maastricht and Philadelphia, 1987); G. Vermes *et al.*, *The History of the Jewish People in the Age of Jesus Christ* by Emile Schürer, 3 vols. (Edinburgh, 1973–87); H. Maccoby, *Early Rabbinic Writings* (Cambridge, 1988); and the forthcoming third and fourth volumes of the *Cambridge History of Judaism.*

2 Israel Abrahams, 'Some Rabbinic Ideas on Prayer', *JQR* 20 (1908), p. 273.

3 Ismar Elbogen, *Der jüdische Gottesdienst in seiner geschichtlichen Entwicklung* (Frankfurt-am-Main, 1931), a work that was based on research undertaken over the previous quarter-century.

4 *Prayer in the Period of the Tanna'im and the Amora'im. Its Nature and its Patterns* (Hebrew; Jerusalem, 1964). See also his *Studies in Jewish Liturgy* (Jerusalem, 1981), posthumously edited by A. Shinan.

5 I. Elbogen, *Ha-Tefillah Beyisra'el Behithpathuthah Ha-Historith* (Tel Aviv, 1972), translated by J. Amir and edited by J. Heinemann, assisted by I. Adler, A. Negev, J. Petuchowski and H. Schirmann; J. Heinemann, *Prayer in the Talmud. Forms and Patterns* (Berlin and New York, 1977), a revised version by the author based on an English version produced by R. S. Sarason. See also J. J. Petuchowski, 'The Liturgy of the Synagogue: History, Structure and Contents' in *Approaches to Ancient Judaism*, vol. IV, ed. W. S. Green (Chico, Ca., 1983), pp. 1–64.

6 E. Fleischer, 'On the Beginnings of Obligatory Jewish Prayer' (Hebrew), *Tarbiz* 59 (1990), pp. 397–441. See also the writer's response to Fleischer in *Tarbiz* 60 (1991), pp. 677–81.

7 L. Ginzberg, 'Jewish Thought as Reflected in the Halakah' in his *Students, Scholars and Saints* (Philadelphia, 1928), p. 116.

8 E. E. Urbach, *The Sages: Their Concepts and Beliefs* (ET, Jerusalem, 1975), vol. I, p. 3.

9 See J. Neusner, 'The Teaching of the Rabbis: Approaches Old and New', *JJS* 27 (1976), pp. 23–35.

10 See the writer's general remarks made in the course of reviewing books on rabbinic subjects in *JJS* 19 (1974), pp. 112–18, 301–5 and 20 (1975), pp. 260–4; *JTS* NS 33 (1982), pp. 537–8 and 37 (1986), pp. 506–8; and *JBL* 102 (1983), pp. 660–3.

11 It should not be forgotten that by its very nature liturgy tends to present more problems for the historian than other areas since

novelty of practice is not only rarely acknowledged but also re-interpreted as established custom. See T. Zahavy, 'Three Stages in the Development of Early Rabbinic Prayer' in *From Ancient Israel to Modern Judaism. Intellect in Quest of Understanding. Essays in Honor of Marvin Fox*, eds. J. Neusner, E. S. Frerichs and N. M. Sarna, vol. 1 (Atlanta, 1989), pp. 233–65.

12 A fuller account of these contexts is given in the previous chapter.

13 Tosefta, *Sukkah* 4.3 (ed. Vilna; ed. M. S. Zuckermandel 4.5, p. 198). It is clear from the notes and comments of Zuckermandel and S. Lieberman (*Tosefta Ki-Fshuṭah, Mo'ed*, New York, 1962, pp. 888–9) that the confused state of the text on the matter of which centres of activity are included in the statement is a reflection of a changing conception of what constituted 'liturgy' on the part of the rabbinic transmitters, and possibly of a lack of sharp distinction between synagogue and academy. See D. Urman, 'The Synagogue and Beth Ha-Midrash. Are they One and the Same? in *Synagogues in Antiquity*, eds. A. Kasher, A. Oppenheimer and U. Rappaport (Hebrew; Jerusalem, 1987), pp. 53–75.

14 The original mishnaic statement is in *'Avoth* 1.2 and the commentary is to be found in Recension A of *'Avoth deRabbi Nathan*, ed. Schechter, pp. 18 and 21–2, trans. J. Goldin (New Haven, 1955), pp. 32 and 34, trans. A. Saldarini (Leiden, 1975), p. 74. Although according to the doctoral dissertation (Cambridge, 1991) of N. Poltzer, *Interpreting the Fathers. A Literary-Structural Comparison of Parallel Narratives in Avot de Rabbi Natan Versions A and B*, the literary form of the tractate, particularly in Recension A, is much later than the talmudic period, the ideas here being cited are clearly part of the core of the traditions which is much earlier.

15 J. Guttmann, *Philosophies of Judaism. The History of Jewish Philosophy from Biblical Times to Franz Rosenzweig* (ET, London, 1964), p. 36.

16 BT, *Qiddushin* f.40b. On the matter of the theological crisis involved, see Urbach, *The Sages*, vol. 1, pp. 351–3.

17 BT, *Sanhedrin* f.74a.

18 Urbach, *The Sages*, vol. 1, p. 608.

19 PT, *Berakhoth* 1.8, f.3c. The stress is on the first two paragraphs since there was still some doubt about the inclusion of the third paragraph; for the sources and Ginzberg's comments, see n. 68 of the previous chapter.

20 BT, *Megillah* f.27a and PT, *Ta'anith* 3.4, f.66c. Growing evidence of the increasing centrality of Torah study in the second century is to be found in attitudes to the outsider on the part of the rabbis;

see A. Oppenheimer, *The 'Am Ha-Aretz. A Study in the Social History of the Jewish People in the Hellenistic-Roman Period* (Leiden, 1977), pp. 170–99. See also Zahavy, 'Three Stages', pp. 242–54.

21 BT, *Megillah* f.27a and *Sanhedrin* f.92a.

22 BT, *Shabbath* f.10a and *Berakhoth* f.6a; PT, *Berakhoth* 5.1, f.8d–9a; BT, *Sukkah* f.16b. It should, however, be acknowledged that texts that refer to both synagogues and academies sometimes have variant readings that cast doubt on whether both institutions were originally mentioned in the core teaching. For a new assessment of the debates between Abbaye and Rava, see R. Kalmin 'Friends and Colleagues, or Barely Acquainted? Relations between Fourth Century Masters in the Babylonian Talmud', *HUCA* (1990), pp. 125–58. See also n. 13 above.

23 *Sifre*, Deuteronomy para. 41, ed. L. Finkelstein, pp. 87–8, and the notes of the editor on the passage.

24 BT, *Pesaḥim* f.109a. Is it possible that this preference for expressing festive joy through wine is the reflection of a growing tendency to accord greater liturgical significance to the use of wine?

25 The 'R. Simeon' is R. Simeon bar Yoḥai according to *Koheleth Rabbah* 7.1.3 but R. Simeon ben Menasya according to *Midrash Shemuel* (ed. S. Buber, Cracow, 1893), pp. 112–13. On the history of the priestly benediction and its changing fortunes in the Jewish liturgy, see Yitschak (Eric) Zimmer in *Sinai* 100 (1987), pp. 452–70 and A. Shapir in *L'Eyla* 31 (1991), pp. 33–5.

26 BT, *Berakhoth* ff.54a and 63a, *Pesaḥim* f.56a, and see the fifth chapter of Heinemann, *Prayer in the Talmud* and *Prayer in the Period of the Tanna'im* and the relevant index references.

27 S. Safrai, 'The Temple and the Synagogue' in *Synagogues in Antiquity*, eds. Kasher *et al.*, pp. 31–51. See chapter 3 above, pp. 85–6 and n. 80. For literary criticism of the fourth chapter of the mishnaic tractate *Rosh Ha-Shanah*, see J. N. Epstein, *Introduction to Tannaitic Literature* (Hebrew; Jerusalem, 1957), p. 366 and for text-critical work on the version in the PT, see E. A. Goldman, 'A Critical Edition of Palestinian Talmud Tractate Rosh Hashana, Chapter Four', *HUCA* 49 (1978), pp. 205–26.

28 BT, *Sukkah* f.45ab and *Megillah* f.10a; see also chapter 3 above, end of n. 34, the last sentence of that note.

29 R. Eleazar's statements are to be found in a string of traditions attached to his name in BT, *Berakhoth* f.32b, all of which emphasise the novel and impressive nature of prayer compared with its cultic forerunner, while R. Yoḥanan's view is recorded in BT, *Berakhoth* f.7a. See also pp. 97 and 106 below for further references to R. Eleazar's statements.

30 The requirement, as reported by R. Jacob ben Aḥa in the name of R. Assi in BT, *Ta'anith* f.27b, would appear to be *qeri'ah*, probably in the sense of formal recitation, while its parallels in BT, *Menaḥoth* f.110a are concerned with the study of the relevant laws. Either way, the concept was regularly used by commentators on the liturgy to justify the inclusion of such passages; see e.g. *Sefer Abudraham* (Warsaw, 1877), p. 16a (ed. A. J. Wertheimer, Jerusalem, 1963, p. 48).

31 BT, *Soṭah* f.9a. No clear statement is made that the 'places of praise' of Moses and David are being distinguished from the first and second Temples but such a coyness on the part of the aggadist would be understandable. On the variants, see the critical edition by Abraham Liss (Jerusalem, 1977).

32 PT, *Berakhoth* 4.5, f.8c and BT, *Berakhoth* f.26b.

33 See Urbach, *The Sages*, vol. I, pp. 318–36 and compare the opposing views of Maimonides and Naḥmanides on whether prayer is indeed a biblically ordained requirement or a rabbinic enactment, neatly summarised by A. Weiss, *Women at Prayer. A Halakhic Analysis of Women's Prayer Groups* (New York, 1990), pp. 14–19.

34 PT, *Berakhoth* 4.1, f.7a. On the later liturgical effects of these views and their harmonisation, see L. Ginzberg, *A Commentary on the Palestinian Talmud* (New York, 1941), vol. III, pp. 22–7.

35 BT, *Ta'anith* ff.23a, 19b–20a and 23a–25a. The variants may be found in H. Malter's critical edition of the tractate published in New York in 1930. Zahavy, 'Three Stages', sees these miraculous powers as evidence of the Yavnean rabbis' conviction that prayer could affect the life of the Jew while the evidence is here being related to pre-Yavnean attitudes to piety. The definition of these prayers as law-court prayers is made by A. Laytner, *Arguing with God. A Jewish Tradition* (Northvale, N.J., and London, 1990), pp. 87–97.

36 See the passages discussed by G. Vermes, *Jesus the Jew. A Historian's Reading of the Gospels* (London, 1973), pp. 58–82 and chapter 3, pp. 59–60 above.

37 BT, *Ta'anith* ff.25b, 24ab and *Sanhedrin* f.106b; see Malter's apparatus to his critical edition.

38 *Berakhoth* 5.1; BT, *'Eruvin* f.65a; Tosefta, *Berakhoth* 3.21 (ed. Vilna; ed. M. S. Zuckermandel 3.21, p. 8); BT, *Berakhoth* f.31a. On the matter of the textual variation regarding the moods listed, see Lieberman, *Tosefta, Zera'im* (New York, 1955), p. 47.

39 BT, *Sanhedrin* f.22a; *Berakhoth* 3.4. Interestingly, Maimonides rules in accordance with the view of R. Simeon in the matter of one's frame of mind but against the Mishnah in the matter of the need for ritual ablution on the grounds that it is based on a decree that

is generally not followed; see his Code on the laws of prayer 4.16 and on the laws of reciting the *shema'* 4.8.

40 Tosefta, *Shabbath* 14.4 (ed. Zuckermandel, 13.4) and BT, *Shabbath* f.115b; Fleischer, 'On the Beginnings', p. 435; M.D. Swartz, *Mystical Prayer in Ancient Judaism. An Analysis of* Ma'aseh Merkavah (Tübingen, 1992).

41 BT, *Berakhoth* f.32b and *Pesaḥim* f.118b.

42 *Devarim Rabbah* (printed edition), 2.12.

43 BT, *Ta'anith* f.23a and *Berakhoth* f.32b. See Laytner, *Arguing with God*, pp. 95–7.

44 BT, *Ḥullin* f.91b and *Soṭah* f.7b. On the matter of the relationship between Israel's prayers and those of the angels, see also chapter 2 above, p. 49. The *Soṭah* passage is paralleled in BT, *Berakhoth* f.34b where the attribution is to R. Kahana and it is clear from there and from the textual variants here that the original text referred to a person rather than a Jew and therefore attracted Christian censorship at a later date. Its original intent was not, however, necessarily aimed outside the Jewish community only.

45 Mishnah, *Berakhoth* 1.3. The passage in BT, *Berakhoth* f.13b is seen as the source of the '*shema'* of R. Judah Ha-Nasi' in the morning benedictions but the history of that earlier recitation of the *shema'* still requires a serious analysis that might give it a more plausible origin than simply a time of persecution. Compare Elbogen, *Der jüdische Gottesdienst*, p. 91 and *Ha-Tefillah*, p. 71 and chapter 6 below, n. 4.

46 BT, *Berakhoth* ff.11b, 48b and 54b.

47 PT, *Rosh Ha-Shanah* 1.3, f.57b. Perhaps there is here the same kind of argument about the nature of the festival as existed with regard to the Day of Atonement; see N. Wieder, *The Judean Scrolls and Karaism* (London, 1962), pp. 161–97.

48 *Mekhilta de-Rabbi Ishmael*, ed. M. Friedmann (Vienna, 1870), p. 37a; eds. S. Horovitz and I. A. Rabin (Frankfurt-am-Main, 1928–31), p. 127; ed. J. Z. Lauterbach (Philadelphia, 1933), vol. II, pp. 26–7.

49 BT, *Berakhoth* f.26a. It seems self-evident that such a piece of exegesis was not simply an intellectual exercise but was polemically aimed at those who neglected or rejected (the passage later speaks of one who deliberately omits) what some of the rabbinic leaders saw as essential prayers.

50 Mishnah, *Berakhoth* 4.3. There is no doubt that Rabban Gamliel championed organised liturgy but some considerable doubt whether Fleischer is justified by the evidence in claiming that he

definitely fixed the text of the *ʿamidah* for talmudic Judaism. The ubiquitousness of alternative views, the existence of other teachers and schools, the Genizah evidence and the problem of transmission all militate against his claim; see *Tarbiẓ* 59 (1990) for Fleischer's views and *Tarbiẓ* 60 (1991) for the writer's response to them.

51 BT, *Berakhoth* ff.27b–28a. The incident is the subject of much scholarly analysis; see, for example, R. Goldenberg, 'The Deposition of Rabban Gamaliel II: An Examination of the Sources', *JJS* 23 (1972), pp. 167–90; and L. Jacobs, *Structure and Form in the Babylonian Talmud* (Cambridge, 1991), pp. 81–6. Cf. also S. Kanter, *Rabban Gamaliel II, The Legal Traditions* (Chico, 1980).

52 BT, *Berakhoth* ff.14b–15a and 60b. See Zahavy, 'Three Stages', especially pp. 242–54.

53 BT, *Sanhedrin* f.94a; on the passage see E. L. Segal, 'The Goat of the Slaughterhouse', *Tarbiẓ* 49 (1979), pp. 43–51.

54 BT, *Rosh Ha-Shanah* f.17b. R. Yoḥanan justifies his interpretation of the verse by pointing to the specific statement of Scripture i.e. the occurrence of the expression *ʿbr ʿl pny* which he takes as equivalent to the rabbinic term *ʿbr lpny htbh* for conducting the service. The exegesis is relevant to the discussion about what the talmudic rabbis meant by the specific statements of Scripture; see R. Loewe, 'The "Plain" Meaning of Scripture in Early Jewish Exegesis', *Papers of the Institute of Jewish Studies* 1 (1964), pp. 140–85.

55 Fleischer in his article 'On the Beginnings' pp. 432–3 fails to distinguish *a* fixed ritual from *the* fixed ritual and is therefore forced to explain the call for innovation in the same non-literal fashion used by the opponents of the concept in talmudic times.

56 Urbach, *The Sages*, vol. 1, p. 122; see also the references and comments in chapter 3, n. 16 above and Swartz, *Mystical Prayer*.

57 BT, *Kethuboth* f.8b.

58 BT, *Berakhoth* f.33b and *Megillah* ff.25a and 18a. Particularly noteworthy for the history of liturgical transmission are the variant readings in the list of epithets that are the subject of the disapproval; cf. *Diqduqey Soferim* on the first two passages just cited.

59 BT, *Shabbath* f.127a, Mishnah, *Peʾah* 1.1, BT, *Shabbath* f.118b. On the text of the mishnaic passage see *Mishnah Zeraʿim*, ed. N. Sachs (Jerusalem, 1972), pp. 94–5.

60 BT, *Bava Bathra* f.164b and *Berakhoth* ff.54b–55a. Is it possible that *qir naṭuy* is a reference to a prayer niche such as those used by fourth-century Byzantine monks? See I. Finkelstein, 'Byzantine Prayer Niches', *IEJ* 31 (1981), pp. 81–91.

61 See e.g. the comments of the printed *Tosafoth* on BT *Berakhoth* f.32b and *Shabbath* f.118b.

62 See Herbert Loewe's remarks in *A Rabbinic Anthology*, eds. C. G. Montefiore and H. Loewe (London, 1938), pp. 407–8.

63 I. Ta-Shema, 'On the Beginning of the Piyyut', *Tarbiẓ* 53 (1984), pp. 285–8.

64 BT, *Soṭah* ff.32b–33a. For fuller references to primary and secondary literature see chapter 3 above, n. 47.

65 On the technical term *prs ʿl shmʿ*, see E. Fleischer on this subject in *Tarbiẓ* 41 (1972), pp. 133–44 and Heinemann, *Studies*, pp. 16–20. On *hallel* see BT, *Soṭah* f.30b. A simple communal response, but a communal response nevertheless, is also recorded in connection with the *qaddish* recitation in *Sifre*, Deuteronomy, para. 306, ed. L. Finkelstein (New York, 1969), p. 342. See also the note by H. Guggenheimer, *Moriah* 13 (1984), p. 89.

66 PT, *Berakhoth* 1.1, f.2b, BT, *Berakhoth* f.21a and *Rosh Ha-Shanah* f.35a.

67 *Tanḥuma*, ed. S. Buber (Vilna, 1885), Genesis, p. 196. The Latin is clearly *vive imperator* but the state of the text makes the Greek more difficult to reconstruct. Buber suggests (κύριε) χατρε clearly to be corrected to χαρτέ, an adjective that greets the emperor as welcome. More likely would be χαῖρε from the verb meaning 'greet'.

68 BT, *Berakhoth* f.34a.

69 BT, *Berakhoth* f.31a. Some readings of the text are more specific about his reason than others but it seems clear from the context.

70 BT, *Berakhoth* f.28b and *Yoma* f.53b; PT, *Berakhoth* 1.8, f.3c.

71 BT, *Berakhoth* ff.16b–17a; Loewe, *A Rabbinic Anthology*, pp. 361–8; BT, *Soṭah* f.22a.

72 BT, *Berakhoth* ff.29b–30a. See Zahavy, 'Three Stages', pp. 242–54.

73 BT, *Berakhoth* ff.3a, 6a, 6b and 8a.

74 Mishnah, *Berakhoth* 4.7; see the traditional commentaries and Albeck's edition of the Mishnah (Jerusalem and Tel Aviv, 1957–60), vol. I, pp. 21–2 and 332 for various explanations of *ḥever haʿir*.

75 BT, *Megillah* f.22a.

76 BT, *Berakhoth* f.7b. There is some confusion in the Munich manuscript as to the correct place of the names Naḥman and Isaac in the attribution.

77 *Pesiqta de-Rav Kahana*, ed. S. Buber (Vilna, 1925, 2nd edn), p. 282; ed. B. Mandelbaum (New York, 1962), vol. II, p. 352.

78 Loewe, *A Rabbinic Anthology*, p. 356.

79 Mishnah, *Sukkah* 5.4; BT, *Bava Bathra* f.25a, *Yevamoth* f.105b and *Berakhoth* f.10b.

80 For aspects of the position adopted by Fleischer and the counter position, see his and Reif's articles in *Tarbiẓ* 59 (1990) and 60 (1991).

5 HOW THE FIRST JEWISH PRAYER-BOOK EVOLVED

1 S. Safrai (ed.), *The Literature of the Sages. First Part: Oral Tora, Halakha, Mishna, Tosefta, Talmud, External Tractates* (Assen and Maastricht and Philadelphia, 1987); D. Weiss-Halivni, *Midrash, Mishnah and Gemara* (Cambridge, Mass., 1986); J. Neusner, *A History of the Jews in Babylonia* I–V (Leiden, 1965–70); G. Alon, *The Jews in their Land in the Talmudic Age 70–640 CE* (Jerusalem, 1980–4).

2 In addition to chapters 3 and 4 above, see M. Meyers and J. F. Strange, *Archaeology, the Rabbis and Early Christianity* (London, 1981); *The Lord's Prayer and Jewish Liturgy*, eds. J. J. Petuchowski and M. Brocke (ET, London, 1978); P. F. Bradshaw, *Daily Prayer in the Early Church* (London, 1981); David A. Fiensy, *Prayers alleged to be Jewish. An Examination of the* Constitutiones Apostolorum (Chico, 1985); P. F. Bradshaw and L. A. Hoffman (eds.), *The Making of Jewish and Christian Worship* (Notre Dame and London, 1991).

3 B. Gerhardsson, *Memory and Manuscript. Oral Tradition and Written Transmission in Rabbinic Judaism and Early Christianity* (Uppsala, 1961); p. 149 below, on the matter of memory, and the exchange between the writer and Fleischer in *Tarbiẓ* 59 (1990), pp. 397–441 and 60 (1991), pp. 677–81; J. Heinemann and J. J. Petuchowski, *Literature of the Synagogue* (New York, 1975); J. J. Petuchowski (ed.), *Contributions to the Scientific Study of Jewish Liturgy* (New York, 1970), pp. xvii–xxi.

4 J. Gutmann (ed.), *Ancient Synagogues. The State of Research* (Chico, 1981); L. I. Levine (ed.), *Ancient Synagogues Revealed* (Jerusalem, 1981) and *The Synagogue in Late Antiquity* (Jerusalem, 1987); *Synagogues in Antiquity*, eds. A. Kasher, A. Oppenheimer and U. Rappaport (Hebrew; Jerusalem, 1987); B. M. Bokser, *The Origins of the Seder. The Passover Rite and Early Rabbinic Judaism* (Berkeley, 1984); J. Schwartz, 'Jubilees, Bethel and the Temple of Jacob', *HUCA* 56 (1985), pp. 63–85; J. Heinemann, *Prayer in the Talmud. Forms and Patterns* (updated and modified ET, Berlin, 1976); B. Brooten, *Women Leaders in the Ancient Synagogue. Inscriptional Evidence and Background Issues* (Chico, 1982); BT, *Megillah* f.10a, *'Avodah Ẓarah* f.52b, *Menaḥoth* f.109b.

5 See chapter 3, pp. 57–61 above. The article on Jewish liturgy by Ezra Fleischer in *Tarbiẓ* 59 (1990) takes a considerably more positive view than Heinemann in *Prayer in the Talmud* about the

degree of formality already in existence in talmudic prayer and has elements of revisionism and apologetics in its uncompromising attitude to the existence of alternative interpretations of the situation at that stage. See also J. Heinemann, *Studies in Jewish Liturgy*, ed. A. Shinan (Jerusalem, 1981), I. Elbogen, *Der jüdische Gottesdienst in seiner geschichtlichen Entwicklung* (Frankfurt-am-Main, 1931; updated Hebrew edition, Tel Aviv, 1972), and J. J. Petuchowski, 'The Liturgy of the Synagogue: History, Structure and Contents' in *Approaches to Ancient Judaism*, vol. IV, ed. W. S. Green (Chico, 1983), pp. 1–50.

6 Robert Goldenberg neatly sums up the problem of using talmudic sources for historical reconstruction in his essay in *Back to the Sources. Reading the Classic Jewish Texts*, ed. B. W. Holtz (New York, 1984), pp. 129–75.

7 S. W. Baron, *A Social and Religious History of the Jews* II (New York, 1952, 2nd edn); Heinemann, *Prayer in the Talmud*, pp. 285–7; A. Oppenheimer, 'Synagogues with a Historic Association in Talmudic Babylonia' in *Synagogues in Antiquity*, eds. Kasher and Oppenheimer, pp.147–54 and I. Gafni, 'Synagogues in Talmudic Babylonia: Traditions and Reality', pp. 155–62 in the same volume.

8 Fiensy, *Prayers alleged to be Jewish*, pp. 215–23; Tosefta, *Sukkah* 4.6 (ed. Zuckermandel, 4.4, p. 198); BT, *Sukkah* f.51b; S. Lieberman (ed.), *Tosefta Ki-Fshuṭa, Mo'ed* (New York, 1962), pp. 889–92; Brooten, *Women Leaders* and L. Roth-Gerson, *The Greek Inscriptions from the Synagogues in Eretz-Israel* (Hebrew; Jerusalem, 1987). Fleischer's interpretation pays little attention to the possibility of such differences; see pp. 401 and 406–11 of his article in *Tarbiẓ* 59 (1990).

9 E.g. Mishnah, *Berakhoth* 1–5, *Ta'anith* 2.2–3, *Yoma* 7.1, *Tamid* 5.1; Tosefta, *Berakhoth* 1–3; BT, *Berakhoth* f.4b and ff.27b–29b. See also L. Ginzberg, *A Commentary on the Palestinian Talmud* (Hebrew; New York, 1941) I, pp. 215–16, III, p. 359; S. C. Reif, 'Liturgical Difficulties and Geniza Manuscripts' in *Studies in Judaism and Islam presented to S. D. Goitein*, eds. S. Morag, I. Ben-Ami, N. A. Stillman (Jerusalem, 1981), pp. 99–122; Heinemann, *Prayer in the Talmud*, pp. 137–92, 218–50 and the various relevant essays in the collection *Studies in Jewish Liturgy* edited by Shinan; and Fleischer, *Tarbiẓ* 59 (1990), pp. 426–44 and Reif (see *Tarbiẓ* 60 (1991), pp. 677–81. See also T. Zahavy, *The Mishnaic Law of Blessings and Prayers* (Decatur, 1988) and 'The Politics of Piety. Social Conflict and the Emergence of Rabbinic Liturgy' in *The Making of Jewish and Christian Worship*, Bradshaw and Hoffmann (eds.), pp. 42–68.

Zahavy is justified in tracing different origins for the *shema'* and the *'amidah* and pointing to their eventual amalgamation. What seems dubious is his linkage of the former to scribal circles and the latter to the priesthood when the opposite may well have been the case, given the respective histories of a close concern with Scripture and the use of the popular *berakhah.*

10 This state of affairs is amply documented in the first two chapters of E. Fleischer, *Eretz-Israel Prayer and Prayer Rituals as portrayed in the Geniza Documents* (Hebrew; Jerusalem, 1988), pp. 19–159, and is specifically noted on p. 93.

11 See chapter 4, pp. 115–17 above; Heinemann, *Prayer in the Talmud*, pp. 139–55; W. J. van Bekkum, *The Qedushta'ot of Yehudah according to Genizah Manuscripts* (Groningen, 1988), pp. 16–17.

12 Philo, 2 Som 15.3.27 and De Opificio Mundi 43.128; Josephus, Contra Apionem 2.17.175; Luke 4:16–21, Acts 13:15 and 15:21; Mishnah, *Megillah* 3–4; BT, *Megillah* ff.21a–32a; Elbogen, *Der jüdische Gottesdienst*, chapter 3, paragraphs 25–6 (German edition, pp. 155–84; Hebrew edition, pp. 117–38); Petuchowski, *Contributions*, pp. xvii–xxi; Heinemann, *Studies in Jewish Liturgy*; G. Vermes, 'The Decalogue and the Minim', *BZAW* 103 (1968), pp. 232–40 reprinted in his *Post-Biblical Jewish Studies* (Leiden, 1975), pp. 169–77; Würthwein, *The Text of the Old Testament. An Introduction to the Biblia Hebraica* (ET of the fourth edition, London, 1980), pp. 75–9; BT, *Pesaḥim* f.117b, *'Arakhin* f.10b, *Berakhoth* f.56a. E. Fleischer has promised a novel approach to the whole problem of lectionary cycles in a forthcoming article in the Hebrew section of *HUCA*. Meanwhile, see his article in *Tarbiz* 59 (1990), pp. 412–14 and his *Eretz-Israel*, pp. 293–320. See also the article by E. E. Urbach, 'The Place of the Ten Commandments in Ritual and Prayer' in *The Ten Commandments as reflected in Tradition and Literature throughout the Ages*, ed. B.-Z. Segal (Hebrew; Jerusalem 1985), pp. 127–45.

13 Heinemann, *Prayer in the Talmud*, pp. 27–9, 218, 256–75; Mishnah, *Berakhoth* 7, 8.1, 5, *Pesaḥim* 10; BT, *Berakhoth* f.20b, *Pesaḥim* ff.53a–54a, 106b, *Kethuboth* ff.7a–8b; M. Bar-Ilan, 'Major Trends in the Formation and Crystallization of the *Qedusha*' (Hebrew), *Daat* 25 (1990), pp. 5–20; Swartz, *Mystical Prayer*; R. Posner, U. Kaploun, S. Cohen, *Jewish Liturgy. Prayer and Synagogue Service through the Ages* (Jerusalem, 1975), pp. 35–8; Reif (chapter 3, pp. 79–82 above), section on liturgical language; Petuchowski, 'The Liturgy of the Synagogue', pp. 33–40.

14 Baron, *Social and Religious History*, VI (1958), pp. 152–313; M. Gil, *Palestine during the first Muslim Period (634–1099)* (Hebrew;

Tel Aviv, 1983; one-volume English version, *A History of Palestine 634–1099*, Cambridge, 1992); M. Ben-Sasson, 'The Jewish Community of Medieval North Africa. Society and Leadership' (Hebrew; doctoral dissertation, Hebrew University of Jerusalem, 1983); M. Beit-Arié, *Hebrew Codicology* (Jerusalem, 1981, 2nd edn), pp. 9–11.

15 For the works of Natronai, Amram, Saadya, Hai, Maimonides, Rashi and Simḥah of Vitry, see L. Ginzberg, *Geonica* II (New York, 1909), pp. 109–10, 114–17; E. D. Goldschmidt, *Seder Rav Amram Gaon* (Jerusalem, 1971); T. Kronholm, *Seder R. Amram Gaon* (Lund, 1974); I. Davidson, S. Assaf, B. I. Joel, *Siddur R. Saadja Gaon* (Jerusalem, 1963, 2nd edn); T. Groner, 'A List of Rav Hai Gaon's Responsa' in *Alei Sefer* 13 (1986); E. D. Goldschmidt, *'Seder Ha-tefillah shel Ha-rambam'*, *Studies of the Research Institute for Hebrew Poetry* VII (1958), pp. 183–213, reprinted in his collected articles *On Jewish Liturgy. Essays on Prayer and Religious Poetry* (Jerusalem, 1978), pp. 187–216; S. Buber and J. Freimann, *Siddur Raschi* (Berlin, 1911); S. Hurwitz, *Maḥzor Vitry* (Nuremburg, 1923, 2nd edn); Baron, *Social and Religious History*, VII (1958), pp. 62–134. For the earliest known Persian and English rites see S. Tal, *The Persian Jewish Prayer Book* (Jerusalem, 1980) and I. Brodie, *The Etz Hayyim* (Jerusalem, 1962–7). See also R. Brody, 'Saadya Gaon on the Limits of Liturgical Flexibility' in *Genizah Research after Ninety Years*, eds. J. Blau and S. C. Reif (Cambridge, 1992), pp. 40–6.

16 E. Fleischer, *Hebrew Liturgical Poetry in the Middle Ages* (Hebrew; Jerusalem, 1975); T. Carmi, *The Penguin Book of Hebrew Verse* (Harmondsworth and New York, 1981), introduction, pp. 13–31. In addition to the standard works of G. G. Scholem, J. Dan and I. Gruenwald, reference may also be made to the recent survey of M. Bar-Ilan, *The Mysteries of Jewish Prayer and Hekhalot* (Hebrew; Ramat Gan, 1987) and to the helpful summary of P. S. Alexander, 'Prayer in the Heikhalot Literature' in *Prière, mystique et judaïsme*, ed. R. Goetschel (Paris, 1987), pp. 43–64. See also A. Laytner, *Arguing with God. A Jewish Tradition* (Northvale, N.J., and London, 1990), pp. 127–76.

17 Baron, *Social and Religious History*, VII (1958), pp. 73–9, 205; Goitein, *A Mediterranean Society* II (Berkeley and Los Angeles and London, 1971), p. 593. See also Swartz, *Mystical Prayer*.

18 Posner *et al.*, *Jewish Liturgy*, pp. 249–53; Idelsohn, *Jewish Liturgy and its Development*, pp. 56–63; L. A. Hoffman, *Beyond the Text. A Holistic Approach to Liturgy* (Bloomington and Indianapolis, 1987), pp. 40–9. See also chapter 6 below.

19 The clearest and most concise and consistent example, written towards the end of the period under discussion, is the prayer-book of Maimonides in Goldschmidt's edition.

20 B. M. Lewin, '*Letoledoth ner shel Shabbath*', *Essays and Studies in Memory of Linda R. Miller*, ed. I. Davidson (New York, 1938), Hebrew part, pp. 55–68; J. Z. Lauterbach, 'The Sabbath in Jewish Ritual and Folklore', *Rabbinic Essays* (Cincinnati, 1951), pp. 454–70; B. S. Jacobson, *Nethiv Binah* II (Tel Aviv, 1968), pp. 25–9; L. A. Hoffman, *The Canonization of the Synagogue Service* (Notre Dame and London, 1979), pp. 86–9.

21 S. C. Reif, *Shabbethai Sofer and his Prayer-book* (Cambridge, 1979); Posner *et al.*, *Jewish Liturgy*; C. Rabin, 'The Linguistic Investigation of the Language of Jewish Prayer' (Hebrew) in *Studies in Aggadah, Targum and Jewish Liturgy in Memory of Joseph Heinemann*, eds. J. J. Petuchowski and E. Fleischer (Jerusalem, 1981), pp. 163–71; Maimonides, *Mishneh Torah, Tefillah* 1.4; Idelsohn, *Jewish Liturgy and its Development*, pp. 56–70.

22 Posner *et al.*, *Jewish Liturgy*, pp. 109–23, 224–6; Idelsohn, *Jewish Liturgy and its Development*, pp. 73–89, 148–9; Jacobson, *Nethiv Binah*, I, pp. 100–3, 127–8, 145–73, 190–2, 276–7, 313, 360–76; II, pp. 388–92; Elbogen *Der jüdische Gottesdienst*, paragraph 53.6; A. Neubauer, *Mediaeval Jewish Chronicles and Chronological Notes* (Oxford, 1887), pp. 83–5; *Massekheth Soferim* 10–14 (ed. M. Higger, New York, 1937, pp. 208–73); Fleischer, *Eretz-Israel*, pp. 275–91. See also M. Ben-Sasson, 'The Structure, Goals and Content of the Story of Nathan Ha-Babli' in *Culture and Society in Medieval Jewry. Studies Dedicated to the Memory of H. H. Ben-Sasson*, eds. M. Ben-Sasson, R. Bonfil and J. R. Hacker (Hebrew; Jerusalem, 1989), pp. 137–96.

23 See J. Gutmann who makes a similar point in 'Sherira Gaon and the Babylonian Origin of the Synagogue' in *Occident and Orient. A Tribute to the Memory of Alexander Scheiber*, ed. R. Dan (Budapest and Leiden, 1988), pp. 209–12; see also the articles by Oppenheimer, 'Synagogues with a Historic Association' and by Gafni, 'Synagogues in Talmudic Babylonia' (n. 7 above).

24 Elbogen, *Der jüdische Gottesdienst*, chapter 3, paragraphs 25–6; Jacobson, *Nethiv Binah*, II, pp. 207–20; M. N. Adler, *The Itinerary of Benjamin of Tudela* (London, 1907), Hebrew section, pp. 62–3, English section, pp. 69–70; *Massekheth Soferim*, ed. Higger; Petuchowski, 'The Liturgy of the Synagogue', p. 30.

25 Fleischer, *Eretz-Israel*, pp. 161–213.

26 All this becomes progressively clearer when one traces and compares the attitudes to prayer and communal worship as they

evolve in the earliest liturgical guides cited in n. 15 above. The writer hopes to return to a more detailed analysis of the theories underlying such attitudes in a future study. By the time of Maimonides it was possible for the philosopher to commit himself fully to authorised prayer texts in his code but to argue elsewhere for a post-cognitive piety that went beyond such a level and had therefore to reinterpret such terms as 'worship' and 'devotion'; see D. R. Blumenthal 'Maimonides: Prayer, Worship and Mysticism' in *Approaches to Judaism in Medieval Times* III, ed. D. R. Blumenthal (Atlanta, 1988), pp. 1–16. On the matter of the talmudic passages, see Jacobson, *Nethiv Binah* II, pp. 256–7.

27 Various presuppositions of the sort just described lie behind much of what is written in such modern treatments as Idelsohn, *Jewish Liturgy and its Development*, Posner *et al.*, *Jewish Liturgy*, A. Millgram, *Jewish Worship* (Philadelphia, 1971), J. M. Cohen, *Horizons of Jewish Prayer* (London, 1986), and E. Klein, *Jewish Prayer. Concepts and Customs* (Columbus, 1986).

28 S. Baer, *'Avodath Yisrael* (Rödelheim, 1868); Elbogen, *Der jüdische Gottesdienst*, German edition, pp. 271–2, Hebrew edition, p. 204; Baron, *Social and Religious History* VII, pp. 62–134.

29 If I have one overall criticism of Hoffman's *Beyond the Text*, it is encapsulated in the fact that in a wide-ranging study of Jewish liturgy covering history, theology, sociology and linguistics, the word *halakhah* does not have to make a single appearance in the index.

30 *Encyclopaedia Judaica* (Jerusalem, 1972), XVI, cols. 1333–42; S. D. Goitein, *A Mediterranean Society*, I (Berkeley and Los Angeles, 1967), pp. 1–28 and *Religion in a Religious Age* (Cambridge, Mass., 1974), pp. 3–17, 139–51; S. C. Reif, *A Guide to the Taylor-Schechter Genizah Collection* (Cambridge, 1973 1st edn, 1979 2nd edn); 'Genizah Collections at Cambridge University Library' (Hebrew), *Te'udah* I, ed. M. A. Friedman (Tel Aviv, 1980), pp. 201–6; 'The Taylor-Schechter Genizah Research Unit' in *Newsletter* no. 19 of the World Union of Jewish Studies (August, 1981), pp. 17*–21*; '1898 Preserved in Letter and Spirit', *The Cambridge Review*, 103, no. 2266 (29 January, 1982), pp. 120–1; (with G. Khan) 'Genizah Material at Cambridge University Library', *Encyclopaedia Judaica Year Book 1983/85* (Jerusalem, 1985), pp. 170–1; *Published Material from the Cambridge Genizah Collections. A Bibliography 1896–1980* (Cambridge, 1988), introduction; 'Cairo Genizah Material at Cambridge University Library', *Bulletin of the Israeli Academic Center in Cairo* 12 (1989),

pp. 29–34; and 'The Genizah Collection at Cambridge University Library' in *Preserving the Jewish Heritage*, ed. T. Kushner (forthcoming).

31 S. Abramson, *Ba-merkazim Uva-tefuṣoth Betequfath Ha-ge'onim* (Jerusalem, 1965) and *'Inyanoth Besifruth Ha-ge'onim* (Jerusalem, 1974); D. M. Goodblatt, *Rabbinic Instruction in Sasanian Babylonia* (Leiden, 1975); T. Groner, *The Legal Methodology of Hai Gaon* (Chico, 1985); R. Brody, 'The Testimony of Geonic Literature to the Text of the Babylonian Talmud' (Hebrew) in *Meḥqarey Talmud*, eds. J. Sussmann and D. Rosenthal (Jerusalem, 1990), pp. 237–303.

32 I. Yeivin, *Introduction to the Tiberian Masorah* (ET, Missoula, 1980); 'Masorah' in *Encyclopaedia Judaica*, XVI, cols. 1401–82; J. Mann, I. Sonne, B. Z. Wacholder, *The Bible as Read and Preached in the Old Synagogue* (Cincinnati, 1940, 1966, 1971); Z. M. Rabinovitz, *Ginzé Midrash* (Tel Aviv, 1976); S. C. Reif, 'A Midrashic Anthology from the Genizah' in *Interpreting the Hebrew Bible*, eds. J. A. Emerton and S. C. Reif (Cambridge,1982), pp. 179–225; M. L. Klein, *Genizah Manuscripts of Palestinian Targum to the Pentateuch* (Cincinnati, 1986) and *Targumic Manuscripts in the Cambridge Genizah Collections* (Cambridge, 1992).

33 N. Wieder, '*Berakhah Bilti Yedu'ah*', *Sinai* 82 (1978), pp. 197–221. The many recent articles of N. Wieder and E. Fleischer in *Sinai* and *Tarbiẓ*, and Fleischer's Hebrew volume *Eretz-Israel*, have taken much further the earlier seminal work of Jacob Mann and the important contributions of Joseph Heinemann. See also M. Margaliot, *Hilkhoth 'Ereṣ Yisrael min Ha-genizah*, ed. I. Ta-Shema (Jerusalem, 1973), pp. 127–52 and E. D. Goldschmidt, *The Passover Haggadah. Its Sources and History* (Hebrew; Jerusalem, 1969). Among younger scholars see T. Groner, '*Ha-berakhah 'al Ha-widui Wegilguleha*', *Bar-Ilan Annual* 13 (1976), pp. 158–68 and *Genizah Fragments* no. 13 (1987), p. 2; Hoffman, *The Canonization*; P. B. Fenton, '*Tefillah be'ad Harashuth*' in *Mi-mizraḥ Umi-ma'arav* IV (1983), pp. 7–21; S. C. Reif, 'Festive Titles in Liturgical Terminology' (Hebrew), *Proceedings of the Ninth World Congress of Jewish Studies*, Division C (Jerusalem, 1986), pp. 63–70; Bar-Ilan, *The Mysteries of Jewish Prayer*; Urbach, 'The Place of the Ten Commandments' (chapter 3, n. 26 above).

34 See e.g. the writer's Hebrew article 'An Aramaic Version of *We'ilu Finu*' in the forthcoming *Festschrift* for Ezra Fleischer.

35 Fleischer in *Tarbiẓ* 59 (1990), pp. 437–41.

36 The pioneering efforts of M. Zulay and J. Schirmann and individual publications by A. Habermann and A. Scheiber have now

been substantially supplemented by E. Fleischer in such works as his *The Yozer. Its Emergence and Development* (Jerusalem, 1984). See also M. Sokoloff and J. Yahalom, 'Aramaic Piyyuṭim from the Byzantine Period', *Jewish Quarterly Review* 75 (1985), pp. 309–21, and van Bekkum, *The Qedushta'ot.*

37 In addition to the work of the scholars cited in the previous note, and that of Petuchowski and Heinemann cited in nn. 3–5 above, see the relevant essays by A. Shinan and J. Yahalom in *The Synagogue in Late Antiquity*, ed. Levine, pp. 97–126 and by Holtz in *Back to the Sources*, pp. 176–211; and G. G. Porton, *Understanding Rabbinic Midrash* (Hoboken, N.J., 1985). See also Fleischer, in *Tarbiz* 59 (1990).

38 Such an interpretation is a common feature of this volume and is also adopted by Petuchowski, *Understanding Jewish Prayer*; Fleischer's view is somewhat at odds with it; see the discussion referred to in n. 3 above.

39 Hoffman's *The Canonization*, by attempting an overview of liturgical developments in the geonic period, contributes to our understanding of this process although he has probably been too ambitious in attempting to identify precise and discrete trends within particular timespans and on the part of individual authorities.

40 For the general history of the period see Baron's *Social and Religious History*, III–VIII; H. H. Ben-Sasson, *A History of the Jewish People* (ET, London, 1976); Cecil Roth, *The World History of the Jewish People. Medieval Period. The Dark Ages* (London, 1966).

41 M. Haran on Scrolls in *Eretz Yisrael* 16 (1982), pp. 86–92; *JJS* 33 (1982), pp. 161–73 and 35 (1984), pp. 84–5; *HUCA* 54 (1983), pp. 111–22 and 56 (1985), pp. 21–62; *Tarbiz* 57 (1988), pp. 151–64 and 58 (1989), pp. 523–4; C. H. Roberts and T. C. Skeat, *The Birth of the Codex* (London, 1983); S. C. Reif, 'Aspects of Mediaeval Jewish Literacy' in *The Uses of Literacy in Early Mediaeval Europe* edited by Rosamond McKitterick (Cambridge, 1989), pp. 146–51.

42 See Mary Carruthers, *The Book of Memory. A Study of Memory in Medieval Culture* (Cambridge, 1990), especially pp. 158 and 215; Gerhardsson, *Memory* and his article on recent research and on the major issues in *A Dictionary of Biblical Interpretation*, eds. R. J. Coggins and J. L. Houlden (London, 1990), pp. 498–501. Contrast Fleischer, 'On the Beginnings', *Tarbiz* 59 (1990), p. 435, n. 97.

43 *Massekheth Soferim*, ed. Higger, with the problematic reference in 3.6, p. 125; Beit-Arié, *Hebrew Codicology*; M. Ben-Sasson,

'Maghreb Libraries in the Genizah', a paper delivered in Cambridge in 1987 but not yet published.

6 AUTHORITIES, RITES AND TEXTS IN THE MIDDLE AGES

1 Just as the tendency in general history has been to uncover important cultural developments not only in pre-Renaissance times but in the early mediaeval period (see e.g. R. McKitterick (ed.), *The Uses of Literacy in Early Mediaeval Europe*, Cambridge, 1990), so have scholars such as S. D. Goitein and H. H. Ben-Sasson demonstrated the extent of Jewish civilisation in the Islamic and Christian worlds long before the major developments in Spain and Italy so much favoured by nineteenth-century Jewish historiography. See e.g. Goitein's *A Mediterranean Society. The Jewish Communities of the Arab World as Portrayed in the Documents of the Cairo Geniza*, 5 volumes (Berkeley and Los Angeles and London, 1967–88) and *A History of the Jewish People* edited by Ben-Sasson (ET, London, 1976). On the relevance of the overall concept of the Middle Ages to Jewish history, see M. D. Herr, 'On the Meaning of the Term "Middle Ages" in Jewish History' in *Culture and Society in Medieval Jewry. Studies Dedicated to the Memory of H. H. Ben-Sasson*, eds. M. Ben-Sasson, R. Bonfil and J. R. Hacker (Hebrew; Jerusalem, 1989), pp. 83–97.

2 See, by way of summary, S. W. Baron, *A Social and Religious History of the Jews*, vol. VII (New York and London and Philadelphia, 1958), pp. 62–134 and J. J. Petuchowski, 'The Liturgy of the Synagogue: History, Structure and Contents' in *Approaches to Ancient Judaism*, vol. IV, ed. W. S. Green (Chico, 1983), pp. 27–45.

3 For the history of liturgical poetry, see E. Fleischer, *Hebrew Liturgical Poetry in the Middle Ages* (Hebrew; Jerusalem, 1975), pp. 115–321; for that of mysticism, see G. Scholem, *Kabbalah* (New York, 1974; an updated amalgam of his contributions to *Encyclopaedia Judaica*), pp. 23–35; for that of liturgy, see I. Elbogen, *Der jüdische Gottesdienst in seiner geschichtlichen Entwicklung* (Frankfurt-am-Main, 1931), pp. 353–93 and its Hebrew updated version *Ha-Tefillah Beyisra'el Behithpatḥutah Ha-Hisṭorith*, eds. J. Amir, J. Heinemann, I. Adler, A. Negev, J. J. Petuchowski and J. Schirmann (Tel Aviv, 1972), pp. 265–91. This section of Elbogen's work is, however, one of the weakest and most tendentious, even when allowance has been made for the period and provenance of the original.

4 See Elbogen, *Der jüdische Gottesdienst*, p. 91 and *Ha-Tefillah*, p. 71,

in the case of the recitation of the *shema'* among the morning benedictions. It was not just the nineteenth-century historiographers who propounded the lachrymose theory of Jewish historical development, pointing to persecution as always the main factor for change and thus attracting the criticism of such modern historians as Salo Baron. Their mediaeval predecessors consistently refer to non-Jewish objections to rites and customs as the reasons for their adjustment or replacement and only rarely with historical justification. Remarkably, Jacob Mann also accepted these explanations as historically valid although he did allude to the possibility of their being *post eventum*; see his 'Changes in the Divine Service of the Synagogue due to Religious Persecutions', *HUCA* 4 (1927), pp. 241–302, especially pp. 245 and 259.

5 E. Ashtor, *The Jews of Moslem Spain*, 3 vols., (ET, Philadelphia, 1973–84), vol. 1, pp. 118–40 and M. Gil, *Palestine During the First Muslim Period (634–1099)*, vol. 1 (Hebrew; Tel Aviv, 1983), pp. 405–626 (ET, *A History of Palestine 634–1099*, Cambridge, 1992, pp. 490–776).

6 N. Rejwan, *The Jews of Iraq* (London, 1985), pp. 155–60 deals with the virtual elimination of the Babylonian community under the Mongols while N. Stillman, *The Jews of Arab Lands* (Philadelphia, 1979), pp. 67–75, describes the Mamluk empire that brought about a decline in the status of the *dhimmi* (Christian and Jewish) communities. The redevelopment of the Palestinian Jewish community in the fifteenth and sixteenth centuries was brought about mainly by the immigration of non-Palestinian Jews, who had little or no link with earlier Palestinian customs, and a similar assessment may be made about the nature of the Iraqi Jewish community in early modern times.

7 The development of the Sefardi and Ashkenazi communities is briefly documented by H. Beinart, 'Hispano-Jewish Society' in *Jewish Society Through the Ages*, ed. H. H. Ben-Sasson (London, 1971), pp. 220–38 and by Ben-Sasson himself in *A History*, pp. 462–627.

8 For examples of the Hebrew codex, see *Hebrew Manuscripts from the Palatine Library. Exhibition* (Jewish National and University Library, Jerusalem, 1985); *Selected Manuscripts and Prints. An Exhibition from the Treasures of the Jewish National and University Library*, eds. M. Nadav and R. Weiser (Jerusalem, 1985); *A Visual Testimony: Judaica from the Vatican Library*, ed. P. Hiat (Florida and New York, 1987); and *A Sign and a Witness: 2,000 Years of Hebrew Books and Illuminated Manuscripts*, ed. L. S. Gold (New York and Oxford, 1988). See also chapter 5 above, n. 41.

9 For the overall history of the community of Eretz Yisrael from the Muslim Conquest until the Crusades, see the work of Gil, *Palestine During the First Muslim Period* and for further assessment of the importance of the Genizah discoveries see chapter 5 above, pp. 141–5.

10 An outstanding treatment of the Palestinian rite and of the Genizah evidence relating to it is to be found in E. Fleischer's *Eretz-Israel Prayer and Prayer Rituals as Portrayed in the Geniza Documents* (Hebrew; Jerusalem, 1988). On mystical liturgy, see P. S. Alexander, 'Prayer in the Heikhalot literature' in *Prière, mystique et judaïsme*, ed. R. Goetschel (Paris, 1987), pp. 43–64; M. Bar-Ilan, 'Major Trends in the Formation and Crystallization of the *Qedusha*' (Hebrew), *Daat* 25 (1990), pp. 5–20; and M. D. Swartz, *Mystical Prayer in Ancient Judaism. An Analysis of* Ma'aseh Merkavah (Tübingen, 1992).

11 References to the general scientific literature on the *Sefer Ha-Ma'asim* traditions, as well as a thorough study of the particular Palestinian *halakhah* relating to the abrogation of vows on New Year, are to be found in M. D. Herr, 'Matters of Palestinian Halakha during the Sixth and Seventh Centuries CE', *Tarbiz* 49 (1979–80), pp. 62–80. See also N. Wieder, '*'Avar We'athid Benusaḥ "Kol Nidrey"*' in *Mikhtam Ledawid*, eds. Y. Gilat, E. Stern and I. Ta-Shema (Ramat Gan, 1977), pp. 189–209.

12 J. Müller, *Ḥilluf Minhagim* in *Haschachar* 7–8 (1876–7), pp. 290–6, 396–9, 579–84, 675–80, 745–50, 424–6, 485–8, 533–6 and 570–4; B. M. Lewin, *Otzar Ḥilluf Minhagim. Thesaurus of Halachic Differences between the Palestinian and Babylonian Schools* (Jerusalem, 1942); M. Margulies (Margaliot), *The Differences Between Babylonian and Palestinian Jews* (Hebrew; Jerusalem, 1938).

13 Fleischer, *Eretz Israel*, pp. 218–24 representing a transcription, translation and analysis of MS Bodley Heb. b. 13; see A. Neubauer and A. E. Cowley (eds), *Catalogue of the Hebrew Manuscripts in the Bodleian Library II*, (Oxford, 1906), no. 2834.22, col. 270.

14 M. Margaliot (Margulies), *Hilkhoth 'Ereṣ Yisra'el min Ha-Genizah*, ed. I. Ta-Shema (Jerusalem, 1973), pp. 127–52.

15 On the general history of Palestinian *piyyuṭ*, see Fleischer, *Hebrew Liturgical Poetry in the Middle Ages*, pp. 77–321; see also J. Yahalom, *Maḥzor Eretz Israel. A Geniza Codex* (Hebrew; Jerusalem, 1987) and the bibliography cited there.

16 M. L. Klein, *Genizah Manuscripts of Palestinian Targum to the Pentateuch*, 2 vols. (Cincinnati, 1986) and *Targumic Manuscripts in the Cambridge Genizah Collections* (Cambridge, 1992).

17 Z. M. Rabinovitz, *Ginzé Midrash. The Oldest Forms of Rabbinic*

Midrashim according to Geniza Manuscripts (Hebrew; Tel Aviv, 1976).

18 *Massekheth Soferim*, ed. M. Higger (New York, 1937), chapters 10–15 and 17–21, pp. 208–82 and 297–361.

19 M. B. Lerner in his article on 'The External Tractates' in *The Literature of the Sages. First Part: Oral Tora, Halakha, Mishna, Tosefta, Talmud, External Tractates*, ed. S. Safrai (Assen and Maastricht and Philadelphia, 1987), pp. 399–400, goes further and tentatively suggests a southern Italian origin for the tractate.

20 Settlements in the Syrian cities are constantly encountered in the history of the Palestinian community. For the Islamic period, see Gil, *Palestine During the First Muslim Period* and for the earlier Christian period, see B. Dinur, 'From Bar Kochba's Revolt to the Turkish Conquest' in *The Jews in their Land*, ed. D. Ben-Gurion (London, 1974, 2nd edn), pp. 164–223 and M. Avi-Yonah, *The Jews of Palestine. A Political History from the Bar Kokhba War to the Arab Conquest* (ET, Oxford, 1976).

21 J. Starr, *Jews in the Byzantine Empire* (Athens, 1939); A. Sharf, *Byzantine Jewry from Justinian to the Fourth Crusade* (London, 1971); see also S. B. Bowman, *The Jews of Byzantium* (Alabama, 1985), especially pp. 129–70.

22 The history of Persian Jewry in pre-Islamic times is covered by J. Neusner, *A History of the Jews in Babylonia*, 5 vols. (Leiden, 1965–70) and important essays on the subject are to be found in *Irano-Judaica. Studies Relating to Jewish Contacts with Persian Culture throughout the Ages*, vols. I and II, eds. S. Shaked and A. Netzer (Jerusalem, 1982 and 1990).

23 See e.g. printed editions *Siddur Tefilloth 'Aram Ṣova* (Venice, 1527) and *Seder Tefilloth Ha-Shanah Leminhag Qehilloth Romania* (Constantinople, 1573–6), as well as *The Persian Jewish Prayer Book. A Facsimile Edition of MS Adler ENA 23 in the Jewish Theological Seminary Library*, ed. S. Tal (Jerusalem, 1980). See also E. D. Goldschmidt, *On Jewish Liturgy. Essays on Prayer and Religious Poetry* (Jerusalem, 1978), pp. 122–52 (originally published in *Sefunot* 8 (1964), pp. 205–36) and n. 24 below.

24 On the similarities and differences, see Goldschmidt, *On Jewish Liturgy*, pp. 217–88 (originally published in *Sefunot* 13 (1971–8), pp. 103–90), especially pp. 250–2, and *Sefunot* 8 (1964), pp. 205–36.

25 A. Z. Idelsohn, *Jewish Liturgy and its Development* (Cincinnati, 1932), p. 59 and Goldschmidt, *On Jewish Liturgy*, index of rites, pp. 466–7 and p. 296. See also *Jewish Liturgy. Prayer and Synagogue Service Through the Ages*, eds. R. Posner, U. Kaploun and S. Cohen (Jerusalem, 1975), pp. 250–3.

26 See pp. 181–206 below.

27 In the subsequent two centuries, however, the waxing of Babylonian influence was matched by the waning of its Palestinian equivalent; see R. Bonfil, 'Tra Due Mondi. Prospettivi di ricerca sulla storia culturale degli Ebrei dell'Italia meridionale nell'alto Medioevo' in *Italia Judaica* (Rome, 1983), vol. 1, pp. 135–58 with an English summary on p. 501 and Fleischer, 'Hebrew Liturgical Poetry in Italy' on pp. 415–26 of the same volume. See also G. Busi, *Libri e Scrittori nella Roma Ebraica del Medioevo* (Rimini, 1990), pp. 15–31.

28 A. I. Schechter, *Studies in Jewish Liturgy based on a Unique Manuscript entitled Seder Ḥibbur Berakot* (Philadelphia, 1930).

29 See the references given in the general index of Fleischer's *Eretz Israel*, p. 352.

30 The characteristics of the old Italian rite are identified by Goldschmidt, *On Jewish Liturgy*, pp. 153–76 (originally published with a new edition of S. D. Luzzatto's introduction, Tel Aviv, 1966); see also Busi, *Libri e Scrittori*, p. 66.

31 *Maḥzor Mikol Ha-Shanah Keminhag K"K Romi* as listed by D. Goldstein in his *Hebrew Incunables in the British Isles. A Preliminary Census* (London, 1985), p. 12, no. 33. A widely available sixteenth-century edition is that of Bologna, 1540, entitled *Maḥzor Kefi Minhag K"K Roma.*

32 Examples may be found in the Bodleian Library and the British Library as well as in the Montefiore Collection at Jews' College; see A. Neubauer, *Catalogue of the Hebrew Manuscripts in the Bodleian Library*, vol. 1 (Oxford, 1886), nos. 1057–72, cols. 243–64; G. Margoliouth, *Catalogue of the Hebrew and Samaritan Manuscripts in the British Museum*, part 2 (London, 1905), nos. 615–48, pp. 207–62; and H. Hirschfeld, *Descriptive Catalogue of the Hebrew MSS of the Montefiore Library* (London, 1904), pp. 63–71.

33 *Shiboley Ha-Leqeṭ Ha-Shalem*, ed. S. Buber (Vilna, 1886) and *Tanya Rabati*, ed. G. Felder, 2 vols. (New York, 1975–80); see also Busi, *Libri e Scrittori*, pp. 35–42 and 54.

34 A full discussion is not possible in the present context but examples may be found in S. C. Reif, *Shabbethai Sofer and his Prayer-book* (Cambridge, 1979), via the index of subjects, p. 365, s.v. 'Franco-German *and* old French rites'.

35 The French rite is often cited, for example in the *Sefer Ha-Manhig* of Abraham ben Nathan Ha-Yarḥi, ed. Y. Raphael, 2 vols. (Jerusalem, 1978), the liturgical commentary of Judah ben Yaqar, ed. S. Yerushalmi, 2 vols. (Jerusalem, 1968–9) and the mystical works of Judah ben Samuel the Pious (see the article by J. Dan, 'The Emergence of Mystical Prayer' in *Studies in Jewish*

Mysticism, eds. J. Dan and F. Talmage (Cambridge, Mass., 1982), pp. 85–120. See also Goldschmidt, *On Jewish Liturgy*, pp. 80–121.

36 *Sefer Ha-Eshkol*, eds. S. and C. Albeck, 2 vols. (Jerusalem, 1935–8); *'Orḥoth Ḥayyim* (Florence, 1759 and partial edition, ed. M. Schlesinger, Berlin, 1899–1902); *Sefer Ha-Minhagoth*, partial edition, ed. S. Assaf in *Sifran shel Rishonim* (Jerusalem, 1935), pp. 121–82. The anonymous halakhic work *Kol Bo*, first printed in Naples, 1490–1, also belongs to this group in a manner yet to be established.

37 See A. Grossman, 'Between Spain and France: Relations between the Jewish Communities of Muslim Spain and France' (Hebrew) in *Galuth 'aḥar Golah (Exile and Diaspora: Studies in the History of the Jewish People Presented to Professor Haim Beinart on the Occasion of his Seventieth Birthday)*, eds. A. Mirski, A. Grossman and Y. Kaplan (Jerusalem, 1988), pp. 75–101; Goldschmidt, *On Jewish Liturgy*, pp. 435–6.

38 *Siddur Rashi*, ed. S. Buber (Berlin, 1910–11); *Sefer Ha-Pardes*, ed. H. Ehrenreich (Deva and Budapest, 1924); *Sefer Ha-'Orah*, ed. S. Buber (Lemberg, 1905). An interesting example of where Rashi seems to presuppose a different liturgical text in his commentary on the Talmud is cited in S. C. Reif, 'Liturgical Difficulties and Geniza Manuscripts' in *Studies in Judaism and Islam presented to Shelomo Dov Goitein*, eds. S. Morag, I. Ben-Ami and N. A. Stillman, English volume (Jerusalem, 1981), pp. 99–122 (especially p. 119).

39 The edition of S. Hurwitz (*Machsor Vitry nach der Handschrift im British Museum*, Berlin, 1893) is based on British Library manuscripts Add. 27200 and 27201 (Margoliouth, *Catalogue of Hebrew and Samaritan MSS*, no. 655, pp. 273–4) and Bodleian manuscript Opp. 59 (Neubauer, *Catalogue of Hebrew MSS*, no. 1100, cols. 306–10) and now requires to be re-assessed on the basis of other evidence; see Goldschmidt, *On Jewish Liturgy*, pp. 66–79.

40 Ed. I. Brodie, 3 vols. (Jerusalem, 1962–7), with important notes provided by N. Wieder in vol. III, pp. 323–7.

41 See *The Sepher haShoham (The Onyx Book) by Moses ben Isaac Hanessiah*, eds. B. Klar and Cecil Roth (London and Jerusalem, 1947) in the grammatical sphere; *The Writings of Rabbi Elijah of London*, eds. M. Y. L. Sacks and Cecil Roth (Jerusalem, 1956) in the halakhic sphere; V. D. Lipman, *The Jews of Medieval Norwich* (London, 1967), in which the poems of Meir of Norwich are edited by A. M. Habermann on pp. 1–45 of the Hebrew section; and M. Beit-Arié, *The Only Dated Medieval Hebrew Manuscript written in England [?]* (London, 1985), dealing with a Hebrew Pentateuch.

42 Edited by J. Freimann in the Hebrew periodical *Haeschkol* 6 (Cracow, 1909), pp. 94–162.

43 Edited by M. Weisz in *Sefer Ha-Yovel Le-Mosheh Aryeh Bloch* (Budapest, 1905), pp. 97–137; see also A. Marx's corrections to that edition in *Zeitschrift für Hebräische Bibliographie* 9 (1905), pp. 143–8.

44 See A. Grossman, 'Relations between the Jewish Communities of Northern France and those of Germany before 1096' (Hebrew) in *'Ummah We-Toledotheha (Nation and History: Studies in the History of the Jewish People based on papers delivered at the Eighth World Congress of Jewish Studies, Jerusalem, 1981)*, volume 1, ed. M. Stern (Jerusalem, 1983), pp. 221–31.

45 The historical background is well sketched by Robert Chazan, *European Jewry and the First Crusade* (Berkeley and Los Angeles and London, 1987).

46 *Der jüdische Gottesdienst*, pp. 370–2 (Hebrew edition, pp. 276–7). Typical are the following two sentences: 'Je mehr die selbständige geistige Tätigkeit unter den Juden zurückging, je mehr das selbständige Denken durch den politischen und sozialen Druck zurückgedrängt wurde, für desto wichtiger galt die Sammlung der Überlieferungen der Vergangenheit . . . Durch die Zerrüttung in den Gemeinden waren frühere Einrichtungen, Bestimmungen und Gewohnheiten in Vergessenheit geraten, man stellte infolgedessen Forschungen darüber an, deren Gründlichkeit heute mehr als verwunderlich erscheint.' For examples of the codices see *The Worms Mahzor*, ed. M. Beit-Arié (Vaduz and Jerusalem, 1985) and *The Amsterdam Mahzor*, ed. A. van der Heide and E. van Voolen (Leiden, 1989) and E. Fleischer's liturgical essays in each of these volumes.

47 'Religious Law and Change: The Medieval Ashkenazic Example', *AJS Review* 12 (1987), pp. 205–21. There may also have been earlier and broader influences at play in the development of Jewish religious authority in Ashkenazi communities, as suggested by I. Ta-Shema in 'Law, Custom and Tradition in Early Jewish Germany' (Hebrew), *Sidra* 3 (1987), pp. 85–161.

48 See responsa nos. 42, 120, 127, 140, 145, 169, 170, 177 and 184 in *Sefer Ha-Ravan*, ed. S. Albeck (Warsaw, 1905) and the helpful article on Eliezer ben Nathan by I. Ta-Shema in *EJ* 6, cols. 626–8.

49 For an excellent summary, see J. Dan, 'The Emergence of Mystical Prayer' in *Studies in Jewish Mysticism*, pp. 85–120. See also P. Schäfer 'The Ideal of Piety of the Ashkenazi Hasidim and its Roots in Jewish Tradition', *Jewish History* 4 (1990), pp. 9–23.

50 Dan, 'The Emergence', p. 93.
51 Dan, *ibid.*, pp. 88–9.
52 M. Beit-Arié, '*Birkhot Ha-'Evarim*', *Tarbiz* 56 (1987), pp. 265–72; *Sefer Ḥasidim*, ed. J. Wistinetski (Berlin, 1891–3) and ed. R. Margaliot (Jerusalem, 1957). There are numerous editions of the *Roqeaḥ*, beginning with that of Soncino (Fano, 1505), and Eleazar's overall importance for the history of Jewish mysticism is covered by Scholem in his various reference works. See also H. Soloveitchik, 'Concerning the Date of *Sefer Ḥasidim*' and J. Dan, 'On the Historical Personality of R. Judah Ḥasid', both in *Culture and Society*, eds. Ben-Sasson *et al.*, pp. 383–98.
53 *Sefer 'Arugath Ha-Bosem*, ed. E. E. Urbach, 4 vols. (Jerusalem, 1939–63).
54 Introduction (Hebrew), p. 12.
55 See, for example, his comments on the grace after meals in section 199. His work (2 vols., Zhitomir, 1862), like so much else, has yet to receive its deserved attention from historians of Jewish liturgy.
56 *Sefer Ravia*, ed. V. Aptowitzer, 2 vols. (Berlin and Jerusalem, 1912–36).
57 On Meir of Rothenburg see I. Elfenbein, *Sefer Minhagim de-bey Maharam b"r Barukh etc.* (New York and Jerusalem, 1938); I. A. Agus, *Rabbi Meir of Rothenburg etc.*, 2 vols. (Philadelphia, 1947); I. Z. Cahana, *Teshuvoth Pesaqim Uminhagim*, 3 vols. (Jerusalem, 1957–62). On Jacob Molin see *Sefer Maharil* (Warsaw, 1974); L. Greenwald, *Maharil Uzemano* (New York, 1944); S. Steiman, *Custom and Survival* (New York, 1963).
58 Ed. H. Ehrenreich, Deva, 1929 (Klausner) and ed. Cracow, 1597 (Tyrnau).
59 For the general linguistic background, see E. Y. Kutscher, *A History of the Hebrew Language*, ed. R. Kutscher (Jerusalem and Leiden, 1982), pp. 148–82.
60 For various details of the Ashkenazi linguistic tradition, see I. Eldar, *The Hebrew Language Tradition in Medieval Ashkenaz (ca. 950–1350 CE)*, vols. I and II (Jerusalem, 1973 and 1979).
61 See Reif, *Shabbethai*, pp. 29–38 and the many examples of controversy on linguistic matters cited throughout that volume. On linguistic variation among the Sefardim, see A. Dodi, 'The Vocalization of a 13th Century Siddur', *Lěšonénu* 53 (1988–9), pp. 67–89.
62 For a summary of the personalities involved in this ongoing dispute, see S. C. Reif, 'Some Observations on Solomon Luria's Prayer-Book', in *Tradition and Transition. Essays Presented to Chief*

Rabbi Sir Immanuel Jakobovits to celebrate twenty years in office, ed. J. Sacks (London, 1986), pp. 247–8 and *Shabbethai*, pp. 58–62.

63 See chapter 5, pp. 148–51 above and pp. 181–5 below.

64 In addition to the catalogues of mediaeval Hebrew manuscripts cited in n. 32 above and the guides to exhibitions cited in n. 8 above, see also R. Posner and I. Ta-Shema, *The Hebrew Book. An Historical Survey* (Jerusalem, 1975); M. Beit-Arié, *Hebrew Codicology* (Jerusalem, 1981, 2nd edn); T. and M. Metzger, *Jewish Life in the Middle Ages. Illuminated Hebrew Manuscripts of the Thirteenth to the Sixteenth Centuries* (London and New York, 1985); D. Goldstein, *Hebrew Manuscript Painting* (London, 1985); and the *maḥzor* editions cited in n. 46 above. See also Cahana, *Teshuvoth*, vol. II, no. 56, pp. 50–2; Agus, *Rabbi Meir*, vol. I, no. 216, p. 266; and Wistinetski, *Sefer Ḥasidim*, p. 184.

65 See the new edition, with an introduction by M. Carmilly-Weinberger (New York, 1969), of William Popper's classic study *The Censorship of Hebrew Books* (New York, 1899).

66 On the Tosafists' general achievements, see E. E. Urbach, *The Tosaphists: their History, Writings and Methods* (Hebrew; Jerusalem, 1955). The German Ḥasidim have already been discussed earlier in this chapter.

67 On the process and various aspects of that settlement, see Baron, *Social and Religious History*, vol. X (New York and London and Philadelphia, 1965), pp. 1–117; Ben-Sasson, *A History*, pp. 462–627; and B. D. Weinryb, *The Jews of Poland. A Social and Economic History of the Jewish Community in Poland from 1100 to 1800* (Philadelphia, 1973), pp. 17–103.

68 On detailed aspects of the Ashkenazi rites, see Goldschmidt, *On Jewish Liturgy*, pp. 9–65; for general description, see Idelsohn, *Jewish Liturgy and its Development*, pp. 61–2 and *Jewish Liturgy*, eds. Posner *et al.*, p. 251.

69 For the general picture (especially as regards relations with North Africa) reconstructed through the recent research of S. Abramson, M. Ben-Sasson and M. Gil, building on the work of J. Mann and S. D. Goitein, see the works cited by M. Gil in an excellent bibliography appended to his article 'The Babylonian Yeshivot and the Maghreb in the Early Middle Ages', *PAAJR* 57 (1991), pp. 69–120. For a summary and some major texts, see A. Grossman, *The Babylonian Exilarchate in the Gaonic Period* (Hebrew; Jerusalem, 1984). Gil is currently working on a history of the Babylonian *yeshivoth* that will demonstrate that they were authoritative communal institutions rather than simply 'academies'; see *Genizah Fragments* 21 (1991), p. 2.

70 On the halakhic work of the geonim and the major compositions, see S. Assaf, *Tequfoth Ha-Ge'onim Wesifruthah* (Jerusalem, 1956); S. Abramson, *Ba-Merkazim Uva-Tefuṣoth* (Jerusalem, 1965) and *'Inyanoth Besifruth Ha-Ge'onim* (Jerusalem, 1974); T. Groner, *The Legal Methodology of Hai Gaon* (Chico, 1985) and R. Brody, *The Textual History of the She'iltot* (Hebrew; New York and Jerusalem, 1991).

71 L. Ginzberg, *Geonica*, vol. II (New York, 1909), pp. 48–53; J. Mann, 'Les "Chapitres" de Ben Bâboi et les Relations de R. Yehoudaï Gaon avec la Palestine', *REJ* 70 (1920), pp. 113–48; L. Ginzberg, *Genizah Studies in Memory of Doctor Solomon Schechter*, vol. II (New York, 1929), pp. 544–73; S. Spiegel, '*Lefarashath Ha-Pulmus shel Pirqoy ben Baboy*' in the Hebrew section of the *Harry Austryn Wolfson Jubilee Volume* (Jerusalem, 1965), pp. 243–74.

72 N. Wieder, 'Genizah Studies in the Babylonian Liturgy' (Hebrew), *Tarbiz* 37 (1968), pp. 135–57 and 240–64, and the same author on a similar theme in *Sinai* 78 (1976), pp. 97–122 and 279–84, and in *Tarbiz* 43 (1973–4), pp. 46–52.

73 See the references cited in nn. 12 and 72 above, Idelsohn, *Jewish Liturgy*, pp. 31–2, and the relevant indexes in Fleischer, *Eretz Israel* and L. A. Hoffman, *The Canonization of the Synagogue Service* (Notre Dame and London, 1979). See also Brody, 'Saadya Gaon', pp. 40–6.

74 J. Müller, *Achter Bericht über die Lehranstalt für die Wissenschaft des Judenthums in Berlin* (Berlin, 1890), p. 10.

75 Ginzberg, *Geonica*, vol. I, pp. 119–20.

76 S. C. Reif, 'Aspects of Mediaeval Jewish Literacy' in *The Uses of Literacy in Early Mediaeval Europe*, ed. R. McKitterick (Cambridge, 1990), pp. 134–55.

77 Y. (Robert) Brody, '*Sifruth Ha-Ge'onim WeHa-Ṭeqsṭ Ha-Talmudi*' in *Meḥqarey Talmud*, eds. Y. Sussmann and D. Rosenthal (Jerusalem, 1990), pp. 237–303.

78 BT, *Menaḥoth* f.43b. Whether the original statement was intended to be taken literally was no longer in question in the geonic period.

79 Ginzberg, *Geonica*, vol. II, pp. 107–21.

80 *Seder Rav Amram Gaon*, ed. N. Coronel (Warsaw, 1865); ed. A. L. Frumkin (Jerusalem, 1912); part 1, ed. D. Hedegård (Lund, 1951) and part 2, ed. T. Kronholm (Lund, 1974); ed. E. D. Goldschmidt (Jerusalem, 1971).

81 *Siddur R. Saadja Gaon*, eds. I. Davidson, S. Assaf and B. I. Joel (Jerusalem, 1941, 1963, 2nd edn); see also Goldschmidt, *On Jewish Liturgy*, pp. 403–20, originally published in *Kiryat Sefer* 18 (1941–2), pp. 336–42.

82 M. R. Cohen and S. Somekh, 'In the Court of Ya'qub ibn Killis: A Fragment from the Cairo Genizah', *JQR* 80 (1990), pp. 283–314.

83 In addition to the relevant parts of the edited text (see n. 81 above), see also the list of contents and introductory essay in that volume.

84 R. Brody, 'Saadya Gaon on the Limits of Liturgical Flexibility' in *Genizah Research after Ninety Years*, eds. J. Blau and S. C. Reif (Cambridge, 1992), pp. 40–6.

85 M. Ben-Sasson, 'The Jewish Community of Medieval North Africa – Society and Leadership Qayrawan 800–1057' (Hebrew; doctoral dissertation, Hebrew University of Jerusalem, 1983).

86 Ben-Sasson, 'Jewish Community', pp. 110–27.

87 Ben-Sasson, *ibid.*, pp. 126–7 and 290–9.

88 Ben-Sasson, *ibid.*, pp. 22–5 and the English summary of twenty-two pages.

89 Groner, *Legal Methodology*, pp. 11, 20–1 and 69–70, including the issues of the fifth cup of wine at the Passover *seder*, the method of shaking the *lulav*, and fasting on a sabbath or festival. Groner deals with other responsa and with the matter of the attribution of responsa in a cautious but conservative manner on pp. 118–31 of that monograph and in his article 'A List of Hai Gaon's Responsa', *Alei Sefer* 13 (1986), pp. 1–123. On the matter of a prayer-book of his, see Groner's wise scepticism on p. 22, n. 11, of his 'List'. See also the articles by H. H. Ben-Sasson and J. Levinger in *EJ* 7, cols. 1130–1 and E. Fleischer, '*'Iyyunim Beshiratho Shel Rav Hay Gaon*' in *Shay Leheyman*, ed. Z. Malachi (Jerusalem, 1977), pp. 239–74.

90 Y. Tobi, 'The *Siddur* of Rabbi Shelomo ben Nathan of Sijilmasa. A Preliminary Study' in *Communautés juives des marges sahariennes du Maghreb*, ed. M. Abitbol (Jerusalem, 1982), pp. 407–25 and the Hebrew version of the same article in the memorial volume for A. M. Habermann, *Yad Leheyman*, ed. Z. Malachi (Lod, 1984), pp. 345–60.

91 The manuscript is Bodley, Poc. 262 (Neubauer, *Catalogue of Hebrew MSS*, no. 896, cols. 190–1), and the history of Jewish Sijilmasa is covered by H. Z. (=J. W.) Hirschberg, *A History of the Jews in North Africa*, 2 vols. (ET of revised edition, Leiden, 1974 and 1981) vol. 1, index, p. 514.

92 Studies of Maimonides are legion. The latest is *Perspectives on Maimonides. Philosophical and Historical Studies*, ed. J. L. Kraemer (Oxford, 1991). For corrections to his biographical details on the basis of Genizah material, see S. D. Goitein, 'Moses Maimonides, Man of Action. A Revision of the Master's Biography in Light of

the Geniza Documents' in *Hommage à Georges Vajda. Etudes d'histoire et de pensée juives*, eds. G. Nahon and C. Touati (Louvain, 1980), pp. 155–67.

93 Bodley, Hunt. 80, Neubauer, *Catalogue of Hebrew MSS*, no. 577, col. 113.

94 The text of the Oxford MS was published by E. D. Goldschmidt in *Studies of the Research Institute for Hebrew Poetry*, vol. VII (Hebrew; Jerusalem, 1958), pp. 183–213 and reprinted in his *On Jewish Liturgy*, pp. 192–216.

95 N. Wieder, *Islamic Influences on the Jewish Worship* (Oxford, 1947; originally published in *Melila* 2, Manchester, 1946, pp. 37–120), pp. 26–30.

96 *Mishneh Torah, Sefer 'Ahavah, Hilkhoth Tefillah*, 15 chapters, published in an English translation in M. Hyamson's edition of the first two parts of the code *The Book of Knowledge* and *The Book of Adoration* (Jerusalem, 1965); see I. Twersky, *Introduction to the Code of Maimonides* (New Haven and London, 1980), pp. 223–4.

97 On the religious philosophy of Maimonides' son, see S. D. Goitein, 'Abraham Maimonides and his Pietist Circle' in *Jewish Medieval and Renaissance Studies*, ed. A. Altmann (Cambridge, Mass., 1967), pp. 145–64 and 'A Treatise in Defence of the Pietists by Abraham Maimonides', *JJS* 16 (1965), pp. 105–14. See also Fenton, *The Treatise of the Pool*, introduction, pp. 1–71, and *Deux Traités de Mystique Juive* (Lagrasse, 1987), pp. 13–111; and D. R. Blumenthal, 'Maimonides' Intellectual Mysticism and the Superiority of the Prophecy of Moses' in *Approaches to Judaism in Medieval Times*, ed. D. R. Blumenthal (Chico, 1984), pp. 27–51.

98 *Sefer Ha-Maspik Le'ovdey Hashem. Kitāb Kifāyat al-'Ābidīn*. Part Two. vol. II, Arabic original with introduction and annotated Hebrew translation by N. Dana (Ramat Gan, 1989).

99 See T-S Ar. 41.105 and AS 182.291; Wieder, *Islamic Influences*, pp. 7–82; P. B. Fenton, '*Tefillah be'ad Ha-Rashuth*', *East and Maghreb* 4 (1983), pp. 7–21; and nos. 65 and 66 in a forthcoming volume entitled *Arabic Legal and Administrative Documents in the Cambridge Genizah Collections* by Geoffrey Khan.

100 Compare the views of Scholem, *Kabbalah*, pp. 35–42 and P. B. Fenton, 'La «Hitbodedut» chez les premiers qabbalistes en Orient et chez les Soufis' in *Prière, Mystique et Judaïsme*, ed. R. Goetschel (Paris, 1987), pp. 133–57 and his monographs *The Treatise of the Pool* and *Deux Traités*.

101 See, for instance, the claims made by Y. Kafiḥ, 'The Ties of Yemenite Jewry with the Jewish Centres' in *The Jews of Yemen*,

eds. Y. Yesha'yahu and Y. Tobi (Hebrew; Jerusalem, 1975), pp. 44–6.

102 The various manuscript collections seem particularly rich in seventeenth-century versions, as in the British Library, Margoliouth, *Catalogue of Hebrew and Samaritan MSS*, vol. II, nos. 711–23, pp. 396–450 and Cambridge University Library, typewritten catalogue of J. D. Pearson and R. Loewe (Or. 1770–2), nos. 411–15.

103 For details of the history and content of the Yemenite rite, see Z. Madmuni, 'Maimonides and the Prayer Rite of the Jews of Yemen' in Yesha'yahu and Tobi, *The Jews of Yemen*, pp. 273–94; see also Y. Kafiḥ, *Halikhoth Teman* (Jerusalem, 1968), especially pp. 66–8.

104 On Yemenite participation in the international commerce of the 'Genizah period', see S. D. Goitein 'Yemenite Jewry and the Indian Trade' in Yesha'yahu and Tobi, *The Jews of Yemen*, pp. 47–69 and in *Molad* 28 (1973), pp. 442–50.

105 For recent editions, translations and studies of the *'Iggereth Teman*, see *Epistle to Yemen*, ed. A. S. Halkin, ET, B. Cohen (New York, 1952); *'Iggeroth Ha-Rambam*, ed. M. D. Rabinovitz (Jerusalem, 1960); *Letters of Maimonides*, ed. L. D. Stitskin (New York, 1977); and *Crisis and Leadership: Epistles of Maimonides*, eds. A. Halkin and D. Hartman (Philadelphia and New York and London, 1985), pp. 91–207.

106 *Siddur R. Saadja*, eds. Davidson *et al.*, introduction, pp. 28–9 and Madmuni, 'Maimonides'.

107 Madmuni, 'Maimonides', pp. 283–91.

108 Kafiḥ, *Halikhoth Teman*, pp. 1–69, with the reference to the reading of the Torah on pp. 67–8; R. Arusi, '*Qeri'ath Ha-Torah Beṣibur*', *Teman* 2 (1990), pp. 29–37.

109 The classic studies are A. A. Neuman, *The Jews in Spain. Their Social, Political and Cultural Life during the Middle Ages*, 2 vols. (Philadelphia, 1942); Y. Baer, *A History of the Jews in Christian Spain* (Philadelphia, 1961 and 1966); and Ashtor, *The Jews* (n. 5).

110 L. Zunz already demonstrates an awareness of the complicated history of the various 'Sefardi' rites in *Die Ritus des synagogalen Gottesdienstes* (Berlin, 1859), pp. 37–59. See also in Hebrew, Goldschmidt, *On Jewish Liturgy*, pp. 265–88 and 297–314, the former originally published in *Sefunot* 13 (1971–8), pp. 103–90, and the latter in *Kiryat Sefer* 20 (1943–4), pp. 171–6 and *'Oṣar Yehudey Sefarad* 4 (1961), pp. 108–13; and in English, Idelsohn, *Jewish Liturgy*, pp. 59–60.

111 Ashtor, *The Jews*, vol. I, pp. 135–6.

112 *The Book of Prayer and Order of Service according to the Custom of the Spanish and Portuguese Jews*, ed. M. Gaster (London, 1901–6), introduction, pp. xiv–xv.

113 Fleischer, *Hebrew Liturgical Poetry*, pp. 333–421.

114 Published by S. Bamberger in *Sha'arey Simḥah* (Fürth, 1861–2); see especially vol. I, pp. 14–16, 19, 20–4, 28–9, 32, 38, 42, 60–2, 64–5, 87, 89, 99, 109–12, 114, 116; vol. II, pp. 2–5, 7, 26, 52, 55, 65–6, 69, 73, 99–100, 102, 105–6, 108–9 and 111.

115 Ed. J. Schor (Berlin and Cracow, 1903), especially pp. 33–42, 170–218, 243–83 and 289–90, with the quoted section on p. 250.

116 Gaster does identify the rite of the London Sefardim as that of Castilia but his view is by no means uncontroversial; see *The Book of Prayer*, pp. xvi–xix. The thirteenth-century prayer-book analysed by Dodi in 'Vocalization', pp. 67–89, is variously described as Catalonian and Provençal and the date is also uncertain.

117 *Peyrush Ha-Tefilloth Weha-berakhoth*, ed. S. Yerushalmi, 2 vols. (Jerusalem, 1968–9); see, for example, pp. 3, 12, 64, 71, 78, 110, 123 and 132 for his citation of various customs in different centres.

118 More attention is given to the importation of the mystical into the Sefardi liturgy in the next chapter; see pp. 240–8 below.

119 Scholem, *Kabbalah*, p. 61 and *Sifrey Ha-Rashba*, ed. M. M. Gerlitz, vol. I (Jerusalem, 1986). For a historical analysis of Adret's responsa, see I. Epstein, *The 'Responsa' of Rabbi Solomon ben Adreth of Barcelona (1235–1310) as a Source of the History of Spain* (London, 1925), especially pp. 57–63. See also Neuman, *The Jews*, vol. II, pp. 156–60.

120 *She'eloth Utheshuvoth . . . Rashba*, parts 1–3 (Bnei Brak, 1958–9), parts 4–7 (New York, 1958, photographic reproductions of eds. Piotrokov, 1808, Vilna, 1884 and Warsaw, 1868); part 3, no. 289; part 1, nos. 380 and 471; part 5, no. 222; part 1, no. 452; part 3, no. 288; part 1, nos. 469 and 473. On the history of the recitation of the Ten Commandments, see E. E. Urbach, 'The Place of the Ten Commandments in Ritual and Prayer' in *The Ten Commandments as reflected in Tradition and Literature throughout the Ages*, ed. B.-Z. Segal (Hebrew; Jerusalem, 1985).

121 Ed. H. G. Enelow, 4 vols. (New York, 1929–32), vol. I, Hebrew introduction, pp. 9–19, English introduction, pp. 11–16; and first part of vol. II.

122 *Sefer Abudraham*, ed. Warsaw, 1877; *Abudraham Ha-Shalem*, ed. S. A. and A. J. Wertheimer (Jerusalem, 1959, 1st edn, 1963, 2nd edn).

123 Abudraham's introduction, ed. Warsaw, p. 3a; ed. Wertheimer, p. 6.

124 E.g. Constantinople 1513, Venice 1546, Venice 1566, Amsterdam 1726, Prague 1784 and 1817, and Lemberg 1857.

125 *She'eloth Utheshuvoth Bar Shesheth* (Vilna, 1879), nos. 37, 334, 84 and 219.

7 FROM PRINTED PRAYERS TO THE SPREAD OF PIETISTIC ONES

1 For ease of reference, the texts will be cited from S. Baer, *'Avodath Yisra'el* (Rödelheim, 1868) and from S. Singer, *The Authorised Daily Prayer Book* (London, 1890). In this case, see Baer, *'Avodath*, pp. 131–2, 75, 129–30, 33, 122, 35, 154, 133–49 and 250–1, and Singer, *Authorised Prayer Book*, pp. 76–7, 37, 75–7, 2, 66, 3, 2–3, 171–3 and 78–80. There are of course differences among the rites concerning the precise use of each of these prayers.

2 See chapter 3 above, pp. 61–4, 85–6; chapter 4 above, p. 110, pp. 113–15; chapter 5 above, pp. 128–30, 136, 138 and 144; chapter 6 above, pp. 165 and 170.

3 See S. Stein, 'The Concept of the "Fence"' in *Studies in Jewish Religious and Intellectual History Presented to Alexander Altmann*, eds. S. Stein and R. Loewe (Alabama, 1979), pp. 301–29.

4 On the general history of the *'aleynu* prayer, see R. Posner, U. Kaploun and S. Cohen, *Jewish Liturgy*, pp. 109–11 and on specific textual problems see Y. Elbaum, 'Concerning Two Textual Emendations in the *'Aleinu*', *Tarbiẓ* 42 (1973), pp. 204–8 and S. C. Reif, 'On a Text of the *'Aleinu* Prayer', *Tarbiẓ* 44 (1975), pp. 202–3 where other literature is cited including N. Wieder's article in *Sinai* 76 (1974), pp. 1–14. See also P. S. Alexander, 'Prayer in the Heikhalōt Literature' in *Prière, mystique et judaïsme*, ed. R. Goetschel (Paris, 1987), pp. 59–61.

5 The text of Ephraim of Bonn's report is to be found in M. Wiener, *Emek Habacha von R. Joseph ha-Cohen* (Leipzig, 1858), Hebrew appendix, p. 8. On persecution as the origin of liturgy, see chapter 6 above, n. 4. See also R. Chazan, *European Jewry and the First Crusade* (Berkeley and Los Angeles and London, 1987), pp. 137–88.

6 See p. 240 below.

7 D. de Sola Pool, *The Kaddish* (Leipzig, 1909); E. Fleischer, *Eretz Israel Prayer and Prayer Rituals as Portrayed in the Geniza Documents* (Hebrew; Jerusalem, 1988), p. 245; B. S. Jacobson, *Nethiv Binah*, vol. 1 (Tel Aviv, 1968), pp. 365–76; and I. Ta-Shema, 'Some

Notes on the Origins of the "*Kaddish Yathom*" (Orphan's Kaddish)', *Tarbiz* 53 (1984), pp. 559–68.

8 See pp. 218–20 below.

9 In addition to the treatment of this theme in earlier chapters (see e.g. n. 2 above), see also J. Heinemann, '*Sefer Tehillim Kimekor Lenusaḥ Ha-Tefillah*' in *Studies in Jewish Liturgy*, ed. A. Shinan (Jerusalem, 1981), pp. 176–9 (originally published in *Dukhan* 5 (1964), pp. 35–43); M. Weitzman, '*Levirur Ha-Yesodoth Ha-Miqra'iyim Ba-Tefillah*' (forthcoming).

10 Baer, *'Avodath*, pp. 33, 122, 125, 222 and 234 and Singer, *Authorised Prayer Book*, pp. 2, 66, 70, 143 and 157. See Jacobson, *Nethiv Binah*, vol. II (Tel Aviv, 1968), pp. 212–17 and 240–4 and A. Berliner, *Kethavim Nivḥarim* (Jerusalem, 1945), pp. 104–6. The Ashkenazi rite has here been used for illustration but similar sets of verses are used in the other rites. See also *Shiboley Ha-Leqeṭ Ha-Shalem*, ed. S. Buber (Vilna, 1886), section 76, p. 56.

11 Baer, *'Avodath*, pp. 156–60 and Singer, *Authorised Prayer Book*, pp. 87–94. This modern liturgical use of the Decalogue may of course be more apologetically motivated than its equivalent in earlier periods; for the earlier history see E. E. Urbach, 'The Place of the Ten Commandments in Ritual and Prayer' in *The Ten Commandments as reflected in Tradition and Literature throughout the Ages*, ed. B.-Z. Segal (Hebrew; Jerusalem, 1985), pp. 127–45.

12 Fifteenth- and sixteenth-century examples of both manuscripts and printed editions according to various rites have been consulted at the British Library, Bodley and Cambridge University Library. For examples, see S. C. Reif, *Shabbethai Sofer and his Prayer-book* (Cambridge, 1979), pp. 333–5. See also R. Loewe, *Ibn Gabirol* (London, 1989), pp. 79–108.

13 I. Elbogen, *Der jüdische Gottesdienst in seiner geschichtlichen Entwicklung* (Frankfurt-am-Main, 1931), pp. 87–9 (Hebrew edition, *Ha-Tefillah Beyisra'el Behithpathuthah Ha-Hisṭorith*, eds. J. Amir, J. Heinemann, I. Adler, A. Negev, J. Petuchowski and Ḥ. (J.) Schirmann (Tel Aviv, 1972), pp. 68–9; Jacobson, *Nethiv Binah*, vol. I, pp. 147–55 and vol. II, pp. 260–72; Berliner, *Kethavim Nivḥarim*, pp. 145–70 and A. M. Habermann, *Shirey Ha-Yiḥud Weha-kavod* (Jerusalem, 1948).

14 S. C. Reif, 'Some Observations on Solomon Luria's Prayer Book' in *Tradition and Transition. Essays presented to Chief Rabbi Sir Immanuel Jakobovits* (London, 1986), pp. 254–55, n. 19. See also Luria's famous responsum no. 64, conveniently translated into English by B. Berliner in *Jews' College Jubilee Volume*, ed. I. Harris (London, 1906), p. 134. On Luria's objection and the general

matter of introductory verses, see A. Hilvitz in *Sinai* 78 (1976), pp. 263–78.

15 Jacobson, *Nethiv Binah*, vol. II, p. 260. See also Shabbethai Sofer's comments on *yigdal* in London Beth Din MS 37, f. 1r.

16 See chapter 6 above, pp. 173–5 and pp. 240–8 and 250–5 below.

17 This is neatly summarised by T. Carmi, *The Penguin Book of Hebrew Verse* (Harmondsworth, 1981), p. 37 although he exaggerates the degree to which printing completed the editorial process for the Hebrew prayer-book; see also n. 61 below.

18 A. Kashtan, 'Synagogue', in *EJ* 15, cols. 601–18; the quotation is from col. 601; see also B. Kern-Ulmer, *Rabbinische Responsen zum Synagogenbau*, vol. I (Hildesheim and Zurich and New York, 1990).

19 R. Wischnitzer, *The Architecture of the European Synagogue* (Philadelphia, 1964), pp. 18–75, especially pp. 40, 43; C. H. Krinsky, *Synagogues of Europe. Architecture, History and Meaning* (Cambridge, Mass., and London, 1985), pp. 38–46; G. Wigoder, *The Story of the Synagogue* (London, 1986), pp. 35–92. See also J. J. Petuchowski, 'The Liturgy of the Synagogue. History, Structure and Contents' in *Approaches to Ancient Judaism*, vol. IV, ed. W. S. Green (Chico, 1983), p. 30.

20 Elbogen, *Der jüdische Gottesdienst*, pp. 203–4 and *Ha-Tefillah*, p. 151; Jacobson, *Nethiv Binah*, vol. II, pp. 230–40.

21 S. C. Reif, '*We'Ilu Finu Nusaḥ 'Arami*' accepted for publication in a forthcoming *Festschrift* for Professor Ezra Fleischer.

22 A. Yaari, 'The Miy Sheberakh Prayers: History and Texts', *Kiryat Sefer* 33 (1957–8), pp. 118–30, 233–50 and 36 (1960), pp. 103–18. Yaari's article is rich in source material but less impressive in the analysis of the early history of the prayers where he is fairly vague and speculative.

23 S. D. Goitein, 'Prayers from the Geniza for Fatimid Caliphs' in *Studies in Judaism, Karaitica and Islamica presented to Leon Nemoy*, ed. S. R. Brunswick (Ramat Gan, 1982), pp. 47–57; P. B. Fenton, '*Tefillah Be'ad Ha-Rashuth*', *East and Maghreb* 4 (1983), pp. 7–21; *Sefer Abudraham* (Warsaw, 1877), p. 37b (foot) and *Sefer Abudraham Ha-Shalem*, ed. A. J. Wertheimer (Jerusalem, 1963), p. 136; Yaari, 'Miy Sheberakh Prayers', p. 247; and B. Schwartz, '*Hanoten Teshua*'. The origin of the traditional Jewish Prayer for the Government', *HUCA* 57 (1986), pp. 113–20.

24 See the original contexts of the verses from Psalms 144, Isaiah 43, Jeremiah 23 and Isaiah 59 (Singer, *Authorised Prayer Book*, p. 153), as pointed out by Schwartz, '*Hanoten Teshua*', p. 119. The arguments for the Jewish liturgical authenticity of the prayer by,

among others, Millgram, *Jewish Worship* (Philadelphia, 1971; p. 189–91), are apologetic rather than historical.

25 Baer, *'Avodath*, pp. 124–5 and Singer, *Authorised Prayer Book*, pp. 69–70. For details of earliest mention and provenance, see Elbogen, *Der jüdische Gottesdienst*, pp. 202–3 and 549, and *Ha-Tefillah*, pp. 150 and 437; Jacobson, *Nethiv Binah*, vol. II, pp. 235–6. The *yehi raṣon* used in the Ashkenazi rite as an introductory prayer for the coming month on the sabbath preceding *Rosh Ḥodesh* (Singer, *Authorised Prayer Book*, p. 154 but not cited by Baer) is borrowed from the personal prayer of Rav, BT, *Berakhoth* f.16b, and was not introduced into the prayer-book with such a function until the early eighteenth century; see Berliner, *Kethavim Nivḥarim*, p. 63.

26 *'Oṣar Ha-Ge'onim, Ḥagigah* (Jerusalem, 1931), responsa, p. 27; Aaron Ha-Kohen of Lunel, *'Orḥoth Ḥayyim* (Florence, 1750), p. 107a; and Abraham bar Ḥiyya, *Sefer Hegjon Ha-Nefesch oder Sitten-Buch*, ed. E. Freimann (Leipzig, 1860), p. 32 (ET, G. Wigoder, *The Meditation of the Sad Soul*, London, 1969, p. 120). See also the discussion by I. Ta-Shema, 'Some Notes on the Origins of the "*Kadish Yathom*" (Orphan's Kaddish)', *Tarbiẓ* 53 (1984), pp. 560–1, and chapter 6 above, n. 89.

27 See Elbogen, *Der jüdische Gottesdienst*, pp. 201–4 and *Ha-Tefillah*, pp. 150–1; Jacobson, *Nethiv Binah*, vol. II, pp. 230–40; S. B. Freehof, 'Hazkarath Neshamoth', *HUCA* 36 (1965), pp. 179–89; Posner *et al.*, *Jewish Liturgy*, pp. 136 and 142–3; Yaari, 'Miy Sheberakh Prayers'; and De Sola Pool, *The Kaddish*, pp. 101–6.

28 Petuchowski, 'The Liturgy of the Synagogue', p. 36; Ta-Shema, 'Some Notes', pp. 559–68. See also *Sefer Ḥasidim*, ed. R. Margaliot (Jerusalem, 1960), nos. 605 and 1171, pp. 393–8 and 578–9.

29 See chapter 5 above, p. 151 and chapter 6 above, pp. 185–7.

30 In all these respects it is perhaps more accurate to refer the complete 'canonisation' process to the period under discussion rather than to the geonic period, as L. A. Hoffman has proposed in his *The Canonization of the Synagogue Service* (Notre Dame and London, 1979). The culmination of the process in Ashkenazi circles was the promotion of an authorised daily prayer-book by the Council of Three Lands in 1610; see p. 232 below.

31 Although Judaeo-Arabic had occasionally been used to translate the statutory Hebrew prayers in the Genizah period (as fragments such as T-S Ar. 8.10 testify; see N. Wieder, *Sinai* 78 (1976), p. 100) this later trend is a more extensive and systematic one. The context for the earlier translation is explained in S. C. Reif, 'Aspects of Mediaeval Jewish Literacy' in *The Uses of Literacy in*

Early Mediaeval Europe, ed. R. McKitterick (Cambridge, 1990), pp. 148–9 and the emergence of widespread translations is noted in the article on 'Prayer-Books' in *JE* 10, pp. 172–6. Unusual targumic and Judaeo-Provençal versions are to be found, for example, in MSS Gaster H61 in the John Rylands University Library of Manchester (see M. Gaster, *MGWJ* 39 (1895), pp. 79–90 and 116) and Roth 32 in the Brotherton Library at the University of Leeds. See also C. Weissler, 'Prayers in Yiddish and the Religious World of Ashkenazic Women' in the volume edited by J. R. Baskin, *Jewish Women in Historical Perspective* (Detroit, 1991), pp. 159–81.

32 One need only examine the final folios of any major collections of late mediaeval or early modern Hebrew codices to encounter the dated signatures of a group of dedicated censors such as those listed in *JE* 3, p. 652. For the influence on the printed prayer-book, see pp. 238–40 below.

33 See chapter 2 above, pp. 28, 30, 39 and 45–6 and chapter 3 above, pp. 78–9.

34 M. Meiselman broached the subject in *Jewish Woman in Jewish Law* (New York, 1978) and among studies that have appeared since then have been R. Biale, *Women and Jewish Law* (New York, 1984), A. Weiss, *Women at Prayer* (New York, 1990), E. Berkovits, *Women in Time and Torah* (New York, 1990), *Jewish Women in Historical Perspective*, ed. Baskin, especially pp. 104–6 and 139–40, and S. Grossman and R. Haut (eds.), *Daughters of the King. Women and the Synagogue* (Philadelphia and New York and Jerusalem, 1992).

35 BT, *Berakhoth* f.26a; *'Oṣar Ha-Ge'onim*, vol. 1, *Berakhoth* (Haifa, 1928), p. 49; Tosafoth on BT, *'Eruvin* f.96a and *Rosh Ha-Shanah* f.33a; Meiselman, *Jewish Woman in Jewish Law*, pp. 147–51.

36 *'Orḥoth Ḥayyim*, *Hilkhoth Tefillin*, section 3, p. 7a.

37 Mordekhai ben Hillel Ha-Kohen, *Sefer Mordekhai* on BT, *Berakhoth* f.47b rejecting the view; Meiri on BT, *Berakhoth* f.23a; *Maharam*, responsum no. 47.

38 Commentary on Alfasi to Mishnah *Megillah* 2.4, to be found on f.6b of that commentary in the Vilna edition.

39 I. Abrahams, *Jewish Life in the Middle Ages* (Philadelphia, 1896), p. 26 and S. Schechter, *Studies in Judaism*, First Series (London and Philadelphia, 1896), p. 324.

40 For a historical overview of the period see H. H. Ben-Sasson, 'The Middle Ages' and S. Ettinger 'The Modern Period', both in *A History of the Jewish People*, ed. H. H. Ben-Sasson (ET, London, 1976), pp. 561–723 and 727–80 respectively.

41 J. Hacker, 'Patterns of the Intellectual Activity of Ottoman Jewry

in the 16th and 17th Centuries', *Tarbiz* 53 (1984), pp. 569–603. See also J. Hacker's English essay on the same subject in *Jewish Thought in the Seventeenth Century*, ed. I. Twersky and B. Septimus (Cambridge, Mass., and London, 1987), pp. 95–135 and M. A. Epstein, *Ottoman Jewish Communities and their Role in the Fifteenth and Sixteenth Centuries* (Freiburg, 1980).

42 L. Zunz, *Die Ritus des synagogalen Gottesdienstes geschichtlich entwickelt* (Berlin, 1859), p. 146.

43 Samuel ben Moses of Medina (= *Mhrshdm*), *She'eloth Utheshuvoth* (Lemberg, 1862), no. 35, fully translated by M. S. Goodblat, *Jewish Life in Turkey in the XVIth Century* (New York, 1952), pp. 139–43 and briefly cited by Ben-Sasson, *A History*, p. 659, wrongly as no. 34.

44 Hacker, 'Patterns', pp. 587–602.

45 H. Z. (= J. W.) Hirschberg, *A History of the Jews in North Africa*, 2 vols. (ET of revised edition, Leiden, 1974 and 1981), vol. I, pp. 362–446.

46 Some caution is advised by M. Beit-Arié who classifies both Iberian and North African manuscripts under 'Sefarad' and notes the adoption of local codicological practices by immigrant scribes; see his *Hebrew Codicology* (Jerusalem, 1981, 2nd edn), especially pp. 9–19 and 104–9. For a summary of Judaeo-Spanish Genizah material, see E. Gutwirth, 'Genizah Fragments in Judaeo-Spanish', *Anuario de filologia* 9 (1983), pp. 219–23.

47 Zeraḥiah ben Isaac Ha-Levi Gerondi, *Ma'or Ha-Qaṭan* on BT, *Beṣah* f.5a. A. David, 'New Information on some Personalities in Jerusalem in the 16th Century', *Shalem* 5 (1987), pp. 229–49; A. David, 'Demographic Changes in the Safed Jewish Community of the Sixteenth Century' in *Occident and Orient. A Tribute to the Memory of Alexander Scheiber*, ed. R. Dan (Budapest and Leiden, 1988), pp. 83–93; A. David, 'New Genizah Documents. Ties of Egyptian Jewry with Eretz Israel in the Sixteenth Century', *Cathedra* 59 (1991), pp. 19–55.

48 Ben-Sasson, *A History*, pp. 631–7 and 659–67.

49 J. Elbaum, *Openness and Insularity* (Hebrew; Jerusalem, 1990); see also chapter 6 above, pp. 171–81.

50 Ben-Sasson, *A History*, pp. 654–6 and 669–87; S. W. Baron, *A Social and Religious History of the Jews*, vol. XVI (New York and London, 1976) devoted to 'Poland–Lithuania 1500–1650'.

51 In addition to Elbaum's overall treatment, *Openness and Insularity*, see the brief background outlined in Reif, *Shabbethai*, pp. 43–52.

52 Reif, *Shabbethai*, pp. 39–41. Others involved in the initiative were

Meshullam Faivush (Phoebus) ben Israel Samuel of Cracow, Jacob Koppel ben Asher Katz of Przemysl, Simon Wolf ben Tebele Auerbach of Posen, Ephraim Luntschitz of Prague and Pinḥas Ha-Levi of Cracow.

53 Reif, *Shabbethai*, pp. 15–27, 33–8, 47–8 and 50–2 and n. 84 below.

54 Reif, *ibid.*, p. 62.

55 See chapter 6, pp. 164–6 above.

56 Numerous examples may be found listed in *JE* 10, p. 174 and in the reprinted articles of Joshua Bloch collected in *Hebrew Printing and Bibliography*, ed. C. Berlin (New York, 1976), pp. 63–142. On the more general historical background, see *Italia Judaica*, 2 vols. (Rome, 1986).

57 Baron, *Social and Religious History*, vol. XIV (New York and London, 1969), p. 92.

58 Baron, *ibid.*, p. 102 (italics are by S. C. R.).

59 C. Roth, *The History of the Jews of Italy* (Philadelphia, 1946), pp. 289–420.

60 R. Bonfil, *Rabbis and Jewish Communities in Renaissance Italy* (ET, Oxford, 1990).

61 A useful summary may be found in *EJ* 13, cols. 1096–110, reproduced with other relevant material from that reference work in *The Hebrew Book. An Historical Survey*, eds. R. Posner and I. Ta-Shema (Jerusalem, 1975). Petuchowski, 'The Liturgy of the Synagogue', rightly stresses the importance of printing for the history of the Hebrew prayer-book text (p. 48) but his own immediate comment about the changes brought about by the system demonstrates that he overstates the case.

62 In addition to *The Hebrew Book*, eds. Posner and Ta-Shema, see the outstanding analysis by E. L. Eisenstein, *The Printing Press as an Agent of Change*, 2 vols. (Cambridge, 1979).

63 These data are derived from a comparative analysis of the rich collection of early printed *siddurim* at the British Library; see J. Zedner, *Catalogue of the Hebrew Books in the Library of the British Museum* (London, 1867), between pp. 458 and 486; see also M. Beit-Arié, 'The Affinity between early Hebrew Printing and Manuscripts' (Hebrew), in *Essays and Studies in Librarianship presented to C. D. Wormann*, eds. M. Nadav and J. Rothschild (Jerusalem, 1975), pp. 27–39, 113.

64 Posner and Ta-Shema, *The Hebrew Book*, p. 209, refer to the liturgies published in Avignon 1765–6, Carpentras 1739–62 and, for the Yemenite rite, Jerusalem, 1894–8.

65 See p. 231 above and chapter 6, pp. 176–8 above.

66 Reif, *Shabbethai*, pp. 15–16 and 34–9.

67 The comparison may be made by examining the illustrations of the synagogue at different periods included in such volumes as U. Kaploun, *The Synagogue* (Philadelphia, 1973), A. Eisenberg, *The Synagogue Through the Ages* (New York, 1974) and Wigoder, *The Story of the Synagogue.*

68 Reif, *Shabbethai*, pp. 39–41; see also pp. 53–8 in that volume for later attempts to use Shabbethai's work for the same purpose.

69 Posner and Ta-Shema, *The Hebrew Book*, pp. 97–103 and 104–12.

70 Eisenstein, *The Printing Press*, pp. 43–159.

71 A. Berliner, *Censur und Confiscation hebräischer Bücher im Kirchenstaate* (Frankfurt-am-Main, 1891); W. Popper, *The Censorshp of Hebrew Books* (New York, 1899), reprinted with an introduction by M. Carmilly-Weinberger (New York, 1969); Posner and Ta-Shema, *The Hebrew Book*, pp. 184–7; and the comments (sometimes apologetic) of Baer, *'Avodath* on pp. 40–1, 93–4, 131, 219, 227, 386 and 448. See also N. Wieder, *'Avar We'athid Benusaḥ 'Kol Nidrey'* in the Gedenkbuch for D. Ochs, *Mikhtam Ledawid*, eds. Y. Gilat, E. Stern and I. Ta-Shema (Ramat Gan, 1977), pp. 189–209.

72 A. Z. Idelsohn, *Jewish Liturgy and its Development* (Cincinnati, 1932), p. 47.

73 Elbogen, *Der jüdische Gottesdienst*, pp. 386–91 and *Ha-Tefillah*, pp. 286–9. Contrast G. Scholem, *Sabbatai Ṣevi. The Mystical Messiah* (ET, Princeton, 1973), pp. 1–8.

74 For recent treatments of Scholem and his work, see D. Biale, *Kabbalah and Counter-History* (Cambridge, Mass., and London, 1979); E. Schweid, *Mysticism and Judaism according to Gershom G. Scholem* (Hebrew; Jerusalem, 1983); J. Dan, *Gershom Scholem and the Mystical Dimension of Jewish History* (New York, 1987); M. Idel, *Kabbalah. New Perspectives* (New Haven and London, 1988); and Alexander, 'Prayer in the Heikhalōt Literature', pp. 43–64. See also above, chapter 2, pp. 48–9; chapter 3, pp. 86–7; chapter 4, pp. 111–13; chapter 5, pp. 130–1, 133 and 144.

75 Scholem, *Kabbalah* (New York, 1974, based on his *EJ* articles), pp. 35–67 and P. B. Fenton, 'La «Hitbodedut» chez les premiers Qabbalistes en Orient et chez les Soufis' in *Prière*, ed. Goetschel, pp. 133–57. See also Fenton's other work cited in chapter 6 above, n. 97.

76 E. Horowitz, 'Coffee, Coffeehouses, and the Nocturnal Rituals of Early Modern Jewry', *AJS Review* 14 (1989), pp. 17–46.

77 S. Schechter, *Studies in Judaism*, Second Series (London and Philadelphia, 1908), pp. 202–85; Scholem, *Kabbalah*, pp. 67–79; and the various biographical entries for these personalities

included in *EJ* and in Scholem, *Kabbalah*, between pp. 391 and 453.

78 G. Scholem, *Major Trends in Jewish Mysticism* (New York, 1954, 3rd edn), pp. 284–6.

79 Elbogen, *Der jüdische Gottesdienst*, pp. 389–93 and *Ha-Tefillah* pp. 288–91; Idelsohn, *Jewish Liturgy and its Development*, pp. 47–55; M. Hallamisch, 'The Influence of the Kabbalah on Jewish Liturgy' and B. Sack, 'Some Remarks on Prayer in the Kabbalah of 16th Century Safed' both in *Prière*, ed. Goetschel, pp. 121–31 and 179–86. The prayers themselves are to be found in an increasing degree in the various rites particularly in the seventeenth and eighteenth centuries, as noted later in this chapter. See also E. D. Goldschmidt 'Prayers for the Eve of the New Moon' in *On Jewish Liturgy*, pp. 322–35.

80 Scholem, *Kabbalah*, p. 79.

81 Reif, *Shabbethai*, pp. 53–6.

82 M. Steinschneider, *Catalogus Librorum Hebraeorum in Bibliotheca Bodleiana* (Berlin, 1852–60), cols. 333–4; *JE* 10, p. 174 and *EJ* 13, col. 987; Posner *et al.*, *Jewish Liturgy*, p. 259.

83 Reif, *Shabbethai*, pp. 56–9.

84 Reif, *ibid.*, pp. 9, 17, 19, 50–2, 227 and 316; Scholem, *Kabbalah*, pp. 41, 76–86, 180, 193–4. See also R. Bonfil, 'Halakhah, Kabbalah and Society. Some Insights into Rabbi Menaḥem Azariah da Fano's Inner World' in *Jewish Thought in the Seventeenth Century*, eds. Twersky and Septimus, pp. 39–61; and M. Idel, 'Major Currents in Italian Kabbalah between 1560 and 1660' in *Italia Judaica*, vol. II, pp. 243–62.

85 Scholem, *Major Trends*, pp. 325–50; see also B. Gross, 'La Prière dans le «Nefesh Ha-Ḥayyim» de R. Ḥayyim de Volozhin' in *Prière*, ed. Goetschel, pp. 225–44.

86 R. Schatz, 'Contemplative Prayer in Ḥasidism', in *Studies in Mysticism and Religion presented to G. G. Scholem*, eds. E. E. Urbach, R. J. Z. Werblowsky and C. Wirszubski (Jerusalem, 1967), pp. 209–26; and J. G. Weiss, 'The Kavvanoth of Prayer in Early Hasidism', *JJS* 9 (1958), pp. 163–92, especially p. 178; see next note.

87 L. Jacobs, *Hasidic Prayer* (London, 1972); E. D. Goldschmidt, 'On the Liturgy of Hassidic Communities' in *On Jewish Liturgy*, pp. 315–21; N. Loewenthal, *Communicating the Infinite. The Emergence of the Habad School* (Chicago and London, 1990), especially pp. 157–9; Y. Mondschein's bibliography of *Sifrey Ha-Halakhah shel Admor Ha-Zaqen* (Brooklyn, 1984), pp. 55–7; *Siddur Torah 'Or* (Brooklyn, 1987), with list of editions. See also Laytner, *Arguing with God*, pp. 177–229.

8 THE CHALLENGE OF THE MODERN WORLD

1 That tendentiousness may also affect the availability of various editions of some *siddurim* as much as it does the explanation of their history and content. The wide use of a prayer-book and the possibility of its regular reproduction provide the opportunity for newly amended versions and the abandonment of earlier texts, not only because of bibliographical neglect but also because of the various vested interests in promoting their replacements. It is astonishing how rarely one finds, even in research libraries, *all* the editions of a particular modern prayer-book.

2 Some important thoughts on the nature of historical research, truth and objectivity have been well expressed by Efraim Shmueli in his chapter on 'Historical Consciousness in the Emancipation Culture' in *Seven Jewish Cultures. A Reinterpretation of Jewish History and Thought* (Cambridge, 1990; translated from the Hebrew edition of Tel Aviv, 1980), pp. 167–202.

3 See, for example, the studies of various aspects of pre-modern Jewish culture contained in A. F. Kleinberger, *The Educational Theory of the Maharal of Prague* (Hebrew; Jerusalem, 1962); S. C. Reif, *Shabbethai Sofer and his Prayer-book* (Cambridge, 1979); D. Téné, 'Comparative Linguistics and Linguistic Knowledge' (Hebrew) in *Hebrew Language Studies presented to Professor Ẓeev Ben-Ḥayyim*, eds. M. Bar-Asher, A. Dotan, G. B. Sarfati and D. Téné (Hebrew; Jerusalem, 1983), pp. 237–87; and R. Bonfil, *Rabbis and Jewish Communities in Renaissance Italy* (Oxford, 1990; translated from the Hebrew edition of Jerusalem, 1979).

4 These elements are to be found in all recent treatments of modern Jewish history, whatever the different approach to their ultimate interpretation. See H. M. Sachar, *The Course of Modern Jewish History* (London, 1958), pp. 25–71; R. Mahler, *A History of Modern Jewry* (London, 1971; an abridged translation of the four-volume Hebrew original, Tel Aviv, 1952–6), pp. xv–xxiii; and S. Ettinger, 'The Modern Period' in *A History of the Jewish People*, ed. H. H. Ben-Sasson (London, 1976; translated from the Hebrew edition of Tel Aviv, 1969), pp. 727–833.

5 Much scholarship has concerned itself with the relationship between Lurianic Kabbalah, Sabbateanism and Ḥasidism. Whatever the degree of their association, their ideas led to the endorsement of new forms of leadership. H. H. Ben-Sasson in his article 'The Middle Ages' in *A History*, p. 703, argues that 'it is clear that the very possibility of acknowledging absolute reverence for a *ẓaddik*, and for his sons after him, had its roots in the

seventeenth century. It is even possible that the response of the Jewish people to . . . Herzl . . . had its roots in the people's reaction to the success of Shabbetai Ẓevi.' Naturally, Scholem and his school make much of this clash between mysticism and rabbinic authority.

6 A. Altmann, *Moses Mendelssohn. A Biographical Study* (London, 1973), p. 719. Altmann's study is more than a biography and, as a valuable analysis of Jewish intellectual history in the eighteenth century, is of relevance to much of the background here being explained.

7 The history of the Jews in Islamic countries in recent centuries and how the position deteriorated between the early Ottoman period and what S. W. Baron has called the 'incipient stagnation' of later times (*A Social and Religious History of the Jews*, vol. XVIII, ch. 77) are well surveyed by Bernard Lewis in *The Jews of Islam* (London, 1984), pp. 107–91; and Chaim Raphael, *The Road from Babylon. The Story of Sephardi and Oriental Jews* (London, 1985), pp. 196–209.

8 Michael Stanislawski has carefully documented the Eastern European enlightenment and pointed out that the story is not one of total Jewish opposition. See his *Tsar Nicholas I and the Jews. The Transformation of Jewish Society in Russia 1825–1855* (Philadelphia, 1983), especially pp. 49–122. See also Emanuel Etkes, 'Immanent Factors and External Influences in the Development of the Haskalah Movement in Russia' in *Towards Modernity. The European Jewish Model*, ed. J. Katz (New Brunswick, 1987), pp. 13–32.

9 The major Jewish demographical changes of the nineteenth and twentieth centuries are clearly demonstrated in the maps between pp. 65 and 112 in Martin Gilbert's *Jewish History Atlas* (London, 1969) and, in more detail, in the Hebrew volume *Carta's Atlas of the Jewish People in Modern Times*, ed. E. Friesel (Jerusalem, 1983), now available in a revised, English edition, *Atlas of Modern Jewish History* (New York and Oxford, 1990).

10 See above, chapter 7, pp. 230–2.

11 Various activities of Satanow (1732–1804) are touched upon by M. Eliav, *Jewish Education in Germany in the period of Enlightenment and Emancipation* (Hebrew; Jerusalem, 1960), p. 241; *EJ* 14, cols. 905–6; Altmann, *Moses Mendelssohn*, pp. 351–4; Reif, *Shabbethai*, p. 60; and N. Rezler-Bersohn, 'Isaac Satanow. An Epitome of an Era', *LBIYB* 25 (1980), pp. 81–99.

12 *'Iggereth Beth Tefillah* (Berlin, 1773); *Wa-Ye'tar Yiṣḥaq* (Berlin, 1784) often together with *Tefillah Mikol Ha-Shanah* (Berlin, 1785); *Seder Haggadah 'al Pesaḥ* (Berlin, 1785); *Seder Seliḥah* (Berlin, 1785).

See M. Steinschneider, 'Hebraïsche Drucke in Deutschland' in *Zeitschrift für die Geschichte der Juden in Deutschland* v (1892), pp. 170–1 and D. Yitshaki, 'The Grammarian Rabbi Zalman Hena and his Fakings', *Tzfunot* 11 (5751), pp. 72–81.

13 The first words of the title, also in Hebrew characters, may be transposed into German as *Gebete der Juden das ganze Jahr* and the volume is described as the second part of the edition *Tefilloth Yisrael*. Cf. Altmann, *Moses Mendelssohn*, p. 352.

14 An appreciation of Ben-Ze'ev's theological, pedagogical and linguistic work is to be found in Mahler's *History*, pp. 600–1. In spite of his short life (1764–1811) and extensive peregrinations, he made a major contribution to the early development of Jewish scholarship.

15 A brief biography of Löwisohn (1788–1821) and details of his work are provided in M. Waxman's *A History of Jewish Literature* (New York, 1960), III, pp. 147–53 and the relevant part of his introduction to the liturgy is cited in Reif, *Shabbethai*, pp. 116–17.

16 On Heidenheim's life and work (1757–1832), see *EJ* 8, cols. 258–9.

17 See Eliav, *Jewish Education*, pp. 140 and 245; I. Schorsch, 'Scholarship in the Service of Reform', *LBIYB* 35 (1990), pp. 82–3; and M. Meyer, *Response to Modernity. A History of the Reform Movement in Judaism* (New York, 1988), pp. 119–21.

18 The Baer–Delitzsch edition, which made its appearance between 1869 and 1895 (from 1891 edited by Baer alone), has been critically evaluated in more recent years by P. Kahle, *The Cairo Geniza* (Oxford, 1959, 2nd edn), pp. 110–16 and by A. Dotan, *EJ* 16, cols. 1478–80.

19 pp. 1–19 in the original edition, after twenty pages of preface and preceding a German translation in Hebrew characters of some of these liturgical laws.

20 pp. v–xiii in the original edition as a preface. In later editions these pages and some others from the original preface replaced the German translation which had become linguistically redundant.

21 See the list given in *EJ* 4, col. 81.

22 N. N. Glatzer in his 'The Beginnings of Modern Jewish Studies' in *Studies in Nineteenth-Century Jewish Intellectual History*, ed. A. Altmann (Cambridge, Mass., 1964), pp. 27–45 offers an assessment of the importance of *Wissenschaft des Judentums* in the shaping of modern Jewish thought while David Biale in *Gershom Scholem. Kabbalah and Counter-History* (Cambridge, Mass., 1979), pp. 1–32, deals with Scholem's animosity towards it. The Steinschneider

quote is cited on p. 1 and documented on p. 227 of the Biale volume. The nature of the movement's historical consciousness is well described by Ismar Schorsch in 'The Ethos of Modern Jewish Scholarship', *LBIYB* 35 (1990), pp. 55–71. See also *The Jew in the Modern World. A Documentary History*, eds. P. R. Mendes-Flohr and J. Reinharz (Oxford, 1980), pp. 182–213, and M. Meyer, *The Origins of the Modern Jew. Jewish Identity and European Culture in Germany, 1749–1824* (Detroit, 1967), pp. 144–82.

23 See N. N. Glatzer, *Leopold Zunz. Jude – Deutscher – Europäer* (Tübingen, 1964) for a full appreciation and details of his correspondence. On the relationship between Jost and Zunz, and their work, see I. Schorsch, 'From Wolfenbüttel to Wissenschaft. The Divergent Paths of Isaak Markus Jost and Leopold Zunz', *LBIYB* 22 (1977), pp. 109–28 and N. N. Glatzer, 'On an Unpublished Letter of Isaak Markus Jost' *LBIYB* 22 (1977), pp. 129–37. See also n. 39 below.

24 L. [Eliezer] Landshuth, *Amude Ha-Aboda (Columnae Cultus). Onomasticon Auctorum Hymnorum Hebraeorum eorumque Carminum cum Notis Biographicis et Bibliographicis*, 2 fascicles (Berlin, 1857–62). Landshuth's commentary, entitled *Meqor Berakhah*, appeared in Edelmann's *Hegyon Lev* published in Königsberg in 1845.

25 *Die gottesdienstlichen Vorträge der Juden historisch entwickelt* (Berlin, 1832), a later edition of which (1892) was used for C. Albeck's revised version in Hebrew *Ha-Derashoth Be-Yisra'el We-Hishtalsheluthan Ha-Hisṭorith* (Jerusalem, 1954). See also chapter 1 above, pp. 2–3.

26 In this respect his relationship with the leading Reformer, Abraham Geiger, is significant; see E. I. J. Rosenthal, 'A Remarkable Friendship. L. Zunz and A. Geiger' in *Tradition, Transition and Transmission. Jubilee Volume in Honor of I. O. Lehman*, ed. B. D. Fox (Cincinnati, 1983), pp. 79–92.

27 *Poesie* appeared in two volumes in Berlin, 1855–9; *Ritus* in Berlin, 1859; and *Literaturgeschichte*, in three volumes, with Nachtrag and Index, in Berlin, 1865–89.

28 See I. Schorsch, 'The Myth of Sephardic Supremacy', *LBIYB* 34 (1989), pp. 47–66.

29 See *The Jew in the Modern World*, eds. Mendes-Flohr and Reinharz, pp. 140–81.

30 Sachar, *Modern Jewish History*, pp. 147–59; Ben-Sasson, *A History*, pp. 834–40; J. J. Petuchowski, *Prayerbook Reform in Europe. The Liturgy of European Liberal and Reform Judaism* (New York, 1968), pp. 31–3 and 44–5; L. A. Hoffman, *Beyond the Text. A Holistic Approach to Liturgy* (Bloomington and Indianapolis, 1987),

pp. 57–9, and I. Schorsch, 'Scholarship in the Service of Reform', *LBIYB* 35 (1990), pp. 73–101.

31 Petuchowski, *Prayerbook Reform*, pp. 48–9. The congregation's novel customs are recorded by Aaron Moses Isaac ben Abraham Graanboom in his *Sefer Meliṣ Yosher* (Amsterdam, 1808–9).

32 Petuchowski, *Prayerbook Reform*, pp. 200–1; Ben-Sasson, *A History*, p. 788.

33 Petuchowski, *Prayerbook Reform*, pp. 49–58.

34 The personality and philosophy of Geiger have attracted much scholarly attention over many years. Max Wiener's *Abraham Geiger and Liberal Judaism*, originally published in the English translation of E. J. Schlochauer (Philadelphia, 1962) and reprinted in Cincinnati, 1981, with a foreword by M. A. Meyer, remains important, but more recent assessments are to be found in *New Perspectives on Abraham Geiger. An HUC–JIR Symposium*, ed. J. J. Petuchowski (Cincinnati, 1975), especially the articles by M. A. Meyer and Petuchowski himself. See also Schorsch, 'Scholarship', pp. 95–7 and n. 39 below, and Meyer, *Response*, pp. 84–99.

35 Petuchowski, *Prayerbook Reform*, pp. 33–5, 56, 99–100, 149–52, 164–75, 274 and 278–81; Meyer in *New Perspectives*, pp. 6–13; Petuchowski in *New Perspectives*, pp. 42–54; Schorsch, 'Scholarship', pp. 95–7; and *Salomon Ludwig Steinheim zum Gedenken. Ein Sammelband*, ed. H.-J. Schoeps (Leiden, 1966).

36 This is clearly demonstrated by Petuchowski, *Prayerbook Reform*, in the fifth chapter of his book, entitled 'The Battle of the Proof Texts', pp. 84–104.

37 Petuchowski, *Prayerbook Reform*, dubs this 'Reform from Within' and deals with it in the third chapter of his book, pp. 31–43. On Steinschneider's role see I. Schorsch, 'Moritz Steinschneider on Liturgical Reform', *HUCA* 53 (1982), pp. 241–64. On Vienna, see M. L. Rozenblit, 'The Struggle over Religious Reform in Nineteenth-Century Vienna', *AJS Review* 14 (1989), pp. 179–221.

38 See Petuchowski, *Prayerbook Reform*, chapters 4 and 6, pp. 44–83 and 105–27.

39 Sachar, *Modern Jewish History*, pp. 154–6; Petuchowski, *Prayerbook Reform*, pp. 55–6; Ben-Sasson, *A History*, pp. 836–8 and 932; *EJ* 7, cols. 80–2; and M. A. Meyer, 'Jewish Religious Reform and Wissenschaft des Judentums. The Positions of Zunz, Geiger and Frankel', *LBIYB* 16 (1971), pp. 19–41, and his *Response*, pp. 84–99.

40 Cf. e.g. the Sefardi prayer-book published by Schlesinger in Vienna in 1873 (*Seder Tefillath Ha-Ḥodesh*); the combination of Jacob Emden's notes and the Ḥasidic rite offered in *Siddur Beth Ya'aqov* (Zhitomir, 1877); and the undated Halberstadt *maḥzor* of

about 1860 which contains a text checked against Heidenheim's and various commentaries by Aaron ben Yeḥiel Michael Ha-Levi.

41 For some examples, see the lists in J. Zedner, *Catalogue of the Hebrew Books in the Library of the British Museum* (London, 1867), pp. 462, 468, 488–92; A. E. Cowley, *A Concise Catalogue of the Hebrew Printed Books in the Bodleian Library* (Oxford, 1929), pp. 551–2. See also chapter 7 above, pp. 251–5 for details of the ḥasidic *siddur*, and the anthology of texts and commentaries to be found in *'Oṣar Ha-Tefilloth*, ed. A. L. Gordon (Vilna, 1915).

42 A brief biography of Lorberbaum (*c.* 1760–1832) appears in *EJ* 11, cols. 492–3 and his liturgical commentary was first published in Zolkiew in 1828. The commentaries of Aaron ben Yeḥiel Michael on the festival prayers, individually named *Beth Lewi*, *Maṭṭeh Lewi* and *Ma'aseh 'Oreg*, were often collectively used and entitled *Qorban 'Aharon* and he also wrote the *Nehora Ha-Shalem* on daily prayers. They were written in the first half of the nineteenth century and the references to them in A. Z. Idelsohn, *Jewish Liturgy and its Development* (Cincinnati, 1932; New York, 1967), pp. 62–3 and *Jewish Liturgy. Prayer and Synagogue Service through the Ages*, eds. R. Posner, U. Kaploun and S. Cohen (Jerusalem, 1975), p. 259, are somewhat lacking in precision.

43 Azulai's commentary was published in Leghorn in 1802 and the anonymous commentary also first appeared in the nineteenth century. On Alnaqar, see *EJ* 2, col. 672.

44 His translations into Italian of the Ashkenazi and Italian rites appeared in Vienna in 1821–2 and 1829 respectively and he published an introduction to the old Roman rite and a text of the Italian rite in Livorno in 1856. A scholarly edition of the introduction was published by E. D. Goldschmidt in Tel Aviv, 1966, and in his *On Jewish Liturgy. Essays on Prayer and Religious Poetry* (Hebrew; Jerusalem, 1978), pp. 153–76.

45 See *The Sephardi Heritage. Volume II. Essays on the History and Cultural Contribution of the Jews of Spain and Portugal. The Western Sephardim*, eds. R. D. Barnett and W. M. Schwab (Grendon, Northants, 1989) and Raphael, *The Road*, pp. 127–95.

46 See above, chapter 3, pp. 79–82; chapter 4, p. 113; and chapter 5, pp. 131, 134, 137 and 145.

47 See, for example the early editions of Ferrara, 1553 (Judaeo-Spanish); Fano, 1505 (Judaeo-Italian); and Ichenhausen, 1544 (Yiddish). For other editions see Zedner, *Catalogue*, pp. 459, 483 and 485 and Cowley, *A Concise Catalogue*, pp. 534 and 555–6.

48 See *JE* 7, p. 325 and *JE* 10, pp. 172–6. In view of the evidence presented there and in the previous note it is difficult to under-

stand the claim by N. H. Rosenbloom, *Tradition in an Age of Reform. The Religious Philosophy of Samson Raphael Hirsch* (Philadelphia, 1976), p. 375, that Friedländer's translation of the prayer-book was a 'precursor of Reform, since the *siddur* had never before been translated into the vernacular'.

49 Rosenbloom, *Tradition* provides details of his life and religious thought and devotes a chapter to his liturgical views on pp. 369–97.

50 Hirsch's prayer-book was published as *Siddur Tefilloth Yisrael. Israels Gebete übersetzt und erläutert* (Frankfurt-am-Main, 1895) and in an English version as *The Hirsch Siddur. The Order of Prayers for the Whole Year. Translation and Commentary by Samson Raphael Hirsch* (Jerusalem and New York, 1969). See p. 138 in both the German and English editions. A modern Israeli edition is promised by Mosad Harav Kook publishers in Jerusalem.

51 See Rosenbloom, *Tradition*, pp. 66–8 and the frontispiece portrait in that volume; Petuchowski, *Prayerbook Reform*, pp. 123–4, on his *Synagogenordnungen*.

52 See e.g. pp. 347–55 of *Siddur* (pp. 347–53 in the English edition) and Rosenbloom, *Tradition*, pp. 69–70.

53 See pp. 108–10 of *Siddur* (same pages in the English edition).

54 For the general historical background see Cecil Roth, *A History of the Jews in England* (Oxford, 1964, 3rd edn), especially pp. 241–66; V. D. Lipman, 'The Age of Emancipation, 1815–1880' in *Three Centuries of Anglo-Jewish History*, ed. V. D. Lipman (Cambridge, 1961), pp. 69–106; Aubrey Newman, *The United Synagogue 1870–1970* (London, 1976), pp. 1–102; and V. D. Lipman, *A History of the Jews in Britain since 1858* (Leicester, 1990), pp. 1–42.

55 Among those responsible for such prayer-books were David Levi, Alexander Alexander and his son Levi, and David Aaron de Sola.

56 See J. M. Shaftesley, 'Religious Controversies' in *A Century of Anglo-Jewish Life 1870–1970*, ed. S. S. Levin (London, 1970), pp. 93–113; Lipman, *A History*, pp. 89–117. To explain Chief Rabbi Hermann Adler's standing among more Orthodox circles one need only cite the fact that when the Machzike Hadath Congregation agreed to recognise his authority they did so 'provided he acts in accordance with the *Shulchan Oruch*'! See B. Homa, *A Fortress in Anglo-Jewry. The Story of the Machzike Hadath* (London, 1953), p. 67.

57 It is interesting to note the theological popularity of the concept of authorisation in nineteenth-century England. It was during that period that the 'King James Version' came to be widely known as

the 'Authorised Version' (e.g. *The Holy Bible according to the Authorized Version*, eds. G. D'Oyly and R. Mant, Cambridge, 1823) and that the epithet 'authorised' was applied to the 1636 liturgy (e.g. *Facsimile of the Black-letter Prayer-book of 1636 . . . authorized by the Act of Uniformity*, London, 1870). Furthermore, the Anglicans of the day, in response to variations of interpretation and practice, were also concerned with establishing a modern but authoritative liturgy that would find general acceptance within the various factions of the church. A Royal Commission was therefore appointed in 1867 'to inquire into the rubrics, orders and directions for regulating the course and conduct of public worship, the administration of the sacraments, and the other services contained in the Book of Common Prayer, according to the use of the United Church of England and Ireland'. The Commission's four lengthy reports were published by the Stationery Office in 1867, 1868 and 1870 and a sentence contained in the eleventh paragraph of the second report summarises its general outlook: 'But this large comprehension seems to us to render it most desirable that in the celebration of the Church's rites there shall be introduced no novel practices, which are welcome only to some, but are offensive to others.' Where alternatives were proposed they were of a minor nature and in the interests of a degree of order and uniformity that did not preclude congregational variation in matters not deemed of central significance.

58 It is not perhaps without significance that the Reform prayer-book published by the West London Synagogue of British Jews in 1840–1 offered a group of specially composed prayers of a similar nature for significant occasions in life, including 'signal deliverance' and 'divine service after childbirth'; see *Forms of Prayer*, pp. 103–10.

59 *The Authorised Daily Prayer Book of the United Hebrew Congregations of the British Empire* (= *ADB*), with a new translation by the Rev. S. Singer, published under the sanction of Chief Rabbi Dr. Nathan Marcus Adler (London, 1890), pp. 311–13, 322–4.

60 *ADB*, pp. 300–3, 314–17, 298–300, 325–6.

61 All these items, with the exception of *'ushpizin* and the *miy sheberakh* entreaties, are cited in full or referred to in the notes in Baer's *'Avodath Yisrael*, pp. 589–738, 196, 199–205, 369–81, 408–9, 345, 230n, 358–61, 337–9, 361n, 406n and 342.

62 *ADB*, pp. 9–14 and 275–7.

63 See *ADB*, pp. 218, 232 and 286 and compare the texts with those in Baer, *'Avodath Yisrael*, pp. 365, 367 (especially the note at the

foot of that page), and 562. See also E. J. Wiesenberg, 'The Shorter Forms of Grace after Meals and of the Amidah', *Niv Hamidrashia* 18–19 (1985–6), pp. 69–84.

64 See e.g. *ADB*, pp. 11–14, 85–6, 120–2, 143–6 and 176–209.

65 *ADB*, pp. 94–101; pp. 85, 143 and 171; and pp. 237–69.

66 See *ADB*, preface, p. viii.

67 See *ADB*, pp. 5 and 76; pp. 121 and 167.

68 For a religious history of United States Jewry during the first half of the nineteenth century, see Sachar, *The Course*, pp. 160–80; Moshe Davis, *The Emergence of Conservative Judaism. The Historical School in 19th Century America* (Philadelphia, 1965), pp. 1–113; Leon A. Jick, *The Americanization of the Synagogue, 1820–1870* (Hanover, 1976), pp. 15–96; Meyer, *Response*, pp. 225–63; M. L. Raphael, *Profiles in American Judaism. The Reform, Conservative, Orthodox, and Reconstructionist Traditions in Historical Perspective* (San Francisco, 1984), pp. 3–19, 129–35; and Michael Meyer, 'German-Jewish Identity in Nineteenth-Century America' in *The American Jewish Experience*, ed. J. D. Sarna (New York, 1986), pp. 43–59, reprinted from *Towards Modernity. The European Jewish Model*, ed. Jacob Katz (New Brunswick, NJ, 1986), pp. 247–67.

69 Sachar, *The Course*, p. 148.

70 See Davis, *The Emergence*, pp. 114–46; Jick, *The Americanization*, pp. 97–113; *Dimensions of Orthodox Judaism*, ed. R. P. Bulka (New York, 1983), the articles on pp. 131–80. See also the articles on the Orthodox, Reform and Conservative synagogues by J. S. Gurock, L. A. Jick and J. Wertheimer in *The American Synagogue. A Sanctuary Transformed*, eds. J. S. Gurock *et al.* (Cambridge and New York, 1987), pp. 37–149.

71 This becomes clear from an examination of the relevant sections on Jewish liturgy of the catalogues of the Library of Congress and the New York Public Library.

72 See I. Leeser's *The Form of Prayers according to the Custom of the Spanish and Portuguese Jews* (Philadelphia, 1837); *Siddur Divrey Ṣadiqim . . . keminhag Ashkenaz* (Philadelphia, 1848); and *'Imrey Lev, Meditations and Prayers for every Situation and Occasion in Life*, translated and adapted from the French by H. Rothschild, revised and corrected by Isaac Leeser (Philadelphia, 1864).

73 See *JE* 10, p. 180; Idelsohn, *Jewish Liturgy and its Development*, pp. 277–80; Posner *et al.*, *Jewish Liturgy*, p. 261; and Hoffman, *Beyond the Text*, pp. 60–3 and 118–24. There seems to be some confusion in these publications about the precise bibliographical details and the references given here are to the first editions. See E. L. Friedland, '*Olath Tamid* by David Einhorn', *HUCA* 45

(1974), pp. 307–32 and L. A. Hoffman, 'The Language of Survival in American Reform Liturgy', *CCAR Journal* 24 (1977), pp. 87–106.

74 For a biography see Israel Knox, *Rabbi in America. The Story of Isaac M. Wise* (Boston, 1957). Cf. also Meyer, *Response*, pp. 235–80. A new biography by S. D. Temkin, *Isaac Mayer Wise. Judaism in the New World* is promised by Oxford University Press in its Littman series.

75 See Hoffman, *Beyond the Text*, pp. 60–3, 70 and 72–3.

76 The general survey here offered of the precursors of the American Conservative movement is substantially based on Davis, *The Emergence*; on Leeser, see pp. 347–9 of that volume.

77 See, in particular, pp. 354–6 of Davis, *The Emergence*.

78 Davis, *ibid.*, pp. 360–2 and 342–4.

79 Such a view is favoured by Abraham Levy in his booklet *The Sephardim. A Problem of Survival* (London, 1972), especially pp. 9–14.

80 Davis, *The Emergence*, pp. 138–46, 288–92 and 305–8.

81 Davis, *ibid.*, pp. 365–6.

9 A BACKGROUND TO CURRENT DEVELOPMENTS

1 Useful summaries of these unique factors are to be found in H. M. Sachar, *The Course of Modern Jewish History* (London, 1958), pp. 305–22, 394–418 and 520–41 and in S. Ettinger, 'The Modern Period' in *A History of the Jewish People*, ed. H. H. Ben-Sasson (London, 1976; translated from the Hebrew edition of Tel Aviv, 1969), pp. 859–69, 939–48 and 1063–74.

2 For details of Jewish religious forms and their history in the twentieth century, particularly in the USA, see J. L. Blau, *Modern Varieties of Judaism* (New York, 1966); M. Sklare, *Conservative Judaism. An American Religious Movement* (Glencoe, 1955); M. Sklare, 'Religion and Ethnicity in the American Jewish Community. Changing Aspects of Reform, Conservative and Orthodox Judaism' in *The Role of Religion in Modern Jewish History*, ed. J. Katz (Cambridge, Mass., 1975), pp. 147–59; R. Bulka (ed.), *Dimensions of Orthodox Judaism* (New York, 1983); M. L. Raphael, *Profiles in American Judaism. The Reform, Conservative, Orthodox, and Reconstructionist Traditions in Historical Perspective* (San Francisco, 1984); M. A. Meyer, *Response to Modernity. A History of the Reform Movement in Judaism* (New York, 1988); and *The American Synagogue: A Sanctuary Transformed*, eds. J. S. Gurock *et al.* (Cambridge and New York, 1987).

3 See C. S. Liebman, 'Orthodoxy in American Jewish Life' in *Dimensions*, ed. Bulka, pp. 33–46; Sklare, *Conservative Judaism*, pp. 19–65.

4 See ch. 8 above, pp. 290–3 and M. Davis, *The Emergence of Conservative Judaism. The Historical School in 19th century America* (Philadelphia, 1965), pp. 311–26. It should of course be borne in mind that both Sklare and Davis were writing before the revival of Orthodoxy that has been characteristic of the last twenty-five years.

5 See Liebman, 'Orthodoxy', pp. 46–72 and J. W. Joselit, *New York's Jewish Jews. The Orthodox Community in the Interwar Years* (Bloomington, 1990), especially pp. 54–84.

6 Any of the editions produced by these companies in the first few decades of the twentieth century illustrate the general point being made. The 'Singer's' was republished by the Hebrew Publishing Company in 1915 and by Bloch in an enlarged edition in 1922. It should also be noted that the latter also published Hertz's British edition, shortly to be discussed, as late as 1957.

7 *Daily Prayer Book. Ha-Siddur Ha-Shalem*, translated and annotated with an introduction by Philip Birnbaum (New York, 1949), pp. 674, 676 and 679.

8 *Siddur Le-Shabbath We-Yom Tov. The Traditional Prayer Book for Sabbath and Festivals*, edited and translated by David de Sola Pool, authorised by the Rabbinical Council of America (New York, 1960), pp. 247–9, 459–569, 597–601, 611–13, and 633–5 compared with the passages cited as missing from the first 'Singer's' in ch. 8 above, pp. 285–7; and pp. 259, 591–3, 475–88, 845–79 for the special needs noted.

9 R. P. Bulka has attempted a useful overview in his 'Orthodoxy Today. An Analysis of the Achievements and the Problems' in the volume that he himself edited entitled *Dimensions of Orthodox Judaism* (New York, 1983), pp. 7–32. For a more general sociological treatment of Jewish religious developments, see C. S. Liebman, 'The Religious Life of American Jewry' in *Understanding American Jewry*, ed. M. Sklare (New Brunswick and London, 1982), pp. 96–124. See also Raphael, *Profiles in American Judaism*, pp. 165–76.

10 L. Kaplan, 'The Ambiguous Modern Orthodox Jew', in Bulka, *Dimensions*, pp. 242–52; originally published in *Judaism* 29 (1979), pp. 439–48.

11 G. Kranzler, 'The Changing Orthodox Jewish Community' in Bulka, *Dimensions*, pp. 121–30; originally published in *Tradition* 16 (1976), pp. 61–72.

12 These brief summaries of the situation are based on the following

articles in Bulka's *Dimensions*: C. S. Liebman, 'Orthodoxy in American Jewish Life' and 'Orthodoxy Today' on pp. 33–120 (originally published in *American Jewish Year Book* 66 (1965), pp. 21–92 and in *Midstream* 25 (1976), pp. 19–28); M. Schick, 'Borough Park: A Jewish Settlement' on pp. 186–98 (originally published in *Jewish Life* (Winter, 1979), pp. 23–35); S. Poll, 'The Impact of Hasidism on American Judaism', on pp. 199–211; and M. D. Angel, 'Religious Life of American Sephardim', on pp. 212–18.

13 L. A. Hoffman, *Beyond the Text. A Holistic Approach to Liturgy* (Bloomington and Indianapolis, 1987), p. 68.

14 The inner tensions to be found in a modern Orthodox synagogue are superbly portrayed by S. C. Heilman, *Synagogue Life* (Chicago, 1976) while the return to a more Eastern European style of Judaism is documented by Schick and Poll in the articles cited in n. 12 above. On more general synagogal developments in the USA, see J. S. Gurock, 'The Emergence of the American Synagogue' in *The American Jewish Experience*, ed. J. D. Sarna (New York and London, 1986), pp. 193–210, reprinted from Gurock's *When Harlem was Jewish* (New York, 1979); the bibliography provided by Liebman in *Understanding American Jewry*, pp. 120–4; A. S. Korres and J. D. Sarna, *American Synagogue History. A Bibliography and State-of-the-Field Study* (New York, 1987); and D. M. Gordis and Y. Ben-Horin, *Jewish Identity in America* (Los Angeles, 1991), especially pp. 159–80.

15 The standard edition of the Ḥabad *siddur* now being used is the *Sidur Tehilas Hashem* (so transliterated on title-page) published in Brooklyn in 1951 and earlier, nineteenth-century editions are discussed in chapter 7 above, pp. 251–5. One of the *siddurim* most widely used in 'strictly' Orthodox communities is the *Siddur Tiqqun Me'ir* (New York, 1933), available in both Ashkenazi and Sefardi (i.e. Ḥasidic) versions.

16 This phenomenon, particularly as it manifests itself in Israel, is helpfully analysed by Janet Aviad, *Return to Judaism. Religious Renewal in Israel* (Chicago and London, 1983), and with regard to American women by D. R. Kaufman, *Rachel's Daughters. Newly Orthodox Jewish Women* (New Brunswick and London, 1991).

17 *Siddur Qol Ya'aqov. The Complete ArtScroll Siddur. A New Translation and Anthological Commentary* by Nosson Scherman (Brooklyn, 1984, 1st edn, 1986, 2nd edn). The ArtScroll series of publications has proved immensely popular but has also attracted criticism from neo-Orthodox circles. See e.g. A. Unterman, 'The ArtScroll Mesorah Series. A Mixed Blessing', *Niv Hamidrashia* 18–19

(1985–6), pp. 59–64. See also B. Barry Levy, 'ArtScroll: An Overview' in *Approaches to Modern Judaism*, ed. M. L. Raphael (Chico, 1983), pp. 111–40.

18 See Liebman, 'Orthodoxy in American Jewish Life', pp. 77–8.

19 *A Prayer Book Printed for the Use of the Oxford University Hebrew Congregation* (London, 1914). The inspiration for the publication of this little volume would appear to have come from Basil Henriques, as Professor Raphael Loewe kindly informs me.

20 The general history of Anglo-Jewry in the twentieth century is covered by L. P. Gartner, *The Jewish Immigrant in England 1870–1914* (London, 1973, 2nd edn); D. Cesarani (ed.), *The Making of Modern Anglo-Jewry* (Oxford, 1990); and V. D. Lipman, *A History of the Jews in Britain since 1858* (Leicester, 1990). For important aspects of the development of the strictly Orthodox wing of Anglo-Jewry, see B. Homa, *A Fortress in Anglo-Jewry. The Story of the Machzike Hadath* (London, 1953), *Orthodoxy in Anglo-Jewry 1880–1940* (JHSE pamphlet, London, 1969), and *Footprints on the Sands of Time* (London, 1990). On the religious evolution of the community, see J. Sacks, *Traditional Alternatives. Orthodoxy and the Future of the Jewish People* (London, 1989). See also ch. 8, pp. 283–4 above. The impact of Jews of German origin is dealt with in *Second Chance. Two Centuries of German-speaking Jews in the United Kingdom*, eds. W. E. Mosse, J. Carlebach, G. Hirschfeld, A. Newman, A. Paucker and P. Pulzer (Tübingen, 1991).

21 By 1912 nine editions had been published, in a total of 133,000 copies, and in 1914 Singer's son-in-law, Israel Abrahams, produced his *Annotated Edition of the Authorised Daily Prayer Book with historical and explanatory notes, and additional matter, compiled in accordance with the plans of the Rev. S. Singer* (London, 1914). For the additional material, inserted without change of pagination, see pp. 124a–c, 238a and 326.

22 *The Authorised Daily Prayer Book of the United Hebrew Congregation of the British Empire*, revised edition and translation with commentary by J. H. Hertz, originally published in three volumes (London, 1942–5), and subsequently in a one-volume edition (London, 1947). He was also responsible for the tenth to the eighteenth editions of the 'Singer's' (1916–44) and his additions may be found on pp. 108, 309a, 316b, and 317a. On the matter of the shorter grace (p. 286), see chapter 8, p. 286 above and E. J. Wiesenberg, 'The Shorter Forms of Grace', *Niv Hamidrashia* 18–19 (1985–6), pp. 69–84.

23 *The Authorised Daily Prayer Book of the United Hebrew Congregations of the British Commonwealth of Nations*, new edition reset and enlarged under the direction of Israel Brodie (London, 1962). The pagi-

nation was new and the innovations are to be found on pp. 167–8, 204–5, 227–32, 307–8, 325–6, 345–6, and 407–10.

24 Ed. Jakobovits, pp. 671–94, 753–8, 709–10, and 663–70.

25 *Ibid.*, pp. 223–4 and 531–2, 703–4, 583–4 and 637–8.

26 *Ibid.*, pp. 833–96, 381–4 and 99–100.

27 *Ibid.*, pp. 169–70 and 739, the latter apparently in response to Wiesenberg's article, 'The Shorter Forms of Grace'.

28 It remains to be seen whether the Jakobovits edition will succeed in challenging the growing interest in the Israeli and American editions of the traditional text discussed elsewhere in this chapter. An attempt was already made by S. Schonfeld in 1969 to provide a more 'Orthodox' *siddur* than the 'Singer's' but it has not proved a popular edition. See his *The Standard Siddur-Prayer Book with an Orthodox English translation and a linear set of references* (London, 1969, 1st edn, 1973, 2nd edn).

29 *The Book of Prayer and Order of Service according to the custom of the Spanish and Portuguese Jews in an English translation based principally on the work of the late Rev. D. A. de Sola* . . . edited and revised by . . . Moses Gaster, vol. I (London, 1901), with a historical introduction on pp. xi–xxviii. The remaining volumes, covering the festival prayers, appeared between 1903 and 1906. On the rites of the Western Sefardim, see also S. Gaguine, *Keter Shem Tob. The Rites and Ceremonies and Liturgical Variants of the Sephardim*, 6 parts (London, 1934–55).

30 Richard Barnett makes some brief and diplomatic references to the influx of these Sefardim in 'The Sephardim of England' in *The Sephardi Heritage. Essays on the History and Cultural Contribution of the Jews of Spain and Portugal*, eds. R. D. Barnett and W. M. Schwab, vol. II (Grendon, Northants, 1989), pp. 5–25, especially p. 22. The two prayer-books mentioned were edited by Ṣalaḥ ben Jacob Manṣur and Menaḥem ben Joseph Baṣri, respectively.

31 There are useful articles by G. Nahon, 'The Sephardim of France' in *The Sephardi Heritage*, eds. Barnett and Schwab, pp. 46–74 and in *EJ* 7, cols. 36–43 but neither deals with those liturgical developments that may be noted in many contemporary synagogues.

32 H. M. Sachar, *A History of Israel* (New York, 1976), pp. 18–35; *EJ* 9, cols. 887–909.

33 S. Halevy, *The Printed Hebrew Books in Jerusalem during the First Half Century (1841–1891)* (Hebrew; Jerusalem, 1963; revised and enlarged, Jerusalem, 1975).

34 Y. Ben-Arieh, *Jerusalem in the Nineteenth Century. Emergence of the New City* (Jerusalem and New York, 1986), pp. 396–8.

35 G. Silberberg, *Torath Ha-Defus* (Merhavya, 1968), pp. 24–6;

Sachar, *A History*, pp. 134–94; *EJ* 13, cols. 1114–16; typical examples are listed, ultimately under *tefillah*, in the bibliographical entries of *Kiryat Sefer* (then *Kirjath Sepher*) during the 1930s and 1940s.

36 On the general history of the religious parties in Israel, see G. S. Schiff, *Tradition and Politics* (Detroit, 1977), and for the more recent history of the National Religious Party (*Mafdal*), the successor of Mizraḥi, see C. S. Liebman and E. Don-Yehiya, *Religion and Politics in Israel* (Bloomington, 1984), pp. 100–18.

37 There are numerous examples of these publications and many of them were produced by such printing houses as Eshkol, Sinai and Beth Raphael, often in photomechanical reprints, small in format and with either decorated silver or plastic covers and inexpensive binding.

38 *Siddur Rinath Yisrael*, edited by Shelomo Tal, was published with the assistance of the Israeli government's ministries of religions and education in Jerusalem in 1970. The Koren *Siddur Tefillah* was published in Jerusalem in 1982 with an introduction by Eliyahu Koren in which acknowledgement is made to Meir Medan for his scholarly assistance. E. D. Goldschmidt's two-volume *maḥzor* for the High Holidays was also printed by Koren but the copyright was vested in the Leo Baeck Institute of New York (1970).

39 See e.g. *Rinath Yisrael*, ed. Tal, pp. 54 and 98; Koren *Siddur*, pp. 40 and 62; Goldschmidt's *Maḥzor*, volume for New Year, pp. 121–5 and 150. See also ch. 7, p. 240 above. On some aspects of the history of the responsive chant, see G. Goldberg, *HUCA* 61 (1990), pp. 203–17, who perhaps understates the degree of innovation in the modern German communities.

40 Published in numerous editions as *Siddur Tefilloth La-Ḥayyal Le-Khol Ha-Shanah* by the chaplaincy of the Israeli Defence Forces in Tel Aviv. On Goren see *EJ* 7, cols. 808–9 and *Who's Who in Israel* (Tel Aviv, 1990–1), p. 96.

41 These developments, which are not without their influences on modern Orthodox practice, are noted by C. S. Liebman and E. Don-Yehiya in *Civil Religion in Israel. Traditional Judaism and Political Culture in the Jewish State* (Berkeley and Los Angeles and London, 1983), pp. 48–58, 113–22 and 167–70.

42 For a variety of approaches, see M. Meiselman, *Jewish Woman in Jewish Law* (New York, 1978); R. Biale, *Women and Jewish Law. An Exploration of Women's Issues in Halakhic Sources* (New York, 1984); E. Berkovits, *Women in Time and Torah* (New York, 1990); and S. Grossman and R. Haut (eds.), *Daughters of the King. Women and the Synagogue* (Philadelphia and New York and Jerusalem, 1992), esp. pp. 227–36.

43 A favourable response to such services from an Orthodox, halakhic viewpoint is to be found in A. Weiss, *Women at Prayer. A Halakhic Analysis of Women's Prayer Groups* (Hoboken, NJ, 1990).
44 Sklare, *Conservative Judaism*, pp. 19–65.
45 *Ibid.*, pp. 66–128.
46 *Maḥzor 'Avodath 'Ohel Mo 'ed. Service of the Synagogue. A New Edition of the Festival Prayers with an English Translation in Prose and Verse*, edited by Herbert M. Adler and Arthur Davis, was issued in six volumes to cover all the festivals (London, 1904–8) and has been reprinted many times in London and New York.
47 Raphael deals with the early history and ideology of the Conservative movement in his *Profiles in American Judaism*, pp. 81–94 and with its institutions and organisations on pp. 112–23.
48 *Maḥzor Le-Shalosh Regalim. Festival Prayer Book. The Hebrew Text of the Synagogue Service for the Three Festivals with English Translations in Prose and Verse* (New York, 1927). See Sklare, *Conservative Judaism*, p. 126 and Jules Harlow's introductory essay 'On the Liturgy of the Conservative Movement' published as a preface to *Siddur Sim Shalom* published by the Rabbinical Assembly in New York, 1985.
49 Richard Libowitz, *Mordecai M. Kaplan and the Development of Reconstructionism* (New York and Toronto, 1983); *The American Judaism of Mordecai M. Kaplan*, eds. E. S. Goldsmith, M. Scult and R. M. Seltzer (New York, 1989); Raphael, *Profiles in American Judaism*, pp. 179–94; Hoffman, *Beyond the Text*, pp. 64–6.
50 Sklare, *Conservative Judaism*, pp. 120–8; Raphael, *Profiles in American Judaism*, p. 122; Hoffman, *Beyond the Text*, pp. 66 and 70; Harlow, 'On the Liturgy', pp. xxi–xxii.
51 Sklare, *Conservative Judaism*, p. 124.
52 Raphael, *Profiles in American Judaism*, pp. 122–3; Hoffman, *Beyond the Text*, p. 74; Harlow, 'On the Liturgy', pp. xxii–xxxi.
53 *Kol Haneshamah. Erev Shabbath. Shabbat Eve* (Wyncote, Pa., 1989) and see pp. xiv–xxiii of the introduction.
54 Raphael, *Profiles in American Judaism*, pp. 94–111.
55 An Institute for Traditional Judaism, to train rabbis, was also founded in Mount Vernon, New York, headed by Weiss-Halivni. The director of the Union was Rabbi Ronald Price and this information is owed to one of its vice-presidents, Rabbi Philip Scheim of Toronto. Even within the Conservative establishment worries began to be expressed about the manner in which institutionalisation had moved Judaism from the home to the synagogue. In the words of Harold M. Schulweis, 'the public institution has robbed the family of its sancta, and the roles of parents have been preempted by the professionals of the public

institutions'. (*Jewish Identity in America*, eds. Gordis and Ben-Horin, pp. 160–1).

56 See Liebman and Don-Yehiya, *Religion and Politics*, pp. 119–37; Raphael, *Profiles in American Judaism*, pp. 106–7; *EJ* 5, cols. 905–6.

57 For details of the 'Jacobs controversy' and the New London Synagogue, which he leads, together with other London Masorti synagogues, see L. Jacobs, *Helping with Inquiries. An Autobiography* (London, 1989), pp. 124–222.

58 Hoffman, *Beyond the Text*, pp. 63, 67 and 70; Meyer, *Response*, p. 279; *Jewish Liturgy, Prayer and Synagogue Service through the Ages*, eds. R. Posner, U. Kaploun and S. Cohen (Jerusalem, 1975), p. 263.

59 The three manifestos are conveniently reprinted by Meyer, *Response*, in an appendix on pp. 387–8 (Pittsburgh), 388–91 (Columbus) and 391–4 (San Francisco).

60 D. Polish, *Renew our Days. The Zionist Issue in Reform Judaism* (Jerusalem, 1976), pp. 115–82; Meyer, *Response*, pp. 302–6 and 326–34. Wise's dates were 1874–1949 and those of Silver 1893–1963.

61 Meyer, *Response*, pp. 298–301. Gamoran lived from 1895 to 1962.

62 Meyer, *Response*, pp. 317–20. A brief appreciation of Cohon by J. J. Petuchowski recently appeared in a posthumous volume of Cohon's work, *Essays in Jewish Theology* (Cincinnati, 1987), xi–xiv. See also the volume by the 'compilers of his literary legacy' *Day Book of Service at the Altar as lived by Samuel S. Cohon 1888–1959* (Los Angeles, 1978).

63 Lauterbach (1873–1942) published important studies of rabbinic literature and custom and Freehof (1892–1990) provided the historical background for Reform's re-assessment of the contemporary relevance of *halakhah*. Idelsohn (1882–1938) was a specialist in Jewish musicology whose study *Jewish Liturgy and its Development* (Cincinnati, 1932) is still a most useful compilation.

64 Meyer, *Response*, devotes his eighth chapter to this theme of 'reorientation' and details the liturgical revisions on pp. 321–2.

65 L. A. Hoffman and N. Wiener, 'The Liturgical State of the World Union for Progressive Judaism', *European Judaism* 24 (1991), p. 13.

66 Hoffman, *Beyond the Text*, p. 67.

67 Hoffman and Wiener, 'The Liturgical State', pp. 17–18.

68 Hoffman, *Beyond the Text*, p. 73.

69 *Ibid.*, p. 74; Meyer, *Response*, pp. 373–82; Raphael, *Profiles in American Judaism*, pp. 63–8.

70 J. J. Petuchowski, *Prayerbook Reform in Europe. The Liturgy of European Liberal and Reform Judaism* (New York, 1968).

71 Petuchowski, *Prayerbook Reform*, pp. 66–8 and 139–41; Meyer, *Response*, pp. 171–80.

72 *Forms of Prayer for Jewish Worship*. Edited for the use of their own and allied congregations by the Ministers of the West London Synagogue of British Jews (Oxford, 1931), preface. See Petuchowski, *Prayerbook Reform*, p. 68.

73 On Montefiore, Montagu and Mattock see, in addition to standard encyclopaedia articles, J. Stein, *Claude Goldsmid Montefiore on the Ancient Rabbis* (Missoula, 1977); E. M. Umansky, *Lily Montagu and the Advancement of Liberal Judaism. From Vision to Vocation* (New York, 1983); Petuchowski, *Prayerbook Reform*, pp. 70–5 and 202–5, and Meyer, *Response*, pp. 212–21; E. Kessler, *An English Jew. The Life and Writings of Claude Montefiore* (London, 1989).

74 Petuchowski, *Prayerbook Reform*, p. 73.

75 Meyer, *Response*, pp. 347–8 and Lipman, *Jews in Britain*, pp. 241–3; Petuchowski, *Prayerbook Reform*, pp. 76–7.

76 *'Avodath Ha-Lev. Service of the Heart. Weekday Sabbath and Festival Services and Prayers for Home and Synagogue* (London, 1967), mostly the work of J. D. Rayner and C. Stern; *Pethaḥ Teshuvah. Gates of Repentance. Services for the High Holydays* (London, 1973), by the same two editors.

77 *Seder Ha-Tefilloth. Forms of Prayer for Jewish Worship. I. Daily, Sabbath and Occasional Prayers* (London, 1977), with an introduction signed by Lionel Blue and Jonathan Magonet but the editing attributed to 'the Assembly of Rabbis of the Reform Synagogues of Great Britain'.

78 Compare the brief allusions to Jews living in the 'land of Israel' in the Liberal *Service of the Heart*, pp. 156, 174, 193, 211 and 285, with the more confident, though still mild, espousal of Zionism to be found in the Reform *Forms of Prayer*, pp. 160 and 259–63. At the time of writing a new, post-modernist Liberal prayer-book was being promised for 1993 that would be more tentative about the rejection of tradition.

79 Hoffman and Wiener, 'The Liturgical State', p. 14.

80 *Ibid.*, pp. 10–22.

81 *Gebetbuch für das ganze Jahr bearbeitet im Auftrag des Liberalen Kultus-Ausschusses des Preussischen Landesverbandes jüdischer Gemeinden*, eds. C. Seligmann, I. Elbogen and H. Vogelstein (Frankfurt-am-Main, 1929). See Petuchowski, *Prayerbook Reform*, pp. 205–13.

82 Meyer, *Response*, pp. 344–6 and Polish, *Renew*, pp. 236–67.

83 See Liebman and Don-Yehiya, *Religion and Politics*, pp. 119–37.

84 Meyer, *Response*, pp. 348–52.

85 *Ha-'Avodah Sheba-lev* (Jerusalem, 1982) and *Kawwanath Ha-Lev* (Jerusalem, 1989). These various Israeli Reform liturgies are examined in detail in an MA dissertation submitted to the Hebrew University of Jerusalem by Zohar Zion in 1990.

Select Bibliography

Abrahams, I., 'Some Rabbinic Ideas on Prayer', *JQR* 20 (1908)

Baillet, M., *Discoveries in the Judaean Desert* VII. *Qumran Grotte 4 III (4Q482 – 4Q520)* (Oxford, 1982)

Bar-Ilan, M., *The Mysteries of Jewish Prayer and Hekhalot* (Hebrew; Ramat Gan, 1987)

'Major Trends in the Formation and Crystallization of the *Qedusha*', *Daat* 25 (1990)

'*Ra'yon Ha-Beḥirah Ba-Tefillah Ha-Yehudith*' in *Ra'yon Ha-Beḥirah Beyisra'el Uva-'amim*, eds. S. Almog and M. Heyd (Jerusalem, 1991)

Barkay, G., *Ketef Hinnom. A Treasure Facing Jerusalem's Walls* (Israel Museum, catalogue no. 274, Jerusalem, 1986)

Baskin, J. R. (ed.), *Jewish Women in Historical Perspective* (Detroit, 1991)

Beit-Arié, M., *Hebrew Codicology* (Jerusalem, 1981, 2nd edn)

'*Birkhot Ha-'Evarim*', *Tarbiẓ* 56 (1987)

Ben-Sasson, M., Bonfil, R., and Hacker, J. R. (eds.), *Culture and Society in Medieval Jewry. Studies Dedicated to the Memory of H. H. Ben-Sasson* (Hebrew; Jerusalem, 1989)

Berkovits, E., *Women in Time and Torah* (New York, 1990)

Berliner, A., *Kethavim Nivḥarim* (Jerusalem, 1945)

Biale, R., *Women and Jewish Law. An Exploration of Women's Issues in Halakhic Sources* (New York, 1984)

Blumenthal, D. R., *Approaches to Judaism in Medieval Times* III (Atlanta, 1988)

Bokser, B. M., *The Origins of the Seder. The Passover Rite and Early Rabbinic Judaism* (Berkeley, 1984)

Bonfil, R., *Rabbis and Jewish Communities in Renaissance Italy* (ET, Oxford, 1990)

Bonfil, R., see also Ben-Sasson, M.

Bradshaw, P. B., *Daily Prayer in the Early Church* (London, 1981)

Bradshaw, P. B. and Hoffman, L. A. (eds.), *The Making of Jewish and Christian Worship* (Notre Dame and London, 1991)

Brocke, M., see Petuchowski, J. J.

Brody, R., 'The Testimony of Geonic Literature to the Text of the Babylonian Talmud' (Hebrew) in *Meḥqarey Talmud*, ed. J. Sussmann and D. Rosenthal (Jerusalem, 1990)

'Saadya Gaon on the Limits of Liturgical Flexibility' in *Genizah Research after Ninety Years*, eds. J. Blau and S. C. Reif (Cambridge, 1992)

Brooten, B., *Women Leaders in the Ancient Synagogue. Inscriptional Evidence and Background Issues* (Chico, 1982)

Bulka, R. P. (ed.), *Dimensions of Orthodox Judaism* (New York, 1983)

Carruthers, M., *The Book of Memory. A Study of Memory in Medieval Culture* (Cambridge, 1990)

Cesarani, D. (ed.), *The Making of Modern Anglo-Jewry* (Oxford, 1990)

Chait, M. J. S., *Handbook of Synagogue Architecture* (Chico, 1982)

Charlesworth, J. H., 'A Prolegomenon to a New Study of the Jewish Background of the Hymns and Prayers in the New Testament', *JJS* 33 (1982)

Clements, R., *The Prayers of the Bible* (London, 1986)

Cohen, J. M., *Horizons of Jewish Prayer* (London, 1986)

Cohen, S., see Posner, R.

Cohn, G. H. (ed.), *Ha-Tefillah Ha-Yehudith. Hemshekh Weḥiddush* (Ramat Gan, 1978)

Dan, J. and Talmage, F. (eds.), *Studies in Jewish Mysticism* (Cambridge, Mass., 1982)

Davis, M., *The Emergence of Conservative Judaism. The Historical School in 19th Century America* (Philadelphia, 1965)

Dimant, D., 'Qumran Sectarian Literature' in *Jewish Writings of the Second Temple Period*, ed. M. E. Stone (Assen and Philadelphia, 1984)

Dodi, A., 'The Vocalization of a 13th Century Siddur', *Lĕšonénu* 53 (1988–9)

Don-Yehiya, E., see Liebman, C. S.

Eisenstein, E. L., *The Printing Press as an Agent of Change*, 2 vols. (Cambridge, 1979)

Elbaum, Y., 'Concerning Two Textual Emendations in the '*Aleinu*', *Tarbiẓ* 42 (1973)

Openness and Insularity (Hebrew; Jerusalem, 1990)

Elbogen, I., *Der jüdische Gottesdienst in seiner geschichtlichen Entwicklung* (Frankfurt-am-Main, 1931)

Ha-Tefillah Beyisra'el Behithpathuthah Ha-Histọrith (updated Hebrew edition of *Gottesdienst*), eds. J. Amir, I. Adler, A. Negev, J. J. Petuchowski and J. (Ḥ.) Schirmann (Tel Aviv, 1972)

Fenton, P. B., *The Treatise of The Pool* (London, 1981)

'*Tefillah be'ad Ha-Rashuth*', *Mi-mizraḥ Umi-ma'arav* IV (1983)

Deux traités de mystique juive (Lagrasse, 1987)

Fiensy, D. A., *Prayers alleged to be Jewish. An Examination of the* Constitutiones Apostolorum (Chico, 1985)

Finkel, A. and Frizzell, L. (eds.), *Standing before God. Studies on Prayer in Scriptures and in Tradition with Essays in Honor of John M. Oesterreicher* (New York, 1981)

Finkelstein, I., 'Byzantine Prayer Niches', *IEJ* 31 (1981)

Finkelstein, L., 'The Origin of the Synagogue', *PAAJR* 1928–30 (1930)

Fleischer, E., 'Towards a Clarification of the Expression "*Poreis 'al Shema*"', *Tarbiz* 41 (1972)

The Yozer. Its Emergence and Development (Hebrew; Jerusalem, 1974)

Hebrew Liturgical Poetry in the Middle Ages (Hebrew; Jerusalem, 1975)

'Hebrew Liturgical Poetry in Italy' in *Italia Judaica* I (Rome, 1983)

Eretz-Israel Prayer and Prayer Rituals as Portrayed in the Geniza Documents (Hebrew; Jerusalem, 1988)

'On the Beginnings of Obligatory Jewish Prayer', *Tarbiz* 59 (1990)

Fleischer, E., see also Petuchowski, J. J.

Flusser, D., 'Psalms, Hymns and Prayers' in *Jewish Writings of the Second Temple Period*, ed. M. E. Stone (Assen and Philadelphia, 1984)

Freehof, S. B., 'Hazkarath Neshamoth', *HUCA* 36 (1965)

Frizzell, L., see Finkel, A.

Gerhardsson, B., *Memory and Manuscript. Oral Tradition and Written Transmission in Rabbinic Judaism and Early Christianity* (Uppsala, 1961)

Gil, M., *Palestine during the First Muslim Period (634–1099)* (Hebrew; 3 vols., Tel Aviv, 1983; one-volume English version *A History of Palestine 634–1099*, Cambridge, 1992)

Goetschel, R. (ed.), *Prière, mystique et judaïsme* (Paris, 1987)

Goitein, S. D., *A Mediterranean Society. The Jewish Communities of the Arab World as Portrayed in the Documents of the Cairo Geniza*, 5 vols. (Berkeley and Los Angeles and London, 1967–88)

'Prayers from the Geniza for Fatimid Caliphs' in *Studies in Judaism, Karaitica and Islamica presented to Leon Nemoy*, ed. S. R. Brunswick (Ramat Gan, 1982)

Goldberg, P. S., *Karaite Liturgy and its Relation to Synagogue Worship* (Manchester, 1957)

Goldschmidt, E. D., 'Studies on Jewish Liturgy by German-Jewish Scholars', *LBIYB* 2 (1957)

The Passover Haggadah. Its Sources and History (Hebrew; Jerusalem, 1969)

On Jewish Liturgy. Essays on Prayer and Religious Poetry (Hebrew; Jerusalem, 1978)

Grabbe, L. L., 'Synagogues in Pre-70 Palestine. A Re-assessment', *JTS* NS 39 (1988)

Greenberg, M., *Biblical Prose Prayer as a Window to the Popular Religion of Ancient Israel* (Berkeley, 1983)

Griffiths, J. G., 'Egypt and the Rise of the Synagogue', *JTS* NS 38 (1987)

Groner, T., '*Ha-Berakhah ʿal Ha-Widui Wegilguleha*', *Bar-Ilan Annual* 13 (1976)

The Legal Methodology of Hai Gaon (Chico, 1985)

'A List of Rav Hai Gaon's Responsa', *Alei Sefer* 13 (1986)

Grossman, A., see Mirski, A.

Gurock, J. S., Jick, L. A. and Wertheimer, J. (eds.), *The American Synagogue. A Sanctuary Transformed* (Cambridge and New York, 1987)

Gutmann, J., *Ancient Synagogues. The State of Research* (Chico, 1981)

'Sherira Gaon and the Babylonian Origin of the Synagogue' in *Occident and Orient. A Tribute to the Memory of Alexander Scheiber*, ed. R. Dan (Budapest and Leiden, 1988)

Habermann, A. M., *Shirey Ha-Yiḥud Weha-Kavod* (Jerusalem, 1948)

Hacker, J., 'Patterns of the Intellectual Activity of Ottoman Jewry in the 16th and 17th Centuries', *Tarbiẓ* 53 (1984)

Hacker, J., see also Ben-Sasson, M.

Hammer, R., 'What Did they Bless? A Study of Mishnah Tamid 5.1', *JQR* 81 (1991)

Haran, M., *Temples and Temple-Service in Ancient Israel* (Oxford, 1978)

'Priest, Temple and Worship', *Tarbiẓ* 48 (1979)

'Priesthood, Temple, Divine Service', *Hebrew Annual Review* 7 (1983)

Heilman, S. C., *Synagogue Life* (Chicago, 1976)

The People of the Book. Drama, Fellowship and Religion (Chicago and London, 1983)

Heinemann, J., *Prayer in the Period of the Tanna'im and the Amora'im. Its Nature and its Patterns* (Hebrew; Jerusalem, 1964)

Prayer in the Talmud (updated English version of his Jerusalem 1964 work, ed. R. Sarason, Berlin, 1977)

'Prayers and Blessings', *Encyclopedia Hebraica* (Hebrew) XXXII (Jerusalem and Tel Aviv, 1981)

Studies in Jewish Liturgy (Hebrew; ed. A. Shinan, Jerusalem, 1981)

Herr, M. D., 'Matters of Palestinian Halakha during the Sixth and Seventh Centuries CE', *Tarbiz* 49 (1979–80)

Hoffman, L. A., 'The Language of Survival in American Reform Liturgy', *CCAR Journal* 24 (1977)

The Canonization of the Synagogue Service (Notre Dame, 1979)

Beyond the Text. A Holistic Approach to Liturgy (Bloomington and Indianapolis, 1987)

Hoffman, L. A., see also Bradshaw, P. B.

Hoffman, L. A. and Wiener, N., 'The Liturgical State of the World Union for Progressive Judaism', *European Judaism* 24 (1991)

Idelsohn, I. Z., *Jewish Liturgy and its Development* (New York, 1932)

Jacobs, L., *Hasidic Prayer* (London, 1972)

Jacobson, B. S., *Nethiv Binah*, 5 vols. (Tel Aviv, 1968–83)

Jick, L. A., *The Americanization of the Synagogue 1820–1870* (Hanover, 1976)

Jick, L. A., see also Gurock, J. S.

Johnson, N. B., *Prayer in the Apocrypha and Pseudepigrapha* (Philadelphia, 1948)

Jones, C., Wainwright, G. and Yarnold, E. (eds.), *The Study of Liturgy* (London, 1978)

Kaplan, Y., see Mirski, A.

Kaploun, U., see Posner, R.

Kasher, A., Oppenheimer, A. and Rappaport, U. (eds.), *Synagogues in Antiquity* (Jerusalem, 1987)

Kavanagh, A., 'Scripture and Worship in Synagogue and Church', *Michigan Quarterly Review* 22 (1983)

Kern-Ulmer, B., *Rabbinische Responsen zum Synagogenbau*, vol. 1 (Hildesheim and Zurich and New York, 1990)

Kilpatrick, G. D., *The Eucharist in Bible and Liturgy* (Cambridge, 1983)

Klein, E., *Jewish Prayer. Concepts and Customs* (Columbus, 1986)

Korres, A. S. and Sarna, J. D., *American Synagogue History. A Bibliography and State-of-the-Field study* (New York, 1987)

Kraus, H.-J., *Worship in Israel. A Cultic History of the Old Testament* (ET, Oxford, 1966)

Krauss, S., *Synagogale Altertümer* (Berlin, 1927)

Krinsky, C. H., *Synagogues of Europe. Architecture, History and Meaning* (Cambridge, Mass., and London, 1985)

Laytner, A., *Arguing with God. A Jewish Tradition* (Northvale, NJ, 1990)

Levi, E., *Yesodoth Ha-Tefillah* (Tel Aviv, 1965, 5th edn)

Levine, L. I. (ed.), *Ancient Synagogues Revealed* (Jerusalem, 1981)

Levine, L. I. (ed.), *The Synagogue in Late Antiquity* (Philadelphia, 1987)

Lewin, B. M., *Otzar Ḥilluf Minhagim. Thesaurus of Halachic Differences Between the Palestinian and Babylonian Schools* (Jerusalem, 1942)

Lewis, B., *The Jews of Islam* (London, 1984)

Liebman, C. S., 'The Religious Life of American Jewry' in *Understanding American Jewry*, ed. M. Sklare (New Brunswick and London, 1982)

Liebman, C. S. and Don-Yehiya, E., *Civil Religion in Israel. Traditional Judaism and Political Culture in the Jewish State* (Berkeley and Los Angeles and London, 1983)

Lipman, V. D., *A History of the Jews in Britain since 1858* (Leicester, 1990)

Loewenthal, N., *Communicating the Infinite. The Emergence of the Habad School* (Chicago and London, 1990)

Mann, J., 'Changes in the Divine Service of the Synagogue due to Religious Persecutions', *HUCA* 4 (1927)

Mann, J. and Sonne, I., *The Bible as Read and Preached in the Old Synagogue*, 2 vols. (Cincinnati, 1940 and 1966)

Margaliot (Margulies), M., *The Differences Between Babylonian and Palestinian Jews* (Hebrew; Jerusalem, 1938)

Hilkhoth 'Ereṣ Yisra'el min Ha-Genizah, ed. I. Ta-Shema (Jerusalem, 1973)

Meiselman, M., *Jewish Woman in Jewish Law* (New York, 1978)

Meyer, M., *Response to Modernity. A History of the Reform Movement in Judaism* (New York, 1988)

Millgram, A., *Jewish Worship* (Philadelphia, 1971)

Mirski, A., Grossman, A. and Kaplan, Y. (eds.), *Exile and Diaspora. Studies in the History of the Jewish People presented to Professor Haim Beinart on the Occasion of his Seventieth Birthday* (Hebrew; Jerusalem, 1988)

Newsom, C., *Songs of the Sabbath Sacrifice. A Critical Edition* (Atlanta, 1985)

Noy, D., 'A Jewish Place of Prayer in Roman Egypt', *JTS* NS 43 (1992)

Oppenheimer, A., see Kasher, A.

Petuchowski, J. J., *Prayerbook Reform in Europe. The Liturgy of Liberal and Reform Judaism* (New York, 1968)

'The Liturgy of the Synagogue. History, Structure and Contents' in *Approaches to Ancient Judaism* IV, ed. W. S. Green (Chico, 1983)

Petuchowski, J. J. (ed.), *Contributions to the Scientific Study of the Jewish Liturgy* (New York, 1970)

Petuchowski, J. J. (ed.), *Understanding Jewish Prayer* (New York, 1972)

Petuchowski, J. J. (ed.), *New Perspectives on Abraham Geiger. An HUC-JIR Symposium* (Cincinnati, 1975)

Petuchowski, J. J. and Brocke, M. (eds.), *The Lord's Prayer and the Jewish Liturgy* (London, 1978)

Petuchowski, J. J., and Fleischer, E. (eds.), *Studies in Aggadah, Targum and Jewish Liturgy in Memory of Joseph Heinemann* (Hebrew; Jerusalem, 1981)

Pool, D. de Sola, *The Kaddish* (Leipzig, 1909)

Popper, W., *The Censorship of Hebrew Books* (New York, 1899); new edition with an introduction by M. Carmilly-Weinberger (New York, 1969)

Porten, B., *Archives from Elephantine. The Life of an Ancient Jewish Military Colony* (Berkeley and Los Angeles, 1968)

Posner, R., Kaploun, U. and Cohen, S. (eds.), *Jewish Liturgy. Prayer and Synagogue Service Through the Ages* (Jerusalem, 1975)

Posner, R. and Ta-Shema, I., *The Hebrew Book. An Historical Survey* (Jerusalem, 1975)

Pritchard, J. B., *Ancient Near Eastern Texts relating to the Old Testament* (Princeton, 1969, 3rd edn)

Raphael, M. L., *Profiles in American Judaism. The Reform, Conservative, Orthodox and Reconstructionist Traditions in Historical Perspective* (San Francisco, 1984)

Rappaport, U., see Kasher, A.

Reif, S. C., *A Guide to the Taylor–Schechter Genizah Collection* (Cambridge, 1973, 1st edn, 1979, 2nd edn)

'On a Text of the '*Aleinu* Prayer', *Tarbiz* 44 (1975)

Shabbethai Sofer and his Prayer-book (Cambridge, 1979)

'Genizah Collections at Cambridge University Library' (Hebrew) in *Te'uda* 1, ed. M. A. Friedman (Tel Aviv, 1980)

'Liturgical Difficulties and Geniza Manuscripts' in *Studies in Judaism and Islam presented to Shelomo Dov Goitein*, eds. S. Morag, I. Ben-Ami, and N. A. Stillman (Jerusalem, 1981)

'Some Issues in Jewish Liturgical Research' (Hebrew), *Proceedings of the Eighth World Congress of Jewish Studies, Jerusalem, 1981*, Division C (Jerusalem, 1982)

'Jewish Liturgical Research. Past, Present and Future' (updated and revised English version of 'Some Issues'), *JJS* 34 (1983)

'Some Observations on Solomon Luria's Prayer-Book' in *Tradition and Transition. Essays Presented to Chief Rabbi Sir Immanuel Jakobovits*, ed. J. Sacks (London, 1986)

'Festive Titles in Liturgical Terminology' (Hebrew), *Proceedings of the Ninth World Congress of Jewish Studies, Jerusalem, 1985*, Division C (Jerusalem, 1986)

Published Material from the Cambridge Genizah Collections. A Bibliography 1896–1980 (Cambridge, 1988)

'Aspects of Mediaeval Jewish Literacy' in *The Uses of Literacy in Early Mediaeval Europe*, ed. R. McKitterick (Cambridge, 1989)

'On the Earliest Development of Jewish Prayer', *Tarbiz* 60 (1991)

'Codicological Aspects of Jewish Liturgical History', *Bulletin of the John Rylands University Library of Manchester* 75 (1993), forthcoming

'An Aramaic Version of *We'ilu Finu*' (Hebrew) in a forthcoming *Festschrift* for Ezra Fleischer

Reif, S. C., see also Preface above, pp. xi–xii

Rezler-Bersohn, N., 'Isaac Satanow. An Epitome of an Era', *LBIYB* 25 (1980)

Rivkin, E., 'Ben Sira and the Nonexistence of the Synagogue' in *In the Time of Harvest. Essays in Honor of Abba Hillel Silver on the Occasion of his 70th Birthday*, ed. D. J. Silver (New York, 1963)

Roberts, C. H. and Skeat, J. C., *The Birth of the Codex* (London, 1983)

Rosenbloom, N. H., *Tradition in an Age of Reform. The Religious Philosophy of Samson Raphael Hirsch* (Philadelphia, 1976)

Roth-Gerson, L., *The Greek Inscriptions from the Synagogues in Eretz-Israel* (Hebrew; Jerusalem, 1987)

Rowley, H. H., *Worship in Ancient Israel. Its Form and Meaning* (London, 1967)

Rozenblit, M., 'The Struggle over Religious Reform in Nineteenth-Century Vienna', *AJS Review* 14 (1989)

Qimron, E., 'Times for Praising God. A Fragment of a Scroll from Qumran (4Q409)', *JQR* 80 (1990)

Sacks, J., *Traditional Alternatives. Orthodoxy and the Future of the Jewish People* (London, 1989)

Safrai, S., 'The Temple and the Divine Service' in *The World History of the Jewish People* (First Series, 7): *The Herodian Period*, ed. M. Avi-Yonah (New Brunswick, 1975)

Sanders, E. P., *Judaism. Practice and Belief. 63 BCE–66 CE* (London and Philadelphia, 1992)

Sarason, R., 'On the Use of Method in the Modern Study of Jewish Liturgy' in *Approaches to Ancient Judaism. Theory and Practice*, ed. W. S. Green (Missoula, 1978)

'Recent Developments in the Study of Jewish Liturgy' in *The Study of Ancient Judaism. I. Mishnah, Midrash, Siddur*, ed. J. Neusner (New York, 1982)

'Religion and Worship. The Case of Judaism' in *Take Judaism, For Example. Studies Towards the Comparison of Religions*, ed. J. Neusner (Chicago, 1983)

Sarna, J. D., see Korres, A. S.

Schäfer, P., *Geniza-Fragmente zur Hekhalot-Literatur* (Tübingen, 1984)

Schechter, A. I., *Studies in Jewish Liturgy based on a Unique Manuscript entitled Seder Ḥibbur Berakot* (Philadelphia, 1930)

Scholem, G., *Kabbalah* (New York, 1974, based on his *EJ* articles)

Schorsch, I., 'Moritz Steinschneider on Liturgical Reform', *HUCA* 53 (1982)

Schwartz, B., '*Hanoten Teshua*'. The Origin of the Traditional Jewish Prayer for the Government', *HUCA* 57 (1986)

Schwartz, J., 'Jubilees, Bethel and the Temple of Jacob', *HUCA* 56 (1985)

Shaftesley, J. M., 'Religious Controversies' in *A Century of Anglo-Jewish Life 1870–1970*, ed. S. S. Levin (London, 1970)

Skeat, J. C., see Roberts, C. H.

Sklare, M., *Conservative Judaism. An American Religious Movement* (Glencoe, 1955)

'Religion and Ethnicity in the American Jewish Community. Changing Aspects of Reform, Conservative and Orthodox Judaism' in *The Role of Religion in Modern Jewish History*, ed. J. Katz (Cambridge, Mass., 1975)

Sokoloff, M. and Yahalom, J., 'Aramaic Piyyuṭim from the Byzantine Period', *JQR* 75 (1985)

Sonne, I., see Mann, J.

Stern, M. (ed.), *Nation and History. Studies in the History of the Jewish People*, vol. 1 (Hebrew; Jerusalem, 1983)

Sussmann, J., 'The History of *Halakha* and the Dead Sea Scrolls – Preliminary Observations on *Miqṣat Ma'ase Ha-Torah* (4QMMT)', *Tarbiẓ* 59 (1990)

Swartz, M. D., *Mystical Prayer in Ancient Judaism. An Analysis of* Ma'aseh Merkavah (Tübingen, 1992)

Talmage, F., see Dan, J.

Ta-Shema, I., 'On the Beginning of the Piyyut', *Tarbiẓ* 53 (1984)

'Some Notes on the Origins of the "Kaddish Yathom"', *Tarbiẓ* 53 (1984)

Ta-Shema, I., see also Posner, R.

Tobi, Y., 'The *Siddur* of Rabbi Shelomo ben Nathan of Sijilmasa. A Preliminary Study' in *Communautés juives des marges sahariennes du Maghreb*, ed. M. Abitbol (Jerusalem, 1982)

Tobi, Y., see also Yesha'yahu, Y.

Urbach, E. E., 'The Place of the Ten Commandments in Ritual and Prayer' in *The Ten Commandments as reflected in Tradition and Literature throughout the Ages*, ed. B.-Z. Segal (Hebrew; Jerusalem, 1985)

Vermes, G., 'The Decalogue and the Minim', *BZAW* 103 (1968) reprinted in his *Post-Biblical Jewish Studies* (Leiden, 1975)

Viviano, B. T., *Study as Worship. Aboth and the New Testament* (Leiden, 1978)

Wainwright, G., see Jones, C.

Weingreen, J., 'The Origin of the Synagogue', *Hermathena* 98 (1964)

Weiss, A., *Women at Prayer. A Halakhic Analysis of Women's Prayer Groups* (Hoboken, N.J., 1990)

Wertheimer, J., see also Gurock, J. S.

Wieder, N., *Islamic Influences on the Jewish Worship* (Hebrew; Oxford, 1947), originally published in *Melila* 2 (Manchester, 1946)

The Judean Scrolls and Karaism (London, 1962)

'Genizah Studies in the Babylonian Liturgy', *Tarbiz* 37 (1968)

'*'Avar We'athid Benusaḥ "Kol Nidrey"*' in *Mikhtam Ledawid*, eds. Y. Gilat, E. Stern and I. Ta-Shema (Ramat Gan, 1977)

'*Berakhah Bilti Yedu'ah*', *Sinai* 82 (1978)

Wiesenberg, E. J., 'The Shorter Forms of Grace after Meals and of the Amidah', *Niv Hamidrashia* 18–19 (1985–6)

Wischnitzer, R., *The Architecture of the European Synagogue* (Philadelphia, 1964)

Würthwein, E., *The Text of the Old Testament. An Introduction to the Biblia Hebraica* (ET of the fourth edition, London, 1980)

Yaari, A., 'The Miy Sheberakh Prayers. History and Texts', *KS* 33 (1957–8) and 36 (1960)

Yadin, Y., *Tefillin from Qumran* (Jerusalem, 1969)

Yahalom, J., *Maḥzor Eretz Israel. A Geniza Codex* (Hebrew; Jerusalem, 1987)

Yahalom, J., see also Sokoloff, M.

Yarnold, E., see Jones, C.

Yesha'yahu, Y. and Tobi, Y. (eds.), *The Jews of Yemen* (Hebrew; Jerusalem, 1975)

Zahavy, T., 'A New Approach to Early Jewish Prayer' in *History of Judaism. The Next Ten Years*, ed. B. M. Bokser (Chico, 1980)

The Mishnaic Law of Blessings and Prayers. Tractate Berakhot (Atlanta, 1987)

'Three Stages in the Development of Early Rabbinic Prayer' in *From Ancient Israel to Modern Judaism. Intellect in Quest of Understanding. Essays in Honor of Marvin Fox*, eds. J. Neusner, E. S. Frerichs and N. M. Sarna, vol. 1 (Atlanta, 1989)

'The Politics of Piety. Social Conflict and the Emergence of Rabbinic Liturgy' in *The Making of Jewish and Christian Worship*, eds. P. F. Bradshaw and L. A. Hoffman (Notre Dame and London, 1991)

Zeitlin, S., 'The Origin of the Synagogue', *PAAJR* 1930–1 (1931)
Zimmer, Y. (Eric), '*Mo'adey Nesi'ath Kapayim*', *Sinai* 100 (1987)
Zunz, L., *Die Ritus des synagogalen Gottesdienstes geschichtlich entwickelt* (Berlin, 1859)

Index of sources

A Hebrew Bible
B Apocrypha and Pseudepigrapha
C Qumran
D Philo and Josephus
E New Testament and early Christian writings
F Talmud and Midrash
G Manuscripts

A Hebrew Bible

B *Apocrypha and Pseudepigrapha*

C *Qumran*

D *Philo and Josephus*

E *New Testament and early Christian writings*

F *Talmud and Midrash*

Index of prayers and rituals

Index of names

Index of subjects and rites